FALL FROM GRACE : THE UNTOLD S

HG4928.5

DATE DUE

~~DE 2 3 '94~~			
~~MR 1 7 '95~~			
~~MY 5 '95~~			
~~MY 1 2 '05~~			

Fall From Grace

The Untold Story of Michael Milken

by Fenton Bailey

with an Introduction by Alan Dershowitz

A BIRCH LANE PRESS BOOK
Published by Carol Publishing Group

To my Mother and Father

A Birch Lane Press Book
Published by Carol Publishing Group
Birch Lane Press is a registered trademark of Carol Communications, Inc.
Editorial Offices: 600 Madison Avenue, New York, N.Y. 10022
Sales & Distribution Offices: 120 Enterprise Avenue, Secaucus, N.J. 07094
In Canada: Canadian Manda Group, P.O. Box 920 Station U, Toronto, Ontario M8Z 5P9
Queries regarding rights and permissions should be addressed to Carol Publishing Group, 600 Madison Avenue, New York, N.Y. 10022

First published in great Britain in 1991, under the title *The Junk Bond Revolution*, by Fourth Estate Limited, London.

Carol Publishing Group books are available at special discounts for bulk purchases, for sales promotions, fund-raising, or educational purposes. Special editions can be created to specifications. For details contact: Special Sales Department, Carol Publishing Group, 120 Enterprise Avenue, Secaucus, N.J. 07094

Manufactured in the United States of America
10 9 8 7 6 5 4 3 2 1

Library of Congress Cataloging-in-Publication Data

Bailey, Fenton.
    Fall from grace : the untold story of Michael Milken / Fenton Bailey : with an introduction by Alan Dershowitz.
        p. cm.
    "Birch Lane Press book."
    Includes bibliographical references and index.
    ISBN 1-55972-135-9
    1. Milken, Michael.   2. Stockbrokers—United States—Biography.
3. Junk bonds—United States.   4. Drexel Burnham Lambert
Incorporated.   5. Securities industry—United States—Corrupt
practices. I. Title.   II. Title: Untold story of MIchael Milken.
HG4928.5.M55B34   1992
364.1'68—dc20
    [B]   92-25285
                                                                        CIP

CONTENTS

INTRODUCTION

by Alan M. Dershowitz

THIS is a book about perception and reality and how, in today's instant-information age, the former can eclipse the latter. Perceptions generated by popular print and broadcast media can make icons of the shallow, and overnight sensations of the mediocre. But this is benign stuff compared to the darkest aspect of the media's power to mold perception: its ability to defame a person of merit—a process which can now be supercharged, thanks to space-age electronics.

The sad truth is that today, the media has more power than ever before to create, out of whole cloth, ersatz individuals to replace the real people whose names they bear, and who make far less 'interesting' copy. This unprecedented power to malign can destroy innocent people so quickly, so thoroughly and so pervasively, that it may take an individual the better part of a lifetime to restore a savaged reputation—if at all.

Our well-designed system of checks and balances, devised by the nineteenth century framers of our Constitution, assures that no branch of government may exercise undue power over the other branches or over the rights of citizens. But as we approach the twenty-first century, we face a danger wholly unanticipated by the authors of our Constitution: That the media—not itself a fourth 'branch', but rather a fourth 'estate'—may be exercising an unchecked power equal to, or in some circumstances even greater than, that exercised by the official agencies of government.

Ironically, those who wrote our Bill of Rights understood the potential importance of the press as a *check* on government. For this reason, the First Amendment assures that government will not abridge the freedom of the press. But the 'press', as it was known to our forefathers, was a weak, local and time-delayed collection of cheaply produced newspapers, leaflets and magazines. Although primitive by today's standards, these journalists could still be an annoyance to the establishment, as evidenced by the likes of John Peter Zenger and Thomas Paine. They also helped achieve important political results. The influence of the Federalist Papers on the adoption of the Constitution is a classic example.

Nevertheless, in writing the laws that govern our land, our founders, along with the myriad authors of federal, state and local statutes, could never have anticipated how quickly and easily an entire nation's mindset can now be contorted by false or misleading information purveyed by the *mass* media. Nor could they have foreseen the impact this phenomenon could have on the due process of law. Today we have come to a dangerous point in history, where the media 'tail', fueled as it is by advanced telecommunications technology, wields the power to wag a 'dog' as big as the United States Government and as important as our system of justice.

The story Fenton Bailey tells in this book is really two stories in one. The surface story is about the rise, decline and resurgence of what was perhaps the most innovative development in modern finance—high yield securities—and the person—Michael Milken—who was largely responsible for its development.

The deeper story is about the unchecked power and unaccountability of a coven of journalists and writers, and how they, in collaboration with prosecutors, federal agents and others, deliberately distorted the high yield bond story and created their own fictitious version of Michael Milken. This deeper story demonstrates the *total commitment* these writers had to their sinister agenda. For nothing less could have persuaded the public that a perfectly viable market with a solid track record, which outperformed U.S. Treasuries and the Dow Jones Industrial Average during the 1980s, was somehow tainted and that there was something wrong with a man who created opportunity, opened the doors for entrepreneurs—including minorities and women—and who gave tirelessly of himself to myriad programs for those in need. Being a criminal defense lawyer, I have seen a spate of such cases in recent years. But this one hit me particularly hard, since I could once count myself among the duped.

Up until December 1990, I was an avid reader of stories about Michael Milken and high yield ('junk') securities. And although I am embarrassed to recall it now, I pretty much believed what I read, even though it did not square with some previous information I had read about the man.

I had first learned about Milken a few years earlier, when I gave a lecture at the Bernard Milken Campus of the West Valley Jewish Community Center in Southern California. I was told that the Center was named in memory of a wonderful man who had recently died of cancer; his family had donated the money to build the facility. His older son, Michael, was described to me as a very private, but extremely generous, multi-millionaire, who was universally respected, indeed loved, by the community.

When I later started reading about his troubles, I recalled this description and wondered how the man I had heard about in California could possibly be the same Michael Milken being depicted in the papers. Unfortunately, I was predisposed to accepting the possibility that two such polar individuals could inhabit the same body. And despite all my professional cynicism about the press, I became part of that large flock of sheep known as public opinion.

Because I accepted the popularized version of Milken, I took a dim view of what were purported to be his transgressions; I said so publicly and even mentioned this once in my syndicated column, although, even then, I argued that his original ten-year sentence was far too harsh for his purported crimes. Later, in December 1990, I met Milken—and agreed to join his legal team—and did a vast amount of research on the man and met scores of individuals who knew and worked with him. Only then did I realize how I too, among the minions, had been taken in by the press. The Michael Milken I got to know quite well over the next several months bears no resemblance either to the media stereotype or to the man I believed he might be.

The real Mike Milken is a thoughtful, conscientious man who cares deeply about the state of the economy, the nation and the world. He is generous, to a fault, in both his business and personal life. And, as Fenton Bailey has described in this book, he is virtually oblivious to the trappings of wealth. His life's work has been based on his philosophy that the private enterprise system and society are inextricably linked with one another, and that they must both be strong in order for each to survive. Furthermore, Milken was regarded by his own colleagues, as well as by competitors and even many of his adversaries, as a highly ethical professional. Perhaps most illuminating of all was the revelation that Milken had not reinvented himself after his investigation began. I learned, instead, that all of his attributes had remained consistent from the time of his youth, through his education and early career, and throughout his rise to success. Indeed, although sorely tested by a prolonged and hideous crisis, these traits continue to remain constant to this day.

It is indeed ironic that Milken, who, in the course of educating others about changes in society and undervalued assets, and had cautioned them about the dangers of falling prey to perception versus reality, would ultimately became a victim of this very phenomenon.

Timing played a major role in this debacle, as well. Many catastrophes recorded throughout history have been the result of a unique confluence of events, trends and crazy happenstance, which, had they all converged at any other time, would never have produced the same results. So too it is with Michael Milken's case. While I don't necessarily agree with everything said in this book, Mr. Bailey hits the nail on the head in juxtaposing the many elements that worked together to bring down Milken and everything he stood for, within a unique time frame that allowed this to happen. By the early 1970s, our world was changing, and there were large groups of people whose economic stability and way of life were suddenly being threatened. Industries and their entrenched managements were being challenged to compete in global markets, where increased productivity, lower labor costs and new technologies were rapidly changing the rules of the game. Many of our leaders in both business and government were slow to recognize the magnitude of this challenge and their reactions were palliative. Most moved reflexively, cutting costs to the bone and laying off thousands of workers. In the meantime, the average citizen, who was reeling from the impact of this problem, had only a rudimentary understanding of its vast, long-term implications. Everyone was searching for someone to blame, and Michael Milken became a handy scapegoat.

As noted in the book, there were three major groups that stood to benefit the most from Milken's 'fall from grace'. They were the government, the press and a group that I would simply call the 'opportunists', under whose umbrella are both individuals and institutions whose agendas were best served by Milken being out of the investment banking picture. This last group comprises some of Drexel's competitors, like Salomon Brothers, whose chairman had derided junk bonds and Michael Milken, and yet today is one of the biggest moneymakers in this market along with the money center banks; corporations such as Unocal, whose CEO, when threatened by a takeover attempt, lobbied Washington to change the rules at all costs; and others at Drexel, who were terrorized into becoming government witnesses.

During the high yield market's evolution in the 1980s, and, in particular, during the era of hostile takeovers initiated primarily by prestigious companies, national law firms got into the action and reaped millions of dollars in fees without having any of their own money at risk. The lawyers won, whether the deal was good or bad.

However, when the cycle slowed down, and some of the deals declined, it was some of these same lawyers, this time representing the self-anointed 'victims', who cried 'foul' and sued everyone in sight—except, of course, themselves and some members of the federal government, who had caused many of the problems and, in some cases, were their pals. In one of the most notorious of these situations, the Resolution Trust Corporation hired Wall Street mega-firm Cravath, Swaine & Moore (which had earned, and continues to earn, millions of dollars in fees by representing principals, including even Drexel, in high yield security offerings), to sue Milken and virtually everyone involved with him.

Indeed, these lawsuits were particularly deceptive, in part, because they sought compensation for losses that didn't even exist, when income and capital gains were taken into account. Despite the fact that over two hundred brokerages, one hundred leading law firms and thousands of investors had gladly participated in this market, including Cravath, this firm ultimately claimed that the high yield bond market was a 'fraud' engineered by Drexel. Of course, later, when market prices surged, everyone positioned themselves to come back in. Although billions were made, Cravath did not refund the multi-hundred-million-dollar settlements and legal fees it had already earned.

In my own view, perhaps the most hypocritical group of opportunists are a few people who worked at Drexel, who first rode Milken's coattails to success and then stabbed him in the back when the going got rough. Drexel's former CEO, Fred Joseph, is an interesting case in point. As Bailey points out in his book, Joseph, who ultimately became a government witness, remained loyal to and protective of Drexel's East Coast operation and its corporate finance mentality, although he was more than happy to cash in on the enormous profits being generated by Milken's High Yield Department in California.

While reporters have virtually ignored this fact, the East Coast/West Coast distinction is critical to understanding the genesis of so many misconceptions regarding Michael Milken. It also sheds light on Joseph's motivation to revise history and shift total responsibility for Drexel's activities onto Milken.

Milken's West Coast department was a trading operation, which was value-driven, provided service to its franchise of investors and maintained a long-term perspective. On the other hand, Joseph's East coast baby, Corporate Finance, including the Mergers & Acquisitions group, was, by definition, deal- and fee-driven. And its focus was short term. Mr. Bailey quotes Joseph as having once told a seminar on ethics that he '...was actually using it, the word "greedy", internally'; that he '...did not want to cut out excessive greed'. Greed was Joseph's credo, not Milken's.

Similarly, it was Joseph and Drexel's Merger & Acquisition Group who, like so many other M&A departments on Wall Street, were keen on using high yield securities to finance takeovers, beating the bushes for opportunities to do so, against Milken's advice when he was still at Drexel, and long after he was out of the picture.

Joseph's pugnacious approach was antithetical to Milken's philosophy of creating value. Furthermore, when Milken returned from meetings in Washington in 1985 and 1986, he understood that the shrill alarm sounded by lobbyists, in reaction to what they perceived to be 'the junk bond bust-up takeover', had such an edge of hysteria to it that it could threaten the entire high yield market. This knowledge convinced him that an aggressive approach could produce a serious backlash. So, he begged the firm and its clients to return to its basic business—financing growing and rebuilding companies. But the higher-ups at Drexel wouldn't listen. By the latter part of the 1980s, Drexel, like so many other investment banking firms, had been taken over by their Merger & Acquisitions departments. While Shearson Lehman/American Express, First Boston/Credit Suisse and Kidder Peabody/General Electric were all bailed out by their wealthy parents, Drexel, which like all the others was not controlled by an overzealous, fee-driven M&A department, no longer had anyone to rescue it from its ruinous course.

Milken's opposition to hostile takeovers has been derided by journalists, yet even Drexel's Chairman of Board Robert Linton said in his letter to Judge Wood, prior to Milken's sentencing:

'From time to time, we had disagreements concerning specific dealings and whenever I had to insist on a course of action for the firm contrary to Michael's wishes, he always adhered to my direction and did so with grace despite our differing points of view.'

But here too, Milken got the blame, not Joseph.

Many of the opportunists publicly rewrote history after Milken's indictment and throughout Drexel's collapse. They were able to claim, without being challenged, that they had always said and done what was politically and economically 'correct' at the time. In sharp contrast, Milken was virtually precluded from saying anything at all. Ever searching for another angle, journalists forged his imposed silence into a rapier with which they have slashed at him time and again. Yet common sense dictates that in the midst of an investigation, a defendant targeted by the prosecution is advised by counsel to remain silent, lest the mere fact of his speaking out in his own defence prejudice his case in the eyes of the judge and prosecutors.

Time is another factor that worked to the opportunists' advantage. The notion that delays and the passage of time are helpful to every defendant in an investigation is out-dated. Today, the burden of proof has shifted to the defendant. Hence, sketchy documentation and faded eye-witness memories have become strategic weapons for the prosecution. It is unlikely that the prosecution could have yielded the same results had the case been undertaken in 1986 or 1987, when the events under scrutiny were much more recent.

Instead, prosecutors, and the 'cooperative' witnesses they enlisted through terrorist tactics, were able to capitalize on the time lapse of four to five years from the events in question. It was clear from the case's inception that Milken would be put on the defencive. And even though the facts brought forth by the defence substantiated his case, without the good will and honesty of others (many of whom were also indicted or under threat of indictment), the true story would never unfold.

Here again the press interfered. Considering the steady stream of leaks (from 'unnamed sources close to the investigation') that fed numerous headline stories in major papers like *The Wall Street Journal* and the *Washington Post* about pending indictments and additional charges (many of which never materialized, or were later thrown out or dismissed), it was never even close to a level playing field for Milken. Bailey cites 325 references in *The Wall Street Journal* and 450 in the *Washington Post* by the time Milken had entered his plea.

Taking into account the virtual gag placed on Milken by his counsel, even his enormous personal wealth was no match for Rudolph Giuliani and his government prosecution team, who had placed their careers on the line in promising to deliver Milken's head on a platter.

Nor could he have countered, in any significant way, the media blitz chiefly implemented by an ambitious reporter, James Stewart, who later became the front-page editor of *The Wall Street Journal*. His baseless allegations and falsehoods spread like a virus from paper to paper, from station to station. News junkies one and all, reporters salivated at the chance to cash in on a 'juicy' story. Who can place a dollar amount on what Stewart (not to mention so many others) had to gain by touting the 'story of the decade', and how likely is it that he would have changed course, even when enough facts emerged to completely undercut his 'conspiracy' theories? To have recanted his errors would have been a courageous undertaking, but he did not rise to the challenge.

Thankfully, not all publications bought into Stewart's conspiracy scoop. For example, James Michaels, editor of *Forbes* magazine, and considered by many to be today's 'dean of financial writers', in his introduction to a March 16, 1992, cover story interview with Michael Milken, rebuffed Stewart without pause. As he put it, 'Our [*Forbes'*] crook-sniffing equipment is sensitive and we can usually smell a phony a good way off. We do not believe the conspiracy theories.'

Another major ingredient that severely influenced the outcome of the Milken case was the government's ability to use RICO and mail and wire fraud as instruments of torture. As Mr. Bailey notes, quoting a former prosecutor,

'"To Federal prosecutors of white collar crime, the mail fraud statute is...[their] Stradivarius..." Since the intent to deceive can constitute fraud and since virtually no business is done in America today without using the wire or mail services of the United States government (phone, fax, letter, telex, modem), one need not even commit a crime in order to have committed the predicate acts necessary to trigger a RICO indictment.'

This is a statute that every business person—indeed, every citizen—in the country should lobby his or her representatives in Congress to change, if not abolish altogether. It became abundantly clear, from abuses of RICO throughout the 1970s and the 1980s, that RICO is a broad, vague dragnet that allows the government to turn virtually any and every activity into a 'racketeering enterprise', to impose Draconian prison sentences on people who rarely get a fair trial, and to confiscate all of their property—frequently doing this prior to trial, so that the defendant cannot even afford to pay for his or her own defence.

For the first few years of its existence, RICO was used, as intended, against 'organized crime' figures, major drug dealers, and murderers. But once RICO's supporting techniques and statutory interpretations were well-honed, ambitious prosecutors like Rudolph Giuliani used them on all sorts of well-meaning citizens. The threat wielded by using RICO against Milken and others will be examined for many years for the ways in which due process can be trampled in the name of 'vigorous' law enforcement.

Mr. Bailey's discussion of the Fatico hearing held by Judge Kimba Wood prior to Milken's sentencing is critical. The hearing was called because of the expectation, loudly trumpeted by the press, that the government had even more evidence against Milken than it would have needed to prove the six counts to which he had already pled guilty. If proven to be true, this could then serve as a sentencing barometer for Judge Wood.

The scales were tipped in the government's favor, in ways that would never have passed muster in the context of a trial. For example, the government had full access to grand jury testimony not available to the defence, and they could dangle the carrot of immunity in front of any one of a number of people who already felt intimidated by the prosecutorial juggernaut. More importantly, the government did not have to meet the 'burden of proof' standard required in a jury trial. Despite this over-whelming bias toward the prosecution, the 'additional evidence' they had promised for months turned to powder in the light of day.

Sadly, none of this benefitted Milken, as it should have. Fatico turned out to be a sham. First, Judge Wood ruled that the prosecution failed to substantiate their allegations with the evidence presented. She also found that the losses incurred by investors, due to Milken's activities, amounted to a little over $300,000. Nevertheless, she sentenced Milken to ten years in prison plus three years of community service, the stiffest penalty, by far, ever meted out for securities laws violations. (Milken had been bludgeoned into pleading guilty to six separate counts involving arguable violations of laws that were as technical as they were vague.) In addition, the press brushed off the critical facts that emerged in the hearing, both in terms of the details of the case and Milken's character.

One incident I found to be particularly offensive, which is retold in these pages, concerns the government's accusation that Mike Milken's charitable works were some sort of eleventh-hour public relations 'stunt' to impress the judge. When evidence was subsequently presented to Judge Wood's satisfaction that Milken's philanthropy had even predated his career on Wall Street, U.S. Assistant Attorney John Carroll claimed that the government had never 'intended' to create the impression that it was otherwise.

Then James Stewart went ahead and wrote about the false charge as if it had *not* been refuted, and, of course, the *Journal* printed this lie. Now, because of this travesty, millions of people all across the country believe that a man who quietly, and modestly, had devoted himself his entire life to significant philanthropic causes, as well as consistently provided personal assistance to friends, associates, employees and others in need, had just been 'posing' as a good guy. Not content to destroy Milken's reputation as a businessman, the government and the press were out to demolish every shred of Michael Milken's character, piece by piece.

Perhaps for the government, this was the only way to vindicate a cavalry charge of ninety-eight counts brought against Milken. Since the government could not prove its case against Milken in the court-room, it was important for it to 'win' its case in the news media, where the assault against Milken at least made good headlines.

By the time Judge Wood presided over Milken's Rule 35 motion hearing to reduce his sentence, in the summer of 1992, government prosecutors had to backtrack even further from their once strident accusations. It began to appear as if they had overreacted on yet another count, obstruction of justice. The U.S. attorney asserted that the 'preponderance of evidence' criterion had not been met.

Thus, so far, every courtroom test of the case against Michael Milken had failed to deliver what had been promised by Giuliani and the press. The 'evidence', long heralded by the prosecution, never materialized, and yet Mike Milken was punished as if it had.

Bailey's notes make it clear that Rudolph Giuliani's hardball tactics knew few bounds. After he wasted millions of taxpayers' dollars on his star-struck prosecutions of prominent Americans and some foreign na-tionals, the appellate courts overturned most of his ill-gotten guilty verdicts, knocking them down like a row of dominoes. Does anyone today worry about the physical, emotional and financial cost to defendants and taxpayers alike in cases like Bess Myerson's, Adnan Kashoggi's, the Mulheren case (where Boesky was the 'star' witness), the Princeton-Newport Case and the famous Wedtech case, all of which were brought down either by juries or on appeal? Today these cases lie on the garbage heap of history, yet much of the damage they wrought can never be undone. One must never forget what former Secretary of Labor Raymond J. Donovan said after he was acquitted of larceny charges, 'Which office do I go to get my reputation back.'

Another Sherman tank in the Milken prosecution was John Shad, then head of the SEC, whom Mr. Bailey quotes as having once said of the Commission, 'We are the judge, jury and prosecutor.' As this book recounts, Shad hired Fred Joseph in 1963 when he was at E.F. Hutton, and became his mentor. Shad later went on to become Chairman of the SEC in 1981, and, in that position, was a key figure in launching the civil investigation of Drexel and Milken. This pattern, in itself, raises serious questions about conflicts of interest for both Shad and Joseph. But the story doesn't end there. At the government's and Joseph's urging, Shad was named Drexel's Chairman of the Board in April of 1989, while Fred Joseph remained CEO. For reasons that continue to elude me, the press has remained virtually silent on the impropriety of his appointment, and has not questioned the past bonds that so closely merged the interests of these two men.

It is important to read about the chain of events that led to Michael Milken's prosecution and its tragic outcome, not only for what it says about Milken and how he has been unconscionably persecuted and scapegoated, but also for what it says about our justice system and our rights as private citizens living in the most democratic nation on Earth.

It is also important to understand how the government and the press manipulated the testimony of the witnesses for the prosecution and were manipulated in turn. Nearly all of the negative descriptions of Michael Milken were based on a handful of sources, each of whom had a powerful incentive to distort the truth and magnify Milken's culpability. Primary among those sources was Ivan Boesky, whose liberty and fortune depended on his ability to persuade government prosecutors and the media that he himself was a small fish compared to Michael Milken, a man with whom Boesky had engaged in sporadic business dealings over several years.

Clearly, in such a situation, the media profits from getting an 'exclusive' story. The prosecutors also have a stake in exaggerating the magnitude of wrongdoing in a particular case, and inflating the roles of unindicted 'suspects'. I recall a public debate with the then-United States Attorney, Rudolph Giuliani, in which he bragged about how he used the media to get reluctant witnesses to join his side and to cooperate against their erstwhile friends and associates. 'The media does the job for me', he explained.

As Bailey retells it in these pages, the implications of Giuliani's approach are chilling. The lack of reliability of the coerced testimony is directly proportional to the amount of pressure exerted by the government on these witnesses and the extent to which they feel that a friend or colleague is vulnerable to whatever tale the government wants to hear. Truth rarely figures into the equation.

This process not only seriously distorts criminal trials and the inevitable civil damage suits that follow, but it threatens as well to distort history. In order to fit the needs and interests of prosecutors, government agencies, intimidated witnesses, and the news media, night is turned into day and day into night. Real criminals suddenly become better than they really are, and the targets of the process become arch-villains who are no longer recognizable to the people who know them well and who, in some cases, were there to witness the truth. Blame is apportioned not in accordance with true culpability, but in accordance with the needs of the prosecution and of the media.

This is precisely what happened to Michael Milken. Ivan Boesky was caught dead to rights stealing tens of millions of dollars from investors by paying valise-fulls of cash for inside information. The secret to Boesky's financial success has little to do with research, intelligence or hard work. It rested on insider trading based on secret information illegally bought for cash from the likes of Martin Siegel. When Boesky got caught, he had only one hope of minimizing his prison sentence and fines. He had to turn in someone who was *perceived* as even more important than he was and whom he could *portray* as a criminal. Immediately after being caught, he started to compose his own lyrics, and eventually he proved to be so 'creative' a composer that the government chose not to continue to vouch for his credibility beyond the one unsuccessful trial in which he testified. But by that time, he had already profited from one of the most favorable plea bargains in history. In exchange for 'giving, the prosecutors Milken and a few others, Boesky and his investors were allowed to keep tens of millions of dollars of illegal profits. And, most ironically, Boesky was allowed by SEC officials and federal prosecutors to liquidate approximately $400 million of his portfolio just *before* the public announcement of his indictment and plea bargain—one of the most striking instances in history of a massive sale of securities on the basis of *material inside information* known to the seller but not the buyers—information that was sure to adversely affect the value of Boesky's securities holdings once it became known to the investing public.

Boesky selected as his bulletin board his long-time ally, James Stewart of *The Wall Street Journal*. Several former colleagues of Stewart at the

Journal confirm this unholy alliance. Dean Rotbart, former reporter and editor of the 'Heard on the Street' column at the *Journal*, recalls that Boesky (as well as Siegel) would 'constantly be on the phone' to Stewart. Jude Wanniski, former associate editor of the *Journal's* 'Op-Ed page', wrote: 'Boesky was even then manipulating the *Journal* . . . for his profit.' It was clearly in Stewart's interest to continue to believe—or pretend to believe—Boesky, since Boesky was *his* 'deep throat'.

It would have been tantamount to committing journalistic suicide for Stewart to doubt Boesky's credibility. And so Stewart regurgitated Boesky's lies about Milken's alleged role in what Stewart had already touted as 'the greatest criminal conspiracy the financial world has ever known'. Even Giuliani, who was motivated to embrace Boesky and Stewart's overstated claims, eventually dropped Boesky like a hot potato and questioned Stewart's credibility. 'I get the sense', Giuliani later said, '[that] Stewart would make Mike Milken responsible for the Second World War.'

Boesky and Siegel formed an alliance with Stewart, steadily feeding him information long before they were caught. And ironically, Stewart continued to use them as sources later on, even though he knew their culpability and lack of credibility had clearly been established. Any journalist would have seriously questioned their motives at that point, but not Stewart. Somehow, he still found their whisperings to be useful, which, in Boesky's case, was even after government prosecutors had washed their hands of him, subsequent to his 'poor performance' at the Mulheren trial.

Indeed, it was eventually learned that just before Boesky made his deal with the government, he had destroyed the documentary evidence that could prove or *disprove* his version of events. Then, after making the deal, he purportedly 'reconstructed' these documents so that they 'corroborated' with his account. Even the government now acknowledges that it can have no confidence as to whether these reconstructions were accurate or were designed to prove that he was telling the truth.

Stewart got plenty out of the bargain himself. The 'information' that Boesky and Siegel fed him before they were indicted helped him win a Pulitzer Prize and a lucrative book contract. The fantasies Boesky (and his representatives) and Siegel continued to funnel to Stewart afterwards, became the heart of Stewart's best-selling book.

The urgency of addressing this problem cannot be overstated. A historical example underscores this need. In the book *Stalin's Apologist*, writer S.J. Taylor chronicles an example of how a crack foreign correspondent for *The New York Times* in the 1920s and 1930s, Walter Duranty, actually helped prolong Stalin's reign of terror by popularizing, through his newspaper stories, the image of the Soviet leader as a benevolent ruler who would lead the Soviet state to a bright future. Duranty's blithe accounts were believed, even though he was a lone voice in lauding Stalin. Like Stewart, Duranty was awarded a Pulitzer Prize and gained substantial prominence as an 'expert' in reporting his subject. And, as in Stewart's situation, it was in the government's best interest at that time to let the lies written go unchallenged, or even to feed into them.

While the First Amendment, which bars the government from playing any abridging role in the dynamics of the press, should remain an absolute, investigative journalists should not be allowed, by the ethical rules of the profession itself, to crush the rights of citizens. Lest anyone doubt it, Stewart knew full well that he could say just about anything with impunity, and he was far from being humble about the implications of being able to wield that kind of power. On the CNN program 'Crossfire', moderator Robert Novak confronted Stewart on this issue. 'You're the judge?' Novak asked. To which Stewart replied, 'Of course. All writers are. This is the court of public opinion.'

At a minimum, what is needed is the application of more rigorous standards for investigative journalists. In fact, I believe it is high time that investigative journalists begin to investigate each other. This process is actually routine in other disciplines that rely so heavily on multiple data sources. In the sphere of scientific research, for example, all experiments reported by one scientist are reviewed and analyzed by other scientists. Unless the results can be replicated, there is the suspicion of scientific fraud. What about journalists?

I cannot, and do not, vouch for the accuracy of every fact and conclusion contained in Fenton Bailey's book. But it certainly presents a far more balanced account of Michael Milken's case, the high yield market and the people involved in it than previous works have done. Bailey began working on this book after Milken's case was already winding down. As a result, he presents his own historical perspective and draws his own conclusions. Although he had met Michael Milken prior to starting the book, neither Milken nor I had any discussion with him regarding his book until after it was published in the United Kingdom.

One fascinating exercise is to contrast how Stewart and Bailey deal so differently with similar, or even identical, facts and situations. Numerous such instances are provided in the Bailey book. Many differences seem to be largely a function of Stewart's conscious decision to create a fictional Michael Milken that fit into a preexisting mold calculated to earn the journalist notoriety and success.

Since the people involved in these events are still here to speak for themselves, it is feasible to reinvestigate Stewart's version of Milken's story and uncover the truth. Mr. Bailey has started this process. Moreover, Bailey's book, unlike others that have been written previously, brings the reader up to date. It includes a current chapter on the high yield story and the events that followed the headlines up until the time Michael Milken was sentenced. It also contains an interview with Michael Milken that ranges in subject from the personal to his views on current events.

Some of the truth has already begun to surface. With regard to allegations that the high yield market was some sort of 'Ponzi' scheme, the market has clearly vindicated itself. First of all, it has always performed well; even during the turbulent 80s it outperformed U.S. Treasury bonds, high-grade corporate bonds, mortgage-backed securities and real estate. Moreover, after reacting in 1990 to its public hanging by the press, by legislators, and by a host of other 'mavens', the market came roaring back in 1991 and 1992, to the tune of $80 billion, and it continues to show positive performance. Empirical evidence has refuted claims that high yield financing destroyed jobs. Instead it created millions of jobs during an era when the *Fortune* 500 companies were laying off millions. In the final analysis, high yield securities continue, as they have for the past fifteen years, to generate social and economic opportunity within the private enterprise system, while affording superior rates of return to investors.

Subsequent to Michael Milken's incarceration, Salomon Brothers admitted to inflating customer orders and filing false reports in its role as a dealer of government-backed securities. In January 1992, the SEC cited ninety-eight leading brokerage firms and banks for creating phony records in order to beat out competition in the government-backed securities market. And in May of 1990, Salomon Brothers settled charges of illegal activities in the U.S. Government securities market. Even though these were similar violations to those to which Milken pled guilty, none of these cases has yet led to criminal charges such as those that destroyed Drexel and annihilated Milken.

For punishment, the firms prosecuted have merely been fined and/or ordered to 'cease and desist', as well as to correct procedures to prevent such abuses in the future. None admitted or denied any wrongdoing. This is the way 'technical' violations were handled in the past. The double standard applied with regard to Michael Milken is conspicuous. Even Judge Louis L. Stanton in the Alan Rosenthal trial in spring of 1992 threw out the count relating to tax fraud involving Milken—the same count that constituted one of the six to which Milken pled guilty. In the dictatorships that still flourish around the world we do not expect to find in force the basic democratic principals that we have all come to take for granted, such as equal justice, due process, innocence until guilt is proven, and freedom of the press. When we think of a dictatorship, we more or less expect that those who are in favor today can be hung in the morning for as trivial an offence as the company they keep. And we expect the local newspapers to faithfully serve their government masters.

It should therefore ring a loud alarm bell for the people in this country that a man can be destroyed by an omnipotent press and by an equally omnipotent government, which not only embolden one another but which at times appear to actually take their cues from one another. What have we come to if the government is 'judge, jury and prosecutor', and our press its willing handmaiden, or, even worse, its catalyst?

When historians look back at what transpired on Wall Street in the 1980s it will be even more clear than it is today that we arrived, through the natural course of events, at a major discontinuity in our nation's history. The old order had to change in order to face the challenges of a new, 'global' world.

Old orders have never given up their reigns easily, whether they represented the Roman Empire, the British Empire or the Soviet 'Empire'. Michael Milken was not a part of the old order on Wall Street, with its strong ties to the government. Nor were most of the individuals whose ventures his High Yield Bond Department helped finance. When all is said and done, this appears to have been his real crime. By being a visionary and an innovator, who lent his support to others of the same persuasion, and by being enormously successful at it, he provoked the wrath of the political and economic power structure.

ACKNOWLEDGMENTS

I OWE a debt of gratitude to anyone who has ever written anything about Michael Milken and in particular the work of Marie Brenner, Connie Bruck, Brian Burrough, Christopher Byron, Gordon Crovitz, Edward Jay Epstein, Jesse Kornbluth, Gail Sheehy, Benjamin Stein, James B. Stewart. Articles in *New York* magazine, *Vanity Fair*, *The Wall Street Journal*, and *The New York Times* were especially helpful. I would like to thank Catherine Bailey, Nikki Kentish Barnes, Domenica Fraser and David Jones at Buffalo Pictures for giving me access to the research material and interviews for the documentary film *Fallen Angel*, as well as Caroline Thomson and Michael Attwell at Channel Four. I would also like to thank Jani Walker and Steven Weinstock at PBS/WNET for their help and guidance in producing the segment 'Milken and the Media' for 'Edge". From early on Victor Weaver was most helpful. I would also like to thank Laurie Weltz and all at Broad Street productions and Louise Gray. Ken Lerer and Ann Brackbill at Robinson Lake and Lerer were co-operative, helpful and fair, as was Steven Anreder at Drexel.

At the beginning of the project I was grateful for the research assistance of William Rapavy and Curtis Cimmons, and I want to thank Robert Farrar for his encouragement, Michael Jones for reading an early version of the manuscript, and Alison Pollet, Maria Silver and all at World of Wonder. I would also like to thank my agent Cat Ledger, my London editor Giles O'Bryen and New York publisher Steven Schragis for their sound advice. I would especially like to thank my partner Randy Barbato. Not only was it his idea to write the book, but also without his support I know that it would never have been written.

1

END OF AN ERA

L OOKING out across the East Village as the dark sky began to give way to
the azure and pinks of dawn, it was hard to believe that there had ever
been a roaring eighties. The view towards Wall Street was a beautiful sight.
The twin peaks of the World Trade Center, now catching the first few rays of
the sun, stuck into the air like the prongs of a giant tuning fork or minimalist
piece of sculpture. But in the immediate foreground the spectacle was not so
pretty. A squatter clambered down the fire escape of an abandoned building
that had only the previous week gone up in flames again. Whether it was arson
– the owner wanting to collect on his insurance – or squatter junkie
carelessness, no one knew. On previous occasions the squatters had moved
right back in and fixed the place up again. This time the roof and the floors in
the centre had collapsed leaving, in the shadow of the dawn, a shell, almost a
gothic ruin. Reagan's trickle down economics hadn't even begun to drip in
places such as this. 'Trickle up economics', one Texan senator had drily
redefined it.

It was the eve of Thanksgiving, Wednesday 21 November 1990, the day
that Milken was scheduled to be sentenced. That day, Milken's horoscope
read: 'Colleagues now appear to be giving you a hard time and trying to settle
old scores.' However, it assured that he would be secure if 'you resolutely
refuse to become involved in unethical practices'. Futhermore, an astrologer
friend had told me that Mars was visible to the human eye, a rare and
portentous event, and truly this day was the end of an era. Never had a decade
ended so precipitously as the eighties. In the space of twelve months Forbes
had died, Trump had gone almost bankrupt, Leona Helmsley had been found
guilty of tax fraud, *Fame* magazine, Forbes's *Egg* magazine and *Manhattan Inc*
had all ceased publication. The $200 billion junk bond market that Milken
had built up had collapsed like the house of cards its opponents had always
said it was and Drexel Burnham, the firm that Milken had turned into Wall
Street's most profitable investment bank became Wall Street's largest bankruptcy. By the end of the day, Margaret Thatcher, another icon of the roaring
eighties, would also know that her time was up.

There was no point in trying to go back to sleep. I had been advised to get down to the courthouse early to get in line if I wanted to be sure of getting a seat at the sentencing. Since the showerhead emitted no more than a trickle of rust-coloured water, it seemed a better idea to stuff a flannel in the plug of the tub and take a bath. I sat in the murky water with that damp wet feeling you get when you can have only a mildly warm bath, and thought about Michael Milken.

He was known to the world at large as the Junk Bond King, and as a result of his record-breaking salary that had earned him a place in the Guiness Book Of Records, as the $550 Million Dollar Man. But as a result of becoming the target of the largest white collar criminal investigation in history, he was seen as a weird, press-shy workaholic who had no need of sleep and who wore a miner's headlamp on the pre-dawn commute into the office so he could work. With junk bonds fuelling the corporate takeover wars that characterized the eighties, he was held responsible for the bust up of corporate America, and for leveraging it to the hilt. That Drexel Burnham went into bankruptcy less than a year after his departure was seen as evidence of the fraudulent nature of the entire enterprise. So much for the cartoon-like dimensions of the perception. The reality is different, though no less compelling.

I had first 'met' Michael Milken at Drexel Burnham. I had a freelance job in the video department editing together lectures and classes on commercial paper, mortgage backs, and other arcana for trainees in the institutional fixed income department. It was not exciting work for someone who did not know the difference between a stock and a bond, and it did not make me want to know. One day someone came into my room and asked me to stop whatever I was doing to edit together something urgently. She clutched to her breast a videotape. It looked like any other videotape except that she held it so tightly her knuckles were white. Having given me my instructions, she gingerly put down the tape as though it were a precious artefact from a long lost civilization. Intrigued, I got to work.

On the screen was a strange but handsome looking man making a speech to an audience. He had black curly hair and deep sunken eyes set in a jowly boyish face. As he spoke he scanned the room, moving his head slowly from side to side in the manner of a practised and accomplished public speaker. Only by scrutinizing his face could you see his brown eyes, set deep inside their dark pools, dart from side to side. Occasionally he would take his hand out of his pocket, pat down the flap, and brush his nose with a finger in a casual gesture reminiscent of Johnny Carson. A Mona Lisa smile flickered perpetually around his lips. He didn't seem to use notes. Instead of a dull monologue about finance packed with facts and figures, his talk was free-ranging and broad themed. He spoke about changes in society and techno-logy, and their implications. He spoke almost slowly at a well-measured pace, and in a lilting monotone that drew you in. He seemed both utterly self-possessed and self-effacing.

'Who was that man speaking?' I asked the woman when she returned to collect the edited piece.

'That,' she said in an awed tone, 'was Michael Milken.'

'Oh, who's he?'

She paused. 'Basically, he's God.'

That was in early 1986. Gradually I found out. Later that summer they arrested Dennis Levine and then, in November, Boesky's plea was made public. Within days there were rumours that Drexel Burnham was under investigation and that Michael Milken, surprisingly, was the criminal mastermind behind an enormous racketeering conspiracy that had corrupted all of Wall Street. In June 1988 Connie Bruck's *The Predator's Ball* had been published. It was a searing indictment of Drexel and Milken and was expected to be followed any day by the real thing, an actual indictment, which did not in fact follow until almost a year later. Meanwhile pieces portraying him as a sinister bewigged recluse, an evil genius and a betrayer of capitalism began to appear in the press. They seemed incongruous with the down-to-earth man on the videotape.

The second time I met him was in the flesh. I had continued working on and off at Drexel and had written a proposal for a documentary about Milken that had been commissioned by Channel Four in Britain. But access to Milken – the single most important thing – proved hardest to come by, perhaps not surprisingly. 'No one meets Michael,' one colleague told me. 'Or if they do it's at 4 a.m. in the morning.' Milken was so brilliant, the demands on his time so great that he had time only for the most important things. In the man's absence, myth had filled the void. Milken was like a god. Whenever the West Coast called with something that needed doing for Michael, people went into a kind of frenzy or overdrive. This seemed as incongruous as the portrayal of Milken as an evil Wizard of Odd. And yet all around him there was this presidential motorcade, and the buzz of drones tending a queen bee.

After months of negotiation we finally got to meet Milken in May 1989. By that time Drexel had settled the government's case and Milken was left to fight alone. As darkness fell we sat out under the poolside sombrero and talked, or rather listened to him talk. With the fading light the pools around his dark black eyes grew and swallowed his face. Eventually we were all sitting in pitch black listening to his soft spoken monologue lapping like the water in the pool nearby, as he spoke on the usual free range of topics. 'His voice pitch was quite remarkable and has a very strange rhythm to it and you were just lulled into it,' said Catherine Bailey, the director who came away thinking that Milken was 'the Reverend Moon of Wall Street' and that his work was the financial version of EST. 'As I sat there listening to him I genuinely believed that this was a man who could solve the problems facing the nineties. Then when you get outside and you leave his company you cannot actually remember a word he said, and then you realize that he was talking this jargon and that it was all absolutely meaningless.'

I disagreed. Milken talked coherently and engagingly. The purpose of the meeting had been to discuss what he would like to see in a film about him, and it did not take him long to warm to his theme, talking about his favourite high yield bond companies all across the country. When we explained that we did not have the resources to go and film them, he offered us the use of a jet to hop around in. As we were obliged to decline this offer, he then suggested high yield bond companies in the New York area. However, the question was virtually academic since almost all the filming – bar an interview with the man himself – had been completed. He also spoke about how workers in America could own their own companies if they agreed to take 10 per cent wage cuts, how gangleaders have proven leadership talents, how bureaucracy was strangling America, and how the drug problem could be tackled by paying farmers not to grow cocoa.

Although there was not much in the way of small talk or conversational give and take, that was because no one else said much. I remembered scribbling notes, and feeling somewhat overawed. Not that he was some godlike presence. He was very straightforward and polite, fetching everybody sodas. But the process of getting through the impenetrable thicket of spokespeople had been such that when it came to the actual meeting I was all but paralysed with expectation and practically at a loss for words. In the end we had to tear ourselves away. He showed us to our car, where he kept talking in the driveway for another forty minutes. 'It's not size – the dinosaurs were big, it's not credit ratings, it's not the money, you've got to get the people to care.' Driving away, I wondered if he was aware of the layers that protected him from public view and if he ever considered how all this wrapping that surrounded him had been received and interpreted by the media and the public. Having finally met him, I could not help thinking that it did him a disservice.

I have not spoken with him since. I had sent an outline of the book I proposed to write but had received no direct reply. I wondered, splashing around that morning in my tepid tub, how he was feeling uptown in his suite of rooms at the Carlyle Hotel. 'What does this nightmare since my indictment feel like? I will answer that I feel as if I am in *Star Wars* and they have just blown up the planet of Obi Wan Kenobi,' he once told a journalist. His life had been a nightmare for so long now that he had stopped wondering when it would end, and now, as he lay under the covers as dawn broke, it must have seemed as if the Evil Emperor was at the foot of his bed, spreading his arms to engulf him in his embrace and pull him down to oblivion.

Lori Milken, his wife, had said she felt like Dorothy in *The Wizard of Oz*, and that she didn't feel she was in Kansas any more. Indeed they were not. They were in New York. Seen through the eyes of Hollywood, New York is urban decay teetering on the brink of collapse. Its subways are filled with toxic ooze engendering Teenage Mutant Ninja Turtles who live in the rank sewers, eat junk food, and fight street crime. It is a city haunted with ghosts and ghouls who slime their victims as in *Ghostbusters*. It is a dark and forbidding Gotham City brooded over by a Batman who, unlike the wholesome original, has been re-cast as a Dark Knight, a dubious do-gooder who believes his violent means justify his ends.

Cleaving to the sun and the future, Milken had left the city behind in the seventies for the West Coast, from where, after almost a decade of California dreaming, he was now dragged back to Gotham City to be broken in to the wheel of tradition and to pay tribute to the past. As Milken once commented of the investigation 'Living in the past when you've lived your whole life in the future is depressing.'

'We're off to see the Wizard, the wonderful Wizard of Odd,' the munchkin's ditty looped in my head as I stepped out of the apartment building. I shared a small, one-bedroom, six floor walk-up apartment in Alphabet City, as it is excitingly known by those who don't live there and so called because the avenues are named with letters instead of numbers. To outsiders it was a dangerous ghetto and was indeed riddled with crack. The brightly coloured caps of the tiny crack vials – red, green and yellow – squished underfoot and littered the sidewalk in confetti profusion. Ninth street, between Avenues B and C, was a twisted yellow brick road, a rollercoaster of narcotic highs and nasty lows. At Avenue B it crosses Tompkins Square Park which for some years now has been a shanty town for the homeless, much to the irritation of the yuppie types who live in the luxurious Christadora Building on the corner, their six-figure condos overlooking the park. Disconsolate, the homeless stand around wire wastebaskets turned into home fires. Just one block East had been the home of Daniel Rakowitz. He had dismembered his ballet dancer girlfriend and allegedly cooked the head into a soup which he had then fed to the homeless whom he had befriended in the park.

I also lived round the corner from where former *Wall Street Journal* reporter and convicted insider trader Foster Winans lived in a six-floor walk-up in equally unfabulous and downwardly mobile surroundings. In his kiss-and-tell book *Trading Secrets* he explained that it was the wretched contrast between the paltriness of his lifestyle, and the glam and glitz of the Wall Street environment in which he worked that first made him think of trading secrets. He wrote a column for the paper called 'Heard on the Street' which was essentially a tip sheet or financial gossip column. His column would often have an impact on the market and profit investors who followed his advice, investors who were often making millions of dollars in salaries and bonuses while he was pulling down $575 a week. For him the roaring eighties was the roar of the whore cursing her crack-dealing pimp on the street below.

So when a millionaire broker had asked him one night 'Wouldn't you like to be a millionaire?', it was not hard to understand why he said yes. Sitting in the cosy exclusivity of the Racquet Club on 51st Street, he would normally have taken the ghetto jet home to his dingy apartment on East 14th Street. Moreover, stepping out onto the corner of Wall Street and Broad Street in the summer of 1986, you could feel the money madness roaring all around you, thundering down the narrow canyon. Only a madman wouldn't have wanted to throw himself in and get soaking rich. I know I did. Working at Drexel Burnham Lambert I was working for $10 an hour, routinely working twelve- to sixteen-hour days. In spite of Drexel's legendary multi-million dollar bonuses, all I ever received was a Christmas bottle of Glen Ellen rosé wine, list price $6.99. Winans, in deciding that he would like to be a millionaire, agreed to trade the contents of his column prior to publication. But instead of becoming a millionaire he got caught.

On the other side of the park Red Ed was earning some loose change by sweeping the sidewalk outside Ray's coffee shop. Ed used to inscribe the sidewalks and lamp posts with stock quote hieroglyphics written in Magic Marker. He also had a teddy bear he used to call the Wall Street Bear; 'Wall Street Bear says buy! buy! buy!' he would say, gesticulating with the bear like a puppeteer. After inheriting a fortune he disappeared for a while and moved to the Mid-West with his girlfriend. But when she had an abortion he returned distraught and garbed himself thenceforward in red drag. He says he used to be on the street, Wall Street, and has one share in every company traded on the New York Stock Exchange. From time to time he would go back to his old stomping ground and hand out a cryptic tip sheet about market trends he wrote and xeroxed. We chatted, and I walked on over to catch the subway down to Brooklyn Bridge.

The US courthouse is an imposing, fifty-four-year-old, neo-classical grey stone building straight out of Batman's Gotham City. Across the width of the base a shallow flight of steps makes gradual ascent to the base of ten imposing pillars of Justice. As I arrived two police officers were putting out the barriers that would hold back the madding crowd of hacks, photographers and tricoters that would gather round the fateful seventeen steps. Apart from a clutch of television vans with microwave relay masts hoisted across the street, no one was in evidence.

I stood at the top of the steps and looked down, visualizing them as they would look to Milken when he would emerge a condemned man. In recent years they had all been here. Bess Myerson, former Miss America and cultural affairs adviser to Mayor Koch, had been acquitted, as had Imelda Marcos, widow of the former Philippines dictator, famous for her three hundred pairs of shoes. In gratitude she had gone straight from the courthouse to St Patrick's Cathedral and walked down the aisle on her knees. Hotel Queen Leona Helmsley had been here too for tax evasion, as had Ivan Boesky, the king of arbitrage.

Former heroes of the eighties, these fallen angels had all been dragged here by one man, former US Attorney Rudolph Giuliani. His headquarters were behind the courthouse and linked to it by a passageway. The prosecutor had used his office to bag high profile cases in a crime crusade of Marvel comic dimensions, which he then tried to parlay into votes as he ran for mayor with the slogan 'He'll Clean Up New York' . He was the Dark Knight, the eighties Batman whose extreme right pursued every perceived wrong. In the end Gotham decided it didn't need his vengeful zeal.

Rudy's victims had all walked the gauntlet of the seventeen steps, and Milken was no exception. The steps were a crucial spectacle, and like walking across hot coals. For those who could not face this ordeal by fire, sneaking in and out of the side entrance merely reinforced their guilt in the public eye. Those who traversed them defiantly with heads held high, even if they turned out to be guilty, nevertheless partially redeemed themselves in the public eye. When Milken was arraigned in April 1989 he had been a hit – in contrast to Boesky who was greeted with boos and jeers. Milken was cheered by hundreds of supporters wearing baseball caps with 'Mike Milken We Believe In You' printed on the front. He had said all along that the most painful thing to him was the publicity of it all, and these short steps must to him have seemed an ordeal by fire. Having already pleaded guilty there was no chance for him to emerge triumphant. Would he be able to face the crowd?

Inside the line had barely begun to form. I was third in line behind Dan Stone, author of *April Fools*, the rush-released 'insider's' account of the collapse of Drexel Burnham Lambert, Wall Street's biggest bankruptcy. Stone had been in the institutional equities department, a safe distance from the core of Drexel's reactor, the junk bond department. He was in a chatty mood, and would be appearing later that day on Financial News Network and NBC with Rudolph Giuliani commenting on the sentence.

Having split the line into two halves – one for press and one for the public – the press were allowed upstairs first. They charged without dignity from the hallway to the elevators, almost running, jockeying with each other for position. Once inside the courtroom illustrators were setting up their boards and pastels in the jury box. Some wore Heath Robinson-esque binoculars that would give them a closer view of their prey, so no micro expression, no shred of remorse, could escape their magnifying eyes. With their necks craned and all their angular bits and pieces they looked like vultures.

Milken, accompanied by his wife Lori and brother Lowell, entered from the back of the courtroom and sat at the table in front of the judge. Inside the courtroom it was hot and getting hotter. It was decided to open a window, only these weren't the kind of windows you could just open. Out of reach, above the judicial wood panelling, you needed to catch a hook with a long pole. Forlornly Milken watched on as someone, embarrassed to be given this task in the first place, tried to hook the window while becoming increasingly flustered. Maybe Milken was figuring out a high yield solution, thinking of a better pole to open the window, a better window that wouldn't need a pole and a better way of financing both. But the spark in his dark eyes had gone, he looked crushed and almost sullen. He had been grounded.

A few minutes before the judge entered, Connie Bruck, author of *The Predator's Ball*, swept in, the belle of the ball. Somehow she had managed to persuade someone to save her a place in the first-come first-served standing-room only crowd. With the the reunion of many lawyers, journalists and loyal friends whose lives had become consumed with the case, there was an almost festive air in the courtroom, emphasized by the imminence of the Thanksgiving holiday. The timing also made this sentencing a symbolic ritual. Thanksgiving is America's oldest holiday, when American familes reunite and over a traditional meal of roast turkey celebrate the arrival of the Pilgrim Fathers in New England and their survival of the first winter. Milken was a Thanksgiving turkey, a sacrifice to history and tradition.

And then the show began. After preliminaries Arthur Liman, Milken's superstar lawyer, roused himself for one final performance. Even though the judge had already made up her mind and was unlikely to be swayed by anything that anyone had to say, it was, he said, 'the only time I can speak to the public'. All along Liman had been tight-lipped and combative with the press, sticking to a few formulaic lines about how he was not at liberty to speak about the case and was reluctant to participate in the trial by press that had typified events thus far.

Today, however, he could speak loud and long, and he did. Had it not been for a faulty microphone, his fifty-minute plea would no doubt have been a good deal more audible. Thus everyone strained to hear him as he set about answering the question he posed himself at the outset: 'What is the real Michael Milken like, not the myth?' Comparing the preceding Fatico proceedings (a pre-trial hearing without a jury intended to allow the Judge to assess the character of the defendant – normally because he is a known mobster) to 'judging a painter on his unsuccessful paintings', he went on to portray a caring man of 'good deeds, good values, good works', which he offered not as a defence for crimes but as part of the total picture. He then went on to speak about Milken's modesty; how he had shunned publicity and cherished privacy; how he cared about his family – not just his wife and children, but the extended family of his colleagues, friends, and in particular their children. Descriptions of Michael as an extraordinarily solicitous employer were illustrated with extracts from letters, including one from a Puerto Rican woman who had been so overwhelmed and frightened of being unable to do the job that she even tried jumping off a chair to break her leg so she could avoid going to work. That drew from the crowd subdued laughter. Diana Perullo's letter went on: 'He took the time to care enough about me to help me believe in myself . . . if it weren't for Michael I would not have succeeded. Today I can say, if it weren't for him I would not have been able to raise my daughter on my own.' In another example an ex-employee wrote about Milken's real concern when he announced his intention of going on a mission to Paris to launch a Mormon Church.

Liman was keen to show that Milken was not 'cut from the same cloth' as Boesky. 'Boesky's most famous quote was . . . "Greed is good". That was his quote'. In contrast Milken was a man with a mission other than the pursuit of wealth. Liman then went on to read from an unpublished letter that Milken had written to *The New York Times* back in 1970 at the age of 24: 'Unlike other crusaders from Berkeley, I have chosen Wall Street as my battleground for improving society because it is here that governments, institutions and industries are financed. While the Wall Street community surrounded by stacks of stocks certainly seems a long way from the egregious gutters of California, the future of both are highly dependent on common factors.'

Maintaining that Milken had 'no interest in material possessions or the perquisites of wealth', Liman went on to illustrate some of Milken's business successes from the point of view of their social significance, before moving on to review Milken's philanthropic contributions and activities. But after a few minutes of this undertaking there was a certain inattentiveness in the courtroom, a feeling that this had all been heard before. Writer Jesse Kornbluth rolled his eyes and others began to shuffle on the benches, which was unfortunate since the seats were covered in leatherette upon which a shifting bottom made farting squeaks.

Tug as Liman might at the heart strings of those present, he seemed unable to knead the material and make it rise like a lump in the throat. He had a rather hoarse voice, and a loose bottom lip that swallowed hard consonants. And although the upside-down triangle of his oddly shaped head no doubt housed a formidable brain, emotional material tumbled out instead of taking quick flight from his tongue into his hearer's hearts. But in one notable exception a response from Michael Milken stirred the assembled from their stupor.

> 'The letter I want to read most is one that Michael doesn't know I am going to read to your honour, because he never sent it to you, and his wife gave it to me and it's a letter from a child at McLaren [a children's help group] who sent it to him on 9 May 1990 after Michael had pled guilty, and I think she wanted him to feel good. It's a child's letter, she wrote two hearts and a balloon: "Dear Mike: Hi. How are you doing? I just want to thank you for everything you do for us. You are a great man. I have grown close to you this last year. I can consider you like a father, a father I never had. I have never met my dad. Well, you guys have been like a family to me with all your love and caring. I love you and your family so much." '

Milken, who had hitherto remained impassive, wept. Liman continued. 'I am not a psychiatrist. I have worked very closely with Michael, and I can't offer your honour an explanation as to how Michael slipped . . . one probation officer found him to be a man overwhelmed by the consequences of his behaviour. The other in California found him to be a broken man.'

On and on he droned while the judge, head cocked prettily to one side, never let her eyes wander from the supplicant, listening, it seemed, with a gentle receptiveness. When her eyes did stray it was to pour herself a cup of water into a polystyrene cup, and as she did so she was sure to look back at Arthur Liman, nodding encouragement. When she bent to take small, delicate sips she would shrug back her long chestnut curls that bounced as they do in shampoo commercials. She was the very picture of Justice. At any moment I expected her to rise, and, unbidden, begin, 'The quality of mercy is not strained, it droppeth as the gentle rain from heaven.' But if Portia she seemed, iron lady she was.

When he was done Judge Wood thanked Mr Liman, in sincere sweetness, for 'a very fine presentation'. She then turned to Milken, asking him if he had anything to add to the letter he had written to the court. Crying, Milken rose. Through the tears and barely audibly he murmured, 'I think in the personal letter I expressed my feelings. What I did violated not just the law but all of my own principles and values. I deeply regret it and will for the rest of my life. I am truly sorry.'

The judge then thanked both him and his wife for 'very moving' letters. One of the defence lawyers felt heartened. As he told *Esquire* magazine, 'If you're going to fuck somebody, you don't look them in the eye and thank them by name for their letter.' Then the judge turned to the government. In contrast to Liman's muffled rasp the voice of Mr Fardella rang out with commanding clarity and the emotional warmth of deep space. Brusquely acknowledging Milken's good qualities, the prosecution then pressed on towards their goal of 'a substantial period of incarceration', which ever since Milken had pleaded guilty had become something of a mantra: 'While the sums that Mr Milken has agreed to pay in fines and restitution reflect substantial deterrence and retribution for his crimes, these penalties do not suffice unless coupled with a substantial period of incarceration . . . even enormous monetary penalties standing alone ultimately become and are perceived as a cost of doing business, especially where other financial resources remain.'

Politely she thanked them too, and then finally it was her turn. It was a big day for her. Although such a historic sentencing required the larger courtroom in the building, some whispered that she had really held out because she wanted to be able to accommodate fifteen of her family and friends to witness her at this milestone in her career.

As she spoke the sweetness and light was tempered with iron, as Mars became increasingly visible in spite of her demure manner. Although she admitted that the special pre-sentencing hearing had 'established neither the government's version of the defendant's conduct nor the defendant's own version', it did establish 'that the defendant engaged in the additional misconduct of attempting to obstruct justice'.

Although she did not allow these stern sentences to cloud her sunny manner, the mood in the courtroom darkened as the thunder clouds piled up. 'When a man of your power in the financial world, at the head of the most important department of one of the most important investment banking houses in this country repeatedly conspires to violate and violates securities and tax laws in order to achieve more power and wealth for himself and his wealthy clients and commits financial crimes that are particularly hard to detect, a significant prison term is required in order to deter others.'

Elsewhere she underlined this particularly strange and, for Milken, dire twist of interpretation: 'You also committed crimes that are hard to detect and crimes that are hard to detect warrant greater punishment in order to be effective in deterring others from committing them.' Evidence that Milken had committed crimes that were hard to detect was in abundance. The judge had been unable to find, as a result of the special Fatico hearing held prior to Milken's sentence for the express purpose of investigating additional crimes, virtually any evidence of Milken's wrongdoing. He had, she found, misled one client, but beyond that nothing more than some ambiguous atmospherics. But it was these atmospherics that she read as the sure signposts of criminal behaviour. Thus the absence of evidence became the proof imperfect of Milken's criminality.

By the time she finally asked Milken to stand, the atmosphere in the courtroom had thickened into that pre-storm silence that precedes the first flash of lightning. For all her soft-spoken gentility Judge Wood was clearly a Zeus in woman's weeds: 'You are unquestionably a man of talent and industry and you have consistently shown a dedication to those less fortunate than you. It is my hope that the rest of your life will fulfill the promise shown early in your career.'

And then she hurled the thunderbolt 'However, for the reasons stated earlier, I sentence you to a total of ten years in prison.'

Neither Milken nor his wife Lori betrayed any emotion. And then, after the little remaining court business, it was all over. The judge rapped her gavel and hurried out with a haste that almost lacked ceremony. Pictured the next day in *The New York Times* attending a luncheon, it was clear that she didn't have much time in which to slip into something more appropiate before getting herself uptown, and it was left to her husband Michael Kramer, a political columnist on *Time* magazine, to utter a few sound bites on the courtroom steps.

Dazed, Milken rose and stepped to the side where he was joined by his wife. They embraced and left. According to James Stewart, prosecutorial journalist for *The Wall Street Journal*, Milken had not been able to take in the sentence at the time and had asked his lawyers what it was that he had been given.

Outside the crowd, mainly hacks, clustered round the barriers, bristling with microphones and cameras. The steps that had seemed so short when they were deserted a few hours ago now stretched out for an eternity. At the bottom the hacks were gathered ten deep, blocking Milken's path to the car that would drive him away. At the top of the steps they jockeyed for position. Bill Tatum, editor and publisher of the *Amsterdam News*, one-time client and long-time supporter of Milken, scrapped with a freelance photographer, threatening fisticuffs unless he desisted from using profanities.

Meanwhile they waited, and waited. This was the moment everybody had been waiting for, the first pictures of Milken finally defeated, the Junk Bond King deposed. Thinking up headlines and captions, everyone agreed that this was the end of eighties. But Milken, who had gamely run the gauntlet when he arrived at the courthouse by purposefully marching up the steps, cheated the media of the spectacle they craved. Milken wasn't going to be coming out. The rumour spread that he had collapsed in a waiting room behind the courtroom and was hyperventilating, and that, once he recovered, they were going to smuggle him out of the back. In fact it was Lori Milken who had finally broken down, her inconsolable cries echoing around the empty courtroom and passageways chilling the few people who lingered there.

A cry went up and the mob ran to the side of the courthouse, intercepting a limousine as it pulled out from a side entrance. One homeboy leapt onto the trunk of the car and began pounding on the roof with his fist. As it turned out it wasn't Milken's car after all, but Arthur Liman's. Uncharacteristically he too had decided to cheat the cameras and make an unobtrusive exit. And Milken had long since gone, somehow escaped.

And that was that. A few anchormen stood on the steps giving their summations. As they all pointed out, this was the biggest and possibly final sentence in the insider trading scandal that had begun with Dennis Levine and led to a total of fourteen convictions. Boesky, who had fingered Milken, had only got three years and most of the sentences averaged between a few months and a year. And yet in spite of this Milken had not even pleaded guilty to insider trading, but merely to a clutch of charges that had previously been treated as civil problems rather than crimes. Although Judge Wood had carefully hedged her summation and made it clear that she was not sentencing Milken for 'a decade of greed', the unprecedented length of the sentence alone – one year for each year of the eighties – suggested otherwise.

I was reminded of a scene from *Reversal Of Fortune*, the film of the book written by celebrity lawyer Alan Dershowitz, who had – in addition to defending other lost causes such as John De Lorean, and Leona Helmsley – successfully argued the appeal of Claus Von Bulow, who had been convicted of attempting to murder his diabetic wife by injecting her with insulin. In the scene reporters clustered around the lawyers and his client on the courthouse steps, while over the hubbub Sunny Von Bulow speaks. She says that she was the only one that really knew what happened, but that, since she was in a coma, she was as good as dead and so her secret remained with her, irretrievable and all but in the grave. Meantime this brouhaha with the court case and the media was really no more than a circus. 'But then,' she added, 'everybody loves a good circus.'

2

HIGH YIELD CHILD

THAT Michael Milken was destined to become a symbol was literally written in the stars. Born on 4 July, American Independence Day, in 1946, Milken would grow to exercise such a brilliant state of mental independence that he would be able to realize the American dream as it had never been realized before. Born on the cusp of a new era, Milken would grow up with American popular culture. The first television set had only been introduced seven years earlier and the first Big Mac was eleven years away and yet by the eighties, when Milken's money machine was operating at full throttle, popular culture would become America's number one export and a global market force.

However, Milken's seemingly unlimited success would not bring him the right to live happily ever after. The totally uncompromising nature of Milken's independent vision, which would not be afraid to consider anything too sacred to be safe from the tide of change, and his commensurate fortune (guesstimated to be between one half and twenty billion dollars) would paradoxically come to be seen as un-American, and turn his dream into a nightmare.

But on that warm summer's evening in 1946 all that lay in the future. As far as Bernard Milken was concerned, the birth of his son on Independence Day must have seemed particularly auspicious, symbolizing for him the fact that he had finally attained against harsh odds his own slice of the American dream, triumphing over the defeats and setbacks of the past. When he heard the news he was having dinner with his aunt and her husband over at their house in the quiet, almost rural Los Angeles suburb of Encino in the San Fernando valley. He had moved there from Wisconsin to start a new life and raise a family.

He himself had never known the joys and securities of family life: his mother had died in childbirth and seven years later his father (who had emigrated to America in 1900) had been killed in a car crash. Then, after contracting polio, he was raised by relatives who had dissipated the little money left for his care with the result that he went into a special home that was practically an orphanage.

But he was determined to build a better life for himself. By working a roster of jobs he put himself through the University of Wisconsin where he met Fern, his future wife. As her best friend Sybil Gordon recalled, 'He was very industrious and would work a number of jobs at the same time, including waiting on tables in sorority houses, reading assignments to blind students and operating peanut routes.' He also taught himself accounting in his spare time.

During the Second World War and after Fern's freshman year, Bernard married her and moved to the West Coast. At this time Bernard Milkevitz also changed the family name to Milken. Apart from the tell-tale limp he had acquired from his battle with polio, Bernard Milken had been victorious in his own personal war with the past, overcoming its setbacks and erasing his defeats.

Two years after Michael's birth followed another son, Lowell, and then, ten years later, a daughter, Joni. For the next thirty years Bernard Milken enjoyed his family life, nestling in the San Fernando Valley, in a reverie of domesticity so cosy that it rivalled even *Wind in the Willows*.

Milken's childhood reads like an enchantment. His great-aunt 'quickly announced that Michael was destined to be an extraordinary individual.' As she lifted him up on the red step chair, 'Michael cracked and chopped every single walnut for her cookies and wiped every single utensil for her sponge cake,' as her daughter remembered. 'Years later when I was at Michael's home I saw him sitting on the floor and playing cards with his children while eating the same cookie recipe he used to help my mother to make as a child.'

It was clear from the start that Michael was a bright button. One friend from third grade remembered that at age 8 he was doing double-digit multiplication while all the others were grappling with the basics of maths. His mother believed that this came from a minor accident she had had just after she had first learned to drive: 'Once when she was driving, we had an accident. My head hit the radio knob and I got a scar. She told me the accident created my intelligence,' said Milken.

He was also extremely competitive. As another boyhood chum recalled, 'I remember in seventh grade we used to have a contest adding up columns of numbers . . . and he was always the fastest.' He also had a prodigious memory. In another game he liked to play, 'One would have to guess from a song title in his large collection of fifties 45s the name of the artist, what was on the flip side, the record label, the publisher and even the catalogue number,' said Harry Horowitz, who grew up with Milken and would later work with him in the high yield bond department. Milken would even compete with himself by trying to do the washing up in record time.

In spite of his love of games and competition, he did not appear to have been a cheat: 'I remember Michael tagging a runner at second base during an important game and the umpire calling the runner out. Unbeknown to this umpire, Michael had dropped the ball. Without hesitation he informed the umpire of his mistake thereby necessitating him to reverse his call,' recalled family friend Sherman Margoles who was the coach of the Encino Little League, the local kids baseball team when Milken was young. Neither was he a poor loser, although in truth he rarely lost anything.

Milken was clearly some kind of boy wonder. Sherman Margoles clarifies, 'He was 12 years old, eager to learn, intelligent, honest, unselfish and co-operative . . . his younger brother Lowell had a slight edge in athletic talent, but Michael had an evident leadership charisma, supported by an early age gift of understanding and compassion for those around him less talented.'

This came out in ballroom dancing classes. 'You used to have to line up and the girls had to choose a partner, and the first one to get Michael, I mean, it was a bee line, because we were eleven and half and he was one of the only boys who could actually dance with you. He didn't step on your toes, he didn't count with his lips, and he could make you laugh while you were dancing,' explained lifelong friend Judy Sherman Wolin who has known Milken since their days at primary school together.

'Now most of us, knowing we wouldn't be dancing at all, much less with Michael, claimed our spots by the wall settling in for an evening we knew would bring us nothing but awful memories and embarrassing moments. I remember clearly that although he could have danced with only the "prettiest girl" or "the most popular girl", Michael danced with every girl in the class – the skinny ones, the plump ones, the ones with glasses and with braces on their teeth (that was me) – making each of us feel special . . . if it is within his power to help a person feel better or believe in himself, Michael does it . . . without artifice, without ego.'

'From the girls' point of view he was certainly one of the the most popular boys . . . and, I think, probably, all the girls had a crush on him. I know I did!' said Wolin. Every Valentine's Day Milken was inundated with cards and the girls who had the task of handing back the papers to the rest of the class once they had been graded would kiss Milken's before returning him his papers. Wolin's puppy love was never reciprocated. Instead Milken's love interest was kindled by Lori Ann Hackel, whom he met when he was in ninth grade and started dating two years later. Her cousin remembered Lori telling her that 'he was very smart, very nice and that she had the feeling that he would always protect her'.

Milken went to Birmingham High School, which combined both junior and senior halves in one six-year school of about 4,500 students. In Milken's mid-year class there were about 138 and over the six years they were there a core of about fifteen or twenty grew to become 'very close and intimate friends', according to eighth-grade girlfriend Hillari Koppelman with whom he shared accelerated classes. Every Friday or Saturday night members of the group would have parties at each other's houses and they would often go on double dates.

Enthusiastically, Milken threw himself into everything. He was class officer, member of the student council, Boys' League, Knights, Squires, and Pep Club, as well as a member of the basketball and track teams. He debated at speech tournaments, received a Junior Chamber of Commerce Award, and was also President of the local AZA chapter affiliated with B'nai Brith. He was voted 'most spirited' and 'friendliest' class member in his senior graduating class in 1964, and prom king (Lori, by now his sweetheart, was school princess and voted 'most likely to succeed'). As then-student body president Richard Hoff remarked, 'He was always the person you wanted on your team.' He was indefatigable, and even as a teenager he supposedly only slept three or four hours a night.

In a rather unusual detail, Milken was also a cheerleader. As he explained, 'I actually thought that one day I was going to be a great basketball player because I was five eleven in the ninth grade and when my mother brings over my old press clippings' – they even had press clippings way back then – 'I was the player of the year in the league.' However, in the intervening summers Milken didn't grow an inch while his peers all shot up. Finally relegated from centre to guard, he was trying out for another team when his coach told him he was trying out for the wrong position. Milken asked him what he meant. 'You should be trying out for the stands over there,' came the reply.

That's exactly what Milken did. Although cheerleading is traditionally perceived as something that girls do, he neither noticed nor cared. In fact he became head yell-leader of a team that included Oscar-winning actress Sally Fields. So even though Milken did have setbacks and was thwarted in his dreams, he was able, for such was the alchemy of his personality, to transform these problems into opportunities. The ability to see value in what others rejected, or thought was worthless, would be the premise of the junk bond revolution, and typified Milken's approach to life. Furthermore, much of Milken's later work involved literally cheering people on, pumping them up with his capital, and giving them the support they needed to realize their dreams. The kid cheerleader was just as successful as the adult cheerleader, in fact so successful that he was even criticized for it. Milken earned himself his first piece of bad press for cheering on his team with a zeal that was considered inappropriate since they were winning 42 to 0. 'I was even controversial as a cheerleader,' he later remarked.

Milken wasn't a total goody two shoes, and would get up to some harmless high jinks, which entailed driving past restaurants and shooting toy machine guns at startled residents. Once he was also supposed to have leapt over a neighbour's fence and practised tennis on their court without permission. He was also a dedicated practical joker. 'Sometimes there'd be a substitute teacher in physics,' Milken remembered. 'When it came time to do the experiments, if things got put in the wrong order, the teacher might be at a serious disadvantage.' Milken also told a story of how he once accumulated seventeen parking tickets in thirty-six hours when he first got a car. Although apocryphal, it was more than ironic in the light of his indictment for stock parking.

If his early life seems like paradise, it probably was. 'It was what I consider a very wholesome background,' said Harry Horowitz. 'Everybody was friendly with everybody else, and the important things were to get your chores done, and take care of your homework, making sure you are taking care of your neighbours . . . they were the values of the neighbourhood.' Such descriptions evoke a golden childhood wrapped in the tissue paper of nostalgia.

Bernard Milken had escaped the nightmare of his past solely by dint of hard work and perseverance. 'To say that he was not a hard worker would be the understatement of the century, and a more upright and morally principled man certainly would have been hard to find,' said a lifelong friend. Together with his wife Fern (who assisted him in his public accounting practice), he sought to instil in his children the same values of hard work and selfless service. Another friend remembered them as 'semi-strict and friendly parents'. From the age of 10 the young Milken earned his pocket money by helping his father with tax returns and sorting cheques.

Milken's critics, such as author Michael Thomas, would argue that this was when he was first bitten by money fever. 'Accountants basically keep the books for people who have a great deal more money than they do, and if you're sitting up late and going to your dad's office on Saturday mornings and seeing how much money other people have and especially how much *more* money other people have, it's going to make you crazy about it.' Milken, on the other hand, claimed that it was his father who taught him about the unimportance of money and the importance of adding value.

Milken recalled, 'I had the opportunity to go and visit my father's clients with him. I remember the days when I used to ask him why he was so attentive to every matter for his clients when by contrast his clients constantly went away on vacation and didn't appear to be worried about their own difficulties. He would tell me that he had a responsibility to them. As he learned about their businesses and got to know their families, he would derive great personal satisfaction from being able to help and seeing his clients achieve. That was his reward. He taught me that helping others was his way of building.'

In describing the parallels between father and son, many family friends have simply said that the apple doesn't fall far from the tree. Milken emulated his father's meticulous conscientiousness. He also shared his abhorrence for any kind of recognition. 'Once we took a family trip to the Grand Teton National Park, Milken remembered. 'It turned out we were the umpteen millionth visitors. They were going to honour us. My father said they'd made a mistake, that it was the car behind us. My brother and I had to push him to accept the free dinner and the raft trip.'

Similarly Milken would shy away from any kind of public acknowledgement. As a schoolboy he always squirmed when they posted the winners of the weekly maths competition on the school board because he was invariably the winner. In later life as headmaster, as it were, of the high yield department on the West Coast, he would make sure that his photo was excluded from the annual yearbook, even though in terms of Drexel's profits he was winning the maths contest hands down.

But of all the fundamentals and beliefs that Milken's father instilled in his son none was more deeply entrenched than the priority of family: 'We are only here for one purpose,' Milken said at the end of his keynote address at his last high yield bond conference in 1988, 'to leave behind a better life for our children and our children's children.' The purpose of all the humility, selflessness and servitude was to plough it back in, folding in all the love, and to repeat the cycle, a closed loop of family security.

Consequently and quite deliberately, little has changed, except that the child now has children of his own and, just like his father, has two sons and one daughter all roughly the same ages apart. The walnut cookie recipe he learnt from his aunt as a child is the same one his family uses today.

'Nothing's changed, we're in a time warp here,' said Judy Wolin outright. When they were growing up, she and Milken's other great boyhood friend Harry Horowitz lived within a few doors of one another – which is exactly where they live today. After graduate business school and after establishing his career in New York, Milken moved back home and burrowed back into the neighbourhood within three miles of where he grew up. Judy lives less than two minutes' drive away while Harry's garden backs onto Michael's. Meanwhile personal lawyer Richard Sandler, another lifelong friend (from elementary school, high school, university and even the same fraternity), has recently built himself a house just across the road. As Harry marvelled, 'If you know their parents . . . they're very, very similar. Both fathers were very, very family-oriented . . . and the mothers both very active . . . and you get a chance to see those same things about their kids. It's almost like going backwards.' 'It's this closed in environment with Michael as King,' said one East Coast ex-Drexelite who spent a lot of time out on the West Coast 'It's just like Shangri-La, that magical kingdom between two mountains where no one ever gets older and everyone's always happy. No one can get in, and no one can get out.'

Time has stood still within this idyllic valley reverie, in so far as Milken in some ways is still a child who seems to have barely grown any older. His boyish looks do not suggest someone in his mid-forties and, it has been argued, his beliefs betray a child-like trust in people, one untainted by the cynicism of the real world. As a kid he worked as a busboy at Du Pars restaurant: 'When someone knocked over a glass they'd yell, "Milken, get out there" and I ran out there with a rag to clean it up,' he recalled. But the same humility still inhabits the body of the billionaire today. Milken was attending a charity luncheon and introducing a writer to the actress and comedienne

Whoopi Goldberg. As they spoke the writer noticed Milken go down on his hands and knees to tie up the laces on Whoopi Goldberg's sneakers. The writer was embarrassed and stunned and thought of Christ washing the feet of his disciples. When Milken stood up again Whoopi cleared the air by saying, 'Michael, you just don't get it, do you . . . they're supposed to be undone.'

There was also, in the opinion of *Vanity Fair* writer Marie Brenner, within this cosy cocoon a fundamental denial of reality. In spite of his limp Milken's father never spoke of the disease that partly crippled him. To protect himself from the cruelties of the past and to protect his family from falling prey to the same tragedies, he created a tightly sealed self-perpetuating family unit, in which the children were the future. As a result of this Brenner argued that Milken could not assess reality accurately. Compounding his father's erasure of the past, Milken maintained that it was not until he was 15 that he noticed his father was handicapped when a schoolmate told him his father had a limp. Instead of acknowledging the orphanage he went to, he preferred instead to think of it as a special home rather like a boarding school. The same schoolmate also marvelled that Milken never mentioned or discussed this with even his closest friends.

However, Milken hardly concealed the fact: speaking at an athletic assembly for the HELP group, a body of disabled children, he told the students that 'they shouldn't think of themselves as disabled or handicapped but rather as children who face special challenges. He shared with them that his father had had polio, yet his father had never thought of himself as disabled . . . he did not even recognize that as a child he was disabled,' according to HELP president Barbara Firestone.

Meanwhile, in the outside world the times were changing, and in 1963, with the assassination of Kennedy, reality did intrude on the dingly dell. At the time Milken was one year away from graduating from high school, and in spite of a basketball game scheduled for the same day, he worked with his friends to arrange a memorial service involving the whole school.

In subsequent years Kennedy's assassination has come to signify the loss of a certain innocence, and his White House has been mythicized as a latter-day Camelot. For many, Kennedy was the beginning and his death was the end of their dreams for a better world and a society that looked after the interests of all its people and discriminated against none. The programme of perestroika that he had planned, one based on a sense of service (ask not what your country can do for you, but what you can do for it), was to be overwhelmed by violent upheaval.

But what left many bitter and disillusioned can only really have hardened Milken's resolve. He had his own ideas. The week after graduating he began at Berkeley, one of the maelstroms of student unrest in the sixties. He was completely unfazed by the fads and crazes of the decade. He didn't drop acid, he didn't do drugs, he didn't smoke, and he didn't drink. Not only did he not drink any alcohol, but he also did not drink soft drinks, like Coca-Cola, and even avoided carbonated water. At the frat beer parties he generally stuck to orange juice, although he has conceded that he may have had one or two beers: 'I didn't enjoy drinking. I didn't like the taste. I didn't feel embarrassed drinking orange juice while others were drinking beer. I did not feel peer pressure.'

In the context of the times Milken was an especially conservative student. Nicknamed Uncle Milty, he was chairman and then president of his fraternity, and helped it stay afloat during a period of financial difficulty. The fraternity became a home away from home, since at one time, in addition to Milken, little brother Lowell and boyhood chums Richard Sandler and Harry Horowitz also lived there (although Harry left after the first semester because of a problem with his grades). When it came to the sexual revolution and the free love generation, he was having none of it, becoming engaged to Lori Ann Hackel who was also enrolled at Berkeley.

In contrast to the quiet conservatism of Encino, Berkeley seemed like a freak show: 'You had a chance to see people ranging from Nazis to communists in the same day . . . boy, the world is a diverse place.' Later in the academic year the university was virtually closed down by the protest strikes of both faculty and students, but Milken was not involved. 'There are better ways to effect change than confrontation,' he said. When asked many years later if he thought he was a revolutionary he deadpanned, 'All the revolutionaries I know are dead.'

However, in the context of the anti-war protests and the activities of the militant left, it was Uncle Milty who was the real rebel. Studying business administration, devouring *The Wall Street Journal* and announcing to colleagues that he would be a millionaire by the time he was 30, the rainbow of Milken's truly contrariant colours began to arch in the sky.

In an era legend for the younger generation's anti-business sentiments, Milken solicited loans from his friends and family friends, paying a premium 10 per cent interest rate. He would also offer to invest their money in exchange for 50 per cent of the losses and 100 per cent of the profits. Milken didn't need to tune in, turn on and drop out because he was already on his own trip.

3

HIGH YIELD BONDS ARE GO

AFTER graduating *summa cum laude* (he failed to win the award as most promising student although two years later his brother would scoop up that particular accolade for the family mantlepiece), Milken first went on honeymoon with Lori to Hawaii (where so many honeymooning couples went in the sixties) and then packed his bags and moved to the East Coast to attend Wharton Business School in Philadelphia.

Having done a stint in the army, Harry Horowitz remembers hooking up with Michael just after the young couple had arrived and attending an orientation dinner with him. He remembers that the Ivy League types (primarily graduates from the Universities of Harvard, Yale, Stanford and Princeton), with their pipes and blue blazers, found the two bright-eyed and bushy-tailed Californians something of an anomaly in their rainy and tradi-tion-drenched cosmology and made fun of them, 'though in a nice sort of way'.

And yet the humour indicates a real divide between the East Coast and the West, and one that would play an extremely significant part in Milken's fate. For New England and California are less like different states of one country than like two independent and utterly different nations. The distance between them is almost as wide as the Atlantic, and has been no less of a cultural divide.

Take the climate. In contrast to the East Coast's moody climate of extremes, the sun always shines in California. Since it never rains on one's parade, the mood is always 'up' and the possibilities are endless. But just as we regard this absence of seasons as somehow immoral, so we regard Califor-nians' ready and sunny smiles as somehow insincere. How can you be really smiling if you smile all the time? How can you be truly happy if you're happy all the time? Non-Californians tend to believe that experience, profondity and value come from a rollercoaster ride of hardship and reward that weather the soul. In this way life's experiences become tattooed and ingrained like furrows on the brow and wrinkles in the heart. But Californians, rather than look like wise old walnuts, go under the knife in order to smooth out the lines and look forever young, and smiling. Lost in the narcissism of the body beautiful and the egomania of celebrity, the Easterners feel that La-la-land or Lotus Land – as these derisions themselves suggest – is a city populated with women like the Stepford Wives, and men like Rambo, fluff-stuffed people inside beautiful tanned skins.

Geographically the differences between East and West are just as marked. In contrast to the stately domes and pillars of the buildings of Washington DC, and the Cleopatra's needle of Manhattan's Empire State Building stuck in solid rock, the foundations of Los Angeles are not built on substance. Instead the city is perched upon the land above the massive San Andreas fault like a vision vouchsafed. Overnight, it could be swallowed up as surely as if it were no more than a dew drop drawn back to heaven. Historically we have been brought up to avoid such risk and insecurity. Since it was the foolish pig that built his house upon the sand, it can only have been a mad pig that would build his house on an earthquake fault.

The movie-set insubstantiality of the city, through the eyes of Eastern prejudice, fits perfectly with the prevalent movie culture where the appearance and surface of things is supremely important. Projected on a screen, movies are no more than flickering images of light and motion, all surface. Everything they touch turns to the shadowy gossamer of celluloid. Even the weight of history becomes 'lite', and grist to the movie mill. Instead of a series of schoolroom lessons to be learned, of received rules and regulations, history is no more than a curiosity chest stuffed with fancy dress, to be plundered at will to clothe the movies in whatever guise is desired.

This absence of history is the most supreme difference. Once upon a time the original frontier, the Eastern seaboard has long since become, with its Ivy League schools, pedigree WASP families, and seat of government, the substance and tradition of America. It is a new England. But the West Coast is a heavenly place of magic and fantasy, and LA is a city of angels. America's final frontier, it is still the wild west, free from tradition. Lured here in their hundreds of thousands by the prospect of gold, people staked all on hitting it big. The gambling spirit did not die with the gold rush. As the shantytown of Los Angeles became the glimmering oasis of Hollywood, they still came with the dream of striking it rich by making it big in the movies. As with the gold rush, the odds were against them and the risks were huge. But the power of the silver screen magically to transform ordinary mortals into immortal stars is just as powerful as the alchemy of gold or incredible wealth. However, this casino mentality stands in marked contrast to the stately East Coast approach to business where the only moral way of making money is to earn it, over time, in a historical process of accumulation.

Together the weather, the city, and the culture, inform Easterners' prejudice of California as a shallow and superficial place. It is literally a world apart. Milken, a California raisin, fell to earth on the East Coast unencumbered with the baggage of the past, and this lightness and lack of form set him slightly apart, and made him something of a curiosity.

Oblivious or fearless, Milken was unfazed by what others might have thought. Performance was what counted, and he was just as competitive as he had ever been. From the outset he had announced his intention of graduating top in his class and had wanted to do this with straight As. However, the instructor teaching the final thesis course didn't give straight As. 'Give me a break Michael, just get an A-minus,' a fellow student was supposed to have told him, but apparently 'that was not of great interest to him' and so he waited until 1978 – by which time he had already made his fortune – to graduate by writing a paper on corporate asset management.

In what appeared to be a small concession to popular tastes Milken feigned slackening off somewhat: Former co-student Harvey Cogen recalled, 'He'd go to the instructors telling them all kinds of things. I think his mother died twelve times that year.' But he only appeared to relax. 'He studied in the middle of the night so people wouldn't know it. He just had to be the best.' As Harry explained, 'I don't think it came easy to Michael because Michael used to study and study hard. It's just that I think he gave the appearance, always has given the appearance (because he does have this quick mind) of being on top of things.' If anything Michael's secret studies signified that he had just given his competitiveness a turn of the screw.

One of Milken's professors at Wharton thought, as did most of his other professors, that he was the most brilliant student that he had ever taught, and so he recommended Milken for a summer job at the Philadelphia branch of Drexel Harriman Ripley, a dwindling investment bank of the old school. Milken was initially despatched to help facilitate the back office transition from old-fashioned bookkeeping to computerized systems but as one executive told Connie Bruck, 'Mike was like a bull in a china shop . . . he was terribly arrogant. And he didn't have the facility to shroud his ability . . . he simply didn't have the patience to listen to another point of view . . . he was useless in a committee, in any situation that called for a group decision. He only cared about bringing the truth. If Mike hadn't gone into the securities business he could have led a religious revival movement.'

Reassigned to another area he made out much better with a plan for overnight delivery of securities which saved the firm millions annually. In 1970 he went to work full time at Drexel, first in Philadelphia and then in New York.

It was from this period that came one of the most powerful and bizarre images to emerge from the eighties: 'At 5.30 a.m. each weekday in the early seventies a bus pulled up to a stop in Cherry Hill, New Jersey, and a young man lugging a bag that bulged with papers mounted its steps . . . ' wrote Connie Bruck in the opening of her book *The Predator's Ball*. 'On winter mornings the sky was still pitch black and the light on the bus was too dim for him to read. He wore a leather aviation cap with the earflaps down [over which] he fitted a miner's headlamp strapped around the back of his head with a huge light projecting from his forehead.'

Milken denies he ever wore a miner's hat, but he was nevertheless something of an oddity. Virtually bald, he had settled on a toupee that one colleague felt moved to describe as 'a hairy mat'. Milken's toupee has of course become one of the media's pet pokes, and the artifice of this vanity has been used as the signifier of Milken's thoroughgoing dishonesty. However, its utter flatness showed such artlessness that only Andy Warhol's outrageous wigs were a more honest declaration of hairlessness. True, Milken did later replace the flat top with a curlier and more current model (one rumour persists that he has thirty of them, each slightly longer than the other, to simulate a cycle of growth and monthly haircut). In contrast to starched cotton shirts and Brooks Brothers suits, Milken was 'no stranger to polyester,' as one writer put it, and much ribbed about his indifference to dress sense.

'It didn't take long to notice Drexel's one public i.e. state-run high school graduate. He was reviled, tormented and every political game that could be played was directed at getting rid of poor Mike,' explained Charles Huber II who was a director of Drexel in 1972. Another former bond trader recalled, 'I never thought he'd make it. I thought he didn't have the personality. In social situations he'd just sort of stand there with his shoulders hunched and this fixed grin on his face.' The grin was like a security blanket to which he clung as steadfastly as a child. It was the last glimmer of California sun, to which he would return.

Indeed, Milken's misfit style was compounded by his offbeat interest in distressed merchandise. Convertible bonds, preferred stocks, and real estate investment trusts were all financial products that had all in their time been popular, but had fallen out of vogue for some reason or another with the result that they could be bought up for a price that was way below their actual value. For example, with preferred stocks, the dividend that these stocks paid was not tax deductible. However, the interest paid on bonds was tax deductible and so this meant it was cheaper for companies to buy back their preferred shares and issue bonds in their place. By buying up preferred stocks, Milken could sell them on again once the continual upward buying pressure had improved their price. He also noticed that if the preferred stock was held by a corporation instead of an individual, then 85 per cent of the dividend was tax deductible after all.

It was essentially the same thinking that informed his interest in 'fallen angels', which were the bonds of companies that had since fallen on hard times, with the result that their bonds were downgraded and rated 'below investment grade'. Milken noticed that the price of these bonds was way below their real value. They could be bought up cheaply and held onto until either the company's fortunes improved or the bond matured, when it was time to repay to the investor his initial investment.

The key to this anomaly was the existence of bond ratings systems in the first place. Although many people – including senators – believed that these credit rating agencies were set up by the government as the result of legislation, they were in fact established to be no more than a guide and service for the investor. There are two main agencies, Moody's, and Standard & Poor's, and their grading systems go from Aaa and AAA respectively all the way down to D. However, once below Baa and BBB, bonds are considered to be 'non-investment grade'. The triple A rated bonds are obviously the safest and represent the largest and most established corporations. Although Ba or BB (double B) bonds are considered to be below non-investment grade this does not mean – although that is exactly what it says – that they are not worthy of investments, they are just riskier. However, over the years the power of the agencies became legend and mere ratings became moral absolutes. As a result bonds that had fallen into disrepute and suffered the disgrace of being defrocked of their investment grade rating were held in more contempt by investors than they deserved to be. And Milken noticed this.

If debased bonds were fallen angels, the bonds of bankrupt companies were homeless bums. But for Milken, the lower they were on the social scale the better, since most investors allowed the smell to put them off. As Tubby Burnham's son, Jon Burnham, recalled, 'Michael made his great fortunes in the early seventies by buying bonds of companies that were supposedly failing bankrupt companies. In many cases he bought them for fifteen cents on the dollar and got paid off at par.' Said Huber, 'Nobody understood those companies, he did immense amounts of work on it and realized there was no way these bonds were not going to get paid off because they had such incredible real estate values . . . and to him buying those bonds was like shooting ducks in a barrel. He said, "There's no way that this is not going to work," and he could prove it to you. He made a fortune for himself and for the firm.'

Once again Milken was questioning the system and was not afraid to trust his contrary findings even though they went against the grain of received, or popular wisdom. He knew that he was right. Even a bankrupt company had tremendous value because of its factories, machinery and property holdings. Research was the key to assess these values, and no one knew the ins and outs of the contents of his junkyard better than Milken. In the case of low-rated bonds, for example, his back-up was Braddock Hickman's study of every corporate bond between 1900 and 1943. 'It's mostly just figures – it's not *Catcher In The Rye*,' he once joked. For Milken the book confirmed what he had been thinking for some time, namely that a portfolio of widely diversified low-grade bonds held over a period of time would be more profitable – even taking into account those companies whose bonds become worthless as a result of going belly up – than the return on a portfolio of investment grade bonds.

Everywhere he went he would cart around large, 60 lb-capacity postal bags stuffed with annual reports, prospectuses, tax filings, proxies, 10Ks, 8Qs, and other financial documents. 'He could run you over with those goddam bags,' one high yield bond colleague remarked ruefully about Milken as, lost in thought, time and space, he would barrel into the office, bags slung over his shoulders. When flying, carry-on hand baggage meant all that he could carry. He preferred two first class seats – one for himself and one for his bags of documents. One reporter who met Milken around Christmastime thought that the bags perhaps contained toys or gifts, until he found himself presented with forty or fifty charts which Milken fished out for the reporter to illustrate his larger points. When he took his daughter Bari for walks he would stack prospectuses on top of her stroller so he could read as he walked. He would even dump them in the seat in his car and read them as he drove to work, which resulted in several accidents ('Michael's focus is not on the road,' his wife said, explaining why he eventually gave in to pressure and got himself a chauffeur).

In some respects the junk man was almost a bag lady. He found value and made use of what other people discarded. Milken's interest in distressed merchandise was an embarrassment to the members of his firm. Bonds traditionally were not supposed to be speculative investments. Unlike shares, which represented an investment in a company and paid a dividend that was a share of the profits, bonds represented a straightforward loan and paid a fixed rate of interest. The purpose of the ratings agencies was to alert investors to high-risk bonds and steer them away from the perils of their 'non-investment grade' status. But in Milken's eyes the concept of risk-free bonds was a contradiction in terms. Since a bond was no more than a loan, it was all about getting paid off in future. To this end a triple A rating that was based on past performance was, as he had seen, no guarantee of what would happen in the future. Thus in spite of the assurances of the ratings agencies, bonds proved over and over again to be a risky business. History was bunk and the future was his junk.

However, Milken did not fit within Drexel Harriman because it had, like much of Wall Street, a tradition-oriented corporate culture. Because a large portion of Wall Street's income derived from fixed rate commissions, houses could not compete with one another by offering discount services. Instead they competed by priding themselves on their heritage and longstanding relationships with *Fortune* 500 companies (*Fortune* magazine's list of the nation's top 500). Drexel Harriman was no exception. Within this historical context Milken's low-grade speculative gambles smacked of the casino and lacked pedigree.

Not only did Milken's colleagues dislike the securities he dealt with, but they also didn't like the way he looked. Such things counted for a great deal in the crusty culture of Drexel Harriman, and Milken was ghettoized with his bags and his junk investments in his own corner of the largely empty office.

'For me the test came,' said Charles Huber, 'when the president, Archie Albright, ordered me to fire Mike. "What's he done," I asked. "The equity salesmen, traders and the preferred stock traders don't like him," said Archie. "He calls on their accounts without telling them . . . he doesn't try to steal commissions, he just embarrasses everybody." "How could he embarrass anyone?" I asked. "Well, for some reason after the customers have talked to Mike, they don't want to talk to the salesmen, the traders or anybody else." I laughed and suggested that we fire the salesmen and the traders and promote Mike.'

According to Huber, 'Mike survived the incredible insults of his peers by simply ignoring them and working harder.' It may be, of course, that he was so lost in his work that he was never aware of them. Milken told one colleague that he did not know if he was necessarily smarter than anybody else (although most people seem to think that he almost certainly knew he was) but that he knew he could work 25 per cent harder. Never having had much need of sleep, he would commute for four hours a day, often not getting home until 1 a.m. and having to get up a few hours later to catch the 5.30 a.m. bus. The synergy of his brain, application, and competitive instinct made him unbeatable.

It was not long before Milken wasn't just trading in preferred stocks, but had a lock-up on the entire market. 'Here was born the fatal flaw which Mike's competitors on Wall Street would never forget. Having set his eyes on a market Mike would seek to dominate that market through his insights and talents,' said Huber. 'Everything about American business tells us to go after 100 per cent market share and don't stop trying till you get it. But woe betide the person who does.' In spite of the fact that the premise of the American dream is success without limitation, most people are prevented through their own limitations – real or perceived – from achieving that, and committing the social crime of success to excess. It was all, Huber ventured, part of 'the illogic of life', and Milken in his logical and flawless analysis of the trees failed to factor into his equation the darker illogic of the wood, its primal shadows, tribal rites and constraints.

Although Milken was frustrated at Drexel because he could not get more than $50,000 to trade with, history was on his side. In 1973 Drexel merged with the Jewish firm of Burnham & Co., a third-tier retail brokerage house. Burnham & Co. was, in the words of Michael Thomas, Lehman veteran and Wall Street bear, 'a chickenshit little firm with rather grand ambitions', while Drexel, in spite of its decline, was what was known as a major 'bracket' firm (bracketing was the Street's time-honoured pecking order, and was a status-based way of carving up new business among the Wall Street pack). In other words, one had the money while the other had the name. A merger was the perfect fit.

As soon as the deal was done Burnham was supposed to have asked if there were any Jews in the firm, and Drexel's management advised Burnham to check out their most brilliant guy Michael Milken, who was then thinking of leaving and returning to Wharton to teach.

As Tubby Burnham, the firm's founder, told Glenn Yago, 'Mike worked away trading securities nobody else was interested in. I offered him $28,000 a year and increased the position he could handle from $500,000 to $2 million. I allowed him to keep a dollar for every three he made. He doubled the position's value in a year. Our deal never changed.'

From being ghettoized in a corner of the trading floor the junk bond bag man had both negotiated the formula that would lead to his controversial record-breaking salary of $550 million in 1987 and secured his position at Drexel, launching his own high yield and convertible bond department which was one of the first specialized niche operations that would be the wave of the future on Wall Street.

Other factors were also working in Milken's favour. In May 1975 fixed rate commissions were abandoned. From being a staple and secure source of income, trading stocks and shares became a money-loser as firms competed with each other in a bidding war, undercutting each other's prices. Within two years revenues on Wall Street plunged $600 million. Bonds were suddenly looked at in a new, speculative light. When, on the eve of the eighties, the government repealed its practice of determining interest rates, setting them free to move with the market, 'overnight the bond market was transformed from a backwater into a casino,' wrote Michael Lewis in *Liar's Poker*. From being a safe and traditional investment area, bonds now became as volatile as shares, a gambler's medium. Milken, with his future-oriented theories, would only welcome this.

But before the junk bond revolution was ready to roll, there was one more piece to fit into place. Again, it hinged on the gap between the perception and the reality of the anomalous credit ratings.

When a company issued new bonds they were rated by the agencies, and of the twenty-three thousand companies in America with sales of over $35 million dollars, only about 5 per cent could issue bonds rated investment grade. The alternative for the remaining 95 per cent not deemed worthy of the investment grade bond market was to turn to the banks or to insurance companies for loans that were expensive because of the high rate of interest, were short term, and came with all sorts of restrictive covenants and other strings attached. Alternatively, they could always issue shares, but shares, unlike bonds, were actual shares of ownership in a company, and issuing them meant diluting control. Because the dividend paid to the shareholders was not tax deductible (unlike the interest paid to the bondholder), they were also a more expensive way of raising money. Of course there would have been another alternative, to issue non investment grade bonds, but there was no market. Sticking with the wisdom of the rating agencies, no Wall Street firms would underwrite them and no investors would buy them. Until Milken came along.

Investment grade companies were so rated because they were perceived by the agencies to be as safe as houses. They arrived at this conclusion by looking at the company's history and balance sheet. But Milken had seen that a triple A rating was not a lifetime award, and depending on how the company performed its debt could be downgraded. In the case of downgraded bonds, Milken, knowing the true value of companies despite their troubles, made his money by buying up these fallen angels at a deep discount. Given that a company's past was no guarantee of its future, it made no sense to Milken to rate them on that basis. 'The value of a company is the sum of two components: its past as represented by its historic balance sheet and its future, represented by its prospects.' Instead it was a question of looking at things not on the balance sheet, such as the quality of management, and the extent of the need and demand for its products. With satisfactory answers to those questions Milken saw no reason not to issue non-investment grade bonds for growing entrepreneurial companies. Although preferable to bank loans, companies would still have to pay a premium for their funds. The bonds would pay a higher interest rate or higher yield than investment grade bonds to compensate investors for the extra risk that they were taking. Drexel would also charge a higher percentage fee for issuing these bonds in addition to taking an equity stake in the company and maybe even a seat on the board.

Contrary to popular opinion, Milken did not invent junk bonds. Bonds that paid a higher yield or rate of interest than was current at the time had been the instrument of choice (or desperation) for entrepreneurs unable to raise money by offering the going rate. 'The tale was familiar enough,' wrote historian Robert Sobel in his essay entitled 'Some Junk! A historical perspective.' 'The young enterprise was foundering, and so a new management took over . . . the firm had several classes of debt, totalling almost eighty million, which required $4.6 million a year in interest payments. The quality of that debt was highly suspect. The evidence was there to be seen in the markets, where some of the firm's bonds, issued at par under the old regime, were selling for around 15 cents on the dollar, and were the objects of intense speculation on Wall Street.' The upshot was that 'the company' issued high yielding debt that paid an interest premium that was fully 1 per cent above the current rate. Initially the 'junk' bonds were ridiculed, but three years later the bonds were trading at par. 'The company' was none other than the United States of America.

But the key to the success of Milken's modern-day junk bonds depended upon his ability to break the psychological lock that the rating agencies had on bond buyers. Generally these consisted of pension funds, life insurance, bank trusts, college endowments and other institutional investors. They relied on the ratings to guide them in making what were thought to be risk-free investments. But as Milken had seen, 'there is no such thing as a risk-free investment', and while it would be fair to say that most of the money managers who were investing their company's funds in these bonds were aware of that, they also had their jobs to think about. If they played it safe and bought only triple A or investment grade bonds, at least if things did go wrong and the bonds went bust as they sometimes did, they wouldn't be blamed and they wouldn't lose their jobs. However, if they left the relative safety of the investment grade high ground and plunged into the wilderness of unrated debt, they were asking for trouble. They would have to do far more research about the companies themselves in order to divine in this volatile netherworld the winners from the losers. And that was as good a reason as any to leave well alone. Why violate the bankers' 3-6-3 code? Borrow money at 3 per cent, lend it out for 6 per cent and on the golf course by 3 p.m.

In trying to persuade money managers to see things his way Milken spoke, as he would often do, in terms of movies. He compared the rating agencies to movie critics. In much the same way that movie critics often give lousy reviews to popular movies, so it was with the rating agencies. 'Recently my son went to see *Lethal Weapon 2* . . . well, the reviews said that *Lethal Weapon 2* was not a good movie and you shouldn't waste your time going to see it. My son saw it anyway and loved it. In fact the film grossed some $20 million the first week it opened . . . even though it got a poor review.' What if a cinema owner had been swayed by one of the bad reviews for *Star Wars*? He might never have booked the film and would have missed one of the box office opportunities of a lifetime. Milken's message was 'ignore the reviewers', or rather, ignore them and listen to him.

Needless to say, Milken's idea got a below investment grade rating from the Wall Street establishment who told would-be investors to call Drexel since they did not deal in that 'junk'. Milken looked West – away from the ingrained prejudice of tradition – for support. 'Deciding that the eastern seaboard managers were unlikely to change,' wrote journalist Jay Epstein, 'Milken turned West to the sun belt focusing his energy on the younger more aggressive fund managers and non-traditional institutions.' As Milken him-self later explained, he looked to managers who were judged by their 'performance rather than conformance'.

And he was successful. In 1977 Merrill Lynch did three issues of junk bonds and then abandoned their embryonic franchise because they thought it was unseemly. The same year Drexel issued $30 million in bonds for Texas International, a petroleum company. The next year they issued $439 million in junk. As compensation for the additional risk Drexel were taking they took a higher fee. Instead of the 1 per cent commission that was typical for the underwriting investment grade bonds, Drexel took 3-4 per cent. Junk bonds were go, and the millions Milken was generating would soon become the firm's profit engine.

4

MILKEN'S PERCEPTION:
HIS HIGH YIELD WORLD

THE LAND OF X, MILK, AND HONEY

MILKEN never really took to the East Coast, and the East Coast would never really take to him.

It is perhaps not surprising that someone who went to Wall Street 'to help improve society', as he had written at the time, and who had felt that 'the egregious gutters of California' depended upon 'common factors', should find himself isolated in his views. Wall Street has never been renowned for its social agenda beyond a self-serving tokenism. A misfit on a street dominated by tradition, Milken, a child of the future, decided to move back to California. As one colleague remarked, 'He had his own ideas, but you could never really figure out where he was coming from. He was a loner.'

The specific reasons for the move were more personal. He had two young children and both were afflicted with juvenile ailments. 'I figured that less rain and less temperature change would mean fewer illnesses. And I wanted to be near my father.' His father had developed a cancerous melanoma on his toe that had spread throughout his body. As Milken would later recall, 'The first time in my life when I felt I really faced a problem that was insolvable was in 1976 when my father was diagnosed as having cancer. Prior to that, there was no situation which I could not either adapt to or for which a solution could not be found.'

Although Milken could not cure his father's cancer, he did come up with a solution of sorts. Most people would hand in their notice, go West and look for another job. But not Milken. He announced to the firm's flabbergasted management that he would be moving back to California and taking his entire department of almost thirty people with him. He made the move over his birthday during the 4 July weekend in 1978. It was an extraordinary declaration of independence.

But it was not a power play. Instead this unprecedented action shows how Milken sought to and succeeded in breaking the bounds of history and shrugging off the weight of tradition. Instead of being forced to be part of the

Wall Street political picture, Milken cut through all constraints and returned to California where he set about financing the future with his high yield bonds. Ultimately, of course, Milken would be plucked out of his high yield orbit and grounded by the piles of power on the East Coast.

One of the management's concerns was that Milken wanted to move to California because he was burning out and wanted to slacken the pace. They could not have been more wrong. Milken's plan was to add three hours to the day. Clocks were set to New York time, and people were expected to be in by 5.30 a.m., an hour and a half before the markets opened in New York. From then until 2 p.m., when the markets closed, they traded. There were none of the two-hour luncheons that were part of a bond trader's culture on Wall Street. After the markets closed the rest of the day would be given over to meetings and company presentations. The day would wind down about fourteen hours after it had started, around 11 p.m. in New York.

'Where else can you work a fourteen-hour day and still be home for dinner?' quipped one trader. As Milken elaborated, 'For all of us in the group, California was a better place to raise families. If a parent leaves home at 5 or 7 a.m., it makes no difference to his or her family – everybody's asleep. But leaving two hours earlier means you're home two hours earlier.' Milken himself rarely left the office until 9 p.m. so it's hard to see how this made much difference to the time he spent with his family. Until his father died in 1979 both he and his brother would stop by the house every day on their way home from work.

The other advantage of the move was that he would get out from under the feet of Drexel's management. Although there were bundles of phone lines tying them together and a procedural umbilical cord that linked the two (every trade was on the screens in New York for review), there was a tremendous difference between being on the end of a telephone three thousand miles away, as opposed to being just down the hall.

'The Department', as it came to be known, was a plain white marble box that had previously housed Gump's department store. It would have seemed quite anonymous were it not for the fact that it was opposite one end of Rodeo Drive, which best-selling sex and shopping novelist Judith Krantz described as 'the most staggering display of luxury in the western world' (it was also California's most popular tourist location after Disneyland). At the other end was Fred Hayman's flagship Giorgio perfume store, whose yellow and white striped bags were almost as big a money-spinner in the eighties as junk bonds. Milken had not originally moved there when he moved back West, but by 1983 they were running out of space in their Century City Quarters (on the Avenue of the Stars) and Milken and his brother (together with a group of other partners) had bought the building which they leased back to Drexel. Milken had originally recommended the property to Drexel as a good investment, but the East Coast were not interested.

'In a town that spawns every excess money can buy Milken chose this as his made-for-the-movies mecca,' snorted Connie Bruck. But Milken himself cared little for displays of wealth. Unlike leverage buyout king Henry Kravis who stuffed his offices overlooking Central Park with fine art and and antiques that were the marvel of all who came there, and unlike arbitrage star Ivan Boesky who worked from an office that looked like the flightdeck of the Starship Enterprise, Milken maintained, 'I have no private office, I never had one in my life.' Instead of glamourizing his power by immolating himself in a fetish of futurism or a museum of art, he said, 'I have to know what's going on.'

Accordingly he worked on the trading floor, which he had customized into an 'X' shape so that from where he sat, at the crux, he could see everyone and hear everything that was going on. Over the years there were several versions but the final version consisted of three Xs strung together like two zigzagging lines. Milken sat in the middle occupying four humanoid spaces (though even this was not his exclusive space. When he was not around he encouraged others to use it). The crucial thing for Milken was that from his vantage point he could see everyone. He could also hear everyone. 'He's got peripheral hearing and seeing,' marvelled Robert Davidow and Milken concurred. As he told the Securities and Exchange Commission in one of their early investigations, 'I have good hearing and over the years it has developed so that I can hear most of the conversations in the department.'

The department was a cybernetic machine, an X-shaped creature of hi-tech and human tech, nerves and wires, quotrons and brains. One hundred people worked the machine, there were over three hundred monitors, two hundred telephone lines and endless miles of cable. There was no flash, no plush, no luxurious trimmings, and its form was purely an expression of its function. Just as the shark had evolved as an eating machine, so the X had evolved as a twelve-legged money-making insect that virtually never slept. It squatted there like a toad, humming and blinking, crunching numbers, spitting out deals and making money. 'The electronic machinery was like the blob; after a while it seemed to take on a life of its own,' commented writer Marie Brenner.

To be sure, life on the X was no picnic. 'We get up at 4 a.m. and we don't go out to lunch and we don't take personal calls, we don't tell jokes, don't talk about the ball game. No one in America works as hard as we do,' said one bond salesman. Wrote Patsy Van Utt, the only woman salesperson who worked on the X a few feet away from Milken: 'He was a demanding person to work for . . . compliments were rarely given . . . he demanded excellence and disdained mediocrity in all of us.'

In explaining this punishing routine Milken compared himself to an Olympic athlete sparing no effort in the competition to be the best. Leading by example, he expected no more but no less from his team members who were expected to join him in his Olympian pursuit of 'going for the gold'. 'It's like running a marathon,' said devoted departmentalist Robert Davidow.

'Sometime in the afternoon you get tired and it's like hitting the wall of pain. You have to run through it, but you get a little spacey.' Just as with the vast gothic generator in *Metropolis*, people worked on the machine and the machine worked them until they were physically exhausted and could work no more.

Awestruck, this is how a journalist who witnessed the spectacle described it: 'Traders and secretaries constantly call out Milken's first name, alerting him to calls, prices, a bid, a potential deal. Milken, with only brief exceptions, is on the phone usually with the device pinned to his right ear, his head cocked right to hold it in place, pen in his left hand. After a time, when that ear is finally exhausted, he will switch, and later stand up and pace slowly. Occasionally he will tap the keyboard on one or two terminals or the calculator on his desk . . . He seems rather calm, actually, among the confusion.'

Milken himself never wrote down orders to buy or sell securities. If it needed to be done he would tell someone to take care of it. Apparently he did this by always saying 'please' and 'thank you' and never raising his voice, which would have been quite unusual for trading floor culture. He had three shifts of assistants who worked before, during, and after the working day screening calls, taking messages and getting people on the phone. One of them estimated that during her shift he would routinely take more than a hundred calls. In another deposition he estimated that he himself handled about five hundred telephone conversations a day (in 1982) and was active in 'potentially one thousand transactions a day'. The telephone on his desk carried a hundred lines, sixteen direct to New York. To one observer watching Milken work was like witnessing a spaceman with ninety-five antennae coming out of his head navigating his spaceship.

Not surprisingly, the sheer volume of work done was mindboggling. At the peak the department was doing one major junk bond issue per day. In terms of trades Milken estimated in a 1986 lawsuit deposition that they were averaging a quarter of a million transactions a month, or within the junk decade (from 1977 to 1987), when Milken held sway, some thirty million transactions.

Another observer who frequently went to the department for meetings recalled, 'Do you remember in those old sci-fi movies they would show how people through robotics and machines would eventually develop their brains to such an extent that they wouldn't need to use their bodies? Well Mike was like this incredible component brain that produced so many ideas at such a high speed that he needed all these people to get the things done that he was thinking up. They would sort of wheel this giant brain into meetings and plug him in. He was never really there. I always wondered what it would be like to get the brain drunk.'

But the brain didn't drink. The brain's meat and drink was work. In a deposition which writer Connie Bruck had to prise from the Securities and

Exchange Commission using the Freedom of Information Act, Milken relayed a typical day.

'I come in in the morning between four thirty and five. I generally read *The Wall Street Journal*. I generally write notes for the people in the department, put them on an administrative person's chair. By five fifteen she's put them on everyone's chair in the department, so if they're not in they can't sit down without picking up their note. I then direct administrative people to make calls for me and get people on the phone, and that generally runs till around two o'clock in the afternoon.

'Sometime around ten forty five to eleven they put some food on my desk which I eat in anywhere from one to five minutes. Sometime in the afternoon it's possible corporations would come in for meetings and there would be meetings in the department with representatives from various corporations.

'Sometime between four and six a position sheet is put out as to what the position is for the department at the end of the [day], which I start to review. And, if I'm not too tired I then start writing out notes for people in the department, asking them why they bought or sold a security, if I have an opinion, or I don't think that's a good idea, or that it might be a good idea.

'When I'm exhausted I go home and get ready for the next day.'

As soon as Milken was ensconced in Beverly Hills people began to make the pilgrimage to go and see him. Oz Mutz, Chief Executive Officer (CEO) of the Forum Group who wanted to raise money for his chain of luxury retirement homes was told by a Drexelite to go to California: 'There's no way he'll travel to Indiana to see you. He's too concerned about spending time with his family to spend it travelling.'

In the afternoon Milken received his supplicants in a series of glass-fronted conference rooms that ran along one side of the X. Filled with black marble tables and black chrome furniture, they were like airport lounges where CEOs would cool their heels waiting for up to two hours for their momentary connection with Mike. Suddenly the brain would be wheeled in, surrounded by a cadre of as many as twenty-five. He had one assistant just to make sure that he kept on schedule. After listening to the presentation or just sparking off a few ideas he would then be wheeled out, and shuttled off to the next room, 'just like a dentist' as one visitor described it.

Perhaps understandably, the supersonic robot was a selective listener. As he himself admitted in an SEC deposition, he 'could be carrying on ten other conversations' at any one time. 'I would say I listen to no more than 25 per cent of the conversations I have with anyone during the trading day . . . I would come in and out, buy and sell securities during any conversations.' People on the other end of this treatment found it rather offputting.

But Milken did not lack the human touch. Even if it meant being late for a meeting he would take time out to play with the kids of his staff if they brought them onto the floor, and he would always take time out to ask about the wives and children of his clients. In the meetings too he would say to his visitors,

'Tell me your hopes and your dreams.' Instead of banking on the balancing sheet – which to Milken was history and thus irrelevant - Milken was betting on the collateral of human creativity.

'We would prepare for these meetings,' said Tom Kalinski, CEO of Mattel toys, 'and we always tried to determine ahead of time what it was that Mike Milken wanted to know about Mattel, but were never able to guess correctly what he was going to ask us. Most of the time he was interested in the toys. He was interested in why Barbie is successful. He was interested in why Masters of the Universe was continuing to grow. He'd offer suggestions on products. Most of the time he was not interested in talking about the nuts and bolts of the business, he was interested in our products.'

If Milken did not listen while they talked it was because he did not need to listen. He already knew (to a depth that often even surprised the CEOs themselves) the information he was pitching to them, because he had committed to his photographic memory every relevant prospectus in his postal bags. So perhaps instead of listening, he watched. As Steven Wynn remembered, when he first met Milken in the office and when he was pitching the idea of building a Golden Nugget casino in Atlantic City, he could feel Milken sizing him up, weighing the unit of human capital before him, and as Milken later explained to him, 'It's not what you've got, it's what you stand for.'

While he invariably asked his clients about their families, Milken had little use for small talk or what most people would call normal conversation. The first time George Gilder met Milken he, as did so many others, simply listened while Milken 'unreeled these oracular spiels'. David Salzman, president of Lorimar Television, a client of Milken's, recalls one of their meetings with about twenty Japanese business leaders: 'We were all spell-bound by Michael's ninety-minute soliloquy on global stability and corporate responsibility.'

Milken's love of the messianic monologue as tool of social discourse would also invade social situations, where it was not always appreciated. Mediatrix Barbara Walters, the cooing interviewer of stars who in the process had become one herself, told her then husband Merv Adelson (founder of Lorimar Pictures) never to repeat the experience after she had to suffer a two-hour lecture on Milken's solution to the problem of Latin American debt. She is since divorced. As even a neighbour commented, 'Periodically when . . . I have a chance to speak with Michael, his conversation is like a stream of consciousness on the welfare of our street and our community.' Apparently she didn't find this all that odd, commending him instead for the voracious-ness of his desire to help.

Robert Sobel, a debt historian and defender of Milken, offered this almost paradoxical insight: 'He's very pleasant and easy to get along with but he's always thinking about five or six other things. He never concentrates upon you, which is a mistake.'

THE THOUGHTS OF CHAIRMAN MIKE

Ultimately, however, a lack of social graces (which Milken didn't generally lack anyway) isn't a crime, and rather than tripping over himself in awkwardness at being a demagogue and an ideologue, Milken maximized. Every year he gathered the faithful for a junk bond jamboree (officially known as the annual Institutional Research Conference). Such a forum was the ideal showcase for the one-way street of Milken's communication skills, and he would tirelessly deliver his junk bond sermons and visions of a high yield world at this modern day Sermon on the Mount.

The first conference, held in 1980, had consisted of fifty or so attendees, but come the final blow-out, there were some 3,200 guests. The cost of this four-day bonanza was estimated to be in excess of $12 million. Over the years those in the house would number politicians and pop stars in addition to some of the most powerful business figures in America. As Dolly Parton put it when she walked on stage to perform at the close of the conference, 'This looks like the original cast of "Lifestyles of the Rich and Famous".'

Although Milken liked to start his day at 4.30 a.m. he compromised, and each day the conference would begin at 6 a.m. with breakfast. The day was then filled with company presentations and panels – generally running four at a time – and would end after dinner around 9 p.m. Not a moment was wasted. Milken would give a keynote address over breakfast and other major speakers such as Ted Turner and W.R. Grace would speak at lunch.

Because Milken felt he was speaking the truth, he did not feel that his message staled with repetition. In his keynote speeches Milken adhered to the same core of ideas that were the building blocks of his junk vision. Invariably it was the inevitability of change and its necessary virtues that was his starting point.

'If you want to be successful, you have to embrace change, not to fight it. But change is a difficult thing to deal with. We don't like to have familiar things change. We don't like it when our kid stops watching the Disney Channel and starts watching MTV. I don't like it when they change my seat at work – it disorients me for a week. And people who have been successful don't like it when the world tells them that they have to change.'

The crucial question was, as times changed and brought new demands, did people alter their perceptions to keep in step with the new realities, or did they, with their bias towards what was familiar and resistance to what was unfamiliar, allow their perceptions to lose touch with reality? Milken believed that this was what had happened to American industry, citing the fact that although it was America that invented and developed the video recorder, not one model was made in America today. The fact that most people stuck with the old instead of venturing with the new was what made people the scarce resource. With his financing he saw himself as empowering the people with the vision to try and build the businesses of tomorrow.

One year Milken planned to illustrate this theme with a video showing the changes in twenty years from 1968, when he was at Berkeley, to 1988. But Milken balked at showing pot-smoking peaceniks and free-love hippies. The past was important only in so far as it related to the future, and the tune-in-turn-on-drop-out make-love-not-war vibe of the sixties was history.

So what were the kind of changes Milken was talking about? They were fundamental social and historical changes: 'Capital is not the scarce resource, people are the scarce resource,' he would announce. 'In an industrial society capital is a scarce resource but in today's information society there's plenty of capital . . . everywhere you go people come up to you and say,"I have money to invest, what should I put it in?"' Although he used it many times, it was a line that would always hook the uninitiated (who were perhaps more excited by the prospect of capital unlimited, traditionally considered to be the scarce resource, than anything else). 'By 1970 there were less people working in industry as a percentage of the population [than] in 1950. By 1970 the major job in this country was a clerk. What did this mean? It meant that the scarce resource was knowledge . . . and so the value of a company and a business was the knowledge and the wisdom and the vision of its employees.'

The failure to see this meant that the way companies were rated in terms of their creditworthiness for loans was based on the wrong set of assumptions. 'The most important asset isn't found on the balance sheet. A company's most important asset is its people; it's human capital, it's managers . . . as I've said before, maybe there's one industry, the sports industry, where you find people on the balance sheet . . . [but] as you look at the *Washington Post* the major assets of these and most of the assets of the American companies aren't on the balance sheets. The publishing and communications companies' assets are not their buildings and not their printing presses, but the people that write and put out that information.'

To illustrate the people factor Milken had a favourite real estate story: 'If we were to turn back the clock forty years we had four pieces of real estate we could get as a gift: one was a little peninsula off the coast of Siberia – no natural resources, terrible weather, very inhospitable neighbours . . . next was an island off the coast of China – no natural resources, devastated (seemed to have lost the war) . . . three was another little island off the coast of China which had its own problems in that the people of the world were going to decide that it didn't exist . . . [fourth] a country with tremendous natural resources, a two thousand mile border with the the United States, tremendous acreage, beautiful weather and tremendous land on both the Atlantic and the Pacific.' The countries were Korea, Japan, Taiwan and Mexico. After a review of the booming economies of the first three when compared with the latter he delivered the punch line: 'The factor we overlooked in the analysis was the people.'

On the home front the credit rating agencies failed to factor people in when they studied the company books in their determination of investment grade from non-investment grade. The result was the yawning gulf between perception and reality. This was another cornerstone of the Milken philosophy, and the theme of the 1987 conference. Milken illustrated this with a video collage of masks, mirrors and drag queens including Dustin Hoffman in *Tootsie* and Julie Andrews in *Victor Victoria*. There was a special significance to this in that junk bonds – more speculative and volatile than investment grade bonds – had often been called 'equity in drag', because they performed more like shares which went up and down according to the company's fortunes.

In the Milken glossary, 'perception' was popular wisdom, surface impressions and erroneous observation often based on the past, while 'reality' was what lay under the surface, the essential truth and what the future would bring. Thus on the one hand, 'The tendency of our financial structure has been to channel loans to industries of the past rather than the future . . . lending money has been based primarily on a balance sheet recording past performance.' On the other hand, 'People and industries of the future are considered risky. Now any future has risk associated with it. It's easy to say that the past is for sure – it's the past. The future and opportunity always have risk.'

According to Milken, the failure to change our ways and attend to the future instead of yielding to the past had created the disarray of the present, and brought about other even more unwelcome changes, which we were still unwilling to accept. To illustrate this, Milken had a favourite basketball story.

'One game that stuck in my mind was the Olympic game between the Soviet Union and the United States in Korea this year. It was a game where I was listening to the announcers and they were telling us that we have really never lost a basketball game in the Olympics. The game we lost in Germany a few years ago, we really deserved to win . . . And listening to the game you got the feeling that it was an American birthright to win. We invented the sport, we were expected to win. And lo and behold in the first half we were behind by ten points . . . they [the announcers] said we were playing poorly and when we started to play well we would, of course, win. But something happened, and what happened was that the other team did, indeed, have ability and the other team went ahead and late in the half the announcer said for the first time that he now thinks that we're not going to win.

'When I think about American business in the past decade, I think about this game. American business at the start of this decade was faced with interest rates going to 21 per cent, was faced with the belief that maybe we had not done a good job modernizing; maybe we hadn't used all the management techniques; and maybe during this decade the dollar was too high. But when the dollar got to its right value and when we used our techniques which were available to us we would once again take our place of leadership in the world. But what happened? . . . The United States is no longer the sun. We're one of the planets of this earth and it's a lot smaller planet.'

Instead of investing in the new entrepreneurial companies of tomorrow, hundreds of billions went instead to Third World countries. 'During the past two decades we really had a situation where loaning money to business in this country was considered too risky, while more than a trillion dollars flowed from the industrially developed nations to other countries around the world especially to Latin American governments.' Instead of going to the less developed countries, Milken argued, the money should have gone to 'our domestic LDCs – the less developed communities'.

'I think we need to understand that investing in people and their business is not risky; it's risk averse. If we don't invest in our people and our businesses, our own country and its cities eventually deteriorate and then we wonder what happened.'

'When you think back over the last decade, you tell me which loan was better risk and created more value – a bank loan to Paraguay or a loan to MCI? . . . It was okay to invest in some distant land in a hope and a dream, but not okay to invest in your own home town.'

Out of this desperate situation Milken, contrary as usual, saw the opportunity to make long-term, fixed rate capital available to companies at a time when the banks, faced by a cash squeeze as a result of loans chasing bad loans down the Third World plughole, were calling in their domestic short-term loans.

Milken was not insensitive to the way others viewed his financing opportunities: 'We can call it junk because if we look back, most new products and ideas are considered junk. Not so long ago a product coming out of Japan, Hong Kong, and Taiwan was considered junk. When Henry Ford was turning out his first Model Ts they were referred to as his "junk" cars.' History is bunk said Henry Ford. The future, added Milken, is junk: 'Junk bond users are the industries of the future'.

THE MAN WHO BUILT LAS VEGAS

This, then, was the premise of the junk bond revolution, and the conference was set up to showcase the world of high yield. Over its four days hundreds of junk companies would make glittering presentations. In 1986 Circus Circus casinos flew in from Las Vegas virtually an entire casino's worth of gaming tables, croupiers, and hostesses (clad in scanty gold lamé) and over a dinner of veal and red wine they were treated to trapeze artists and circus acts on stage. Four years earlier, when the conference was considerably smaller, everyone had flown to Vegas for the day.

The renaissance of Las Vegas was perhaps the jewel in the crown of the junk bond revolution. Milken had irrigated this desert with his junk bonds, creating phenomenal growth and, supposedly, one out of every three jobs in the state of Nevada.

Outlawed by Congress in 1894, and branded as a sinful vice by the puritan ethic, gambling was the domain of organized crime, an image both exaggerated and perpetuated by Hollywood and television. Vegas itself has fared little better. Stuck on the desert like a gaudy coloured band-aid, its strip was a nasty neon gash, a runway of casinos and sleaze. Besides the gambling vice all it had to offer were quick weddings, cheap motels and instant divorces. And Liberace.

Fear and loathing, yes, but a wholesome family destination resort, themed like Disneyland? Surely not. Milken saw things differently. He didn't see gangsters, he saw numbers, magic numbers. 'In the late seventies I'd take money managers and pension fund people into the casinos and show them that it wasn't a gambling business, it was a business that was built on the laws of probability and statistics.' The odds were simple and inexorable. For every ten dollars gambled, the casinos gave back nine and took one. This 10 per cent profit margin made gambling almost like any other business. Continued Milken, 'We'd go up in the catwalks looking down on the gaming tables and really see the inner workings of the industry. Once these people had all these stereotypes stripped away and they saw that it was a business their attitudes changed.'

It was a classic Milken insight, a golden opportunity overlooked by an entrenched perception that defied the underlying realities. That Milken should see it this way was not surprising, gambling was a model of his own business philosophy. As Philip Sartre, CEO of Harrah's (the casino chain that began to turn around gambling's crime-grimed image in the sixties) argued, 'Wherever there is a way to win, somebody will attempt it. Call it what you will: competitiveness . . . the will to win . . . human nature . . . foolhardiness . . . or, in its most obnoxious form, greed. No law will ever suppress that instinct.' Milken liked to compete and Milken liked to win.

The risk-taking of gambling was synonymous with the essence of the American entrepreneurial spirit. In a country where 'You bet' is one of the most common expressions, gambling is inherently part of the American dream – the romantic notion of risking all and winning big. Congress funded the revolutionary army in 1776 with lottery tickets, and George Washington bought the first one. 'Where gambling is legal, it will prosper . . . and where it is illegal, gambling will persist. How can you stop the world's second oldest profession?' asked Philip Sartre. In 1989 Americans legally gambled $220 billion (more than the Pentagon's budget).

Milken was aware of the respectability that Bill Harrah, the company's founder, had brought to the chain. He was also aware that Harrah's had approached Drexel Burnham for financing and had been rejected. But that was on the East Coast. Barely more than ten days after Milken had moved out West, Steve Wynn, who owned a small downtown Vegas casino called the Golden Nugget, went to see him. Milken's cousin Stanley Zax had set up the meeting.

Wynn, who like Milken was a graduate of Wharton Business School, had come to Vegas to make his fortune and parlayed a liquor distributorship into a controlling share of Golden Nugget casino. At that time New Jersey State had recently legalized gambling to revive the dwindling fortunes of Atlantic City, a former seaside resort town. The crowds were flocking there, and Wynn wanted to be in on it. The only problem was he didn't have any money. He figured he needed $65 million to build a Golden Nugget on the East Coast.

Wynn is a showman and delivers a consummately seamless performance, whether it be one on one or starring in his own television commercials upstaging his pals Frank Sinatra or Dolly Parton. And one of his favourite shows, even after countless performances all these years, is to tell the story of how he met Michael Milken.

Although he normally wore a suit, Wynn had to wear jeans to the meeting because he had just broken his leg and it was in plaster. But Milken, who did not have the same excuse, was equally informally attired: 'Stan [Zax] introduces me to this young kid, who's also wearing Levis and a plaid short-sleeved shirt. We sit down, I drape my busted leg over the couch, and Mike, taking notes on a yellow legal pad, says "Tell me about the Golden Nugget in Atlantic City." '

'I told him about how I wanted to build a property from scratch, not remodel, because although I'd lose a little time, I'd make up in overhead, and in the long run the guy with the better mousetrap would have a major advantage. . . . I said that my message to him was that it wasn't the dog in the fight, it was the fight in the dog.'

'He didn't say a word. He just sat there and listened. I talked to him for an hour. He asked me only one question, for clarification. When it was all through he leaned back and put his hand behind his head and said, "I think we'll do it." '

Milken then explained that he was sending him to New York to persuade the committment committee. 'This company is an old company and very respectable. And they turned down Harrah's and they turned down Bally's. I don't think they should have turned down Harrah's, but I didn't think it was my place to say so.' Continued Wynn, 'He asked me, "Do you have any laces for your shoes?" I said "No". But I said I didn't wear silk suits and a pinkie ring either . . . I told him I dressed conservatively, that I'd always dressed conservatively, that I didn't wear yellow pants and pink shirts.'

Wynn got the money and built his hotel. In three years Wynn made back his $150 million investment, and sold the casino in 1986 for $450 million. The buyers of his junk bonds 'all made out like bandits,' he said.

The same day that Wynn first made his pilgrimage to the junk oasis in Beverly Hills, Milken also blessed him with a vision of the future. 'The gaming industry needs a White Knight. They need somebody they can believe in who's not just capable but stands for integrity . . . if someone emerges like that the marketplace will give him everything he wants. You can be that guy,

Steve. You've got an unblemished career. But I'm gonna tell you, there's no home runs. You hit singles, and hit singles, and some day you can do anything you want. That's the way it works. The most important thing is to keep your promises [and] if you do good, the day will come when you'll be able to raise a billion dollars.'

This prophecy, with its overtones of the wise old Obe Wan Kenobi from *Star Wars*, gave Wynn pause. 'When he said that I thought the man was certifiably insane. I was willing to sell my soul that day for $65 million. But look what's happened. Counting all the deals, I've done $1.6 billion so far, and we're just getting going.'

'Mike made me,' says Wynn, without a trace of discomfort. 'I love him. He is my favourite living human. He and my wife.' And he has faithfully followed the map of Milken's visionary business plan ever since.

Wynn also introduced Bill Bennett, chairman of Circus Circus, to Milken. Bennett's concept was to remove the taint of sin city for adults only and turn gambling into a family affair. This he did with his circus theme casinos and small-stake tables. While trapeze artists frolicked overhead you could feed quarters, dimes and even nickels into the cheapest slots around. This idea made his casinos the most profitable of all in Vegas in the eighties.

It was Wynn who took the concept of the theme venue to the next stage with the Mirage. With its palm trees and orange glass towers, this oasis come Polynesian atoll is a vision of luxuriance in the middle of the baked dirt and neon boxes that constitute the rest of the strip. The three-thousand-room hotel cost $620 million to build, $500 million of which was raised by Milken in a complex tiering of bonds to create a total package that Wynn, with typical understatement, called 'the most perfectly financed building in the history of the world'.

To enter the pleasure dome visitors cross a lagoon framed by a waterfall and volcano. Every fifteen minutes the $40 million volcano (manned by a crew of twelve) erupts and billows smoke and flames 100 feet into the air. Any unpleasant combustion odours are dispelled by pina colada gas (purchased at a cost of $180 a gallon). Inside the visitors walk into a rain forest and make their way through banana and palm trees to the reception desk, which fronts a shark stocked aquarium. There is also an eighteen-hole golf course, dolphin and white tiger habitats and five floors of penthouses consisting of 10,000-square feet villa suites. Out at the back Michael Jackson is supposed to be landscaping a re-creation of Hawaii's Diamond Head.

This, says Wynn, is Vegas 'at its fantasy best'. The significance of this 'resort destination' is that it is the pure realization of fantasy. When Milken told Wynn to tell him his dreams he did, and Milken helped turn them into a reality. Instead of being an oppressive force, the past is appropriated at whim. Instead of its weight of tradition, rules and lessons, history only exists as a motif book for decorative fantasies. Up the strip Circus Circus have also opened a four-thousand-room medieval castle, with crenellated turrets and a drawbridge. Excalibur boasts a daily jousting tournament in the dungeons and, themed to the ridiculous, it even contains a restaurant called Lancelotta Pasta. Also financed with Drexel junk, Kirk Kerkorian will soon be opening the five-thousand-room Metro Goldwyn Mayer Grand Hotel and Theme Park.

Jack Sheehan, who wrote a seven-part special on Milken for the *Las Vegas Sun* (also financed with junk bonds) thought of calling the series 'The Man Who Built Las Vegas' because 'he really was that instrumental'. In addition to Circus Circus and the Golden Nugget, Milken financed Bally's, Caesar's Palace, Harrah's, Holiday Inns, Sahara Resorts, Sands, Showboat and Tropicana – almost every casino on the strip – and raised a total of $2.5 billion dollars. As a result Nevada is one of the fastest growing states in the country.

WIRING THE GLOBAL VILLAGE

However, compared to the revolution in telecommunications, the gaming industry, although neat and self-contained, was a small-fry example of the impact junk bonds could have.

As Steve Wynn pointed out Milken's junk was 'venture capital masquerading as debt financing'. But traditionally venture capital comes in relatively small amounts, and compared to the lakes of money Milken was able to provide through junk the funds coming from private fortunes were chump change. As a venture capitalist writ large, Milken's knack was both for identifying future needs, and for making available capital in sufficiently large and long-term projects so as to be effective competition with the patient and limitless finance provided by the Japanese banks for huge projects such as multi-billion dollar telecommunications systems.

Originally many thought that cable television would only be worth the scrap copper that could be retrieved from the coaxial cables that were used to transmit the television signal that was normally broadcast over the air. Serving areas with poor broadcast reception, cable did not offer any more choice, it was just an alternative mode of transmission and limited itself to network reruns. Market research showed that the networks gave the people what they want, and in the late sixties, with only 6 per cent of America subscribing to cable, it looked as if they were right.

The turnaround came with 'narrowcasting', the targeting of special tastes instead of pandering to mass appeal. Home Box Office, the first of the narrowcasters, went after movie lovers with a subscription service that broadcast uncut and uninterrupted films. By 1989 cable TV enjoyed revenues of $16 billion, with 58 per cent of American homes cabled up. The American cable company Tele-Communications was financed by $800 million of Milken's junk bonds, so that it would emerge from this boom period of growth the largest cable company in the States.

Narrowcasting gave the lie to the popular executive wisdom that television was called a boob tube because the people watching it were boobs. As George Gilder further elaborated in his *Life after Television*, 'Those who thought they could never go broke underestimating the intelligence of the American people are going to discover that they are wrong . . . appealing to a mass audience worked only when people cannot gratify their special interests.' Cable could satisfy those interests.

HBO was followed in 1980 by Ted Turner's CNN. Like so many of the entrepreneurs Milken has financed, Turner lacked all the usual credible credentials, and was certainly a wild card. As a student he had kept an alligator. When his father killed himself, all he was left with was a billboard company and a loony vision for a twenty-four-hour global news network, or the 'Chicken Noodle Network' as it was nicknamed when it was first launched.

However, like Milken, he had limitless energy and was obsessively competitive. When he won the America's Cup one of his colleagues subsequently remarked that he didn't think Turner enjoyed sailing at all, all he wanted to do was win. Removed from the present, Turner, again like Milken, was fixated on the future, and driven by a vision of a better world: 'You, I, most people – we live in 1989. We worry a couple of weeks ahead, a month ahead. Ted lives five years ahead. This is all behind him. Ted is thinking about what's going on in 1995,' said a colleague.

A regular and popular speaker at Milken's annual high yield bond conference, he would always speak about global social issues and formed Turner's Better World Society to campaign through television against the nuclear arms race, the cold war and pollution of the environment. He also sponsored his own Olympics, the Goodwill Games, and used the network for a series called 'Waging Peace' aimed at the ending of regional wars.

Operating on $100 million in junk, the Chicken Noodle Network got off to a shaky start in 1980. CNN reporters were thrown off Senator Kennedy's campaign plane because they didn't have enough money to pay their air fare. However, by dint of sheer persistence, the news joke became a newsbreaker and people turned to it to watch live events unfolding. Audiences could watch the Oliver North hearings, Tiananmen Square, and the war in the Gulf for themselves instead of being dictated to by potted reruns every three hours, which was the standard headline fare offered by the networks. With CNN's global reach came a much greater impact. Routinely watched in eighty-six countries and by heads of state from Fidel Castro (who did a station identification for Turner) to George Bush, the newsbreaker has now become a newsmaker, a kind of global uplink that played a sizeable role in bringing East Germany, Romania and almost China in from the cold. America watched the students in Beijing and the students in Beijing watched themselves on CNN.

Milken also financed Turner's $1.25 billion acquisition of MGM/UA's film library from Kirk Kerkorian. Although the acquisition nearly bankrupted him, it has since become the backbone of his highly successful TNT movie and entertainment channel.

Where Ted Turner kept an alligator in his room, Bill McGowan, CEO of MCI, peddled alligator purses as a younger entrepreneur. Having set up a small defence contracting firm, McGowan then turned his sights on AT&T, the telephone behemoth known fondly to most Americans as Ma Bell. 'For too long, a dynamic, innovative telecommunications industry was held hostage by an all-powerful, slow-to-change monopoly. The Bell system monopoly did all it could to prevent competitors from entering the field,' claimed McGowan, whose long-distance company MCI was a minnow compared to the whale of AT&T.

'Ten years ago,' read a contemporary piece of Drexel literature, 'the term "telecommunications" meant little more than lifting the phone and placing a call through AT&T.' However in an anti-trust suit the cartel was broken up, unleashing at a stroke the telecommunications revolution, indeed even creating the very concept of one. For instead of being able to trickle down their technology at a leisurely rate, Ma Bell suddenly had to compete with rival companies and work to keep its customers by offering them better service and more services, in addition to providing the plain old telephone service (known in the business as POTS) that had hitherto defined telecommunications.

In order to do this, however, AT&T needed to overhaul their network. Quite apart from the scarcity and ever-escalating expense of copper, it was subject to electrical interference and eventual erosion. Copper wires were also limited in the capacity of calls that they could handle. In contrast fibre optic cables, thinner than a human hair, were capable of handling far more information and weren't subject to erosion or interference. Made out of sand, these glass wires were also cheaper.

Developed over a seventeen-year period, Corning Glass were trying to make good on their investment in fibre optics by selling their wares to AT&T while at the same time trying to beat out the Japanese who were developing the same technology. But AT&T weren't buying. For regulatory reasons they were obliged to depreciate the value of their equipment over a fifty-year period and thus treat their copper network as a 'historical object to be preserved', as Gilder put it, instead of as a tool to be replaced the moment it became obsolete and non-competitive.

McGowan saw this was an opportunity that had to be seized. His only problem was that with revenues of only $230 million in 1981, he didn't have the money. The nationwide fibre optic network he had in mind would cost $3 billion, and venture capitalists – to whom people would normally look to take a bet on the future – had never put that kind of money down. 'When we started, emerging companies could turn to venture capital firms for early rounds of financing. But they had few places to go when their needs grew larger,' said

McGowan. 'The heart of the problem was that banks and institutional investors did not know how to finance growth companies . . . they wrote elaborate restrictions into their lending agreement . . . an unending series of renegotiations would follow and the cost in management time and flexibility would be astronomical.'

McGowan, originally only looking for $500 million, was persuaded by Milken that he needed a billion. At the time (in mid-1983), not only was it a record-breaking junk bond issue, but it was also the largest securities issue ever. As a result of a total of $3 billion in financing, MCI has expanded 772 per cent within ten years, employing just under twenty thousand people. Of course this wasn't a closed-end effort, and there were plenty of knock-on effects; with his order of 110,000 kilometres of fibre optic wire, Corning secured the manufacturing volume to recover their investment and keep developing the technology. AT&T were pushed to compete and keep up ordering more fibre optics themselves, and, as a result of the improved and expanded competing services of AT&T and MCI, businesses have been able to expand their services and their markets.

One of the long-term results of junk financing fibre optics is that, eventually, the phone companies will provide PANS as well as POTS. Where POTS is Plain Old Telephone Service, PANS is Pictures And News Services. The significance of this is that phone users will be able to dial up almost any kind of information – pictures, films, text, programmes – ultimately dispensing with the need for broadcasting networks. With fibre optics this is technically possible although currently prohibited by regulation.

As a result of another regulatory glitsch much like the one crimping AT&T's dulled competitive spirit, the government in the seventies was actually giving away licences to operate cellular phones to whoever applied for them. The problem was that the FCC, which regulates these things, was forbidden from auctioning off franchises to operate a part of the radio frequency, and instead they had a lottery-style free for all. The result of this was that the spectrum fell into the hands of a lot of lawyers and savvy professionals who weren't going to look a gift horse in the mouth but who had neither the means nor the intention of using that gift. Milken estimated one entrepreneur, John Kluge, made over a billon dollars for himself by sending in applications for these franchises which he later auctioned off. It was Craig McCaw who came round to buy up the franchises financed with junk bonds, to create the only nationwide cellular network. Given the fact that silicon-based technology becomes 90 per cent cheaper every seven years, it is only a matter of time before pocket phones become virtually free goods and the rates and quality of wireless telephony better than their immobile equivalents. In other words, despite the risk and the billions initially needed, the rewards will be vast. Between 1986 and 1988 Milken raised $1.7 billion for McCaw, who later sold a 20 per cent stake to British Telecom for an estimated $2–3 billion.

Media and telecommunication were the third largest issuer of high yield bonds, but there was a wide array of other users. Milken's penchant and forte was for reading the entrails of demographics and financing the results. For example, in the area of health care Milken noticed that with over a million new cases of cancer every year, one in three Americans will contract cancer at some point in their lives. This was not for Milken an abstract statistic. He had lost his own father to the disease, and many of the families of his colleagues and friends and those around him were battling with cancer.

In the course of seeking treatment for his own daughter who had bone cancer, Dr Bernard Salick had noticed how demoralized were patients interred in institutional hospitals and how isolated from the support of their families, at a time when the hospitals themselves were staggering through an endless series of financial crises. Salick went to Milken with the idea of treating people with cancer on an outpatient basis so that they could come in for their chemotherapy and then go home at night.

With the over-65 population growing three times as fast as the population as a whole and on course to double by the year 2000, Milken saw opportunities in the greying of America. Oz Mutz's Forum Group had spotted a lucrative niche among the affluent and elderly wishing to remain in the urban areas where they had spent much of their lives. Accordingly, he is building a chain of luxury retirement communities across the nation, which are leased on an annual basis instead of the usual life-remaining basis. With the health care market growing as a whole Milken has financed, to name but a few examples, inexpensive mail order drugs, psychiatric beds, and shared scanning equipment for hospitals, to the tune of $6.4 billion.

'Business and society are intertwined, the best businessman, the best investor, has always been a social scientist. He has always been concerned with people; he's always tried to figure out what people want and what the people's needs are,' said Milken. His social engineering took him beyond financing companies into the area of race relations and management/worker relations. While junk bonds would come to be remembered as the deadly weapon of hostile takeovers, Milken himself was more interested in the possibilities of Employee Stock Ownership Programmes (or ESOPs) whereby employees – instead of management or raiders – could buy the companies they worked for.

He argued that traditional divisions between workers and management, for example, had to be superseded by new partnerships, new bonds. Often, taking an ownership position meant rolling back wages, and this was anathema to unions locked into the old adversarial relationship with management built on a mutual mistrust. 'By insisting on getting high wages and not being in an ownership situation, the unions are in a heads you lose tails you win situation . . . they keep thinking that "we are labour, you are management", but the more successful they are at getting high wages, the less competitive the company becomes,' argued Milken. 'By not having ownership, they don't participate in the value of the company if it does well. If the company does poorly, then they lose their jobs.' Milken described his ESOPs, from Avis (the largest of its kind) to Unimar (a small tug boat company), as 'democratizing capital'.

Similarly, the traditional discrimination between native and foreign had to give way to a more embracing approach. 'The change in ethnic mixture has underlined many opportunities that are available and many problems that exist in the country today. For example, in New York and in LA where I live, more than 80 per cent of the children in public school are either Asian, black or Hispanic . . . I'm sure we'll be able to figure out how long it's going to be before the majority of people's ancestors in this country come from Latin America, from Asia and from Africa . . . not from Europe.' With a population of twenty million hispanics in the US, and growing at five times the rate of the rest of the population, Milken saw the necessity and good sense in financing hispanic services, such as television (Telemundo) and grocery chains (Vons).

When investment grading was put in the wider context of changing demographics it became discrimination. 'There are almost no companies in the United States that are headed by blacks, Asians or hispanics that would qualify as "Investment grade credits." In fact there is only one – the Coca-Cola company is headed by a Cuban. Similarly there is only one investment grade company – the *Washington Post* is headed by a woman.'

Junk financing, as Milken saw it, wasn't just a business, it was a social imperative of the greatest magnitude. 'If people don't feel they have an opportunity then you don't have an underpinning for a society,' he would say, or, more bluntly, 'There will be no future for the United States unless there is a future and a feeling of opportunity for these people.'

This inevitably led to the crowning theme of Milken's high yield philosophy, the importance of education. 'Are we going to be prepared to cope with the tremendous change and tremendous opportunity in this country that this change makes? We are not going to be able to cope without education because the easiest thing to do is to blame your misfortunes on another person of another religion, another race.' For Milken, the children were the future. 'The future of America is not in the boardrooms of America, it is in the classrooms of America.' The undeniable logic of this was the cornerstone of Milken's philosophy: 'We are only here for one purpose, to leave a better life for our children and for our children's children.'

Over the years, as the annual conference grew in size, these people and humanistic concerns began to preoccupy Milken more and more. 'By 1986 I had moved away from many of the traditional aspects of the business. To the continued dismay of some of my associates and clients, I devoted more and more of my time, thought and resources to addressing societal problems in non-conventional ways. In fact due to my urging even at the firm's annual research conference, the number of speakers on education and social issues was constantly increased.' Panels on employee ownership, Third World debt, and education abounded to the vexation of some of his colleagues who felt it was more important to stick to the company presentations.

SPACE JUNK

But whether the emphasis fell on social issues or specific companies, the objective was the same, to show that the junk bond revolution was for real. It was not sufficent for Milken to compare junk bonds to Henry Ford's junk cars. The Model T, especially since it had become an historical classic, was something instantly recognisable by all. It was also tangible. But in spite of the fact that they were the building bricks of the information age, junk bonds were just pieces of paper. No matter that these promissory notes stood for an idea or a future need, and as such were the coinage of the information age, in the popular perception pieces of paper were pieces of paper, which were as nothing and worthless when compared to tangible things, or real products with real value.

It was this problem that caused Sherman McCoy almost more humiliation than anything else in *Bonfire of the Vanities*, when he tried to explain to his young daughter exactly what it is that a bond salesman did for a living. In the end he settled on the unprepossessing metaphor of a large slice of cake. Every time he handed out a slice of cake he crumbled a little bit off, and these crumbs were how he made a living. His daughter was as unimpressed as he was with this analogy, which belied his self-characterization as a Master of the Universe and indicated to the reader that the bonds were bunk or a phony way of making a living. Milken, sensitive to the popular notion that his line of work was merely paper shuffling that created no value, took pains to show his kids what it was he built. He bought a map of the States and used coloured pins to illustrate all the locations of high yield companies. He took them off to Las Vegas, to show them how high yield bonds were transforming a desert into an oasis. In the early days of the conference it was possible to repeat the exercise and fly all the attendees there.

As the years went on Milken came up with other equally extravagant ways of illustrating the high yield world. Each evening at the conference dinner was centred around some high yield entertainment that was a combination of instruction and recreation. For Entertainment Night, for example, they took over one of the larger aircraft hangars at Santa Monica airport, and filled it with sideshows, an electronic playland in which people could star in their own MTV music video, be an anchor on the news, appear in the classic sitcom 'Cheers' or audition for a Miller beer commercial. Look-alikes of celebrities vogued through the crowd available for photo-opportunities. In 1988 they staged a high yield fashion show with only junk designers on the catwalk.

Working with the East Coast video department, Milken virtually created his own private media, turning out an increasing number of music clips, spoofs and corporate profiles to illustrate his themes. Although he was himself shy of the media, he knew what a powerful medium television was and how effective a vehicle it could be to express his high yield dreams. He had grown up during its golden age, and movies peppered his frame of reference as much as actual examples. He intuitively knew what 'buzz' was and how to create it. (Given this it is hard to believe, as an aside, that Milken was both unaware of the power of the media to determine his fate and unable to package himself sympathetically for the American public.)

Every year Milken found a new way to catalogue the high yield bond achievement, each more cheeky and ingenious than the last. In 1988 the Drexel Burnham Orchestra – a Hoffnung confusion of classical musicians playing their instruments and Drexel traders playing theirs (quotrons, computer keyboards, phones) – performed 'The First Quarter Symphony, Opus $11 Billion', which, as the name suggested, catalogued the $11 billion worth of deals Drexel had done in the first three months of the year.

But the music videos were the most popular. Madonna doing 'Material Girl' but singing new junk lyrics: 'Everybody's living in a material world, and I am a material girl' became 'Everybody's living in a high yield world and I am a double B girl.' In previous years they had re-made the theme from *Ghostbusters* – 'Who ya gonna Call? Call Drexel!' (ultimately the ghouls of the establishment would win the day and slime the debtbusters), and the Pointer Sisters' classic hit 'Jump' became in their marauding hands 'Junk!'. Whitney Houston sang that famous ballad about 'The Greatest Bonds Of All' and James Brown's 'Living In America' became, natch, 'Financing America'. The cutest of all was the California Raisins, the silly Philly soul group of animated raisins, doing 'Raisin' Capital on the Street' to the tune of 'Dancin' in the Street'. This abundance of junk TV led one regular attendee to complain that the conference had become 'a visual gangbang.'

However, amusing and entertaining though all these were, Milken still strived for something that could illustrate the all-embracing nature of the high yield world, and the fact that it was a whole world. As Glenn Yago wrote in his book *Junk Bonds*, 'Today working families might leave their children in a day care centre financed by high yield bonds (Kinder-Care or La Petite Academie); seek medical treatment through high-yield financed health care (Maxicare, Salick, Charter Medical); read a 'high yield' newspaper (Ingersoll) or book (Macmillan, Maxwell); go to work at any number of manufacturing or service companies financed by high yield securities (steel, paper products, chemical processing, financing services); return to high yield financed homes (Hovnanian Enterprises); let their children watch cable television (almost exclusively financed in the high yield market, and go out either to shop (Macy's), eat (Chi Chi's, Denny's) or see a movie (Lorimar, Warner, Ohio).' Moreover, come 1987, as Milken liked to remind his audience, the average high yield company had 4,000 employees, had been in business for thirty-six years, and had over $1 billion in assets. According to Milken, these companies were responsible for 'all the new jobs in this country in the last twenty years in the private sector.'

It was the High Yield Bond Spaceship that would come to be seen as the most visceral articulation of Milken's concepts. At home he had a model of a cruise ship of the future that could accommodate twenty thousand passengers in skyscrapers built on the foredecks: 'This will cost $1.8 billion to build and I can't get anyone interested in it,' he lamented to a reporter. Perhaps it was this eccentric scheme that gave Milken the idea of building a model city exclusively out of the companies that had used high yield bonds, and thus showing what they had wrought.

'He came in free-associating: "I see all these high yield companies in one city" he said,' remembered one Drexelite assigned to the project, 'and he's throwing out all these germs – I mean gems – little seeds, it was going to be a city surrounded by rural areas too.' But once it was decided to pirate the Starship hit 'We Built This City on Rock and Roll', and change the title to 'We Built This City on High Yield Bonds', the model makers suggested that a space station might be more appropriate than an earth-bound city. The idea was approved, and for a cost of approximately $150,000, a 2001-style space wheel was built.

The finished model – with a diameter of some 10 feet – was replete with video monitors which showed a trip through deep space. As the occasional high yield planet loomed up out of the void and whooshed past, a soothing female voice informed the audience of the facts of the non-investment grade universe. Perhaps the neutrality of the voice was supposed to discharge the strong emotional reaction always triggered by discussions of debt, but its anodyne tones instead evoked the blankness of supercomputer Hal, the villain in *2001*. Finally, after our long journey through the void of deep space we approach home, the junk bond space station, and, to the tune of 'We Built This City on Rock and Roll', the heavens burst into song:

> Right from the beginning
> A city is alive
> It's gotta learn to grow
> If it's gonna thrive.
> Gotta keep the people working
> Keep them happy too
> And give them the resources
> To do what they want to do.
>
> Nursing homes and drug stores
> Cable TV too
> Hotels and bowling alleys
> So many things to do
> From real estate and lumber

To carpet on the floor
So many jobs created
And those jobs keep creating more

To buy and build a future
For our daughters and our sons
And remember that's the reason
We built this city on high yield bonds.

When the model was first shown in 1988 (ironically at the last conference Milken would ever attend), it was a huge success. Did it symbolize Milken's sky-high aspirations? Was Milken – like Blofeld in *Moonraker* – launching his own space programme? One can almost hear Shirley Bassey singing the theme, 'Junk Bonds Are Forever'.

If Milken had gone for the idea because of his love for the future and fondness for referencing the film *Star Wars*, the space wheel and its context much more evoked Nic Roeg's *The Man Who Fell To Earth*, although probably no parallel was intended. The central character of the film was a man who had literally fallen to earth from outer space. He quickly became fabulously wealthy from the invention and marketing of a string of innovative products. In order to return whence he came he then took the fatal and overreaching step of launching his own space programme. At this point, even though he had done nothing wrong, the government decided that it had to stop him because his wealth, monopoly, and power had become so great. He was dragged away from the launch pad as he made his way to his spaceship during the final countdown.

Of course, this is no more than a brittle piece of science fiction and yet it was a perfect model for Milken, whose intensity, brilliance, and private manner were not unlike the character of Newton played by David Bowie in the film. With his darting eyes in deep-sunk hollows and fixed, spacey grin, it does not take too much to imagine that Milken did fall to earth from another planet. But more than this, the message of the film was that even in the free world, and even in a capitalist environment where market forces are supposed to have free reign, there is some kind of limit to the wealth and monopoly powers to be enjoyed by one man. The implication was that with the American dream the sky actually was the limit – no crossing beyond this point for the heavens belong to God and government. Milken's model spaceship was a kind of hubris, a step too far. He would have to be stopped. Indeed once Milken's vision of a high yield world had been through the wringers of the establishment, it would, like Newton's space programme, be no more than pie in the sky, and a pipe dream, just like the model of the space wheel and the $2 billion boat in Milken's living room.

Having been shipped to Tokyo for the last high yield bond conference of all, the intergalactic folly was delayed at customs by inspecting officers who thought they had stumbled upon some secret new high-tech weapon. By the time it finally arrived back in America Drexel was teetering on the verge of bankruptcy and the $8,000 shipping bill went unpaid. To this day the High Yield Bond spaceship, the pride and model of a whole world vision, languishes unwanted in a warehouse in Los Angeles.

5

THE DREXEL REALITY

THE DARK SIDE OF THE FORCE

FOR Milken the conference was an opportunity for his clients to glimpse the promised land of high yield, a kindler, gentler world, from cities to – with a small leap of the imagination – even space stations. But the conference was not always received in the spirit in which it was given.

Perhaps for the same reason that Milken had relocated to one of the most swank locations in Hollywood, the high yield bond conference was a lavish affair. It showed vistors that this was truly a land of Milken honey. For four days attendees were Drexel's guests. They put them up and gave them breakfast, lunch and dinner. Milken laid on a gourmet spread. There was no sign of rubber chicken. They dined on Chateaubriand, filet mignon, fine wines and mountains of chocolate mousse with strawberries and whipped cream. In addition there were private dinners for the elite at Spago's, Chasen's, Jimmy's and The Ivy. Companies vied with one another to lay on the most lavish presentation. As part of Merv Adelson's pitch for Lorimar (the makers of 'Dallas', 'Knot's Landing' and 'Falcon's Crest'), guests grazed on a global smorgasbord of food; pizza, hot dogs, shish kebab, brownies, candy floss, ice cream sundaes, noodles, tacos, etc. Every conference ended with 'The Friday Night Extravaganza', at which some stellar entertainer would appear. Generally Steve Wynn provided the superstar; Frank Sinatra, Dolly Parton, Diana Ross and Kenny Rogers all performed. At the last conference it was Sheena Easton.

Because he did not stint in putting on the glitz, many came less to hear a sermon than feed at the trough while paying lip service to Milken's incredible bread machine. The more they were showered with corporate largesse, the more they gobbled it up. There seemed to be no limit to their appetites. 'On arriving at the Drexel conference, seemingly normal people became possessed by possessing,' an eye witness declared one year. When RJR Nabisco reps, dressed as giant Oreo Cookies or as Mr Planter (the giant peanut man), roamed the lobby handing out free product samples, they were almost torn apart in the resulting feeding frenzy.

'The high-powered investors at Drexel Burnham Lambert's "Junk Bond" conference this week in Beverly Hills, California, almost came to blows over some prize acquisitions; "Top Gun" hats and Gumby dolls,' reported *The Wall Street Journal* in 1987 under the headline 'You mean this is about securities? I came for one of those neat caps.' 'They were lined up thirty-five deep pushing and shoving,' one harrowed staffer told the paper. His job was to distribute ALF (the furry friendly Alien Life Form critter who was the star of a popular television sitcom) T-shirts to the mob. The one person who told the newspaper that he found the scrum *déclassé* and that he would 'sooner go out and pay retail' was clearly the exception. Conferees actually dived in and started helping themselves as they looted 'Top Gun' caps from storage boxes before attendants had a chance to unpack them. 'Very few people wanted to talk about the company. They just wanted to get the stuff,' groused a spokesman for Twentieth Century Fox who had been bombarded with abuse when people who had lined up to get their free copy of *The Fly* had to make do with *Alien* instead, after they ran out of the former.

An attendee recalled losing her conference virginity: 'My first junk bond conference was like my first niteclub opening . . . free-flowing booze, free-spending guys in suits, conspicuously phony conversations, the constant wondering if that person next to you was Anybody Important, and the definite knowledge that, later on, somebody somewhere was going to get screwed.' A few nights later she attended the conference's movie night at the local cineplex in Century City which Drexel had blanket-booked: 'The fully-stocked snack bar was free causing hundreds to line up for free popcorn with extra butter.' When she asked one wealthy investment banker if there wasn't something inappropriate about this greed for freebies he replied, 'Never pass up the opportunity to get something for nothing.' Although she herself admitted to being troubled by the fact that it was usually those who can usually afford it who get things for free, she also admitted that she hadn't had to spend, thanks to the conference, any money on shampoo for years.

The point of the movie evening was that pre-release films were being shown in the various cinemas. 'Vestron was screening *The Unholy* [and] to get people in they were giving out free videos of their previous hit *Dirty Dancing*. Clever executives figured that they could enter the theatre, get their free videos, then pretend to go to the bathroom and leave without having to watch the movie. Vestron caught on to this one fairly quickly and refused to dispense the videos until after *The Unholy* was shown. This nearly caused a riot. Additional security was called for . . . later when I saw them leaving the theatre, I thought they might have the decency to look at least somewhat sheepish. But no, they came out loudly admitting that the film was the worst they'd ever seen and brandishing their free *Dirty Dancing* videos as though they were trophies from a battle well fought and won.' Experienced executives brought along an extra suitcase for all the booty or had it Fed Exed (at Drexel's expense) back home.

For the inside track there was supposedly some real sleaze.

The speck of dirt that spun this pearl was Bungalow 8, a small secluded chalet in the grounds of Boesky's Beverly Hills Hotel. One of Milken's colleagues, Don Engel, used to occupy this pink three-bedroomed outhouse during the conference and host a champagne cocktail party that combined business with pleasure. In one corner would be twenty of the most powerful financiers in America, and in another (the back bedroom, according to the artist's rendition of the affair in *Manhattan Inc* magazine) 'would be actresses and fashion models' who had been 'brought in to cozy up the event'. But, the caption copy concluded, 'Gentleman preferred bonds' to leggy blondes. To hear Connie Bruck tell it – although she never attended such an occasion – they did considerably more than cozy things up. In her book she quoted one former Drexel associate as hearing Engel say, 'I understand CEOs. CEOs don't care about money, power or fame. They have all that. What they want is pussy. And I'm going to make sure that they get it.' However, one woman who did attend and who vouchsafed that she was not a prostitute said, 'It was very sedate. All these men wanted to do was talk about business and lie to one another about who made more money.' After cocktails the guests were chauffeured in stretch limousines to a private room at Chasen's for dinner.

Who knows how much Milken's preoccupations may have shielded him from these realities. In any event he was not in attendance. During the day Milken talked about raising $6 out of every $10 to build homes for American families, and then in the evening he went home to his. He did not go to Bungalow 8. As one Drexel Vice President recalled, 'I remember him late one evening at the conference . . . while every pipsqueak with a Drexel business card was holding court in places like the Polo Lounge and Chasen's, the most powerful financier in the world was quibbling over rush charges on slides he wanted made up overnight for his keynote address the next day. "If it's $100 per slide, have them produce them all," he specified, "but if it's $300, I only want these ten." '

Milken could not prevent his high yield bonds from being called junk bonds, and neither could he prevent the 'Institutional Research Conference' from being called 'The Predator's Ball'. What made the conference so newsworthy was its sheer intensity (few other business conferences served breakfast at 6 a.m.), coupled with the fact that until the last two years the press were not invited. Inevitably this frustrated fascination created, when it came to rumour, a pressure-cooker atmosphere.

As the years went by, and as the line of stretch limos lined up outside the Beverly Hilton in the pre-dawn gloom grew, so too did the rumour and speculation that Milken's secretive network was in fact a sinister cabal, an incestuous daisy chain of manipulating marketeers operating in concert. If this wasn't the case, the argument went, then why was everything so intense and secret?

In 1984 a cover story ran in *Forbes* magazine depicting a merry-go-round with some of America's biggest and most notorious dealmakers perched on horses and going round and round. Off to the side and winding the whole mechanism up was a beaming Milken. The article was titled 'Taking in Each Other's Laundry' and detailed the incestuous knitting of Milken's network. Featured in the illustration were takeover artists Saul Steinberg, Carl Lindner, the Belzberg Brothers and Victor Posner. Also appearing was Thomas Spiegel, the colourful head of Columbia Savings & Loans, and Fred Carr, the head of First Executive, an insurance company. A second tier of players included arbitrageur Ivan Boesky, Steve Wynn, and Meshulam Riklis (whose Rapid American Company had offices in Milken's building).

This network shared many ventures in common. For example, First Stratford was a Delaware based re-insurance outfit owned by Milken and Carr. When Saul Steinberg created a spin-off of his First Reliance insurance business called Reliance Capital, the primary investors were Ronald Perelman, Ivan Boesky, Tom Spiegel, and Mantar Associates (a partnership consisting of Milken and partners). Then there were the funds that were run by ex-departmentalists such as the Atlantic Corporation, and the Solomon Asset Fund run by David Solomon and Pacific Asset Holdings (run by ex-Milkenite Gary Winnick).

This network, then, would invest in each other's deals in a way that was considered sinister or bogus. As *Forbes* wrote, 'I'll finance you by buying stocks and bonds that you issue, because I think they're a good investment. You buy my securities because you think my issues are a good investment. Some of the capital I raise becomes capital for you, and some of the capital you raise becomes capital for me. Because we all believe our paper is good and Drexel helps make liquid, stable markets in it, our paper really is good. A self-fulfilling prophecy.'

But as Steve Wynn maintained, 'They would say, well, "Milken would raise money for a company like the Golden Nugget and then the Golden Nugget would invest in a deal like Ron Perelman". That's a perfect example, because that's exactly what I did do. I did in fact invest fifty million dollars with Ron Perelman when he did Revlon. . . . The fact that we would invest in other Milken deals was testimony not to any kind of secret arrangement, which is preposterous, but testimony to the fact that Michael's judgements in companies represented the best judgements in companies available on the planet earth at any given moment.'

Another criticism was that Drexel, as a matter of course, would overfund its deals, raising more money for clients than they wanted or needed. Because Drexel's fee was based on a percentage of the size of the deal this was to their advantage. It also meant, since the client was paying a high rate of interest on this surfeit of cash, that they would want to re-invest it in some equally high yielding investment. And thus they would buy more junk. Wynn argued that he felt that he needed the extra money as a cushion in case things did not pan out as planned. Other critics of overfunding argued that the extra money was used to prop up an otherwise unworkable deal by providing money to pay the interest on the money borrowed.

This would lead to the criticism that hidden behind the nameplates of seemingly independent companies lay an interconnectedness that gave the impression of a liquid market while concealing a rigged reality. Writer Connie Bruck, using an intoxicating brew of words like 'soldered' and 'matrixing', and making reference to generative connections, tried to give Milken's *modus operandi* a sinister spin. But there was nothing necessarily illegal in these interacting ventures, which were no more than the expedient meshing that weaves the business fabric. That they did not publicize their activities did not mean that they did not fulfill their filing obligations to the letter.

To be sure, not all of his clients displayed the moral integrity that motivated Milken himself, and for this he would be held, somewhat illogically, responsible. Generally people are held responsible for their own ethics, and not those of their clients or business associates. Milken was made an exception to this, because of the intensity of his network and the fact that it especially revolved around him.

It was certain key players that aroused the most suspicion. Tom Spiegel was the unapologetic and go-getting head of Columbia Savings & Loans. Savings & Loans organizations were initially created to finance families in their pursuit of the American dream by providing mortgages so they could own their own homes. In 1982 they were deregulated and allowed to diversify their investments. They were allowed to become venture capitalists and, unlike most risk-takers, enjoyed the extraordinary benefit of a safety net, since the government guaranteed deposits of up to $100,000. Tom Spiegel invested some $4 billion (40 per cent of Columbia's assets) in junk bonds. The company had a branch in Milken's office building and by the end of the eighties was constructing its own lavish headquarters nearby. Never finished, the walls were leather-bound, the floors of stainless steel and, in an unusual touch, the bullet-proof bathrooms were also intended to double as bomb shelters. Spiegel caused a scandal when he paid himself $9 million in 1985, which he cut back the following year to $3.8 million. When he travelled – on one of two company jets – he would often take his karate coach with him. He once gave his Chief Financial Officer a Mercedes Benz and provided Milken with a set of wheels and a share in a jet. He also cultivated political connections that would later add to the junk bond controversy, leading to the resignation of Congressman Tony Coelho to whom he had lent money to invest in junk, and to the investigation of Los Angeles mayor Tom Bradley, who had also invested in junk bonds.

One of the junk bond users that Drexel canonized as an example of the kinder, gentler face of the high yield revolution was Kinder-Care, a day care centre for kids. In 1988 there were over ten million working mothers with children under 6 in the US, by which time Kinder-Care had grown to be the largest day care facility in the country with 1,150 day care centres in operation. 'Someone was going to have to take care of the children of the females who were entering the labour force in droves' said a Kinder-Care executive sounding like a social worker. With over $350 million raised for Kinder-Care over the years, it was a favoured example of Milken's and featured in Drexel's series of television ads.

The perception was that here was a company that wasn't really a company at all, but more of a benevolent social force. The reality turned out to be different. Kinder-Care had not stuck to its inspiration of helping out working moms. It had diversified into financial services, buying up a Savings & Loans operation, and a number of retail facilities. The true nature of their diversifications was cloaked in this improbable rhetoric: 'it behoves us to make the most of the relationships we have built with the working family, and to extend it beyond school age,' said CEO and co-founder Perry Mendel. One journalist visiting the headquarters observed, 'The impression that kids come low on the list of Kinder-Care's corporate priorities is reinforced by a visit to the company's well-appointed headquarters. A romper room the place is not. Mendel and Grassgreen [his partner] have blinking quotrons within reach on their desks . . . '. As profits plumeted Grassgreen defrauded the company by, as he has admitted, misappropriating monies to his own account. All of this was unbeknown to Milken. In 1990, Grassgreen resigned and pleaded guilty to two felony counts.

Of Milken's network the *Forbes* article concluded, 'It's a community of interest, not a cabal. Its ties are thus stronger than any formal agreement could forge.' Connie Bruck's verdict was also vague but sinister: 'every business and profession has its network through which referrals and favors are exchanged. What set this one apart was its utter dominance by a single individual.' But because Milken had created a market virtually from scratch it is not surprising that the bonds within the network were more intense than if Milken had merely patched into an existing consortium of interests. Nevertheless the suspicion in both cases was that despite an absence of verifiable wrongdoing, the whole arrangement did not pass the smell test.

Unfortunately, Milken also knitted his department in the same way that he modelled his client relationships. Ultimately this would create the damaging public perception that he was running a cult. When Milken moved to the West Coast – although everyone would deny this – he all but left Drexel. For months after he moved there was no Drexel sign on the door. Essentially what he did when he moved was begin to create an alternative organization, a mutant hydra that grew out of the head of Drexel. Multiple and diffuse, this organization had no single identity. Instead it consisted of some 517 partnerships registered in different states all across America, and numbered a seemingly limitless variety of partners, from family members to work colleagues to favoured clients. Partners even included folk singer Kenny Rogers, according to Dan Stone.

This alternative organization was built around a familial core, a trinity that consisted of Milken's younger brother Lowell, his personal lawyer and boyhood friend Richard Sandler and another boyhood friend Harry Horowitz (both of whom lived next door to him in Encino). It was a soft hierarchy, and the roles within this cadre were fuzzy. Sandler was the principal partner in a number of the partnerships (a token figurehead for Milken, critics argued). He had recently built himself a house opposite Milken.

Harry has variously been described as Milken's 'eyes and ears', 'valet', 'traffic controller', and 'Jeeves'. One colleague remarked, 'Harry doesn't tolerate fools gladly', while others suggest he might not be all that brilliant himself. When another asked Harry what it was exactly that Lowell did, he felt that Harry's answer was the kind that one would expect from 'the other girlfriend'.

But of the three, Lowell's role was probably the most important and the most shrouded in mystery. 'His duties are very broad based,' a Drexel spokesman once volunteered illuminatingly. As with Harry and Sandler, Lowell, a rising tax attorney, joined forces with Milken a few months after his move back West. He brought with him Craig Cogut (who would become Drexel's General Counsel) and is believed to have been the lynchpin in the myriad of partnerships set up by the Milken brothers for themselves, their families, inner-track colleagues and selected clients. (The 1989 indictment stated that Lowell's duties 'have included administering certain investment partnerships created by the high yield department and providing tax-related and other advice to Drexel clients'.)

The full extent of the partnerships has yet to be calculated. According to documents leaked from the congressional investigation, the biggest twenty-five partnerships paid out some $2 billion in the eighties (with some $1 billion estimated to have been paid to Milken). However, according to Milken's spokespeople, these figures represented gross payments and not net profits and had been in some cases double and triple-counted.

Such partnerships were not an uncommon practice on Wall Street. Generally it was more acceptable for investment bankers to have their own trading accounts with the firm they worked in order to prevent them from trading on inside information, which they could do undetected if they had their account with an outside firm. In-house, however, a restricted list of stocks and securities would prevent them from either insider trading or from putting their own interests over and above those of their clients. But what was so remarkable about Milken's partnerships was their profusion.

These partnerships not only profited those who were included in them, but also served Drexel a useful purpose. As Drexel's chairman in 1984, Bob Linton, had pointed out, Milken had made so much money for the firm that he was a source of capital to Drexel. It was not uncommon for 'merchant bankers like us', he explained, to take positions in the companies with which they did business. Thus when Drexel considered a deal too risky, Milken and an array of his partnerships would often step up to the plate and bear the brunt of the risk, with Drexel buying in at a later, safer date.

The partnerships also made Milken's favoured rich beyond their wildest dreams. The earnings of the high yield bond department were legend on the street. A former Salomon Brothers colleague of Michael Lewis's who defected to Drexel's junk bond department – as did at least a dozen others – told him, 'Twenty or thirty are worth ten million dollars or more, and five or six have made more than a hundred million' (quoted in *Liar's Poker*). One was supposed to have found a $100,000 error in his weekly pay cheque, and when he asked Milken about it he was told that it wasn't an error.

Milken himself was keen that his colleagues should re-invest in the partnerships – whose dealings were blind to their investors – because he felt that money was a distraction. He didn't want his staff sitting around counting up how much they were worth (and he himself, contrary to the myth that he posted his net worth above his bed, claimed not to know how much he was worth since he had last calculated it back in the seventies). Milken hoped that out of sight meant out of mind when it came to the money squirrelled away in secret pockets and pools of the partnerships.

But this privacy coupled with the fact that no one, inside as well as outside the department, really knew how much anyone was making, only fuelled the fever of outside speculation and promulgated the idea of Milken's junk bond department as a kind of religious cult.

'Unlike most of Wall Street, there were virtually no politics in our department,' said one of his colleagues. 'Everyone was motivated by Mike. Mike was very demanding and critical.' This virtual contradiction encapsulates the dynamics of the department. Milken and his punishing example-led routine inspired awe, fear and performance anxiety in many people. In addition to the woman who jumped off her chair in attempt to break her leg, one person lost twenty pounds in the first four weeks, and another was hospitalized with 'life-threatening symptoms'.

One trader recalled his first meeting with the great man: 'It took place in one of the men's restrooms. He was washing his hands when I entered. He looked at me with his stern/serious look . . . I thought I had done something wrong because I remember that day he bought frozen yogurt for the entire trading floor. I distinctly remember that he saw me coming out of the lunch room with about ten scoops on my plate. Well, I naturally got embarrassed. As we both washed our hands he looked at me in the mirror and said, "Hello James, how are you?" I replied, "Just fine, thank-you sir." He said, "Don't call me sir, call me Mike." I said, "Okay sir, uh, I mean Mike." He said, "So, did you have enough frozen yogurt?" I said, "Plenty, thank-you again Mike." He said, "You're welcome." That made me feel good because no other senior executive at his level had ever acknowledged my existence at any of the other companies I had been employed with.'

The warm glow that suffused people when Milken knew their name and talked to them was the organizing principle in the office. Everyone jockeyed for proximity and scrambled for his attention. 'The two biggest political things out on the West Coast were how close you sat to him and where you parked your car. How much time he spent with you was the measure of how successful you were . . . that was how you were measured by your peers. How he measured you, well, only Michael knows . . . you had to prove your worth to him and the worst thing in the world was if he didn't call on you, it meant he didn't value your opinion. If he talked to you, you felt like a million bucks' (this notwithstanding the fact that many of them *were* worth a million bucks, and some considerably more).

The politics of the department, therefore, were that Milken ruled. When I asked one old faithful about Milken's management structure the answer came back, 'He didn't manage, he ruled. The high yield bond department was a kingdom and a kingdom rules. The object of a manager is to provide an organization that can run without him. Mike wasn't like that and the department couldn't – didn't – run without him.' When Milken left Peter Ackerman, the most obvious successor, refused the post, leaving a reluctant John Kissick to step up to the throne. Try though he did to wield the rhetoric of high yield, the shoes were too big for him and he rattled around in the role like a tiny pea in a giant pod.

With Milken as the undisputed lord and master, a rigid hierarchy or bureaucratic top-down structure was unnecessary. Ostensibly there was no hierarchy. 'He made certain that each person had their name listed alphabetically on our Christmas cards to show that all employees were equally important,' said Harry Horowitz. Unlike Wall Street, which tended to have a two-tier structure of white professionals and then an ethnic back office staff, Milken collapsed the divide. The group responsible for recruiting analysts, for example, consisted of a Bangladeshi Muslim, a Japanese American woman, a black male and an Italian. Milken was as close to and as admired by his chauffeurs and bodyguards as he was by his hard-ball traders. Moreover, Ivy League WASPs straight out of business school were a rarity in the department.

Milken would never speak in terms of people who worked *for* him. People worked with him as co-workers, colleagues or partners, and had no hierarchical title. As Gerry Finneran, who worked with Milken on the debt of less developed countries, recalled, 'When I asked what my title would be, he responded, whatever you need to get your job done. I'm a senior vice president but if you need to be a "president" we'll make you a president.'

In another Securities and Exchange Commission deposition regulators had this almost comic exchange with Milken:

'I don't necessarily view them as subordinate.'

'Well, how many people are subordinate to you in the hierarchical structure of the firm?'

'We don't really have a pecking order.'

'How many people are assigned to the high yield and convertible bond department in addition to yourself?'

Milken gave his answer.

'Now do each of these people report to you?'

'Since I'm the manager you could say that [but] I may not speak to them for eight months.'

'But you don't report to them?'

'No.'

'You're not subordinate to any of these . . . people in your department?'

'By subordinate you mean accountable?'

'Yes.'

'I'm not – I'm accountable in I'm trying to do a good job. Again we don't have people that check in with one another.'

'Well, do these people report to you? Are you the denominated boss?'

'Yes.'

Teasing the regulators with his contra-thinking, Milken's wind-up is a distraction from the obvious fact that although they were all equals, he created them equal, and as the source he was the boss. Furthermore, the way the boss cat plays with the regulatory mice in this exchange simply underlines this.

Instead of a hierarchy of titles he favoured and fostered the feeling of an extended family. 'He was paternalistic, regarding his department as a family and being very supportive of its individual members,' wrote David Bergman, bond salesman. In addition to paying for the frozen yogurt, he paid for the catered lunches, the department's Christmas party and the Summer picnic for members of the department and their families. Only Marie Antoinette would call it a 'picnic'; it resembled rather a fully fledged fair.

He urged his colleagues to raise families of their own: 'Having a happy home life allows you to have the courage to try new ideas and accept constructive criticism, because you know that even if you've had a difficult time at work, there is someone at home who will give you a hug and love you for who you are,' he once explained. There was a bulletin board in the department covered with pictures of the team's kids.

When one of his assistants went into hospital with anorexia, he offered an unlimited supply of Haagen Dazs ice cream; when one of his relay assistants went out of town to visit her father for his birthday a huge basket of fruit and cheese arrived for him before even she did. When a member of an assistant's family got cancer he would phone around seeking out the best doctors and treatment. When one had chicken pox he sent over libraries of videotapes for the patient to watch while stuck in bed. When a client of one of his traders had a cocaine problem, Milken himself became actively involved in his rehabilitation. If it was a miscarriage, a mugging, breast cancer or alcoholism, he would be involved. On and on and on and on. 'He plunges in, with both feet in a blur of activity. To look at him you would gather that he believes it is impossible for him to spread himself too thin,' said one of his colleagues.

In these actions and many others Milken was basically Big Daddy and the people around him were his kids: 'I know that Michael has recently spent a considerable amount of time teaching math to young inner city children. Let there be no mistake that Michael was teaching for many years prior to this – it was just that we were slightly older students with more formal degrees,' clarified departmentalist Kenneth Moelis. (Milken also disciplined them with some of the same rules that one imposes on Boy Scouts, such as forbidding swearing. Although most trading floors are cesspits of profanity – few traders are sensitive poets, it would be a contradiction in terms – Milken forbade it in his presence. 'I even recall Michael stopping me mid-sentence once to correct my using a slang and slightly derogatory term to describe a person of a particular nationality,' added a mortified Moelis.)

Milken wasn't just a father to them, he was 'Our Father', little short of God, and many literally worshipped him. Although he said he looked for people with 'a strong self-image and a secure personal life', he appeared to hire people who weren't quite complete in themselves, often reaching out to people when they were most in need and at their most vulnerable. 'He surrounded himself with people who were losers,' remembers one colleague, 'a lot of lost people who would find religion – he would convert them.' He made them, moulded them, and they seemed to be only too happy to be putty in his hands.

Lorraine Spurge joined the high yield department after she had been left by her husband for a 16-year-old girl, and she had sold up, packed up and moved lock stock and barrel with her two young daughters to start a new life. Another person came to the department after the loss of her family and the dwindling of her financial resources. Another was an old family friend whose business had failed (Milken had lent him money to start it). Others came from all walks of life: a car salesman, a furniture salesman, a missionary for the Latter Day Saints just back from Italy, and a frightened immigrant. One trading assistant was a young runaway called Lisa Jones. She had lied about her age and background and also had come to California from the East coast to start a new life. After her break-up with her fiancé Drexel became her life and her family. She worshipped Milken.

That is not to say that Milken deliberately picked up wounded birds, but a consequence of his kindness was that many reciprocated with blind loyalty. 'Everyone Milken comes into contact with he wants to help. He wants to help them do whatever it is they are trying to do better,' said Ken Lerer. This is not to say that Milken is a saint, for he is certainly very shrewd. People struggling with their own fulfillment are going to try harder, work harder and so yield more.

But the return on facilitating people's personal fulfillment can be too much, and the people Milken picked have ultimately done him the disservice of mythologizing him as messiah. Placing the man on a pedestal and describing him in terms that seem impossibly good have had the inevitable effect of turning him in outsiders' eyes into a cult leader. And in demurring from the role that his people thrust upon him – by excluding his picture from the annual report for example – he has, with this selfless humility, merely reinforced the myth they have made for him.

It is not entirely coincidental that religious imagery abounds when people describe Milken. His former Wharton professor spoke of his messianism, Reginald Lewis said, 'Michael walks on water.' So many journalists spoke of his evangelical fervour when talking about junk bonds that it became a cliché. However, it is worth pointing out that while Milken was undeniably charismatic and even compelling, much of the messianism was projected onto him by his disciples rather than projected by him. (This perhaps explains why Connie Bruck, author of *The Predator's Ball*, was disappointed when she finally met Milken. Not a messiah at all, she found him rather transparent. This is hardly surprising. She had been expecting the myth created by others instead of the ordinary man.)

For example, the following story told by Gerry Finneran is but one of hundreds from the letters that flooded to Judge Wood pleading for a lenient sentence. 'In the summer of 1987 Michael asked us to organize a business trip to Mexico that would begin with a breakfast Saturday morning and end on Monday evening. We explained to Michael that . . . it would be impossible to set up meetings on Saturday and Sunday. Whenever Michael would disagree with someone he would never raise his voice. He would simply say, "You don't understand." We didn't.' Without relating exactly how they were set up, the letter then goes on to list the many meetings that were held that weekend. Although he did not include it in the letter to the judge – no doubt because he thought it would be inappropriate – on another occasion he related how Milken used the same mantra to get Finneran to cash out a portfolio of investments on the eve of the October 1987 crash.

While on the one hand he allowed people to put him on a pedestal, on the other he allowed other people in the department, such as some of his hardball traders and biggest producers, to take advantage of him.

Again and again friends and working colleagues reiterated the notion that Milken could not say no, and would always see the good in someone instead of the bad. 'If Michael has a fault, it is the way he often is blind to the bad in a person, preferring to focus on any small good. To this end, he was often led astray by someone in whom he continued to believe even when it was patently obvious that such an association was dubious,' said one colleague on the X. Another opined, 'His greatest strength is his greatest weakness: his willingness to help . . . [and] his inability not to be taken advantage of.' Said Harry Horowitz, 'He assumes or chooses to view only the good in people. He is constantly trying to make lemonade out of lemons. He has never fired anyone and everyone knew that, and I believe many took advantage of him.' At departmental meetings there were frequent discussions about clearing out the dead wood which Milken would always conclude by saying that he would take care of it. His way of taking care of it was to juggle and shuffle, eliminate old jobs only by creating new ones and moving people sideways.

Because Milken tended to see only the good in people and because he believed that people were equal, he refused to judge them even when it would have been in his interests to do so. Many at Drexel on the East Coast believed that Milken had surrounded himself with 'a notorious goon squad', as Margaret Laws put it. Even within the department people described some of Milken's pet traders as 'scumbags' whom they wouldn't even want to sit next to. So naive was Milken that, 'If a guy was doing drugs in the bathroom he wouldn't notice, if there was an office romance he wouldn't notice until he got the invitation to the wedding,' as one insider said.

Thus although the image of a Wizard of Odd enslaving his followers by paying them millions of dollars, feeding them magic frozen yogurt, and seducing them with fatherly little kindnesses makes for exciting copy, it simply doesn't fit. The sheer volume and variety of his selflessness put it beyond the reach of mere technique. The problem was not that he cared, but that he cared too much and he allowed his compassion to blind him to his own interests. He made many of them everything that they were. Out of the void of their loves he made them richer than they could have ever dreamed of being under their own mediocre steam. Those that weren't gorging themselves at the trough bowed down in gratitude and made him their cult leader.

Reinforcing the image of a cult, they made outsiders of everyone who was not an insider, even within their own firm. As a result there was an 'us and them' relationship between the East and West. The West considered themselves the 'us', and scorned the East as the 'them'. They thought they were lazy and would often taunt them by calling first thing California time (i.e. 4 a.m. which was 7 a.m. in New York) and leaving messages before the East Coast had even made it to their desks. 'We couldn't stand them,' said one of the high yield bond team not quite as forthrightly as some others. 'They were incompetent, they always got in our way, they didn't know what they were doing and they didn't understand what we were doing. There was this feeling that we were always dragging them along, supporting their growth.'

Aware of this, although the East respected the West, 'Respect didn't mean popularity,' as Dan Stone wrote in *April Fools*. 'They weren't exactly the Trapp family singers – they fought for every dollar as though it were their first.' According to his account the West Coast would sell ahead on deals, telling the East Coast not to sell a new issue until it had been officially filed with the SEC. They would then use this lead time to place the issue with their clients. Finally a conference call was arranged to resolve the issue. As Stone recalls, a 'mystery guest' came on the line at the top of the meeting.

' "This is Mike. Can we take care of this another time?" '
"Sure, Mike."
End of meeting.'

Milken even made a speech to the equity department in October 1986 upbraiding them for 'lack of effort and intensity', according to Stone. 'We were the poor stepchild,' commented one member. Another member of retail talked about HITS, High Income Trust Securities, which were junk securities bundled together, starting in 1983, in a mutual fund in which the general public could buy shares (in general only very few wealthy individuals invested in junk). 'They got the right letters, but the wrong order.' According to this retailer, 'The Department' 'was taking the real crap off the street and giving it to us instead of their institutional investors'. Not only did they rarely contain any of the department's own junk issues for their clients, but the trashy junk that they did contain was 'obscenely marked up'.

Furthermore, 'The Department' shrouded itself in secrecy. They resisted any and all press – who were the ultimate outsiders and despoilers of the secrecy. As an East Coast Vice President explained, 'They wanted to create and preserve an air of mystery so they said "let's not tell anybody what we do, let's preserve the mystique of our department." '. But why? 'They had a lot of proprietary research on distressed companies and they didn't want their competitors to know any more than they needed to know.' But it was also fun. Cloaked in mystery, they could out-psyche their competitors.

It would be futile to try and argue that Milken did not, albeit indirectly and even unintentionally, create these results. Leading by example, this competition supremo roused his colleagues to a competitiveness that was so razor sharp it did not hesitate to shark on its own firm. As in 1972, when the equity and preferred staff had wanted to fire Milken because their clients no longer wanted to deal with anyone else once they had talked with him, so it was now, with Milken's department honing the art of being a complete one-stop service. Milken's pursuit of 100 per cent market share, which many argue was obsessive and his fatal flaw, fired people on to make extraordinary efforts to get business, to make money, to please Mike.

But by surrounding himself with people who so crudely and selfishly misappropriated his motives, Milken allowed himself to be represented – often misrepresented – by them. As co-worker Robert Fisher recalls, 'Whenever extraordinary feats were required and we needed more power to complete a specific task, we would frequently take Mike's name as our ally . . . "Mike wants you to do this" . . . Mike's name was an effective tool and many people used it without his approval or knowledge.' Thus while Milken ruled from the centre of the X, he was also at the same time putty in the myth-making hands of those he surrounded himself with.

As Drexel executive Chris Anderson remarked, 'He is our product,' which was one that 'bears as little resemblance to the true character of Michael Milken as the image of Kentucky Fried Chicken bears to the character of

Colonel Sanders'. To the outside world Milken would appear to be by turns sinister cult leader or capo of a mafia-style securities manipulating family, as Milken the man began to be buried by the myth created by those around him.

LIFE IN WARTIME

Had Milken stuck to underwriting high yield bonds for the companies of the future he might have been left to indulge his ideology of a people's capitalism, and pursue the democratization of capital undisturbed.

He may have exchanged his corner ghetto in the office for a swank place on Rodeo Drive, but he was still operating out of his own corner of the market. He wasn't really stepping on anybody's toes, at least not yet. But the high yield bond conference did not come to be called the Predator's Ball for nothing. Named after corporate raiders who gathered there, Milken's vision of a kinder, gentler high yield world would come to be seen instead as a revolution red in tooth and claw once it was decided to use junk bonds in hostile takeovers.

Milken's partner in the great takeover caper was Fred Joseph, who had come to head up the corporate finance department in 1974. As the name suggests, corporate finance worked on the financing of corporations, figuring out what instruments – stocks, bonds or hybrids – were most appropriate for a company's capital structure, conceptualizing their financing needs. But as a colleague remembered Fred once acknowledging in a meeting, 'Nobody conceptualizes like Mike does.' Athough Milken's department was techni- cally known as the high yield and convertible bond department, and therefore would in most other firms have limited itself to trading and underwriting these items, it was much more the one stop whatever-you-want department. Corporate finance could either twist in the wind or team up with Milken. Wisely Fred Joseph chose the latter (in later years corporate finance all but merged with Milken, moving its centre of operations out to Beverly Hills where it was linked, via passageway, to the Milken building).

Joseph recalled their first meeting. 'I remember the first time I met Michael. He was on the phone and very frenetic. That was in 1974 . . . he'd have been 28 and I was 37. An investor I respect told me I ought to go find this very smart young man who was trading bonds for us at that time. I went down to the trading floor, introduced myself, and got into a very strange, disjointed conversation. I was pitching the idea that we could probably do a lot together. He was very friendly, but he had one ear on me and one on the phone, executing trades, watching the tapes, quoting prices to people on the other end, and telling his own people what to do. This went on for some time, and I couldn't be sure if he paid any attention to what I'd been saying.'

But he did keep at it. Indeed it was Fred Joseph who had first suggested to Milken that they get together and get into issuing junk originals. He was also supposed to have originally suggested using junk to finance hostile takeovers.

The son of a cab driver and a former amateur boxer, the young Joseph had led a Boston street gang called the Vikings. With their blue and gold satin jackets, the Vikings were like something out of *West Side Story*. CEO of Drexel since 1985, was on the face of it the nice guy. His ability, in direct inverse proportion to Milken's, was to project a suavity and face. He did not suffer from the cosmetic handicap of walking round with a toupee that looked as though a small mammal had died on his head (as Michael Lewis described it). Instead he had silvery grey hair and could sit in a chair in such a way – draping one foot over the other and waggling his foot – as to project a candour so polished and smooth that nothing, and particularly not the burrs of misfortune, could stick to it.

Appearances can be beguiling, and indeed one Drexel partner remarked that he knew all was lost the moment he noticed that Fred Joseph parted his hair like Ted Kennedy. For all the silvery haired beneficence, there was a real predatory streak in Joseph. *Institutional Investor* pictured him up a tree togged out in jungle fatigues, face smeared with camouflage blacking and sporting a high-tech crossbow. Just like Rambo. Joseph's hobby was deerstalking.

'The way I do it, it's a gentle form of hunting. The deer win most of the time. The reason I love it is that you just disappear . . . up a tree with scents on. Don't move for hours. And you get to see immense amounts of nature in action.' However, the whole purpose of the scents – things like essence of doe in heat – was to attract the deer, presumably so that from his vantage point up in the trees, he could shoot them right between the eyes.

He was certainly ambitious. When he came to Drexel 'we ranked twenty first out of twenty-one major firms on Wall Street. . . . what you had here was the squish together of the old Burnham and the old Drexel investment banking operations with no direction, no identity.' His idea was for 'developing what I call competitive advantages, niches, edges. They can be a product and then you extend the product. You take high yield bonds into high premium converts, into notes and warrants, into financing leveraged buyouts.' Having gained this toehold it was his ambition to parlay that into one of the grand old firms of yore, indeed, he was supposed to have announced that given ten years he could have built something like Goldman Sachs – the most revered of firms on Wall Street.

Once Joseph was asked on television, 'If you couldn't be CEO of Drexel, what would you do?' Quick as a flash the answer came back, 'Be CEO of Goldman Sachs.' Joseph did not cherish these longings just because he wanted to belong to the grand old tradition of Wall Street. No, Goldman Sachs was the tops, king of the heap, the grand old man of the whole kaboodle. It didn't get any better than that. But the interviewer was not to be fobbed off with such an easy answer. 'Well, if you couldn't work on Wall Street, what would you do?' Barely a beat passed before Joseph came back with the answer, 'Go to work for a Japanese securities firm and take over Wall Street.' Earlier on the interviewer had asked, 'You like taking on the establishment, don't you?' 'No, not particularly,' said Fred. 'What I like doing is winning . . . and I like to win the investment banking game.'

Like Milken, Joseph was an unapologetic iconoclast. He regarded the old syndication process as 'a group of things that just don't have much important business application', and something they had suffered at the mercy of for long enough. Traditionally on Wall Street an investment bank would set up a syndicate to share in major financings. Other houses, according to their place in the Wall Street hierarchy (determined by pedigree, history and track record), would be given a share of the new issue to sell to their clients. While this meant less profit for the managing firm, it protected the lead bank from getting stuck with securities it could not sell. But what Joseph objected to was the way old firms, 'using their historic position as a tool of personal prejudice . . . [would say] "this one's an old wire house" and therefore they'd treat the firm like an old wire house for years after they'd ceased to be an old wire house and had become an investment banking power'. In this way Wall Street's powerhouses could minimize the share of securities that firms like Drexel would get to distribute in any underwriting syndication, thus maximizing their own profits while minimizing those of their competitors. 'The establishment . . . had a real stake in maintaining the status quo because the firms that were on top of the heap had a real stake in staying there and a real stake in not letting others into that level of club participation.' But with Milken Drexel no longer needed to kowtow to the tradition. If his department could place all the bonds within his network of clients and private syndicate of partnerships, what was the point of going outside to other companies to get them to help you do work you could perfectly well do yourself? What was the point in wasting time and losing money propping up a historical vestigial tradition just for the sake of appearances?

These were not the tactics that were going to win Drexel any friends on the street. On the occasions when Drexel did put together a syndicate their partners sometimes complained of being misled or choked off in their supply of securities, but this may have been sour grapes. In one case a company protesting against this unfair treatment bought only one $1,000 bond in the issue after Drexel failed to come through with the $15 million bonds they said they had been promised.

Not only was Drexel not interested in cutting other companies in on their business, they were also not beyond poaching clients. In this Drexel was merely taking the trend on the Street one step further. Since the abolition of fixed commissions the ties that had bound investment houses and their industrial clients in virtual wedlock had been disintegrating. Casual transactional relationships had replaced long-term relationships. John Gutfreund (pronounced 'Good friend') of the giant bond house Salomon Brothers had been ruthless in taking advantage of this new environment, but he did not like it when it happened to him. In one infamous case Drexel reportedly snatched Wickes away from a done deal with Salomon after they had printed a prospectus for a bond offering. According to Harry Horowitz, Gutfreund 'told his employees and senior management that he was going to bury Drexel, and together they all worked towards that.' Drexel also ended up taking Beatrice Foods, Uniroyal, TWA, Pacific Lumber and National Can away from Salomon. 'You tell that trader of yours on the Coast that I'm going to cut his nuts off. He can't have all our business,' Gutfreund told Joseph, according to Marie Brenner.

Anyone who got up in the morning boasting that they were 'ready to bite the ass off a bear' (as Gutfreund did) was bound to get sore when it was their own ass that was being bitten off. Salomon Brothers reportedly mailed out copies of lawsuits to clients, and fed stories to the press at the same time as the government's investigation was going on, which can only have further tainted Drexel's stained reputation. Although there are no laws against competitiveness, there is a point beyond which it becomes counterproductive. Competition does not always pay.

But what would really seal Drexel's reputation in the eyes of others was their idea of using junk bonds in hostile takeovers. 'I can tell you that [the] decision to finance hostile takeovers was nothing more than probably a two minute presentation I made,' Fred Joseph said. 'We had done a strategy session for ourselves in December '83 and the issue was, "How can we expand our merger and acquisitions activities so that they will grow at a pace like our financing activities?"' The growth of Milken's department was leaving all others in the shade. 'And we concluded that, you know, we can do difficult financing. We're in the merger business, is it hard to finance? Well unfriendlies are hard to finance. Could we finance them? And within three days, five of Mike's guys and five of my guys effectively figured out that we could do that. And by the time of the high yield conference we had already done that Gulf transaction, which another firm had tried to do and couldn't.'

The Gulf transaction was Boone Pickens's attempted raid on the massive Gulf Oil with his tinpot Mesa Petroleum corporation in 1984. Gulf, the sixth of the seven largest oil companies in the States (which were known as the Seven Sisters), was almost thirty times the size of Mesa (and would ultimately sell for $13.3 billion compared to Mesa's measly net worth of under $400 million). Traditionally hostile takeovers were limited to larger companies snaffling up smaller companies. This seemed to reflect a natural order. A small company would have neither the resources nor the money to take on a company many times its size. Unless, of course, it could borrow the money. But who was going to lend it?

The banks would never in a million years dream of lending to a Texan cowpoke like Pickens, who called himself Boone because he claimed he was a distant relative of the legendary frontiersman Daniel Boone. Seen through establishment eyes, these raiders were fast-buck buccaneers whose companies were no more than tax shelters that they carried on their backs like shells. To lend to a single individual (and his shell corporation) to take on an institution that was part of America's corporate heritage was antipodian.

But Milken didn't see it that way. 'The long and the short of it is, if you haven't inherited wealth, or if you haven't inherited a large company through succession, it's unfair for someone to tell you that you are too risky to borrow the money to fulfill your dream.' The puniness of their corporations was irrelevant since in Milken's books the assets of a company were its people, especially its management, and it was this human capital that was the critical resource. The fact that they were not blue chips off the old block was not a problem – because of their background Milken saw the entrepreneurial zeal burning in people like Saul Steinberg, Ted Turner, William Farley, Reginald Lewis. Neither did the fact that they didn't already head up a large company count against them. It presented him with the opportunity to get them the corporation of their dreams.

The challenge they faced back in 1983 was how to finesse it. From the raider's point of view the crucial thing for a credible takeover bid was to have the financing in place before he started. If it was going to take him months of protracted negotiations with a number of different parties to get that financing, news of his intentions would inevitably leak, speculation driving the stock up and closing the window of opportunity. But with Pickens's Gulf raid, Milken's one-stop service was able to raise $1.7 billion in just forty-eight hours. Having obtained commitment letters from investors (for which they were paid a fee whether the deal went through or not), Drexel would then provide the raider with a letter stating that it was 'highly confident' that they could raise the necessary funds. Although no more than a piece of paper, the highly confident letter would come to be more valuable than paper money, promising to pay the bearer on demand all the junk bonds he would need (and sometimes more than he would need) with which to go shopping for a corporation. In the event of the Gulf deal Drexel was never called upon to underwrite and sell the junk bonds because Pickens sold his accumulation of Gulf shares to Chevron (who went on to buy the rest of the company for $13.3 billion) for a profit of $446 million.

Once this technique had been developed and refined, the sky would be the limit. 'We now felt that we could do very large high yield bond financings of unfriendly acquisitions with a transaction where the prospective owners withstood credit analysis – and this might tip the scales a little bit, making it possible for larger companies to be acquired targets. I've said it in about the same words I've said it to you. It was just, "Hey guys, notice this." '

'Hey guys, notice this' was not some little anomaly. It was the potential to invert the corporate world order. One of the things that defines any establishment is the stability of its hierarchy. If you were number 50 in the *Fortune* 500, the assumption was that you could only be taken over by the top 49. The 450 companies below you could pose no threat, since you were bigger, and further up in the pecking order. The reasoning behind this was simple. Whoever could buy up all the shares of a public company owned the company and it was assumed – until junk bonds came along – that only a bigger company could muster the resources needed to buy up all the shares. Junk bonds changed all that by empowering the entrepreneurial individual. Whether the companies liked it or not – and generally management did not – raiders could snap up the shares without having to ask anyone's permission – hence the notion of the hostile takeover. Thus junk bonds showed that the corporate ladder of the *Fortune* 500 was no more than an idea, an historical abstract as opposed to an inviolable reality. Like the rating agencies and their investment grade credits, these were merely indicators of past performance that had nothing to do with what might happen in the future. But over time an aura of absolute authority had gradually accreted around them causing them to be enshrined as institutions, national treasures even.

In other words, 'Hey guys, notice this' was the clarion call of a revolution. Suddenly no company was safe from 'the junk bond bust up takeover' as its opponents would call it. By 1986, at the height of merger-mania, there would be fifteen takeovers a day. Were there no limits? There were some, as David Kay, head of mergers and acquisitions at Drexel, explained to *The Wall Street Journal*: 'From a purely mechanical point of view we could do any size acquisition, but from the real world point of view it wouldn't be appropriate to create the perception that our technique has the potential of toppling American institutions that are at the top of the pile. IBM isn't a candidate for takeover because it's an exquisitely run company.' Clearly there were no limits to Drexel's arrogance.

'We understood the implications of getting into the financing of large acquisitions before we did it. And we understood the heat that would result from our doing that,' said Joseph. People were duly outraged. When Ted Turner's Chicken Noodle Network tried to take over CBS in 1985 *The New York Times* mocked Turner as the mouse that tried to swallow the elephant, but he forced CBS into a costly restructuring implementing many of the changes he would have made had his takeover bid succeeded.

'But an awful lot of the heat is just rhetoric,' countered Joseph dismissively, 'it's yelling "junk bond bust up break up takeover artists." ' This was the mantra chanted throughout the land against the raiders and their financiers, because often the favoured transaction for the takeover itself was the leveraged buyout. In a leveraged buyout, junk bonds were the lever a raider used to get control of his target company. Since the raider did not personally have the billions needed to acquire a major American corporation, Milken would help him raise the money by lending him cash in the form of junk bonds. The raider could negotiate such a loan by providing as collateral the target company. Once the raider had acquired the company he could sell company assets either to make the interest payments on his junk bonds, which were higher yielding, or, better still, sell off more assets and save the expense of the high interest rate by retiring as much of the expensive debt as soon as possible. As Michael Brown, West Coast head of mergers at Drexel, put it,

'We take a minnow, identify a whale, and then look to its assets to finance the transaction.'

This break up was also the way the raider took his profit. Every acquisition was based on the simple notion that there was some hidden value in the company as a result of which it was undervalued in the market place. This enabled him to buy up the shares at a discount. He could then make any necessary adjustments before cashing in his investment at a profit. Often this meant no more than selling off the individual pieces which were worth more than the whole. Embedded in the concrete of the conglomerate, these gems had not shined and had not therefore been properly valued.

The CEOs of the whales objected to being torn apart by these minnows which in their eyes more resembled piranhas. They denounced the raiders as sharks, 'terrorists in three-piece suits', and claimed that the reason why junk bonds were so called was because their users were reducing companies to piles of junk, dismembering companies that had been built over generations.

But the raiders countered that the structure of a company was not a sacred architecture. Indeed as a result of a zealous anti-trust culture in the sixties and seventies that believed that monopolies or even large concentrations of economic power were not in the public interest, companies, in order to fulfill their economic *raison d'être* of expansion, were obliged to diversify laterally, becoming vast and unwieldy baskets of unrelated businesses, misshapen conglomerates. By the eighties, with increased competition from abroad making performance a premium, the economic climate had turned against these hybrid reactions to regulation. The raiders argued that in busting up the conglomerate they weren't cannibalizing the company but performing a necessary service, liberating divisions and spinning them off so they could perform more effectively.

As William Farley, the junk bond underwear king, explained, 'If you go back to after World War 2, what you saw was the emergence and strength of American Industry. We dominated, America dominated steel, and ship building and chemicals, and pharmaceuticals, and automotive . . . gradually the rest of the world became more competitive, and American companies became sort of fat and lazy and there was no way to restructure these companies. What happened is that over the last five or six years you have entrepreneurs like myself who have relatively little equity but who have got the ambition, who have the experience, who have talent, were able to get control of these companies, restructure them, cut the bureaucracy, improve their operations, build additional product lines and make them more competitive.'

At this point the raiders argued that they were the solution to the problem and not the problem. The problem was not bust up break up takoevers, the problem was 'entrenched management' and corpocrats who, had they been doing their job properly, would have seen the need to restructure and would have done it years ago.

'There is a club in America that has no name. Most of its members would barely acknowledge it, but its influence extends from coast to coast and is indirectly felt by most people in the nation. The club is a loose network of executives who run large, publicly owned corporations. It has no bylaws or official headquarters, and no official recruitment,' wrote Boone Pickens in *Boone!*. 'The Good Ol' Boys', as he also liked to call them, could be known by their entrenched rituals. The richest and most powerful (and most entrenched) would foregather in Bohemian Grove, an adult boy scout camp in California where they banished care and where there wasn't a phone for miles. Or they would go on hunting trips. Before Boone became a raider *non grata* within the establishment he went on some of these field trips. The 'hunting' consisted of shooting ducks reared in captivity that had been fed salty grain. Then, when they were released near a lake, the thirsty ducks immediately flew towards it, straight into the jolly CEOs with their jolly guns who had craftily placed themselves between duck and lake.

Carl Icahn, the junk bond backed takeover artist best known for his acquisition of TWA, argued that management were like gardeners who had made the mistake of thinking that they owned the estates they were paid to take care of. In fact they had been hired by the true owners of the estates – the shareholders – to look after them for them. Boone Pickens maintained that the shareholders had been forgotten and in 1986 he formed the United Shareholders Association to champion their rights. Said Saul Steinberg, 'The corporate raider helps keep management honest . . . many managements thought they owned the company . . . many companies had shooting lodges and apartments all over. They were like kings.' To be sure, even after retirement a CEO would enjoy an office, a secretary and a salary for life. It is not hard to imagine the august headquarters of America's most revered corporations housing entire wings of musty CEOs, as though these companies were museums. And then there were the perks. In the case of TWA there were golden passes, which a director could use to fly himself and his family around for free and for life. And then there were the corporate jets, a pet concern of many an entrenched CEO who customized their 727s with little luxuries, a gun rack for Bergerac (CEO of Revlon) and a grand piano for Hartley (CEO of Unocal).

This enjoyment of their entrenchedness was complemented by a kind of in-breeding. As Icahn commented, 'American CEOs, while not the best and the brightest, are politically astute and possess finely honed survival instincts, which may explain why they generally select seconds in command who are not quite as bright as they are; smarter ones would constitute a threat. When the CEO retires, however, that second in command takes the reins. We clearly have an anti-Darwinian principle working in our executive suite; the survival of the unfittest. At the same time companies are burdened by layers of Vice Presidents, who not only don't produce, but are counterproductive. We have, therefore, created a corporate welfare state.'

When attacked, entrenched management could respond viciously in self-defence. And the lengths to which boards would go to ward off their attackers underlined this. An impressive array of sexy-sounding tactics were invented and deployed to frustrate the raider. One solution was to go out and find an alternative friendly buyer, who came to be known as a White Knight. Hostile raider Sir James Goldsmith once ridiculed this concept by announcing to one startled board 'Well, I'm white and I'm a knight, what more could you want?' In a myriad of ways the board would make life difficult for the raider while smoothing the path of the White Knight. The Knight might get an·inside discount price or be treated to a lock-up agreement in which the board simply closed out other bids even if they were more competitive.

This tactic was more benign than the array of other 'shark repellants' that were devised at vast expense by lawyers specializing in this kind of litigation to drive away the raider. In the 'Pac Man' defence, the attacked tried to gobble up the raider by taking him over in return. There was the 'poison pill' which, simply explained, was designed to poison the raider's investment, triggering all sorts of treacherous boobytraps once the raider swallowed the pill through the accumulation of a certain amount of stock. 'Scorched earth' was similarly designed to sow salt and render the acquisition so barren so that it would no longer be of interest to the raider. 'Special voting rights' included the distribution of hybrid shares to friendly insiders that carried special voting privileges, thus obviating the fundamental shareholder right of one share, one vote. If it came to a proxy fight and the issue was going to be decided at a shareholders' meeting, an inside cabal whose friendly vote was assured could thus thwart the raider's attempts. Another device was the 'staggered board' by which only a certain number of board members could be replaced every year, thus frustrating the raider's desire to flush out entrenched management by protracting the process over an impractically lengthy period of time. Another key stratagem was called 'selling the crown jewels'. All the board did was sell to a friendly buyer the key or core operations that were the apple of the raider's eye.

'Greenmail' was another popular device. That it sounded like blackmail was no accident, since only a question of legality distinguished blackmail from greenmail which was basically an offer to buy back a raider's stock at a premium price. Because this was offered only to the raider as opposed to the other ordinary shareholders, it was basically a bribe. Although opprobium was heaped on the raiders who took this pay-off (and people like Steinberg gladly took it), the real scandal was that boards were willing to make it in the first place for no other reason than to keep their jobs. In so doing they showed a disregard for shareholder rights, treating some more equally than others. This self-interest and self-dealing reached a new pitch with the bail out feature of 'golden parachutes', lavish compensation packages for board members in the event that all the above lines of defence failed, and a successful takeover could not be avoided.

In short, as Icahn once lamented, 'There are some kamikaze boards out there that will do anything – blow up the company – to keep me out' (quoted in *Takeover* by Moira Johnston). The raiders were not slow to point out that virtually all of these manoeuvres were designed to frustrate the shareholders' basic right to decide on the future of the company they owned, while protecting management's jobs.

As the violence of these terms suggests, the takeover wars were no picnic. Indeed a report for the US Senate Committee on Banking spoke of the 'lexical violence' of takeover language, and that its vocabulary of 'predations, crime, and warfare' was evidence alone of the need for reform. In *Powershift* – revealingly subtitled 'Knowledge, wealth and violence at the edge of the 21st century' – Alvin Toffler noted that brute force had been sublimated into legal force. Lawyers were referred to as 'hired guns', and some white collar workers took delight in strapping their portable phones in holsters as though they were gunmen in the Wild West. Given that lawyers were the footsoldiers of the takeover wars, it was not surprising that the takeover game suggested full blown war. Insisting on anonymity for fear of takeover retribution, one industrialist even told *Manhattan Inc*, 'It's nothing short of war.' He was not exaggerating.

Because the media loves colourful conflicts, it was the perfect arena for the battle. On the one side there were the raiders, upstarts, underdogs and outsiders (the kind of anti-heroes the media loves to worship). They were not dwarves in borrowed robes. Larger than life and twice as rich, they filled the stage with their spectacle. Lacking blue-blooded ancestry, they were instead more like Mutant Ninja Turtles, up from the sewers and with no nose for dry sherry, posing as companies with their half-shell tax shelters on their backs.

Steinberg was the *enfant terrible* of the pack. Large and jowly, he had a way of rolling his eyes that made him look misleadingly jolly. At night his wife Gayfryd padlocked the refrigerator to prevent midnight raids in which he has been known to consume entire gallons of Haagen Dazs ice cream. 'I've greenmailed more companies than anyone else,' he boasted cheerfully. With Nelson Peltz he was supposed to have hosted at his house in Quoque, Long Island, topless tennis tournaments for female model doubles. But it was his business shenanigans that earned him the headline 'Fear and Loathing in the Corporate Boardroom'. In 1984 he celebrated Mickey Mouse's 50th birthday by announcing that he was storming the Magic Kingdom in a takeover attack that was generally seen as anti-American (in the end he walked away with $60 million in greenmail). He was just 29 when, in 1969, he first made his mark with a run at the Chemical Bank.

Nelson Peltz, Steinberg's 'tennis' partner, was a small food business and snack vending operator, when he bought Triangle Industries in 1985 for $1 billion. 'If you don't inherit it, you've got to borrow it,' he chirped, happily echoing the Milken line. A business school drop-out, he kept a book he had written called *All I Know About Business* on the desk of his lavish triplex penthouse offices on Lexington Avenue. He would show it to visitors who would politely flick through it, only to see that all the pages were blank. And yet in spite of this he had enough know-how to re-sell Triangle three years later for a personal profit of $520 million. He had a $2 million apartment in Paris, acres of seafront property on the French Riviera, a 106 acre estate in Bedford, New York, an $18 million estate in Palm Beach Florida, and travelled by limousine, helicopter and Lear jet. The size of his wife's diamond ring, which one friend described as covering the base of the finger to the knuckle ring, was legend.

Striking another note was William Farley, the go-go entrepreneur who also in 1985 made his first billion dollar acquisition of Northwest Industries which included the classic American underwear manufacturers Fruit of the Loom. It was a perfect fit. Farley fancied himself as a ladies' man, and was constantly in the company of models or former Miss Americas. As a wearer of Superman underwear, he has been reported to have asked prospective dates if they would like to see Superman fly. But it was not only his underwear that made Farley a superman. He was a fitness fanatic and has modelled his companies in his own image, making them lean and mean, and installing gymnasiums for his employees. He toyed with a presidential campaign in 1988, splurging $2.5 million on television advertisements. When he made his $3 billion bid for Westpoint Pepperell the chairman vowed to fight Farley 'until hell freezes over'. Farley went to the town and went on a walkabout with the mayor courting the people. On one such occasion the multi-millionaire and fitness fanatic saw a pair of trainers in the window that he liked. He had to borrow $40 from the mayor to make the purchase. According to *The Wall Street Journal* it took Farley a year to pay him back.

Then there was Boone Pickens, the self-styled Texan who titled his immodest best seller *Boone!* (perhaps also imitating Iacocca's two million seller *Iacocca*). The title sounds like a distant cannon, and of course his raids on Big Oil were the first shots in the takeover war. Having compared him to J.R. Ewing, CBS anchorwoman Diane Sawyer swooned, 'We've turned you into a mythical giant,' perhaps overwhelmed in equal measure by the media's myth-making powers and the stature of Boone. To create this effect Boone had a penchant for giving interviews on his private jet. 'I was introduced to the subject of corporate takeovers at twenty thousand feet sharing a Mesa jet with T. Boone Pickens as he launched his bid for Phillips Petroleum. It was a rare and privileged introduction,' raved Moira Johnston in the foreword to her book *Takeover: The New Wall Street Warriors*. However, it turned out to be not so rare, as one comes across many similar tales of induction into Boone's mile-high club: 'There are some first sentences you never forget,' wrote Joseph Nocera critiquing Johnston. 'The reason is that I too had first learned about takeovers at 20,000 feet, sitting across from T. Boone Pickens.'

The account continued, 'I can still picture those plane rides in my mind's eye; Pickens would have his jacket off and his tie pulled down, casually munching apple slices as he talked about anything that popped into his head. He was so relaxed that he might as well have been flying to a vacation on the beach. Next to him sat his wife Bea, half-reading a book and half eavesdropping, kibitzing whenever she had a detail to add to some story he was telling that showed – again! – the stupidity of entrenched management. Behind them might be seated a lawyer or an investment banker, reading through stacks of documents. Here was the tip off that we were not on a joy ride, but rather we were headed to New York, to the Waldorf Astoria to engage in corporate battle.'

The spectacle of corporate battle was *magnifique*, as the mangy raiders left their corner to take on what they saw as the fat and lazy corpocrats, the villains of entrenched management.

Michel Bergerac of Revlon and Fred Hartley of Unocal were the targets of two spectacular takeover battles. Bergerac's love of executive comfort was lampooned as excessive. He indulged his love of game hunting, shooting tigers in Africa and grouse on the moors of Scotland, travelling in a personalized 727 equipped with gun racks. His Madison Avenue apartment was packed with stuffed dead things, and littered with elephant tusks and zebra skins. On the wall painted in the style of the old masters hung an oil portrait of Bergerac and friends hunting on the moors. 'I am not afraid of this,' he said of the attack on Revlon by Perelman and his tax loss shell corporation Pantry Pride which he dismissed as Panty Pride. 'I am a big game hunter,' he told Connie Bruck. 'I sit there and a tiger charges me and when it gets to ten feet from me I shoot it between the eyes.'

The hunter had become the hunted in what was essentially a class war. 'At around midnight on October 9th Perelman and his entourage arrived for the first time in Revlon's gilded rococo foyer on the thirty-ninth floor of the General Motors building,' wrote Bruck in *The Predator's Ball*. 'I'll never forget those twenty or thirty guys coming off the elevators,' recalled Bergerac. 'All short, bald, with big cigars! it was incredible! If central casting had had to produce thirty guys like that they couldn't do it . . . .' Arthur Liman, who was at the time helping Revlon with its corporate defence, said, 'What a scene, all the Drexels were in one room – these guys with their feet up on Michel's tables, spilling their cigar ash onto his rugs.' In time Liman would come to represent the king of the Drexels and the man who had made Perelman's raid possible, Michael Milken (Milken was supposed to have advised against the Revlon transaction, but to have gone along with it nonetheless). In the end Perelman bought Revlon for $1.8 billion, and Bergerac pulled the string on a whopping $35 million golden parachute.

Fred Hartley, chairman of Unocal Petroleum, had a penchant for shooting quail in Spain. Not blessed with the warmest of manners, his face had a cold look to it, consisting of lidless shark eyes, thin lips and a pasty-white vampire's complexion with bits flaking off, like the Evil Emperor in *Star Wars*. His utterances did little to dispel the chill. Commenting on a Unocal oil spill he was quoted in *The Wall Street Journal* as having said, 'I'm amazed at the publicity for the loss of a few birds.' In fact what he had really said was, 'I am always tremendously impressed at the publicity that death of birds receives versus the loss of people in this day and age' (although unfairly misrepresented, the fact is that the person who fails to talk in bites in the media age gets bitten).

Embittered by Boone's smooth talking raid, Hartley never bothered to conceal his disdain. Although Hartley once shared the same golf cart with him, pre-raid, there was no executive bonding. 'He's a small time operator . . . in fact he announced he was giving up mining oil, because it was a losing game. The reason it was a losing game to him was he wasn't capable of finding very much.' Hartley ridiculed him as a 'paper driller . . . drilling on Wall Street'. Again it was the industry prejudice against the information entrepreneur.

Boone matched Hartley's contempt with amused criticism. What, he asked, was the point of spending billions, as Unocal had, on a complex oil-extracting shale operation when cheaper oil could be had from abroad? At what point did one stop squandering shareholder dollars and stop doing what one had always done even though it no longer made economic sense?

Of the voluntary, self-imposed restructuring and the $3.6 billion in debt that Unocal had to take on, Hartley said that either they would have had to do it or let 'the barbarians do it'. Perish the thought! On the eve of victory Hartley proposed a board luncheon and, since they had so much to do, a flunky suggested a working lunch of sandwiches. 'No!' yelled Hartley, barking mad. 'We are not barbarians.' He saw himself as the final stalwart of civilization stemming the tide of barbarism. Wall Street were all vermin and he would even avoid saying the words 'investment banking'.

But king of the buyouts and the man behind the biggest transaction in the history of the planet was Henry Kravis of Kravis, Kohlberg & Roberts, a leveraged buyout boutique. In 1986 KKR had been behind what was then the biggest LBO ever, the $8.2 billion buyout of Beatrice, a sprawling conglomerate including Avis Rent-a-cars, Playtex bras, Samsonite luggage, Tropicana orange juice and a bunch of other global food businesses. Milken's high yield bond department not only provided $2.5 billion in junk bonds, but also ended up owning just under 25 per cent of Beatrice. While KKR set about the spin off, bust up, what-you-will of Beatrice, the papers drooled over the potential profits: $400 million for Kravis out of a total of $2.5 billion for KKR (and for only $417 million down in cash!), $86 million for Drexel and perhaps a $1 billion profit on their investment. The day *The New York Times* printed the profit guesstimates for the Beatrice deal, Adam Smith, author of *The Roaring Eighties*, was on the phone to a friend:

'It's lucky I love my work because otherwise I would think I was in the wrong business,' he said.

'This morning everyone thinks he is in the wrong business and that's what's wrong with America,' came the apropos reply.

Buyout fever had seized the nation, making Henry Kravis the most celebrated of all the takeover artists. Only 5 feet 6 inches tall, the press mythicized him as the pint-sized buyout king, the Little Mr Big of Business. What King Henry lacked in stature he made up for in capital. With holdings of $45 billion KKR would rank seventh in the *Fortune* 500 if it was a publicly traded company. 'He's quite tall when he stands on his wallet,' said his Amazonian wife (just shy of 6 feet) to someone who once remarked on the disparity of their size.

Henry cut a swathe through society with his fashion designer wife (who had her own Henry-financed line), appearing – reluctantly he said – in gossip and society columns. Kravis claimed it was because of his wife that he appeared so frequently in *Women's Wear Daily*, while his wife claimed that she wanted to stay home and that Henry was 'the most gregarious person on Earth'. He was a close friend of Hollywood producer and actor Michael Douglas (they went to the same prep school) who looked to him in preparing for his Boeskyesque role as Gordon Gekko in the film *Wall Street*. As was par for the times, Kravis was obsessively competitive. He hated to lose at ping-pong and had been known to play with an opponent for as long as it took him to win one game.

Of all the battles and all the characters, the 1989 takeover of RJR Nabisco enshrined the follies of the period in the greatest LBO of all. Celebrated in the epic book *Barbarians At The Gate* – a title of which Fred Hartley would have thoroughly approved – the almost comic antics brought the language of lexical violence to a new pitch. The sheer greed and grasping self-interest of almost all those involved defied belief (and was also testimony to how hopelessly twisted Milken's original junk bond revolution had become).

The story began when Ross Johnson, CEO of RJR Nabisco, announced that he wanted to take the company private in an LBO. In other words, he wanted to buy out the public shareholders and become the owner (along with a group of others) of the company. The rationale for this was that the company's shares were trading at a price beneath their true value, and as a manager it was his fiduciary responsibility to make sure that the shares of the company in his charge traded at the highest price. He claimed he had tried everything, but that nothing had worked. He had an idea. He would buy out the shareholders and offer them a premium price for their shares, thus solving the problem of share price once and for all. Of course to do this he would need to borrow vast amounts.

But the altruism of these arguments did not alter the fact that by taking the company private in an LBO he stood to become a very rich man. He estimated that he might make $100 million, although others suggested the figure was more like $1 billion. Neither could his rhetoric hide the fact that he was trying to spirit the company away from its true owners, the shareholders. As anti-LBO fanatic Ben Stein queried in *Barrons*, 'If management is required to put the shareholder's interest ahead of its own, why doesn't management sell off those units and pay the value to the stockholders? Is it not the clear duty of management to realize that value for the stockholders and not partly for the stockholders and mostly for themselves?' The argument went that it was not within the scope of Johnson's brief to unburden the shareholders of their stock, relieving them of their investment at a price that would enable him to then extract monopoly profits for himself.

Because of his position as a manager, Ross Johnson had unique knowledge of the value of the company. He put in what was generally regarded as a lowball offer of $70 per share for a total cost of $16 billion. Having paid off the shareholders and acquired the company he could then sell off the parts to repay the purchase price of the whole. This restructuring – although it would reverse the merger of the R.J. Reynolds tobacco and Nabisco foods that he himself had encouraged only three years earlier – would be the way to make the company fulfill its potential and maximize value.

In *Barbarians At The Gate* Ross Johnson's managerial skills are presented as colourfully *manqué*. In his career it would appear that his only bright idea (apart from a modestly successful lightbulb) was for a wine called French Kiss (a disaster) and a gravy bar that came in the form of a margarine stick (ditto). He also presided over RJR's multi-million dollar attempt to launch a tobacco-free cigarette called Premier. The very notion that a tobacco company should try and create a non-tobacco cigarette, selling itself as 'the world's cleanest cigarette' and thus implying that its other brands were dirty and unsafe, seemed to evade all. In the event it too was a disaster. As Johnson was quoted as saying, 'This tastes like a fart.'

What Johnson lacked in creativity he made up for with his fondness for corporate largesse. Team Nabisco was an assortment of celebrity athletes on annual retainers of a quarter of a million dollars or more, and then there was the RJR air force of ten corporate jets which Johnson proudly housed in a new no-expense-spared hangar at a cost of $12 million. On one occasion flight records list a passenger G. Shepherd – Ross Johnson's German shepherd – who was airlifted out of trouble after he had bitten a security guard. He liked to tip generously and frequently ('Get me an inch of fifties,' he once commanded his secretary) and won favour by showing the board members a good time. As Ross Johnson knew, he was a very lucky guy. 'Some genius invented the Oreo cookie and we're just living off the inheritance,' he pronounced as the heir apparent.

Having tried to persuade Johnson to do a deal with KKR for RJR, Kravis was dismayed to see him try and do it without him. It is claimed that he said he had a franchise and that he was going to protect it. Kravis liked to think of himself as a White Knight. He was not a raider, he did not do hostiles. But this was semantics. He did a raider's work, the only difference was that he worked with incumbent management who often came to him when staring down the barrel of a raider's gun. KKR would benefit from the inside information management possessed, which would help them decide how best to downsize, restructure and carve up complex industries and businesses they knew nothing about. In return, management would become even more entrenched by being rewarded with an ownership chunk of the business they had previously only overseen. 'When management has its own dollars up,' said Kravis, 'they say, "Do we really need all the limousines?"' This is a sad reflection on management who were unable to do their jobs before they owned their jobs.

In the unholy battle that followed few came out ahead, and at several points people almost came to blows. One of the most memorable conflicts of the war was the 'Drexel problem', Gutfreund's refusal to take second place to Drexel on the tombstone advertisment announcing the underwriting syndicate. As Bryan Burrough incredulously put it, 'Through all the machismo, through all the greed, through all the discussion of shareholder value it came down to this: John Gutfreund [was] prepared to scrap the largest takeover of all time because [his] firm's name would go on the right, not the left side, of a tombstone advertisment buried among the stock tables at the back of *The Wall Street Journal* and *The New York Times*.'

On another occasion, when negotiations were particularly tense at a Literary Lions dinner at the New York Public Library, Kravis attacked William Norwich, the social columnist for the *Daily News*. In spite of the fact that Kravis seemed to enjoy cutting a swathe through society he took a different line when talking to the press. 'When she [his wife] gets her picture taken I get my picture taken, and we're in *Women's Wear Daily* and the magazines, and I don't like that.' In addition to not liking the press he especially did not like it when the press accused him of loathing the press as Norwich had done. Kravis attacked, calling him an 'arsehole', and threatened to break both his kneecaps. As a British guest commented afterwards, it was something she would have expected to see 'at a low-life party', but not the Literary Lions.

Finally KKR beat out Ross Johnson with a higher bid for the company (total cost $25 billion). But the end result was less interesting than the process. 'In takeovers,' said Icahn, 'the metaphor is war', and the war in question in RJR Nabisco was 'Nam. At one point, Kravis described his strategy thus: 'We were charging though the rice paddies, not stopping for anything and taking no prisoners,' elsewhere people spoke of napalming the corporate air force and perks. But no one embodied the Viet vet theme better than the Drexel rainmaker Jeff 'Mad Dog' Beck who liked to take the credit for making both the Beatrice deal and the RJR deal come to pass. Living up to his nickname, Beck could synthesize madness and doggedness. It is said that when he was given a packet of Milk Bone dog biscuits by Ross Johnson he wolfed down the lot during the course of the meeting, though Beck has denied this. Beck claimed that the nickname came from his service in 'Nam, highlights of which included wiping out an entire battalion of enemy nips single-handed and being peppered with shrapnel. During the junk bond conference he would lure beauties back to his bunker at the Bel Air Hotel, and offer to show them the shrapnel in his butt or thrill them with his multi-orgasmic prowess. At more staid dinner parties he would content himself with sporting the small scar on his wrist – apparently his life had been saved by his wristwatch.

Claiming to have met Oliver Stone, the director of *Platoon*, while serving in 'Nam, he served as an adviser on the making of *Wall Street*, the movie which Stone also directed. He contributed to this a small cameo role and some pieces of dialogue, such as 'lock and load', one of his pet war cries prior to big meetings. Oliver Stone was impressed by Beck ('To me he really was the new Wall Street'), as was Michael Douglas who put Beck together with a screenwriter with a view to producing a movie about the Mad Dog's life.

Douglas even went so far as to take him to the Oscar awards ceremony one year. As Beck stepped out of the limo and into 'an adoring sound-and-light show of cameras clicking and flashes illuminating the evening', he recalled that he was 'on an orgasmic journey of total impression since there was no content. It was the greatest show on earth, the adult version of a Ringling Brothers circus.' Later, comparing himself to his companion, he said: 'We were both chameleons, both stars bringing our own fantasies of life to others. The only difference was that he was a professional actor known as such and I was in disguise as an investment banker.' Shortly afterwards, Beck received a telegram from the famed Mike Ovitz at Creative Artists Associated, jokingly inviting him to sign up, which he did. Beck had also put into the works a book about his life, to be called *Rainmaker*.

Beck was fond of making the analogy between Wall Street and the paddy fields of 'Nam. One confidante remembers him saying that he thought Milken was like some person who had been badly shell shocked on some mission in the jungle and that as a result he was an AWOL automaton figure with miswired nerves and jerking about in a mad frenzy. He dubbed Milken 'The Terminator'. If the government had not stopped Milken, they would have had to stop him by locking him in a padded cell, he reportedly argued.

In the upshot it was Beck who should have been put in a padded cell. For as was so typical of the eighties, nothing was as it seemed. Although he claimed to be a Vietnamese hero he had all but dodged the draft, and as for his claims that he was heir to the Beck's beer fortune, he was in fact no relation. But Beck was a tenacious actor. When confronted by *The Wall Street Journal* over lunch, 'Mr Beck first looks away, then stares at the ceiling for a moment. Under the table his left leg begins rapidly bobbing. A thin mist falls over his eyes. "I can't talk about it," he says after a long silence.' But he did. He claimed that the real truth was that he led a double life as a secret agent. In January 1990, Douglas, furious at having been deceived, cancelled the movie project. After the *Journal* printed its *exposé* Beck also received a sympathy cake from his colleagues. Shaped like a female organ it bore, in pink icing, the legend 'Lock and load'.

Beck's scam was up. He levelled with his biographer, and Anthony Bianco graciously allowed Beck to append his own confessional epilogue to *Rainmaker*, in which he made, from the sadder and wiser vantage point of the New Age nineties, an almost stereotypical confession renouncing his lifestyle: 'Spending money on apartments, charitable donations, country homes, vacations at the Hotel du Cap, New Year's Eves in Paris, jewelry, designer dresses, private schools, chauffeurs, housekeepers, nannies, laundresses, antiques, interior decorators, and architectural designers was the outer manifestation of a personality out of control. It seemed that the more money I made, the less it sufficed.' To celebrate his deals he bejewelled his 'socially prominent' wife and bought himself horses, which scared him to death. 'In the disjointed atmosphere of the 1980s, even marriage and love became a deal, it seemed, and were talked about in material terms rather than in terms of emotion.' This rot of materialism was the context for Beck's self-mythification. 'On Wall Street during the 1980s there were no boundaries, and my creations took on a life of their own . . . while it became a challenge to my complex mind to keep re-inventing this wheel of deception, I was also addicted to this escapist form of pain relief.' The upshot was that instead of winning an Oscar, as Douglas had done for his role as Gekko, Beck claimed he found 'something much more meaningful to me' than a gold statuette: 'understanding and self-awareness'.

Beck and his vainglorious delusions of grandeur will doubtless be remembered as one of the symbols of Wall Street in the eighties. As author Michael Thomas, an old time Wall Streeter and author of *Hanover Place*, a Wall Street novel that has languished in the shadow of *Bonfire of the Vanities*, once commented about the takeover wars, 'This is a very compelling game. It's like a gambler's addiction, you can't stop playing . . . There's a terrific feeling when you're 25 years old and you're kicking around a 30-billion dollar corporation with 15,000 small-time people who don't understand anything more than having a house to live in and putting food on the table. That is pretty heady stuff and you get a crazed level of near hysterical enthusiasm when a big deal is going down . . . There's a lot of play acting in all of this, the glorification of stress and expenditure of time. Parkinson said "work expands to fill the time" and today work expands to fill all time, and I think it makes people feel tough. This is a generation that has never known war and the oldest among them paid their way out of Vietnam, so war is a game to them and they're storming paper beach heads.'

For all the machismo and posturing, for all the sublimated violence, the metaphor of war was merely metaphor. The fashion of slinging portable phones around one's waist cowboy-style was a poor substitute for packing a real pistol. The quick call could never surpass the quick draw. Commented another observer who was drawn to merger mania only to quit in disgust,

'Real men don't work on Wall Street. All the shouting, all the yelling, was really no more than the squealing of a bunch of men who had had their balls cut off by technology. Working the phones they thought they were gunslingers, but they didn't even have the guts of a secretary pool. They thought they were "big swinging dicks" but they were eunuchs. They weren't really men at all.'

So mired in cliché and popular mythology has Wolfe's image of masters of the universe become that we tend to forget that its source was a children's cartoon, and that far from being towering Ozymandians bestriding the canyon of the street, they were infantile fantasists, scampering around rat-a-tat-tatting with their toy guns, consumed with their game and consumed with winning. When one Drexelite exclaimed in ecstasy that Drexel was 'Disneyland for adults' he only got one thing wrong – it wasn't for adults, it was for overgrown kids.

Beck's Rambo image was in part a colourful creation of the Wall Street Universe. As the titles of two books about the boom – *Takeover Madness* and *Merger Mania* (the latter 'written' by Ivan Boesky) – show, insanity was sanctioned. An infantile hyperexcitement was part of the mix. And Wall Street's madness was in turn a creation of America in the eighties. 'We have every right to dream heroic dreams,' announced Reagan in his inaugural address, and with this abracadabra the Mickey Mouse president, speaking from his Disneyland White House, transformed the empire state into a dream state. In this fantasy decade the only limit would be the extent of your imagination, for nothing else would limit your powers of self-invention.

THE DOBERMANS OF WALL STREET

One of the interesting things about the Beck debacle was that Drexel had ever hired him in the first place. Beck's wild stories had got him fired from Oppenheimer where he had once pledged to prop up a deal with his Beck's billions. Fred Joseph called the CEO of Oppenheimer and said, 'This is one of the most controversial guys I've ever checked references on, what's the truth?' So the CEO told him, and still Joseph hired him.

Beck was hired as a rainmaker, to bring in business and feed the twinned machine of mergers and acquisitions and the West Coast junk bond department. Since he wasn't going to be working closely on deal details, the thinking can only have been that his fictive lives would not be able to mess with delicate realities. However, Drexel so revelled in its gun-toting corporate culture that it is not hard to imagine Joseph feeling that the Mad Dog would make an excellent addition to the platoon he was modelling.

Joseph created an environment at Drexel where winning was God. Instead of a rigid hierarchy Drexel consisted of a number of profit centres. One Drexelite compared it to a department store with leased booths. People were using Drexel as a nameplate only. Or as Dan Stone described it, Drexel was 'a bunch of businesses under a big tent'. For a Wall Street house this bazaar was bizarre: 'It was far too entrepreneurial, this was an investment bank for God's sake,' commented one East Coaster. The overriding credo was: go for it. 'There's less reverence for tradition, but not a violation of the unwritten rules,' countered Fred.

Small wonder then that Drexel earned itself a strong reputation. They were variously known as 'The JR of Wall Street', 'the Libya of investment banking', or 'the Dobermans of Wall Street'. In a television interview Fred empathized with their hatred: 'We've grown faster than any firm in the past decade . . . and we've been aggressive about doing it, we've grown so fast we've had to hire people from other firms and they don't like it . . . we've taken their accounts because we're doing larger deals than they can do . . . there have been eleven deals of over $1 billion in the history of Wall Street and we've done nine of them . . . and they don't like it, and if I were one of them I wouldn't like it.' Although he was aware that Drexel's success and attitude was breeding antagonism that he knew was 'out there in spades', he seemed supremely unconcerned. 'I wish I could hide my competitiveness as well as Goldman Sachs . . . I try to make our people understand that we don't want to be excessively aggressive,' he said, striking a tone of mock wonderment that can only have been designed to enrage the competition all the more. 'We try not to spite them with our success,' he added, spiting them further.

Far from being apologetic, Drexel revelled in its predatoriness. In 1984 they had decided that it was time to switch advertisers, and after an exhaustive search they settled on Chiat & Day, the LA company best known for its controversial ads for Apple in which legions of uniformly grey and blind-folded businessmen, IBM clones, walked lemming-like over the edge of a cliff. But one, the Apple guy, removed his blindfold and pulled back from the brink.

Scrapping the gentle animal fables that had been the spine of the old advertising campaign, Chiat & Day began with a series of controversial ads that complemented Drexel's aggressiveness perhaps too much. In one ad, 'An Idea Whose Time Has Come', Drexel thumbed its nose at the white shoe world it was trouncing, reprinting among others a quote from *Time*: 'Investment banking is beginning to lose its old genteel overtones of Ivy League colleges and gentlemen's social clubs.' Underneath the copy read, 'A few years ago Drexel Burnham came out of nowhere with a tough aggressive attitude, a hard entrepreneurial spirit and a relative indifference to the staid traditions of business . . . why follow the pack when you can follow the leader?' Other ads were even more controversial: '95 per cent of American Companies were considered Junk.' Not all of the 95 per cent relished the pun. 'End Capital Punishment' depicted a guy with a money bag over his head and a rope tied to his neck. Even Drexel thought that 'How to attempt and how to avoid a takeover' was perhaps a little strong, and the ad only ran once in *Institutional Investor*.

In 1986 Drexel aired at the conference its Titanium credit card commercial, a sketch based on the American Express Platinum Card which perfectly encapsulated the American excess that was the spirit of the times. A yacht-long Rolls Royce pulled up outside the towering headquarters of 'The Fat And Lethargic Corp'. Waving a silvery credit card at the guards, our unidentified raider passed unimpeded up to the executive floors and straight into the boardroom where a meeting was in progress. While the chairman produced a credit card imprinter, other members of the board strapped on golden parachutes and began jumping out of the windows. Finally we saw that the card was the Drexel Titanium card, good for credit of up to $10 billion and it was brandished by none other than Larry Hagman as J.R. Ewing. 'Apply today for the Drexel Titanium Card,' he said, 'don't go huntin' without it!'.

When it came to the bad publicity that hostile takeovers were generating, the East Coast made a point of wallowing in it and smearing the mud slung all over themselves as though it were a kind of tribal warpaint. 'At the time it felt good,' said a senior Drexel executive of their posturing as G.I. Joe meets J. R. Ewing. 'I know that sounds awfully naive but it was the way we saw the world and the way the world saw us.'

More than this, Drexel East just didn't care. They thought that the grumblings of the competition were just sour grapes. Wallowing in fees, the money was pouring in and they just revelled in it. Bonuses for non-management Drexel employees went as high as 42 per cent of their annual salary. This was streaks ahead of Goldman Sachs whose average bonus was 25 per cent. When challenged about the pay Drexel lavished on its youngest and most inexperienced, Joseph replied, 'In an environment of phenomenal profits and unprecedented fees, what difference does it make. The difference amounts to a rounding error.' Knowing that they were the chosen race, Drexel trainees ate – at the company's expense – in the most expensive restaurants in town. They ordered Roederer Cristal by the caseload, and when they had drunk their fill they sprayed each other with it (this piggery inspired one disgusted old-timer at Drexel to draw up a list of restaurants where trainees could have dinner for under $50.00).

Meanwhile Joseph rushed to build the full-service Goldman Sachs of his dreams. Drexel went on a massive hiring binge, one of the most rapid expansions in Wall Street history. In late 1986 the firm hired their ten thousandth employee. On the eve of the eighties Drexel had been just three thousand strong. One department, mortgage back securities, was built from scratch by Fred Joseph's brother Stephen by hiring 280 employees in eighteen months. Earlier that year Drexel had signed an agreement to move into Seven World Trade Center, the recently completed forty-seven-storey building that squatted in the shadow of the twin towers. Tubby Burnham had attended the building's topping off ceremony. With two million square feet, there would be plenty of room to house the ten thousand.

Even in its hiring policies Drexel was not afraid to be controversial. Joseph reportedly told a a seminar on ethics that he 'hired excessively aggressive guys because it fit with our aggressive image. I did not want to cut off that aggression, I was actually using it, the word "greedy" internally. I did not want to cut out excessive greed.' And so the greedy flocked to Drexel like bees to honey. Since Drexel was trying to build up a blue chip client base, so that they could secure their future by graduating from outlaw to establishment once the takeover jamboree slowed, it was regarded as a great coup when they hired Martin Siegel, the charming takeover defence specialist from Kidder Peabody who brought in tow a bunch of big blue clients. But as would be revealed, Siegel was up to his ears in insider trading, as was, coincidentally, the man who shared his office next door, Dennis Levine. And there were others. Although Joseph would dismiss it as a coincidence, Drexel had more than its fair share of people whose greed knew no bounds.

Indeed in Milken's defence it has been argued that Milken was always opposed to Fred Joseph's idea of using junk bonds in hostile takeovers, and only reluctantly acquiesced. 'Michael thought it would get them a lot of bad publicity. He didn't think it was good for the market in that it would cloud the point of junk bonds – and he was right,' claims Milken's PR man Ken Lerer. However, there is some division on this; 'he just flat-out didn't,' a former senior executive at Drexel told Dan Stone. 'If Michael had been opposed, it never would have been launched as a major strategy.' But it was, and if he had been opposed something made him change his mind. Milken would often argue that if he didn't do the business someone else would, but if this was his thinking in this case, it seems extraordinarily naive – especially from someone who had said back in the sixties that there were better ways to achieve things than through confrontation.

If Milken did find this 'predatory capitalism' distasteful, he did little to try and peddle his 'people's capitalism' outside of his small circle of converts and lip servants who gathered at the junk bond conference (closed to the press until 1988). Where smooth talking Boone could deflect criticism by talking about shareholder rights, portraying himself as 'the people's raider', and Drexel East was unapologetically aggressive, out of the West came nothing other than the usual radio silence. In today's media world the absence of a score creates a sinister effect that makes the public uneasy and suspicious.

One projecting secrecy, the other swanky, the two Drexels were projecting two distinct images that did not make for a complementary fit. In retrospect the East should have made Milken welcome the media in and go out and tell his story. For their part the West should have stopped the East from rubbing people's noses in it. Had the relationship been more equal, that might have happened. But as it was, they didn't even have the same goals. Fred Joseph wanted a full-service bank, but Milken wasn't interested in status or size. 'The dinosaurs were big,' he liked to say. 'Look what happened to them.' Moreover, the West was making all the money and the East was not going to kill the goose that laid the golden egg. But the roar from the torrent of money pouring in would have drowned out their voices even if anyone had decided to speak up. In fact founder 'Tubby' Burnham had grave doubts about the use of junk bonds in takeovers, the mega-bonuses and some of the hybrid bonds they were peddling. But 'I stand in awe of your achievement' was all he wrote in a memo to Milken.

Unable to move forward together, the push-me-pull-you creature of the two Drexels was setting itself up as the target of a political unpopularity that easily could – and would – spark massive popular resentment. But in spite of this unperceived flaw that this schizophrenic corporate culture represented, Drexel's and Milken's real problems would be caused by the real predator's ball – the rich and famous lifestyles of the junk bond jillionaires and their Marie Antoinettes.

6

THE JUNK BOND JILLIONAIRES AND
THEIR MARIE ANTOINETTES

IN their campaign to restructure corporate America, one of the raiders'
favourite complaints was the way entrenched management squandered
public shareholder money on personal extravagances. However, the truth was
that the raiders rarely scrimped on themselves. Steinberg, who had complained of CEOs living like kings, flagrantly lived like one himself and even
had Jacob Jordaen's massive masterpiece *The King Drinks* hanging in his
dining room, as befitted a king.

Ron Perelman, owner of Revlon, considered to be the third richest man in
America, may have lampooned Bergerac's golden parachute, but he retained
James, Bergerac's former butler. In other words, little had changed. As
Bergerac lamented, 'You know it's fairly common practice in America for a
chief executive of a large company to have easy transport like an aeroplane . . .
and the raiders say that these are terrible people, they are so interested in
gadgets and toys that they will do anything to protect and preserve them . . .
but what is more amusing to see is when some of these so-called raiders
manage to get hold of one of these large companies and a mysterious process
of osmosis seems to take place. They go to London to get their suits, they hire
French chefs, they drink good French wine, one plane is not enough for them
and some of them have two or three planes. So all I can tell you is that either
the demands of the job create these things or that the good life is contagious.'

While the demands of the job may well have created these things – subject
to an indulgent definition of demand – the notion of the good life as a
contagious disease is much more illuminating. Shut out of the feast for so
long, the raiders fell upon the good life and glutted themselves on it. They
lived their lives in a fever of acquisition, not just of companies, but of
apartments, paintings, jets, and charitable causes. In a delirium of consumption they quaffed lakes of Cristal and mountains of caviar that were piled so
high one guest dispensed with the toast points altogether and called for a
spoon with which to shovel the Iranian gold. And the conspicuousness of the

consumption was the thing. Everyone had to see, so that by witnessing their gargantuan appetites we would know that the grand acquisitors truly were Supermen.

With his second wife Claudia Cohen, a former *New York Post* gossip columnist turned television news anchor, Perelman set out to scale the heights of old money society just as surely as he had vaulted the citadel of the corpocracy. He hired a former editor of *Town & Country* magazine as a social secretary, and assembled a glitzy board that would include Ann Getty and Henry Kissinger. Indeed it was hard to separate the business from the pleasure. *Forbes* magazine commented, 'Perelman's role in running Revlon seems heavily concentrated on what might be called the celebrity and image sides of the business. He is very involved in selecting celebrities for the company's television and print advertising campaigns. They include Frank and Barbara Sinatra, Melanie Griffith and Don Johnson.' Junkophobe Teddy Forstmann, an LBO specialist who did not use junk bonds and who took every opportunity to discredit them, commented that Perelman's acquisition of Revlon was 'the highest price ever paid in the history of this country to get a good table at a New York restaurant'.

That table was at Le Cirque, where Perelman would lunch most days always at the same table 'by the door at the far end of the room . . . sitting as always on the outside of the table, he takes pleasure in greeting every passer by,' according to Fairchild, the publisher of the trade publications *Women's Wear Daily* and *M*. On that particular day Alice Mason the realtor, Saul Steinberg and Barbara Walters were also there. The restaurant was also a favourite watering hole of the Kravises and the Gutfreunds. According to myth, Fairchild suddenly realized that he was staring down the barrel of a new world order.

In his book *Chic Savages* he recalled the epiphany more prosaically; 'Picture the scene: a rainy Monday morning, yet another cover to think up for W, and all I'm drawing is a great big blank . . . "You know," I begin, "there's been a big change in society; today it's all money and power and greed . . . we have to give this society a name that means something to the reader. Not 'nouveau riche'; but nouveau something. We've got nouvelle cuisine, we've got nouvelle . . . . That's it! Nouvelle Society."'

He warmed to his theme. 'Nouvelle Society wants them[selves] covered. It's not enough that these people have trouble spending all their new money; they seem to have an insatiable desire for publicity about how they go about trying,' said Fairchild.

'The equestrian classes promenade through the mirrored galleries of the media, their least movements accompanied by a ceaseless murmuring of praise,' sputtered Lewis Lapham in *Money and Class in America*, his attack on what he calls 'the pathologies of wealth'. 'The media, both print and electronic, dote on the iconography of wealth.' But Lapham, dilettante editor of *Harper's Magazine* and host of a television book programme, came from old money, and, as he explained, old money only wanted to see its name in the paper three times; birth, marriage and death. As he elaborated in his distinctions between old money and new money, 'Old money reads the gossip columns with faint amusement, as if reading restoration comedy or an account of some remarkable tribe in the uplands of New Guinea. To the new money, the columns are as serious as the stock market reports.'

In their desperate need to be recognized the nouvelles found an ally in certain publishing outfits which had an equally desperate need to sell magazines. Condé Nast's relaunch of their jazz age intellectual magazine *Vanity Fair* was headed for disaster until *Tatler* editrix Tina Brown took the helm and replaced the *literati* with *glitterati*. With its stable of celebrity writers like Dominick Dunne it became the diary of the vanities of nouvelle, celebrating the 'If you were indicted, you're invited' celebrity world order; the good, the bad but not the ugly paraded across its covers from Ronald Reagan to Claus Von Bulow.

Now that business was glamorous the glittery nouvelles were a perfect fit, and provided copy that in the *Vanity Fair*'s own words was 'a pop-up book of the *Time*'s business news, a cabaret of corporate life'. For example: 'September 17th 1985. Alice Mason's season-premiere black-tie dinner for fifty in her art stuffed rooms. Conversation: At Alice's table Carl Icahn, not content with grabbing TWA, made a takeover bid, fended off only by the wit of Malcolm Forbes . . . Icahn accused all CEOs of being "Waspy guys who sit on blue-ribbon boards and cheat the shareholders out of their rightful dues". Aileen Mehle [who under the pseudonym 'Suzy' wrote the gossip column in the *New York Post*] defended the Revlon board [on which she sat at the time]; "A fine board, an honorable board, Mr Icahn!" "Don't patronize me, Aileen!" roared Icahn. In fact the tycoon preying upon Revlon, Ron Perelman, was craning his ears at the next table. Minutes: . . . Forbes walked away with half a million bucks from Icahn for Princeton.' This kind of gossip (from the December 1985 issue which reviewed the most spectacular parties all around the globe that year) sold magazines by the truck load.

Vanity Fair was the quintessential style magazine and in print media it was style mags that ruled in the eighties, from *Spy* to the various shelter magazines, from *Manhattan Inc* to *Women's Wear Daily* (a trade rag which charted the lifestyles of the ladies who lunch, and which Nancy Reagan had specially couriered to the White House every day). In their different styles these magazines all – to borrow Lapham's words – doted on the iconography of wealth. Glossies ruled not least because colour photographs on their wet-look slippery paper mouth-wateringly represented the gorgeous colours and textures of money, success, fame, glamour, the official mantra of the eighties.

On the television – where the supercolour saturation of the electronic page rivalled the sensuality of gloss – it was no different. Instead of the lifestyles of the poor and ordinary, people wanted and got 'Lifestyles of the Rich and

Famous', an actual television programme which in the words of its inimitable British ex-patriot creator and host Robin Leach presented their 'champagne wishes and caviar dreams'. The spectacle of their excess played to rapt audiences. Audiences were also glued to their screen every Wednesday night for 'Dynasty' in which Alexis and Blake Carrington, lovers and heads of rival corporations, wrangled from the boardroom to the bedroom.

The public seemed to have an insatiable voyeuristic appetite to see the lifestyles of the rich and famous splayed out, to be teased and tormented by all the money and beautiful things that they did not have, and thanks to both a wealth of media and the media of wealth we know more about the nouvelles than we might care to know.

Author Michael Thomas complained about the corruption of hard journalism by the desire of journalists to dine with their subjects rather than on them. Tina Brown became a society fixture, a surrogate Princess Di (whom she uncannily resembled in the magazine's advertising campaign in which she featured). But there was some limit to the sycophancy. Neither Wolfe's *Bonfire of Vanities* nor Dunne's *People Like Us* – a *roman à clef* so thinly veiled that you could throw away the clef – were particularly flattering to the nouvelles and their excessive wealth. But when *Women's Wear Daily* managed to get hold of an early draft of *People Like Us* and published an extract naming names, Dunne was surprised in the uproar that followed that no one was really mad at him. As Oscar Wilde might have said, there was only one thing worse than being in it, and that was not being in it. However unflattering inclusion in Dunne's book might have been, it was not nearly as devastating as exclusion, which would have meant that one's impact on the social Richter scale was negligible. Whether you looked good or bad, the thing in the new media morality was to be seen. Impact was all.

'So what's different about today's Nouvelle Society, obsessed with buyouts, takeovers, stocks, bonds and mergers?' Fairchild asked himself rhetorically. 'It's the money. The aspirations of Nouvelle Society have moved on to a lavishness beyond most people's richest dreams.' American Express introduced their platinum card in the eighties. 'If you have less than $150 million, you didn't make it,' ran an advertisement for the *Forbes* 400, a listing of the richest people in America.

But it wasn't just that you needed more, people counted it more and it counted more. 'Money doesn't talk anymore, it shrieks,' wrote Suzy, gossip columnist for the *New York Post*. As Dominick Dunne, commenting on the very existence of the *Forbes* list (which only began in 1982) explained, 'This new wealth likes to talk about how much they've spent. You can be at a party and somebody will walk in and say "Oh, there's Mr So and So", and everybody says he's worth 600 million or he's worth 800 million, or he's worth a billion . . . and we know before dinner how much people are worth. We sit down to dinner and we invariably find out before dinner's over that the very apartment whose dining room we're seated in was sold to this very rich person by someone like Alice Mason, the great realtor in New York, for seven million dollars or nine million dollars or ten million dollars. We know that the curtains on the window cost a thousand dollars a window and we know that the flowers in the centre piece of the table which was arranged by Marlo cost six hundred dollars. We know that the hostess's dress by Christian Lacroix cost twenty-five thousand dollars and people talk about money all the time.'

Earning it was one thing, but the spectacle of spending it was no less important. To this end many of the junk bond jillionaires had what was known in Nouvelle Society as 'trophy wives', beautiful second wives younger than their husbands. However, they were not bimbos. Beautiful, alert and ambitious, their spending patterns complemented the earning power of their mates. Because of their couture junkets to Paris in their husbands' 727s – where they would think nothing of dropping $37,000 on a beaded Lacroix jacket – they also came to be known as the Marie Antoinettes. Indeed, as was noticed at the time when Lacroix was the darling of the fashion world and came to America with his Luxe collection (just six weeks after the October crash in 1987), his clothes with all their bustles, hoops, lace, tassle, fringe, plumes, ropes and beads reminded many fashion commentators of the costumes of the 1770s: 'Clothes of such brilliant luxury and defiance probably haven't been seen since eighteenth century French aristocrats rattled in carts over the cobblestones on their way to the guillotine,' wrote a transported Julie Baumgold of the new *Crash Chic*. There were other things as well, silly little things, like Ann Bass's penchant for sending her napkins on Concorde to Paris for cleaning (because they didn't shrink).

'My wife has spent all my money, but it's worth it,' John Gutfreund, chairman of Salomon, was supposed to have complained of his wife Susan, trophy non-pareil. On another occasion he told a reporter, 'She collects things. I don't. She has enriched my life.' An air stewardess from Texas, Susan Gutfreund knew which buttons to push: 'When older guys discover their sexuality, they're gone,' one of their friends told *New York* magazine, under the cover of anonymity.

'It's like living in a fairy tale,' Mrs Gutfreund told *The New York Times*. Unreality was, as ever, the keynote, and unbridled fantasy the theme. A refrigerator in the bathroom to chill her perfume, and in the living room a million-dollar Robert Adam rug on the floor. When they entertained 'le tout New York attended to swill champagne and feed at the troughs of caviar' (of which they offered four kinds). They garlanded the chairs with roses (ladies with backless dresses got thorns in their backs), they flew in monkey bread from a favourite restaurant in Dallas, and arranged the fruit so beautifully that one guest, unwittingly echoing Prufrock, recalled, 'John insisted that I have a peach, but I was afraid to take one.' But nothing would compare to the iridescent apples made of spun sugar they served as dessert at a dinner they threw for Henry Kissinger. Their chef had, she announced, acquired the technique from the glass-blowers of Murano, Italy. 'When I come home, I have to ask Susan, "Who's coming for dinner?" It doesn't matter if I ask her because I don't know most of them.' Not that she always knew her guests all that intimately either. They were all part of the shopping spree, the necessary figurines one would need to have on the mantelpiece.

On another occasion they rented Blenheim Palace and hosted a party for 350 Salomon Brothers clients and friends. The engraved invitation read, incredibly, 'Mr and Mrs John Gutfreund, At Home, Blenheim'. However, the Gutfreunds earned their footnote in the annals of the History Nouvelle with their Christmas parties, held at their real home this time, in Manhattan. Resolving to have a traditional English Christmas, she decided their River House penthouse duplex would house a floor-to-ceiling Christmas tree, which at 22 feet would be 2 feet higher than the White House's. Although the tree, planted in 1953 (when Susan was only 7), only cost $400 it would cost another $6,000 to hoist this half ton of greenery – since the tree did not fit in the elevator – up twenty-four floors and in through a window. The only problem was that even though Susan Gutfreund spoke about their penthouse, they did not in fact live in a penthouse, and, what was worse, their upstairs neighbours expressly forbade the use of their roof for the hoist. This resulted in a lawsuit, and, in following years, sawing the tree in half and then bolting it back together. In the fullness of time the Gutfreunds moved to a $6.5 million apartment which – *naturellement* – had to be gutted and redecorated for a rumoured cost of $20 million.

Trophy of trophies, Susan Gutfreund even appeared to be modelling herself on Marie Antoinette, and embarked on a crash course of frenchification tutored by decorator and close friend of the First Lady, Jane Wrightsman, who even owned Marie Antoinette's velvet-lined dog kennel. After the crash Susan moved on to Paris, buying a town house on the Rive Gauche which they shared with Givenchy. The underground car park they had built cost $1 million alone. She liked to sprinkle her social intercourse with a little French ('Bonsoir, Madame' she said when presented to Nancy Reagan), and sent her butler to Versailles for her string beans. As an ingratiating gift for one of the Rothschilds she snapped up Marie Antoinette's original letters, and she has even uttered her own little Antoinettisms, most famously at a lunch thrown by Malcolm Forbes for Mitterrand's wife. Two weeks after Black Monday, and cheerfully prattling on about the hassle of running two households, she sighed to the assembled, 'It's so expensive to be rich!' (even though the line was in fact embroidered on a cushion in Forbes's office, it was nevertheless as *bon* a *mot* as if she had shrieked 'Let them eat cake'). One of her Antoinettish trifles was a subway bracelet. Although it was unlikely that she had ever ridden the subway, the bracelet had sliding doors so that the jewels could be hidden in covered compartments. It was so called because, disguised in this way, it would not attract the attention of muggers.

Endearingly, Susan claimed that she did not seek publicity, it was thrust upon her. This was why, she maintained, when her picture was in *Women's Wear Daily* it was always in profile, unlike the full frontals of everyone else in the frame who were publicity seekers. 'She's straight out of Trollope,' remarked Eleanor Lambert, fashion publicist.

Not all the trophy wives were as Antoinettish as Susan. Gayfryd, third wife of raider Saul Steinberg, had her own tubular steel business. 'We were the Drexel Burnham of the pipe business,' she once remarked. Before Steinberg she was married to a shady oil tycoon from New Orleans who later jumped off a building. 'It was a classic vignette of the Reagan era in which life imitates mini-series,' gushed *Vanity Fair*'s revival artist Tina Brown, turning herself inside out on this occasion in a raver's delight: 'One windy Saturday night there was a knock at my beach house door: a billion dollars blew in. Gayfryd, wearing skintight pants and Bulgari gold bracelets, and full maquillage . . . wanted to phone their electrician to deal with a blackout. "This is a bit much," she mused, "considering Saul is the major stockholder in LILCO (Long Island Lighting Company)." '

We marvel at the buying power of massive wealth: 'Last Christmas they went for two weeks skiing in Vail and Saul found the service so bad he went out the next day and bought an apartment' (add this to the cottage in Key Largo and the entire hotel in the south of France). We are dumbstruck at the sheer wealth of things: 'The Steinbergs' thirty-four room apartment has the treasure stuffed look of a Walt Disney Blenheim.' And the scale: 28,000 square feet, fifteen staff and fifteen wood-burning fireplaces. Even their summer home is the size of an 'ocean liner', and 'an enormous rubber Loch Ness monster bobs in the acres of swimming pool'.

'The nouvelles are forever playing a form of Monopoly in the painting, fine art and antiques market,' explained Fairchild of his pet social set, 'and there appears to be no end to their insatiable appetite to acquire and show off their precious – and sky high expensive – possessions.' But none more than the Steinbergs' who retained their own curator to preside over their collection of sixty Rodins, Titians and Rubens that filled their thirty-four-room apartment. They were works worthy of a predator, and included Titian's *Salome With the Head of John the Baptist* and a Francis Bacon. There was even a Renoir in the powder room. Gayfryd Steinberg had also commissioned an essay on each piece from the Metropolitan Museum so she could bone up on the collection. 'Such art belongs in a museum but fewer and fewer pieces of real quality are getting there because of Nouvelle Society's zeal for hanging masterpieces on their own wall,' enthused Fairchild.

Then there was the spectacle of the Steinberg Tisch wedding, a merger of two nouvelle jillionaire families. Hailed by our Tina as 'a baronial alliance on the scale of Castile and Aragon in the fifteenth century', she didn't queer her pitch for an invitation to what turned out to be one of the extravaganzas of the decade. The gala reception for five hundred was held in the great hall of the Metropolitan Museum, which, with twelve thousand white tulips (at $9 a bloom) flown in from Holland, fifty thousand French roses (at $7.50), an entire harvest of peonies, and angels in satin playing gold harps with white garlands, was transformed into an arcadia, or, as one wag put it, 'a private dutch-y'. Rumour had it that the tulips had failed to open by the appointed day, necessitating a battery of frantic servants coaxing the flowers open with hairdryers in the final few hours before the reception.

'It was a fairy tale,' exclaimed a Trump. 'Trumpeters in medieval costumes called the guests to a dinner of poached Coho salmon in a pink champagne aspic, a trio of veal, lamb and chicken, orzo with porcini mushrooms, and spring vegetables . . . and a seven foot high Grand marnier wedding cake festooned with sugar flowers. They drank vintage wines – Corton Charlemagne, Chateau Latour, and Roederer Cristal Champagne – all from Saul Steinberg's private collection,' read one report. 'Post-Caligulan Rome,' snorted Michael Thomas.

Carolyn Roehm, Henry Kravis's second wife, was a different kind of Antoinette. It was she who had observed that her husband was tall when he stood on his wallet, and when asked about some particularly extravagant emeralds she wore, claimed she found them under her pillow. 'And where have you been sleeping?' came the follow-up. 'In the right bed,' she answered, without missing a beat. Asked by the Mad Dog what she wanted out of life, she is supposed to have replied that she wanted to be rich and famous. She succeeded on both counts. Thanks to a multi-million dollar investment from her husband, she also had her own business as a fashion designer with her own line. While she may have liked playing the working woman just as Marie Antoinette enjoyed playing the lowly milk maid (*Women's Wear Daily* dubbed her debut collection as 'Too rich'), she appeared to be, like her husband, a *bona fide* workaholic driven by the manic energy that coloured eighties endeavour.

They set themselves up in a sixteen-room $5.5 million apartment on Park Avenue, the same building in which the Steinbergs live, and like their neighbours, stuffed it with antique furniture and art – Monets, Renoirs, Tissots, and a Sargent as big as a sail. Also like the Steinbergs, they made use of the Metropolitan Museum as a personal annexe. In 1988 the Kravises held a small intimate party there for 110 of their friends to preview the Degas exhibit. 'Oh what is so rare as the perfect party?' babbled syntaxless Suzy of the *New York Post*, 'the one to be measured against by any host or hostess seeking to entertain with wondrous taste and big dollops of flair?' Foliage-crowned trellises! Tables covered with hunt tapestries trimmed with heavy bullion fringe! Centrepieces of miniature fruits in gilded baskets! Rabbit pie and baba au rhum! 'It was Medi-chichi,' raved one. Indeed Marlo Phillips, the preferred florist of the nouvelles, who would charge up to $5,000 for a single bouquet, observed of her clients that 'they are a teeny weeny group of people who are living the lives of fifteenth, sixteenth and seventeenth century royalty. They are the kings and queens of today.'

But no matter how much the merchant princes wallowed in their wealth, they were cursed with not really being kings or queens at all. Of the interior of the Kravis apartment (which along with all the other nouvelle nests was sumptuously photographed for the 'shelter magazines' like *House and Garden* and *Architectural Digest*), one unnamed friend told a journalist that the effect was 'instant old'. The remark revealed a method to the madness of excess. Nouvelle Society stood – to its despair – agonizingly apart from old money. Nouvelle felt so gauche, so arriviste, so embarrassingly awkward. What was wanted was the ease and grace that only old money had acquired over time. And they wanted it now, as part of their spree of instant acquisition.

As Tom Wolfe observed in an interview, today's pop society is 'made up of people whose status rests not on . . . ancestry, but on various brilliant ephemera'. The jumble of jumbos, jets, crystal, caviar, couture, soirées, Christmas trees, and all the grand old masters you could find wall space for, were the bargaining chips which Nouvelle Society hoped to be able to trade into old money. 'Social rank has always been one of the pricier commodities sold in the great American department store,' lamented Lapham, who defined new money as someone who can say, speaking of paintings by Picasso, 'I'll take two of the blue ones.' They buy up 'the best of the past, as if they could, in so doing, back-date their own provenance,' wrote social expert Jesse Kornbluth. The wall-sized Sargent of the Sixth Marquess of London jammed between wall and ceiling in King Henry's dining room led the father to ask his Gatsby son, 'Which one of our relatives is this?'

CHARITY BALLS

The most effective way to buy social status, especially the cachet of old money class, was through philanthropy. Regular charitable contributions and appearances gradually gilded the rough hewn, bear-ass-biting pit bull with the silvery haired patina of benevolence. And thus the nouvelles became socially entrenched. In return for large donations they ended up sitting on any number of boards, or had a wing named after them. 'I was taught to give something back,' said Kravis, who has given $10 million to the Metropolitan Museum. But they were not giving it away just for kicks. 'Nouvelles donate willingly but require a speedy return on their investment,' observed Fairchild. The Met is in the course of building a wing that will be named after Kravis, and he sits on the board. He also sits on the board of the Mount Sinai Medical Center (to whom he also gave $10 million) and the New York City Ballet. Saul Steinberg also gave generously to the Metropolitan, underwriting the cost of the Frank Lloyd Wright room, in which he has been pictured casually leaning on one priceless chair as though it were his own personal living room. Then there was the $11 million he gave to his alma mater, Wharton Business School. He has estimated that over the years he has given away $50 million.

If they had been taught to give something back, the nouvelles instinctively knew not to give it anonymously, and in the eighties the charity trudge erupted in conspicuous compassion. 'Instead of raising a few thousand dollars so a hospital could have a few linen napkins on a Sunday they raised hundreds of thousands, half a million to two million, to save a library. The concerns were bigger and it became an entire cottage industry,' said William Norwich, society columnist for the *Daily News*. And instead of quietly sending off a cheque, which had been the old WASP style, the new rich liked to season their giving with glittery galas and expensive plate dinners. Saul Steinberg's Metropolitan club dinners raised around $250,000 a time for PEN (a literary charity), and John Gutfreund was a trustee of the New York Public Library where the Literary Lions held their annual bashes (it was at such an event that Kravis bashed writer William Norwich). Carolyn Roehm Kravis headed the New York City Ballet board and raised close to a million dollars one year. Together with Metropolitan Costume benefit and the Winter Antiques show, there were about twenty major events on the calendar every season. However, on occasions when the sole purpose was, ostensibly, to help those less fortunate than their nouvelle selves, putting on the glitz seemed increasingly inappropriate.

Felix Rohatyn, partner at the white shoe Wall Street bank Lazard Freres, finally spoke out. Rohatyn, although technically nouvelle, had made his stash before the eighties and had assumed the mantle of elder statesman, not least for his role in saving New York from its fiscal crisis in 1976. But he had also, and with considerably less success, been retained by Bergerac to defend Revlon and keep it out of Perelman's raiding arms. Perhaps not surprisingly he became a critic of junk bonds and their jillionaires. A speech he made in November 1985 was picked up by the press: 'While dazzling benefit dinners are attended by our richest and most elegant New Yorkers, and millions of dollars are raised for our golden institutions, it is increasingly difficult to find money for less glamorous needs.' Some causes were more attractive than others, and generally the needs of the poor were the least attractive of all, especially when compared with the august status of the New York Library, Ballet, and Metropolitan Museum.

In a subsequent cover interview in *Manhattan Inc*, Rohatyn went on to criticize the lavishness of the charity circuit. 'Here is Mr XYZ, who's got a billion dollars and is just moving into the city of New York from Squeedunk. And what project can we figure to bring him in so that he gives us $10 million, and we can put his name on the door?' It was not too hard to figure out to whom Rohatyn referred; the interview was interrupted for 'an off-the-record discussion about a certain squeedunkian who has achieved new heights of civic respectability and top dinner invites in part by making huge donations to the most glamorous and social of charities'. 'But darling,' said Elizabeth [his socialite wife], 'these are what the people who go to them buy . . . [this] whole kind of social movement has moved into the bought party. And so if Mr and Mrs So-and-So want to pay $5,000 to go to a party so they can say they sat at the same table with Mr and Mrs X, and their picture is going to be in *W* – well, you can't really fault that ... social climbing has always been that ... Trollope wrote about it, Dickens wrote about it, Edith Wharton wrote about it. I mean it's always been the same thing.'

'I just feel that we've crossed some lines in terms of excess,' replied Felix. 'People in our world are swimming in money ... but in order to get the city's rich to give a lousy thousand dollars to the poor who are drowning in front of their eyes you have to parade little black kids in front of them and give them party favours. I've read all of Dickens and most of Edith Wharton but I can't recall coming across anything quite so monstrous. Perhaps I should read more Trollope.'

Although the brouhaha boosted the pot raised by the Rohatyns' own fund-raiser for the Lenox Hill Neighbourhood Association (to the tune of half a million), the elder statesman's attempts at social engineering did little more than generate good copy. *W* magazine took 'Felix the Cat' to task for criticizing women flying on Concorde to Paris for dress fittings while his own 'Snow White' wife commissioned designer dresses (had Felix known that Ann Bass's table napkins were also on board Concorde he might have had a heart attack).

'Why do we have to have a dinner?' wondered William Norwich. 'I don't know. It must go back to some primal tribal thing where the meal is some kind of communion done in ritual clothes. It's a way to participate as an animal.' For sure, people did not eat the exquisitely catered meal – invariably by Glorious Foods – for nourishment or substance. 'You can never be too rich or too thin,' someone once said, and the ladies of both Nouvelle and Vieille Society specialized in a skeletality that vied with the profile of an After Eight mint, and was celebrated by Tom Wolfe with his 'social X-rays'. This was *anorexia richosa*.

The 'painfully thin' and 'greyhound slim' complemented their look with the rictus grin. Given that the meal was no more than communion for these sleek beasts, the real purpose of these events was the photographs recording the occasion and destined for the tombstones of the social columns. 'A truly fashionable event ended the moment it began, once everybody had been seen or not seen,' wrote Lapham. 'The rest of the evening was superfluous. The guests might as well be spun sugar blown into the shapes of venetian glass and filled with lemon mousse. The photographs of the party appearing in the next day's paper, or the next week's issue, belong to the iconography of wealth. The dinner guests might as well be standing in the foreground of a renaissance religious painting.'

Except that in such paintings you don't find people grinning like wildebeests, dazzling the viewer with a display of perfectly shaped and radiantly white teeth. The laws of body language dictate that the baring of one's teeth is an act of aggression. Dogs peel back their gums before attacking. Accordingly, in past society the seemly smile was simply a smile, not a ghastly grin of fang-baring all, the kind one gives before falling on the feast. So when Norwich speaks of participating as an animal we can only think of the Tyrannosaurus Rex, legendary for its predatory rapacity, and a perfect mascot for the relentless appetites and acquisitiveness of nouvelle.

MILKEN, AT HOME

All of which has nothing to do with Milken. Milken didn't lunch at Le Cirque, and when he went to the circus it was with thousands of underprivileged children. Milken was conspicuously absent from the nouvelle parties and the social rounds of the status seekers. His name was not checked in the Liz, Suzy or Billy columns. His wife was neither trophy nor Antoinette. She did not preside over PEN or the Literary Lions. Instead she spent much of her time ferrying her and her neighbour's kids, working on her own writing and the activities of the Milken Foundation.

The humble homely lifestyle of the Milkens is quite a comedown after the wretched excess and extravagant follies of the nouvelles. 'Michael's the easiest man in the world to locate. You either call him at home or at the office. He doesn't go flitting about the globe. He doesn't have yachts and stuff like that. He's either working or he's with his kids,' asserted Steve Wynn.

Tara Drive sounds like something out of *Gone With The Wind*, and was so called (along with all the other streets in the vicinity) because the land was part of Clark Gable's estate. But for all the grandeur it evoked, Tara Drive was a quiet little *cul-de-sac* on a gentle slope just minutes from Venture Boulevard, the main drag of Encino, a suburb that one writer described as the New Jersey of LA. Milken lived in the same neighbourhood in which he grew up, and just under three miles away from his old home where his mother still lives. Milken bought the house – which used to be the guest house on the estate – for $750,000 in 1978 when he moved back to California. Two white gates lean lazily open – it doesn't seem as if anybody bothers to close them – and trash cans sit on the left. You walk through the gates up a brick driveway that curves up a gentle slope and round to the left. The vegetation rearing up on either side creates a closed-in feel, as though one were entering a warren. At the end of the drive it is possible to glimpse the cobalt blue house peeking out, almost hidden from view by the overarching greenery. There's a three-car garage on the right with a basket ball hoop above it, just like Anyhouse, Anytown USA. A crazy paving path winds to the front door passing through a small trellis construction and past a huge weeping willow that further shades the house from view. On the left is a small lawn with trees and a children's playhouse leading to a tall shrubbery that hides the road behind, and on the other side, behind a flowerbed, a small patio with four chairs and a round table and a large pink and white striped umbrella. Behind that is a small swimming pool and tennis court. The two storey, four-bedroomed house seems low from the outside, and snuggles down into the hillside on which it was built.

In the den, there is a bar that has been converted into a video library overflowing with cassettes, and there is also a video jukebox. Some of the furniture is the same as the Milkens had in Cherry Hill in New Jersey. In the living room there are large red chintz sofas, a grand piano, reproduction end tables. Over the fireplace hangs a large colour photograph of the family, retouched with an airbrush. In addition to bookcases filled with books, there are volumes of photo albums looking like old leather bound tomes in maroon with 'Milken Family Vol. 1' in gold tooling. Tucked away on the first floor Milken also has a study which contains the token globe and a large desk topped with green leather. Instead of a quotron there's an old TV. Milken said he used the room for storage and the office treadmill as coat rack. Up on the landing outside the boys' bedroom there is a xerox machine.

Although Michael Jackson used to live in Encino, the neighbourhood still does not compare with Beverly Hills. Milken's abode stands in bold contrast to the mansions of Beverly Hills where the fashion in the eighties was for teardowns: buying a plot with a house on it, and tearing it down to build a bigger, better one. Aaron Spelling, the television producer whose productions – 'Dynasty', 'The Colbys' – set in electronic amber the champagne wishes and caviar dreams of the decade, was himself a Milken client. At a reported cost of $12 million he bought a property and tore it down to build in its stead a 50,000-square foot French chateau, containing guest wing, ice rink and discotheque, for a reported additional $50 million. If Milken were to build on this scale in relation to his fortune, he could have built an entire city, or had his own space programme, building for real the model of the high yield bond spaceship.

However, when the journalist Jay Epstein asked Milken about his lifestyle he replied, 'I have one house, one wife, one cat and one car.' Milken has no Art Nouvelle – no Renoirs, Monets, or Reubens – except for a collection of antiquities, including a marble head of Nero circa AD 54 and a bronze shield with the inscription of Anatolian King Pharnaces, first century BC, most of which are on permanent loan or donated to museums, and none of which are exhibited in his home. True, he did have a share in a private jet that was given to him by a major client, Fred Carr of First Executive, and Carr is also supposed to have advanced Milken the black mercedes he is now chauffeured around in (prior to this he would drive himself to work in the family wagon).

His one wife, is petite, almost bird-like. She seems almost as tightly wound as her corkscrew black hair, coiled up inside and tensed against misfortune, giving the simultaneous impression of strength and frailty. She is simply at odds with the glitz and glam of corporate culture. She doesn't own a mink, and many remark on the fact that she was forever turning out in her homely style. Recalled a close friend of Milken's, 'I saw Nelson Peltz's wife once wearing so much fake gaudy jewellery, that I just thought it had to be fake, she needs her arm in a sling just to hold it up. There they all were dressed up to the nines, dripping with fur and jewellery and in comes Lori with her republican cloth coat.'

Instead she seems more comfortable at home. The neighbours send their children over when it is time to learn to ride a bicycle without stabilisers, and two hours later she sends them back home proudly clutching the stabilisers in their hands. Many local parents have her listed on school cards as a contact in case of an emergency.

She is an avid writer, and although she has never had anything published she said, 'I've had some nice rejection letters.' Milken rented her a small office a few minutes away from their home, where she went to write when the children were in school. Every other Monday night she went with a friend to her literature class, and Michael stayed at home, helping with the homework and cooking dinner for the children. Of their vast wealth she has simply said, 'I knew Michael would be good at whatever he did, but this level of success is a total shock. Obviously I feel well-off. I can pay my bills. And I can buy any book I want. That's wonderful.'

Milken's critics nod sagely at this almost embarrassing humility and utter lack of assumption, suggesting that she was a 'mob wife' who had no conception of what it was that her husband did. Indeed when Milken had a surprise videotape made for her, he managed to get it hosted by Barbara Walters (presumably because her husband Merv Adelson, head of Lorimar Pictures, was a client of Milken's). When she was given the tape she could not believe that it really was *the* Barbara Walters on tape. On the other hand Peter Magowan, CEO of Safeway, remembered Lori telling his wife, 'If Michael had only listened to me and not gotten involved with some of these people he wouldn't be in this problem right now.'

When Milken got home he played with his children on whom he doted. He romped with his 9-year-old daughter Bari on the sofa or tested her spelling: 'How do you spell circus?' According to the director of the Castlemont School, 'they are each other's "special person". . . . Bari often brings to her classroom special childish treasures given to her by her father (stuffed animals, photgraphs of father and daughter together).' Milken would always take her to her Saturday morning ballet class. A family friend recalled an afternoon at their house. 'Michael's 9-year-old daughter Bari had just finished making several bracelets out of cloth. She was sitting on her dad's lap while he was on the phone . . . Michael got off the phone a few minutes later and asked Bari what she was going to do with the bracelets. Bari suggested setting up a stand similar to her lemonade stand at the base of the driveway to sell her wares. Michael sat there patiently encouraging her to determine on her own how much she should charge for her bracelets and who might be potential customers. The next thing I knew there were Michael and Bari setting up her table of $1 bracelets in front of the house eagerly awaiting the neighbourhood clientele.'

No less devoted to his two sons Greg and Lance, he would forever quiz them on maths and pit them against each other in solving problems. When he travelled he would pack an algebra textbook so he could help them with their homework. Although, due to a myriad of investment partnerships to which they belonged, the children were individually worth millions, they made do on allowances of $10 a week. 'I have very normal children. When they save up and buy something, that's a big thing. I think that's great,' Milken once said.

En famille, they all bicycled around the neighbourhood, skipped Le Cirque and trooped off to the local coffee shop.

Friends and colleagues who have visited their home have described it as snug and cosy. Meals, normally buffet style, were served in the kitchen and then eaten in the breakfast nook, a small, informal dining room off to the side. Sometimes the housekeeper, who was treated as one of the family, was there to help out, sometimes she was not. Often the house was filled with visitors, from house guests to the children's friends, as well as the babies of their neighbours. 'It was like a three ring circus,' recalled one.

Leon Black, co-head of Mergers and Acquisitions at Drexel, remembered a lunchtime there: 'Mike served us on paper plates and played with our little boys, pushing them on the swings and regaling them with a myriad of children's riddles and games of which I had never heard. While sitting outside with Lori Milken, she scolded her own two older boys for not cleaning the outdoor furniture for the guest and threatening no allowance if their chores weren't completed. After a lovely afternoon with our two boys delighting in following Mike around like the Pied Piper, we departed.'

Wrote Marie Brenner of her visit: 'We helped ourselves to dinner in the kitchen, poured our own Kraft bottled dressing over a salad made with iceberg lettuce and served ourselves green beans and barbecued chicken from Pyrex dishes . . . Although Milken has earned an estimated two billion, he and Lori have an almost chilling indifference to living in any other way than they did as children of the San Fernando Valley thirty years ago. The table was set in the breakfast 'nook' with stainless steel flatware and paper napkins, not the fine quality Servaides, but the supermarket special, the Colortex hamper-size container, which the local Gelsons sells, three hundred for $2.09.'

Milken's lifestyle was hard to believe and easy to resent. A tribal morality demands that the rich let us know that they are rich. We expect them to walk a path between decadence and economy. Sending your linen napkins to Paris to be cleaned may be one extreme, but using paper serviettes is the other. Only people who can't afford to eat off anything else eat off paper plates, and for billionaires to behave like white trash was clearly beyond the pale. Thus the billionaires' use of paper napkins was produced as evidence of a 'chilling indifference' to their wealth.

But it wasn't so much that the paper napkins were cheap, it was that they were so unstylish. There was no self-conscious polishing of surfaces in an attempt to make things more attractive than they are, sexier, and therefore more befitting the glossy pages of *Vanity Fair*. The napkins symbolized a lifestyle entirely lacking in style, and unstylish in the eighties was like un-American in the fifties. The Milkens rounded out their style crimes with Lori's cotton top with matching trousers 'in Pepto Bismol pink' and Michael's sister Joni's unicorn fur-tipped slippers.

Several other publications picked up on the paper napkins, and tore into Milken about it. *Playboy*, applying its 'philosophy' of wine, women and song, concluded that the reason why the public loathe him was that here was a man 'incapable of enjoying his wealth', or of 'having fun'. The paper napkins would join the miner's headlamp and the toupee as the cartoon costume of Milken as whacky weirdo villain. Had Milken heeded the generalized politics of his society, and stocked up on art, apartments, jets, politicians and all the other junk that money can buy it might have been different. But 'Milken loathed extravagance and ostentation,' said Leon Black, and Milken himself said, 'I can't overstate the importance of my family and the lack of importance of money.' But what Milken could not comprehend was that he lived in a society and a decade where those values were reversed.

Over dinner, Brenner, coping with the paper plates and paper napkins, pressed Milken about money. 'Even at the height of the takeover spree, he seemed uncomprehending of the New York world of his tycoons . . . Milken, in love with the same girl since age 15, was perplexed by the tales of the new wives with their husbands' new fortunes, their walls covered with Sargent portraits . . . their tables with new Georgian silver and Marlo's embryonic roses; their flower bills often running ten thousand a month.' Of two people whose fortunes he made he was supposed to have once said, 'I can't tell people how to act. My guys are consenting adults. I can't believe people in New York would regard some of these people as social leaders.'

Where Boesky gave the decade its motto, 'Greed works', Milken said, considerably less quotably, 'People who seek wealth don't normally find it . . . people who have created tremendous wealth did it by having a vision and making it work. They generally created something of value, they produced something society needed and produced wealth as a by-product.' Whatever kind of pathology money was for Milken he was simply not interested in what it could buy. Money to Milken was an electronic blip, a way, many argued on his behalf, of keeping the score. 'Are you the man with all the money?' Milken once was challenged by a group of inner-city kids. 'We all sat down on the playground before school started . . . and we emptied our pockets that day and found that I had only $1.35 and they each had between $.75 and $4 . . . they still said that I was the man; but we all agreed that it was what we learn and share with others that is the true measure of a person's worth,' Milken recalled in a letter to Judge Wood.

Milken may have been crazy to believe that anyone other than children would believe him, but he did sincerely believe and practise what he preached. In contrast to the famed $1 million birthday party Saul Steinberg threw for himself in Long Island, Milken went for a down-home 4th of July party. Instead of nude tableaux vivants of all his Monets, Milken had a plain old picnic on the grass and a barbecue in his back garden. It was more of a kids' party than a party for Milken, and the rule of admission was that every adult had to bring a child. All afternoon there were party games – potato sack races, pie-eating contests, egg toss – and then the day ended with fireworks.

One annual guest remarked on how old-fashioned it was, which would appear to contrast with his image of himself as an iconoclast. Like the junk bond jillionaires he minted he had no time for obsolete traditions, and cared little about sweeping them aside. But here he and his clients parted ways. The iconoclasm of the raiders was merely sabre rattling, the rationale to justify their overleaping ambition. They applied this self-serving iconoclasm to their personal lives as well. Marriage was not for life, and wives were assets to be traded. Instead of growing old together, spouses were spun off for younger models, they were trophies befitting new-found wealth and power, and with these the raiders went about shoring up the breach their iconoclasm had made in the castle's walls through an accumulation of fine and civilized things. They also did civilized things, philanthropically parading the battlements, making the rounds of charity galas. In this way the raiders sought to entrench themselves as kings of the castle.

But Milken's iconoclasm, although aped by those he financed to their own acquisitive ends, was genuine. He would, for example, come to believe more and more in partnerships between management and workers who would co-operate in shared ownership. Had his beliefs masked his hunger for power he might have sought to become chairman of Drexel (as many persuasively argued he should). Instead his iconoclasm was limited to his notions of people's capitalism, and ended when he walked through the front door. A wife was an asset you did not trade, and marriage was not a bond of convenience that lasted just so long as it was convenient.

In this respect, then, the vision that he brought to business was tempered by a conservative sensibility in the home. 'You can call me old-fashioned but I think a child should be raised by both parents, and that children should grow up with knowledge, security and respect for their elders,' Milken once said in an interview. Concerned that 45 per cent of American children under the age of 1 have only a single parent at home he asked, 'What's this going to do to our human capital?' As disconcerting as such facts might be, his phrasing was no less startling, although it was the key to his philanthropy. Instead of being a glittery round of charity events, philanthropy for Milken was the logical extension of his business vision. At work he was concerned about the democratization of capital, equipping the scarce resource of human capital with junk bonds and other tools, while outside the office he sought to nurture and raise human capital through the work of the Milken Family Foundation.

MILK OF HUMAN KINDNESS

Rohatyn, who was not shy to speak out against Milken and junk bonds, would have found his views about New York's charity circuit showiness and inattention to the needier yet less glamorous charities implicit in the work of the Milken Family Foundation. It deliberately eschewed the glitzy charities – such as the highly publicized *cause célèbres* for the arts which abounded as much in LA as New York – and instead supported approximately seven hundred causes from the Anti-Defamation League to Camp Ronald McDonald for children with cancer; from Habilitat, a rehabilitation centre for addicts in Hawaii to the Todd Morsilli Fund, an organization started after the founder's son was run over by a drunk driver. The list also included animals, energy research, the local branch of the Boy Scouts, the Harlem Boys Choir, Down's syndrome sufferers, people with AIDS, rape victims, the blind, the homeless, Indian heritage, the aged, a local science and engineering fair, illiteracy programmes, 100 Black Men of America, battered wives, and many more.

This apparently scattershot approach might seem an unfocused attempt to please as many people as possible. However, said Richard Hoff, Director of CARE, 'He has a global view of the world which everything fits within. The CARE work we are doing in Mexico fits with investments in Latin America. He put us together with the Mexican and American Foundation [a business organization for involving entrepreneurs from both countries], and said, "You both have a lot in common, you could work together, get to know each other." And because of the synergy of working together, the whole becomes greater than the individual parts.'

Milken therefore was the force that bound the global scope of the Foundation, which he tried to encompass by networking its beneficiaries. But he did not limit himself to this. In addition to supporting and networking many existing programmes, he also created many of the the foundation's own programmes. At Wharton, his alma mater, he started the West Philadelphia Project, which teamed young entrepreneurs from the depressed neighbourhood with students at the business school who performed as mentors. Said Milken 'Wharton has thousands of students, yet you find that less than 5 per cent and closer to 1 per cent of the students that were brought from all over the world to Philadelphia stayed in Philadelphia. After they graduate they leave. What an unbelievable opportunity Philadelphia is missing.'

Believing that many of the nation's heroes laboured unrecognized and unrewarded, Milken instituted the Educator Awards Programme, which began in 1987 by honouring twenty-five of California's outstanding teachers and presenting them with a cheque for $25,000. The programme has since spread to thirteen states. Milken added to the idea by creating a three-day educator retreat where teachers could meet and network. The idea has also been extended to both cancer and epilepsy researchers.

All of this Milken did in his own trademark style. 'This is another of my crazy ideas,' he told the university's president Sheldon Hackney when he went to visit Milken in Beverly Hills.'Let's say we go out and buy up these [West Philadelphia] houses at $10,000 to $15,000 each. We can buy 100 per cent for $8 million. I think the houses could be worth $50,000 once the whole neighbourhood is brought back up. We give away half to the community, get kids instead of writing graffiti on the walls to work in the houses. People have a lot of pride in a building if they are working on it.' Then he would get Penn students to do four or five hours' community service in West Philadelphia, and bring in small minority-owned businesses that were proven success stories 'and give them the capital and let them grow'. 'The renaissance of West Philadelphia seemed nearly complete,' wrote David Vyse, the *Washington Post* writer who was covering the meeting. 'Then a secretary entered the room and brought the two back to Beverly Hills. Milken was late for a meeting with the chief executive of a health care company. Before Hackney was ushered to the elevators Milken told him, "Dream One is financing. Dream Two is West Philadelphia . . . I appreciate your stopping here today." '

In addition to his own involvement Milken also sought to include Drexel. 'Even though we work long hours there is still time for the community and charities.' Henry Wilf, a colleague in Milken's department, remembered him saying, 'I put in more time than any of you at the office yet I am the only representative from our department who attends these functions and helps them. We work in the community and there are those who are not as fortunate as we are. Let us show that we are interested in more than our business.' As a result of his initiative, Drexel became closely involved with Variety, the children's charity. Through its national and international network, each local branch of Drexel could get involved with a local branch of Variety. Milken thought it would be popular with people at Drexel, on the assumption that everyone got along well with kids. Drexel accordingly sponsored the annual telethon and awareness day, a thirty-five-city-wide event in which tens of thousands of children were taken on outings to the zoo, the circus, and baseball games (after Drexel's collapse, the Foundation assumed the costs). Also as a result of Milken's urging, Drexel sponsored from 1985 on the Cedar Sinai sports spectacular, which raised half a million dollars annually for the hospital's birth defects programme. The Foundation matched Drexel's contribution dollar for dollar.

Out of this spread of activities, a pattern emerges: 40 per cent of the Foundation's resources go to education (followed by 20 per cent for health care and medical research and the remainder to community services and human welfare). This links up with many of the presentations at the high yield bond conference where Milken's speeches would have education as a central theme, stressing that the children are the future, and the importance of America's nurseries in growing human capital. Beyond writing cheques, knitting together the activities of the various causes and devising new programmes, he spent a great deal of time hands on, and predictably his favourite activities were projects involving children.

Take, for example, Milken's involvement with one his favourite concerns, the HELP group, a juvenile centre for problem children who have run away, have been abused or have mental impairments. President Barbara Firestone recalled her first encounter with Milken at the first Drexel Variety Children's Awareness Day, which involved taking a thousand children on a tour of Universal Studios. 'During the lunch period one of our children had a tantrum and I saw a man looking on with a very concerned expression as if to say, "What can I do to help?" I told him that this non-verbal child was autistic and retarded and was experiencing behavioural difficulties most likely related to the fact that he had not yet eaten. He disappeared for a few moments and returned with a tray full of food.'

Shortly afterwards Milken became a direct sponsor of the HELP group. Typical of all his philanthropy was its anonymity. The only building named after the family is the Bernard Milken Jewish Community Campus. Until 1987 the Foundation did not even publish a report. But after a sizeable donation he agreed to let HELP honour him in the spring of 1989 at a luncheon and to name the wing they were going to build the Milken Family Campus West. The event included many performances by disabled children singing, dancing, playing the piano or just saying 'Hi!' to Michael. Many were painful to watch. The child that sang 'Over the Rainbow' in a frail and shaky voice reduced Milken and certainly many others to tears. After her home had burnt down when she was 4 she had lived in a car for eleven years where she was repeatedly molested by her father. People listened in agony, and then erupted in applause when it was over.

When he got up to speak, Milken described what he had just seen as children fulfilling their potential far beyond what most people challenge themselves to achieve. 'All of us should have such problems,' he said. It was typical contrarian Milken, who at the time was facing a ninety-eight-count indictment.

Milken, in the words of one colleague, 'never liked to give up on people.' Whether one of his traders was battling against cocaine addiction or a child was fighting multiple sclerosis, Milken persisted. In his math club, for instance, he got a child with cerebral palsy who had withdrawn into his own world to be his assistant. To Milken this was proof that the potential was unlimited and that anyone could do anything.

Milken did not speak in tongues, but he did speak in the language of added value. The prosaic routine of a simple meeting in Milken's mouth might become 'the opportunity of visiting with'. When speaking about how as a child his mother had wanted him to become a doctor but that he was squeamish at the sight of blood, he commented that he had the 'opportunity' to choose another profession. Where others spoke of problem children, Milken saw only opportunities. Although the Foundation report did not bear his name, it smacked of Milken, speaking about 'people undeterred by the myth that nothing works'.

In Milken's eyes, not only could everyone play but everyone could also win. Lorraine Spurge's 15-year-old daughter recalled the annual summer Drexel picnic: 'This was an unbelievable event with riding, hot air balloons, races and games. What I loved most of all were the carnival games and prizes. Michael made sure the kids always went home with a prize. You couldn't lose at any of these games. This was special when you're little . . . because it's almost impossible to win at these games. You can never quite reach or get three in a row, [but] at these picnics you were always a winner. It was like a dream come true!' Competition in Milken's eyes was not a zero sum game, where one person's gain was another's loss. It was predicated on 100 per cent participation.

To this extent Milken was a typical Californian. Like Reagan, he believed in the importance of dreams and strove to make them come true. His language of unlimited upside, of unbounded potential, was the only possible syntax in a movie-making culture where making the unreal real – or at least real enough to suspend the disbelief of cynics – was all important, and doubly so in a city built on a massive earthquake fault in bold-faced defiance of inevitability. How else to conjure up the future in defiance of the gravitational pull of the past? In this, then, he would inevitably fall foul of the ruling East Coast prejudice against this West Coast language, which it condemned as superficial, insincere and duplicitous.

Another of Milken's pet projects was the math club, which started out as a way of keeping the kids amused when they were all out at the local diner waiting for their food. Subsequently it evolved into a whacky maths class he taught to problem children. Of course in Milkenspeak 'problem' spelt 'opportunity', and he taught these two-hour classes first thing in the morning to abused, physically handicapped and mentally retarded children, handing out T-shirts and calculators.

Milken's brother-in-law helped out as the wizard: 'Mike and I have a routine we do where I go out of the room "guarded" by several children so I can't hear what's going on. Mike gives the kids a series of calculations to do that only I can know and I come back into the room and "guess" the answer. It's incredible to see these young faces come alive with surprise and delight, and when we explain how the trick was done they all go home to try it on their friends and parents.' In this way he made the subject come alive by skipping the drudgery with his tricks and giving out 'handy hints'.

Although Connie Bruck was supposed to have got it wrong when she said that he was a magician who performed tricks for his friends and family, there is something of the magician in him. He could provide magic not to dumbfound but to show what could be done. He also took a child-like delight in making people's dreams come true, from cash-starved entrepreneurs to love-starved children. For the former he provided junk bonds and for the latter he laid on Michael Jackson, organizing trips for children of the HELP group, among others, to Jackson's Los Olivos ranch in Santa Barbara.

Michael Jackson had also gone along on Milken's outings to the circus. Apparently the two were introduced by Steve Wynn, and since then Milken has become something of a father figure to the gloved one and even helped him out with his maths. Jackson has also spoken out for his newfound friend: 'Our mutual love and concern for children, from the affluent to the disadvantaged, was the catalysis [sic] for our fateful meeting and ensuing friendship.' Of the visits to his ranch he observed, 'I am very mindful that children gravitate toward positive energy and retreat from negative energy. They are generally unbias [sic] and unaffected by media hype. The children I encountered were exceedingly happy to share these moments with Michael.'

Milken did indeed seem to have a special ability to bond with children. 'Their reaction to his walking in the door is sort of a combination of a loving father they hadn't seen in some time and Santa Claus. Some of them, by no means small, literally jump up and hang on his neck,' wrote Joan Brooks, a colleague. 'I saw the children greet Milken with the same sort of enthusiasm that they would greet a rock star or a sports figure,' commented another who had helped Milken out in the maths club team. Around children Milken would become as frisky as Bambi: 'When he's with children he's like a child himself. Laughing, joking and playing, jumping. Very playful,' said a friend. Accordingly, when children came over to the house to play they would often ask, if Milken's children were not in, if Milken could come out and play. 'Sometimes I am far more comfortable with children than I am with adults,' Milken admitted. 'They say very few things that they don't believe. They have few pretences.'

Although Michael Jackson and Michael Milken are very different (most vividly illustrated by the fact that Jackson has bought the remains of the Elephant Man, while Milken bought the diary of Anne Frank for the Simon Wiesenthal centre), more than one friend of the pair has observed that there was something similar and child-like about both of them. In spite of the fact that both have dominated and carved out empires in their respective worlds of entertainment and finance, they were both child rulers. Of the two Milken would appear to be less at the mercy of the outside world, and less in need of protection. But in the people he surrounded himself with he showed a child-like naivety and trust; would the rest of the world beyond his enchanted circle living in happy valley share his views, and could he get them to abandon their perceptions for his reality?

His vision of a high yield world in all its aspects – from growth companies to financing raiders to helping handicapped children – was that of an innocent, and while it was precisely this that made his ideas so powerfully appealing because of their radiant, relevant simplicity, it also left him vulnerable, since he was unable to anticipate the probable political consequences or comprehend cynical judgements of his motives.

'He was like a nuclear physicist isolated at Los Alamos in 1944,' wrote Marie Brenner, 'so focused on the splitting of one atom, so assured that his work would help to win the war, that he couldn't see that he might be creating a lethal instrument capable of jeopardizing his own security.' Milken did more than split one atom. It was as a result of the junk bond revolution that fully one half of the *Fortune* 500 were restructured by the decade's end.

He had sowed the wind and now he would reap the storm.

7

THE ESTABLISHMENT STRIKES BACK

IN the fullness of time Drexel would downplay their aggressive image as junketeers and stress instead that junk bonds accounted for only 30 per cent of the financing in a leveraged buyout. But the miracle of leverage was that a little could go a long way. Junk bonds provided the mezzanine financing, which was so called because it represented the entry-level money necessary to lever up the remaining 60 per cent of the financing that would come from commercial banks. Drexel would also argue that only 4 per cent of junk bonds were ever used for hostile takeovers. But this is somewhat like saying that the fuse is only a small percentage part of a stick of dynamite. When asked if he thought it had been wise for Drexel to have supported the restructuring of Big Oil, Drexel's David Kay replied bleakly, 'The numbers made sense.' Numbers and statistics, for their sheer irrelevance, are a weak defence.

As Sir James Goldsmith once remarked, 'I don't know whether or not Mike Milken realized it at the time that he had found a way of financing an immense revolution in America.' Bill Tatum, the publisher of the black newspaper *The Amsterdam News*, who was backed by Milken in his bid to buy the *New York Post*, saw Establishment America as a closed club: 'There is a sign on the door and it says, "Oh no my friend, you do not enter here." Mike dared to say not only will I enter, I will make it possible for those who have never entered to enter too. You won't give it to me? For that which is just good and fair . . . I'll take it, I'll take it with all the instrumentalities that I can create and then muster . . . I'll take it for the workers, for the women, for blacks, for hispanics. I'll take it for those who have been traditionally locked out.' (Tatum had experienced this first hand. No other investment bank would return his calls when he tried to raise the money for his bid: 'The assumption was that if you're black you can't or won't pay it back.'). As Sir James Goldsmith concluded, 'Now he [Milken] has witnessed the full power of the Establishment triangle: big business, big unions and big government.'

'We understood the implications of getting into the financing of large acquisitions before we did it. And we understood the heat that would result from our doing that. And we succeeded beyond our expectations, and the heat was greater than we expected.' Fred Joseph could certainly be a master of understatement. The *perestroika* that the junk bond revolution forced on corporate America was, given the fact that business is America's cultural core and supreme political body, no less radical or significant than its Russian parallel. 'But,' Fred told *Manhattan Inc* in 1986, 'an awful lot of the heat is just rhetoric, it's yelling "junk bond bust up break up takeover artists".'

He would soon see that the heat generated by using junk bonds in hostile takeovers was more than the rhetoric he had dismissed it as, for the Establishment was not going to stand idly by as it was dispossessed. In March 1985 Hartley, the unsimpatico CEO of Unocal, wrote to Paul Volcker, Chairman of the Federal Reserve Board, urging him to investigate 'abuses by some banks and financiers that are feeding a takeover frenzy that strikes at the economic well being of this country'. Unocal's long-term bank had turned and lent money to raider Boone Pickens. Hartley also had, on a Saturday morning, a copy of the letter hand delivered in plain brown envelopes to the home of every congressman. The sinister packages so frightened some wives that they even called their husbands up on the golf course.

Volcker responded publicly by recommending that regulation G, hitherto applied to stocks, should also be applied to bonds. Regulation G was one of the reforms introduced after the 1929 crash, limiting to 50 per cent the amount an investor could borrow in addition to the cash he had to purchase stocks.

The night before the recommendation, Volcker had had dinner with Andrew Sigler, chairman of the policy committee of the Business Round-table. The Business Roundtable was the official organization of 'The Club' Boone wrote about in *Boone!*, and represented the top two hundred Corporations of America: 'In 1985, the Roundtable called a meeting and one of the CEOs . . . called and told me about it. I think it was Roger Smith [CEO of General Motors, and target of the film *Roger and Me*] who asked for $50,000 from each member. I understand they raised $9 million for a PR and lobbying campaign to get Boone.' He also claimed that they approached the banks to cut him off.

Hartley also retained Nicholas Brady, chairman of Dillon Reade and the epitome of white shoe banking (with whom Unocal had an extraordinary thirty-year relationship), to defend Unocal against Drexel-backed Boone. In the words of John Gutfreund, 'Brady is a patrician – the old white shoe mould of banker, from a time when bankers don't mix with traders who were the immigrant classes of the time.' Brady grew up on a 2,500 acre estate next door, as luck would have it, to their good friends the Dillons. In spite of a reading disability Brady nevertheless did Yale, Harvard and then for an inevitably successful career chose Dillon Reade, becoming, by the age of 30, a partner and Vice President. Twelve years later he was chairman.

Said *Fortune* magazine, 'Brady is no visionary. Nor is he a master of management. And don't look to him for an articulate explanation of complicated economic philosophies.' Thus it was on the basis of his friendship with George Bush, rather than this sparkling recommendation, that he became Secretary to the Treasury. In Washington circles Brady, who did not strive to do the social rounds or to dazzle (he is supposed to have worn the same cardigan with a hole in it for the last ten years, and delighted in serving roast beef sandwiches wrapped in wax paper at his boardroom table), was known as the 'First Friend'. He was also a member of Bohemian Grove, the California retreat for the wealthy and successful. Although no one could have been very surprised by Brady's appointment, it did not bode well for the raiders, especially their financiers.

Needless to say Brady did not like junk bonds. In 1985 while in the service of Unocal he wrote an op-ed piece for *The New York Times* entitled 'Equity is lost in junk bondage', complaining about the defunding of corporate America, whereby cash stocks were bought up and replaced with debt as a result of the junk bond-financed hostile takeovers and leveraged buyouts.

Snared in a shared taxi ride by a syndicated columnist (admittedly before Brady became Treasury Secretary), he chatted happily, revealing his inbred prejudice. The journalist wrote of the encounter, 'I wanted to try out my then favorite theory: the problem with go-go grab-grab glorification of money and greed, that it was luring the best and the brightest of young Americans away from work and ambitions that would better serve their fellow men and women. Brady looked at me as if I were crazy. "These aren't the best. This is all they can do. These are the people you want to keep off the streets . . . the best you can say is that they are gamblers and hustlers."' Establishment Wall Street abhorred the notion of the market as a casino.

In 1985, legislation loomed on the horizon with the Junk Bond Limitation Act, a bill that proposed to restrict the use of junk bonds in hostile takeovers. According to one West Coast Drexelite who lobbied in Washington, this was also the result of Hartley's handiwork. Hartley was supposed to have leaned on Big Oil man Robert Anderson, whose towering ARCO headquarters were across the street from the Unocal building. Anderson, whose massive ranches in New Mexico also made him the nation's largest individual landowner, had, perhaps not surprisingly, a strong connection with New Mexico's Representative Pete Dominici, whom Anderson and Hartley persuaded to sponsor the bill. The Business Roundtable supported the bill, and played hardball to get it through. According to Harry Horowitz, 'All the blue chip companies told their brokerage houses not to get in the way of the bill or they would drop them. They told them that we were crooks, that we were trying to bust up break up junk bond takeover America, and they told it every day, twenty four hours a day.'

Towards the end of 1985 Volcker wrote to congressman Proxmire, the chairman of the Senate Banking Committee, to express his concern about 'the speed of debt growth', and Proxmire set up a series of hearings to consider his Corporate Productivity Act which was, he said, designed 'to slow down the current wave of hostile corporate takeovers and raids'. Altogether, according to Fred Joseph, there were thirty-one bills proposed in 1985 alone to limit takeover activity.

However, the ability of the conservative business establishment to pull together and call on connections did not enable them to bypass the quagmire of debate. Like the tar pits of the Jurassic age, representatives sank into the morass as surely as the dinosaurs of yore, weighed down by their own slow-wittedness, verbosity and viscose due process. The problem, as one representative was once brave enough to admit, was their own ignorance. 'The truth about Congress is that most members don't know the difference between an LBO and a UFO,' said Carroll Hubbard Jr, a Democrat from Kentucky. Fred Joseph remembered going to see Dominici at the time he was proposing the Junk Bond Limitation Act. 'I said, "Do you know what a junk bond is?" He said, "Nope, but I bet you I am going to learn now." ' Either he was a quick studier or he had a ghost writer, since by May he had written an op-ed editorial piece entitled 'Fools and their junk bonds' for *The Wall Street Journal* in which he urged a moratorium on the use of junk bonds in hostile takeovers.

In trying to understand junk bonds and LBOs, many of the debates focused on debt. They were hardly clarified by the fact that they were therefore played out against a highly charged background, since historically we are acculturated to fear debt.

'Never a borrower or a lender be' goes the old saying. It reflects the historical distaste for usury. Ever since Christ threw the money changers out of the temple, charging that they had turned a house of prayer into a den of thieves, the business of making money with money has always been tainted. (Often this has also been an anti-Semitic taint.) But the truism is also a perfect way of maintaining the status quo. If you don't borrow it, you will, to use another cliché, 'live within your means'. 'Your means' is defined as what is available to you, and 'live within' discourages reaching out for what lies beyond a circumscribing circle. The risk and gamble involved in trying to realize an idea or make a dream come true is thus outlawed. Enshrined in cliché, these sentiments have thus long since taken on the resonance of Grand Truths, Absolute Values. However, they are no more than cultural conditioning. Those who don't have it don't borrow it, and those who have it don't lend it. In this way the rich get richer and the poor get poorer.

In America the puritan phobia of debt was given a schizoid twist by the fact that the country was built on it. Americans could not afford to let the stigma of debt put them off. They didn't inherit it, so they had to borrow it. America happily borrowed from the British and the Europeans to build the railway network at the beginning of the nineteenth century. They equally happily defaulted on many of the loans. In the twentieth century America created the credit card which, when introduced on English shores, triggered an orgy of debtphobia, pundits conjured up images of people, unable to control themselves, going on spending sprees that could only end in economic ruin. But in America there was no such fear of debt. Debt was the instrument of risk upon which the pioneering spirit of the country had been built. There was even a children's game called 'Mall Madness' in which players went on a shopping spree, and enjoyed unlimited purchasing power thanks to the game's 'Easy Money' credit card, as it was appropriately called.

But after a six-trillion-dollar shopping spree in which American consumers rung up nearly a trillion in outstanding debt, the government nearly three trillion and corporations two trillion, the spectre of debt which had been sleeping in some dark corner of the puritan psyche was awakened. After the orgy a period of blood letting and retribution would surely follow.

The debates played to the galleries of these emotions. When Hartley testified in Congress about Unocal's forced $3.5 billion recapitalization he spoke of 'a highly engineered conspiracy that has the whole world laughing at us . . . But we had to do it . . . or let the barbarians do it. We had to exchange the warm blood of equity for the cold water of debt.' On other occasions Hartley would rant and rave that America had become a Third World country, because it was now the number one debtor nation in the world ahead of Brazil. Senators spoke emotively about a trillion-dollar rollercoaster ride as America's corporations piled debt on top of debt, recklessly leveraging themselves to the hilt.

'It's an emotional subject,' Milken once said euphemistically. 'It's hard to convince people that debt may be good.' Washington was convinced that debt was bad. Although Milken did not take his case to Washington he argued that debt was neither good nor bad, it was simply a tool to be used. 'So, you just don't take seriously all the arguments that an overloaded corporate debt structure is dangerous to the economy?' he was asked in an interview in *New Perspectives Quarterly*. 'Debt isn't good, debt isn't bad. To put it in the extreme, for some companies no debt is too much leverage. For others a debt of 100 per cent can easily be absorbed. People assume the capital structure of a company is burned in stone. The capital structure, like the individual, is constantly changing . . . More or less debt is beside the point. The company that is well managed is adapting its capital structure to today's environment and the circumstances at hand. And the circumstances mean different things for different companies.'

To understand how to use it one had to distinguish between different kinds. 'Who is the worst risk? Countries head the list. The Soviet Union has defaulted on its debt. The new government of Iran isn't recognizing the debt of the former government. [US consumers] are the second-worst credit-risk of all. Credit card losses are accumulating at a 6 per cent default rate . . . ' But federal debt and consumer debt were less easy to attack than corporate debt, resulting in the 'junk bond bust up break up shut down' floor show.

One of the fundamental fears of debt is not being able to pay it back. In a recession, for example, cash flow would dip and debtors would not be able to pay the interest on the debt. The cushion that equity provided was gone. Proof of this was offered in two forms; the first was a Brookings Institute computer model study that indicated that, yes indeed, in a recession 10 per cent of leveraged companies would be unable to meet the interest payment on their junk bonds which would go into default with the result that the company went bankrupt. This look into the future was complemented by Asquith's re-evaluation of the junk bond default rates in the past which were about ten times higher than had previously been considered. However, the sexy statistic proved to be no more than the result of different methodologies. Asquith's study was a percentage of junk bonds that went into default over a ten-year period. The more quoted figure of a 3 per cent default rate was an annual figure. Multiplying this by ten, to calculate the default rate over a ten-year period, creates a figure of 30 per cent, which is not significantly less than Asquith's figure of 34 per cent.

But even here a popular misconception was colouring the debate. In America even in bankruptcy companies are not shut down or liquidated. 'Most companies get into trouble not because of their capital structure, but because of a change in the business for some reason. And, in those very few circumstances where a company actually goes bankrupt, the enterprises generally don't go out of business . . . Texaco went bankrupt, but you could still go into a Texaco station and put gas in your tank, get your window washed and your car fixed. Texaco emerged from bankruptcy with its stock selling as much as 35 per cent higher than before bankruptcy.' Milken argued that there were tremendous forces trying to keep companies in business. 'Companies don't have to fail when they're sick. Companies can survive, what they need is the help . . . when a company is in trouble a lot of people come to its assistance. Whether its employees, bankers, a lot of people have invested interest.' Milken compared this to the traditional community act of barn raising and saw the role of financing as analagous to medicine.

However, even in healthy times the medicine of debt was seen as voodoo financing. Debt demanded a focus on the short term necessitating that every effort be put into maximizing profits to pay off the principal and make the huge interest payments. This emphasis on the short term was at the expense of the long term, with less research and development for new products, it was argued. But research and development, as evidenced by Nabisco's multi-million smoke-free cigarette and Unocal's billion dollar oil shale folly, was no magic touchstone.

In his editorial 'Fools and their takeover bonds', Pete Dominici said he was alarmed to read in the prospectus for Metromedia's issue of junk bonds that 'Based on current levels of operations and anticipated growth, the company does not expect to be able to generate sufficient cash flow to make all principal payments due on the notes . . . '. The bonds were lampooned as 'toxic waste' and 'securities swill'. However, the offering sold out within two hours. The reason for this, according to Milken, was simple. You only had to look at the assets to see what they were worth. Once sold there would be no problem with the debt. Indeed Kluge, who had paid $2 billion to buy Metromedia, sold it piecemeal for a total of $3.6 billion.

But this triggered the 'junk bond break up bust up shut down' mantra, in which 'shut down' carried special power. Milken once noted that the shut down of obsolete plants and the elimination of jobs in the normal course of business went unremarked upon, implying that it had unfairly become the nub of the junk bond takeover debate. But for congressmen grappling with abstract concepts of leverage it provided a welcome concreteness. As representatives of their states they had a clear mandate to look after the interests of the workforce and protect jobs. They didn't have to think about this, they simply had a duty to discharge.

Furthermore, management played on their employees fear of losing their jobs to create a spectacle that would win public support. When Boone Pickens made his run at Phillips (prior to his attack on Unocal), well-stoked ignorance and fear moved the people of Bartlesville to pull out all the stops. There were Boone Buster T-shirts, heart-shaped 'I love Phillips' cookies, balloons and even an anti-Boone float in the Christmas parade. The television crews poured in to broadcast the spectacle, and of course in so doing fuelled it. When the good people of Bartlesville held a special service to pray for the board of directors it was mentioned on the national news that evening.

Then there was Safeway. The supermarket chain had been rescued by KKR playing their preferred role of White Knight. As a result Safeway had to be broken up with divisions sold off to pay down the debt incurred in the purchase. There were buyers for all the pieces, with the exception of the Dallas division, where a single buyer failed to emerge for the entire block of stores. Safeway unions had negotiated higher wages than was standard for the industry with the result that they were non-competitive and warded off buyers. As a result individual stores were closed or sold to non-unionized operations with the total loss of about ten thousand jobs. Workers were filmed burning their uniforms outside stores as they were boarded up. Although Peter Magowan, the Safeway CEO after the buyout maintained, 'I think you could make a very good case that the Safeway employees lost ten thousand jobs, but the buyers might well have replaced those . . . with thirteen or fourteen thousand employees,' a year after the buyout only 40 per cent had been re-employed.

A front page Pullitzer Prize winning *Wall Street Journal* article also dwelt on the human cost of the buyout: 'Safeway LBO yields vast profits but exacts a heavy human toll' read the headline. The article was a moving portrayal of the misery caused by the changes that followed in the wake of the takeover. On the anniversary of losing his job one man 'told his wife he loved her, then he locked the bathroom door, loaded his .22 caliber hunting rifle and blew his brains out.' Two others attempted suicide. Another believed it killed his wife, and another lost his fiancée – who would not marry an unemployed man. 'I am ashamed' one worker was quoted staring at his big empty hands. 'I am like an old thrown out mop.' Against this emotional backdrop Glenn Yago's conclusion that 'only 6.6 per cent of jobs lost through plant closings and layoff can be attributed to changes in ownership' (and LBOs represented only a fraction of ownership changes), made little impact. When confronted about the deaths Peter Magowan commented, 'If it's true I'm obviously sorry about such a tragic thing, but any attempt to associate this directly with the LBO shows a disposition to want to believe the worst of LBOs.'

Not only did people believe the worst, but also in their eyes junk bonds and Milken were to blame. This is an extract from one of the many letters written to Judge Wood urging a stiff sentence 'for the guru behind the wave of leveraged buyouts': 'My cousin Dick is a hardworking guy who got a job in a local factory and worked his way up to supervisor while making extra money working nights as a basketball referee in his central Massachusetts town.

'He and his wife rebuilt an abandoned house out in the country and raised three beautiful kids on food they grew in the garden. Dick is what they call a hot ticket, always full of fun and jokes, without a mean bone in his body. When I last saw Dick a year ago he didn't look so good. He had a series of health problems and was probably drinking too much. Seems like Dick's company was bought out in some kind of Wall Street scheme and the workforce was let go and then allowed to bid on their old jobs at two-thirds of their prior pay. Dick, like many other folks, didn't have a lot of room to manoeuvre with kids of college age and he took the job at pay he had earned five or six years ago. As he related this story Dick seemed deeply humiliated and beaten down.'

All of this begged the wider question of just what a corporation was. Was a corporation just a money making-machine or was it a social institution? Did a company have a responsibility to its workers beyond paying them? Should it protect them from change, guarantee their jobs and keep the plants open even in the teeth of economic changes? Before the takeover the Safeway motto was 'Safeway offers security', and the workers in the Dallas division had been with the company for an average of seventeen years. Post LBO the motto read, in part, 'Targeted returns on current investment'. But as Magowan, in chiding *The Wall Street Journal* for their advocacy, pointed out, 'guaranteed lifetime employment was never a corporate precondition'.

Felix Rohatyn, in addition to sounding the alarm on charity glitz, also began to make public service announcements about the market for corporate control. He had spoken out in April 1985 using the forum of *The Wall Street Journal* in a piece headed 'junk bonds and other securities swill' in which he named (or identified by company) Merv Adelson, Sir James Goldsmith, Carl Icahn, Steve Wynn, Boone Pickens, Nelson Peltz, William Farley and Ted Turner as the swill eaters and junk junkies. He asked 'whether large corporations can be treated like artichokes and simply torn apart without any regard for employees, communities or customers, solely in order to pay off speculative debt', and suggested the question should be one of public policy.

In his corporation-as-artichoke theory, Rohatyn was cosying up to Washington and the Establishment in which capitalists were silver-haired patricians pottering around the market garden and corporations were exotic vegetables of the public weal. In a television taping for a PBS series on 'Ethics in America' in 1988, Senator Wirth enshrined this notion with a vision of the 'Peach Tree Corporation' in 'Plum Valley', USA. As a fantasy board member, Wirth was waxing poetic in response to a 'junk bond bust up shut down' takeover threat.

'For a long time now we've been trying to get corporations to be more responsible and at Peach Tree we've done it, we're reaching out, supporting this university, supporting cultural activities and so on, we are the ultimate of what America believes corporate responsibility is . . . and you lawyers from Wall Street come in and tell us what to do with our communities and responsibilities and we're gonna make this as difficult as we can for you.'

It was a defiant and convincing moment. But then this wasn't just any television taping. Assembled were most of the key players on the takeover scene, including Fred Mercer, Boone Pickens, Sir James Goldsmith, John Gutfreund, Arthur Liman, Fred Joseph and the US Attorney Rudolph Giuliani. It was an historic event, to assemble these egos together to speak on the record and in one room. (Fred Joseph sat next to Rudolph Giuliani who was at the time leading the investigation into Drexel. It was the first time they had met.)

'How do you defend today?' fired back Goldsmith. 'You don't defend on economic grounds, on being able to get a better offer, you defend on being able to go to Washington, to Senate and to Congress, who believe in the sort of stuff Senator Wirth just talked about which is a pastoral America, with a little company and a little church and a little university, and the whole thing is going to be there forever, they don't have to compete and competition is awful and totally mixing up the difference between doing business and doing good. Doing business is what gives you the fuel to do good, don't mix them up.' For good measure he threw in his own natural analogy: 'The bee doesn't make honey because he's doing good. He doesn't go through a lot of soul searching and say am I doing good when I make honey?'

'What about the plant in Plum Valley and the people there?' asked Wirth. 'You modernize it, make it more efficient, and if you can't of course it's got to be closed. What are you running, a charity or a business?' came the answer. There was the crux of the matter. Goldsmith, arguing that a corporation was not an architectural monument or national treasure to be preserved at all costs, maintained that form should follow function.

He had made these arguments in Washington when he had had to provide an account of his attack on Goodyear before Congress. Mercer, CEO of Goodyear, had run to Washington arguing that it had taken ninety years to build the company, and that Goldsmith's motive was 'to buy up and bust up and cash it out and run to a Swiss bank account.'

Goldsmith, who, unlike Milken, did not shy away from Washington, told the hearing that he saw the dead hand of the corpocrat in the classic tyre maker, and that it had strayed into non-automotive areas which it knew nothing about, buying at vast expense an oil company and announcing that it would build at monumental expense a transcontinental pipeline. 'Mr Mercer in a letter to Goodyear employees stated that I was responsible for introducing "this corporation to a new and not very pretty world". What he means, of course, is the rough and tough world of competition, a world in which you don't just throw away hundreds of millions of dollars chasing after scatter-brained dreams; a world in which you run a business as a business and not as an institution.'

He also took the opportunity to put the debate in a wider global perspective. 'I come from Europe, and I have seen European freedom and prosperity destroyed by what I call the triangular alliance, the triangular Establishment: big business, big unions, big government, all absolutely throttling out entre-preneurialism.' Goldsmith further argued that effete values, an upstairs downstairs society and a distaste for risk takers, who were dismissed as vulgar and uncouth, had turned England and France into cultures of decay. Which was why Goldsmith had come to America. 'I happen to believe in this country, I believe in America, I believe that this country is the hope of the western world . . . and if all this nonsense that I have heard this morning here, with all respect, is actually believed by your citizens, then you have got the European disease good and proper.'

As soon as he had completed his prepared statement Goldsmith was slapped in the face with evidence of what he was saying. 'Who in the hell are you?' demanded Congressman Sieberling to cheers and applause. His great grandfather had founded Goodyear, the company Goldsmith was raiding and the reason why he had been summoned to Washington.

Thus far we have seen that the minutiae of the Washington debates were informed by the fear of debt and the fear of change. A response to this was to discredit the threats as unreal. Milken's junk bonds weren't real money. Although known as the Junk Bond King Milken saw himself as providing a wide variety of prescription securities to suit each case. With convertible bonds, (which could be converted into stock), commodity-backed bonds (whose value and interest rate was based on the market value of a commodity), increasing rate notes (whose interest rate increased according to pre-set conditions), 'companies can borrow for twenty-five or thirty years at some-times as little as half the cost', said Milken. With zero coupon bonds (where interest payment was delayed) and payment in kind bonds (where the interest was paid with further bonds or securities) it was possible to avoid paying interest on the debt for up to five years. 'The right capital instrument becomes the function of the period of the time,' Doctor Milken would intone before prescribing one of his medicinal securities. But his opponents trashed his hybrid bonds as mutant freaks from the immorality of debt: 'toxic waste', 'securities swill', 'wampum'.

Theodore Forstmann, a leveraged buyout specialist who vowed never to use a junk bond and who was a player in the scramble for RJR Nabisco, was one of Milken's most vociferous opponents. He once called Milken 'a piece of slime' and compared him to a hooker who had got the rest of Wall Street on the game, as brokerage houses became junk bond bordellos. He particularly objected to PIKs: ' "payment-in-kind" is based on the notion that when a borrower is too broke to pay his interest in cash, he can "pay" by issuing an additional note, which he also can't afford to service. This is the intellectual equivalent of doubling your money by folding it in half.' He reserved special venom for the triumphant Kravis, who only won by using vast amounts of this 'play dough' or 'funny money'. 'We', he liked to say, 'are real people with real money.' There are those who disagree, arguing that Forstmann's bonds paid the same rate as high yield bonds and were therefore no different from junk.

Since this paper money wasn't real money, the people who worked with it weren't doing real work. 'Let me tell you about what's wrong with Mike Milken and company,' Fred Mercer, the CEO of Goodyear, recalled telling an audience after Milken had given a speech against entrenched management. 'You have to start by asking, what does he provide for society? What does he create? What actually happens in the way of building products that help our standard of living to be either maintained or improved? And the answer is nothing . . . and incidentally it pays quite well. It pays a lot better than what I've been paid.'

In this one can detect the good old-fashioned prejudice that all finance is nothing more than the shifting around of pieces of paper. It is an industrial perspective that cannot conceive of the modes of the information age, and feels that its symbols and services are as worthless as they are demeaning: 'We're slowly having to cash out the industrial basis of this country . . . we still represent the biggest market in the world, and if we're going to deny our own corporations to serve that market, through this whole break up process, then we're going to have to import just about everything that we need, and we'll end up as a service economy, cutting each other's hair and making pizzas for one another and taking in each other's laundry. That is not the way you stay a leader in this global economy.'

This unreal work was done for unreal pay. As one lobbyist explained to Connie Bruck, it was hard for congressmen to feel sympathetic towards these people: 'Kravis in his five-thousand-dollar chair, with his hundred-and-twenty-five-dollar-a-yard wallpaper behind him . . . why isn't he in his shirtsleeves at his desk? Is this guy always in his living room? Ross Johnson is the only guy in the world who makes Henry Kravis look good.' Ross Johnson stood to make $100 million out of his LBO of RJR Nabisco. When asked by *Time* about the unreal size of the sum he answered in kind: 'It's kind of monopoly money.' Congressman Proxmire told the Senate, 'I do not begrudge an honest person an honest day's pay for his or her work, but . . . we are paying some of this country's best talent unbelievable sums of money for an essentially non-productive use . . . No new plants are built, no jobs created, no wealth enhanced.' To make things worse, the combination of unreal work and unreal returns was luring MBAs away from the real world of industry to the unreal world of Wall Street, creating a brain drain. It did not escape the congressmen's baleful eye that magazines and newspapers everywhere were reporting that students, straight out of college, were picking up salaries of $100,000 or more.

In response to this assortment of fear and prejudice, Drexel launched a vigorous lobbying campaign to try and educate Washington, opening a Washington office, hiring a former White House aide and retaining various outside lobbyists. Politicians were invited to attend to speak at the high yield bond conference. 'You are democratizing capital in some senses, but you're gonna have to sell it. The hostile takeover thing has certainly hurt your industry,' Congressman Thomas McMillen told the assembled in 1987. 'My recommendation to you is do this conference in Washington next year.' That same year Chic Hecht of the Senate Banking Committee was in attendance, as was Mayor Tom Bradley, who introduced Milken. The previous year Senator Edward Kennedy, Representative Tim Wirth, and Senator Alan Cranston had been among the politicians present.

No differently from any other special interest group, Drexel lobbied with words and with dollars in the form of campaign contributions. Senator Alfonse D'Amato, jumping on the regulatory bandwagon, supported legislation in the spring of 1985 to restrict Savings & Loans from investing in junk bonds and to limit their use in takeovers. Drexel participated in a fund raiser dinner for D'Amato at Chasens' in Beverly Hills, attended by twenty-three Drexelites and some close clients. The dinner raised $33,000. All in all D'Amato, famous for his ability to raise campaign funds, took in approximately half a million from the investment community and the proposed legislation fizzled. D'Amato, once quizzed about any possible connection between the donations and the diluting of his anti-junk zeal, said, 'The fact is that junk bonds have produced millions of jobs, and don't forget I'm not a patsy for these guys. I've introduced bills to crack down on insider trading.'

Some argue that it was the high yield bond department's idea to start up the Alliance for Capital Access, a lobbying organization of Drexel clients and high yield bond users that would attempt to counter that of the Business Roundtable. Drexel also published and distributed State books, which let representatives know about the non-investment grade companies and the high yield bond users in their states. And they worked. Thomas Bliley (Republican, Virginia) told the 1988 conference (in return for a $1,000 speaking fee), 'I didn't realize that some thirty-two firms in Virginia employing 64,000 people had used high yield bonds to make acquisitions and expand facilities.'

Drexel's lobbying came to an abrupt end after its settlement with the government. One lobbyist spoke for them all when he said, 'They're pariahs. I wouldn't carry anything to the Hill on Drexel stationery.' However, they had successfully fended off the first two waves of righteous regulation – the first in 1984 and 1985 concerning itself with the raiders, and then in 1987 the concerns over the taxation of acquisition debt. But with the record-breaking leveraged buyout of RJR Nabisco there was a third wave, and, appropriately, Kohlberg, Kravis & Roberts galloped into the breach.

KKR presented a glossy and optimistic study they had commissioned on the effect of leveraged buyouts. However, at a congressional hearing an academic from the Brookings Institute noticed some 'inconsistencies' in the findings. The study followed the performance of seventeen leveraged buyouts for three years after KKR had made them private (when data about these companies is no longer publicly available). But because seven of these transactions were not yet three years old, they could project the necessary figures without indicating this in the study. Furthermore, the projected seven were six times as big as the other ten with the result that the report's findings were 85 per cent speculation. When it came to evaluating whether LBOs created or cost jobs, KKR did not include divisions that were sold off after the deal. Thus the closing of Safeway's Dallas division and the ten thousand jobs lost there were not included. Conversely they did include in their calculations acquisitions, and as one person commented, 'KKR made no distinction between making the pie bigger and buying a bigger piece of the pie.'

Michael Lewis attended the hearing and witnessed the KKR representatives pose of 'benign condescension' turn into 'malignant indignation' as these revelations were made. 'Each time a point was made against him the man from KKR rocked back and forth in his chair. He frantically sifted a growing chaos of paper on his table as if somewhere in the mess a rebuttal might be found. It was hard not to feel sorry for him. He was like the boy in high school assigned to argue an impossible case – say, genocide as a means of population control.' Another study that claimed to be 'a survey of the existing academic literature' proved to be equally partial. Debunking this was Professor Bernanke, who made the unforgettable pronouncement that 'using high leverage to improve corporate performance is much like encouraging safe driving by putting a dagger, pointed at the driver's chest, in every car's steering wheel; it may improve driving but may lead to disaster during a snowstorm.'

The one truth that emerges from the blizzard of studies was that they obscured more than they revealed. There was a dearth of studies using hard data, and since most had an ideological axe to grind their numerical findings were less revealing than the attitudes and assumptions they betrayed. As Connie Bruck explained in *The New Yorker* 'most members of Congress are easily intimidated by the apparent complexity of high finance – a response that has been encouraged by people on the Street, who for decades have promulgated the notion that what goes on there is beyond the ken of any outsider . . . the lack of respect is no doubt genuine, but is also a kind of conceptual amulet, to ward off intrusive oversight.' Wall Street was eager to keep the ways and means of its money-making cloaked in mystery, and Congress was fearful of doing anything that might cause the market to crash and create a recession.

Previous regulation had even created the very environment Congress was so eager to reform. The Hart Scott Rodino anti-trust law had created the unwieldy conglomerates, and the Williams Act (1967) had set up the arbitrageurs as key players in the takeover wars. Thus it could be argued that the entire insider trading scandal was in fact the creation of regulation. The act required that investors make public their holdings and their intentions by filing a form called a 13D within ten days of acquiring a 5 per cent stake in a company. The law was designed to prevent overnight takeovers, or 'Saturday night specials' as they were known, and slow the process down. However it created a window of opportunity for arbitrageurs who, hearing of a possible takeover in the works, would buy up huge blocks of stock which they would then hold and, if the deal went through, sell to the raider at a handsome profit. This high-risk activity created such a demand for hot information that it pushed the arbs right to the line dividing legal and public information from inside information upon which it was illegal to trade.

But the most graphic of regulation back-firing came when Congress tried to tackle the debt/equity issue. Again, Congress had itself created the leveraging of America through their own regulation. For Washington taxed stock dividends while making the interest payable on bonds tax-deductible. Bonds were thus cheaper for a company than shares, and by loading up with bonds, they could lower their tax profile to zero. This made debt cheaper than equity, and, so long as the rule continued, preferable for the capital structure. Congress, out of its concern for overleverage, and perhaps feeling a little cheated of its tax dollars, wondered about revising the tax policy so that bonds would no longer be such a tax break.

The only problem, was when was a bond a bond and when was a bond not a bond? Deregulation had created a roaring market for boring old bonds which were bought and sold with all the frenzy and adrenalin of shares. The demand created led to a plethora of new products, half breed bonds that were like shares, or 'equity in drag' which were shares dressed up as bonds so that they would not miss out on the tax advantage. Traditionally bonds paid a fixed rate of interest, were non-speculative, and, in the event of disaster, were senior to stock on the repayment schedule. Neo-bonds did not necessarily pay a fixed rate of interest but might, like a share dividend, pay a rate that reflected the changing fortunes of the company. They were a bet on the future and came with virtually no guarantee of repayment. Highly speculative, these bonds were also known as 'synthetic equities'. 'The creative juices of the Elizabethans may have gone into the sonnet; the creative juices of the eighties went into thinking up new securities,' wrote Adam Smith in *The Roaring Eighties*. According to one colleague, Milken alone was responsible for issuing over ninety variations of bonds.

Congress had never had to make this Solomon's judgement between debt and equity before (ironically, it was the Secretary to the Treasury who had the power to decide what was debt and what was equity, none other than James Brady), and the prospect alone of regulation was enough to create the very result it was trying to avoid. On 14 October 1987 the House Ways and Means Committee announced it was filing legislation to make the interest paid on bonds issued for takeovers (i.e. junk bonds) taxable. Although this was only the first step along the path to becoming law, it is widely acknowledged that this announcement triggered the market crash the following Monday.

In the end, of the thirty bills that dealt with regulating takeovers in 1984 and 1985, not one passed. However there was plenty of state legislation. Within eighteen months thirty-seven states passed laws restricting takeover activity, somewhat confirming Pickens's view that powerful companies treated the state legislature 'like it was their own banana republic'. Goldsmith claimed that in certain cases the company lawyers went so far as to draft the legislation for the state legislature themselves. In Delaware, a wide range of anti-takeover laws catered to over half of the *Fortune* 500 who were registered there. In return for registration fees – which generated 17 per cent of Delaware's income – the state looked after their interests. Furthermore, in New York, Maryland, Florida and Texas there were caps on the amounts that insurance companies were allowed to invest in junk. Glenn Yago argued that the purposes of this legislation were purely self serving. In New York, for example, the Equitable & Metropolitan Life led the battle to restrict insurance investment in high yield bonds to 20 per cent. At the time there were only two other insurance companies whose portfolios exceeded 20 per cent and they happened to be Equitable & Metropolitan's two main rivals.

Where Rohatyn saw Milken and his crowd as tearing apart corporations as though they were erector sets, Milken saw himself differently, remembering the time he had spent as a child building homes and machines with erector sets. In his eyes it was regulation that was the destructive force, and it caused him to view Washington as 'a city that tears down'. Harry Horowitz, who spent a spell lobbying in Washington, remarked, 'There's only four or five senators who have actually been in business for themselves. The rest of them are – guess what – lawyers, who don't know what it means to build something.' (Indeed statistically 63 per cent of Congress and 44 per cent of the House of Representatives went to law school and/or are practising lawyers.)

Milken saw this regulation mania as a defensive reaction to America's declining competitiveness. 'Just imagine there was a baseball team – like the

New York Yankees – that won all the time. It even came to believe it had a divine right to win. Then a new team came along whose pitchers knew how to throw curveballs and sliders which its hitters couldn't hit. It began to lose. So its manager decided, rather than teaching them how to hit these pitches, to go to the commission – and have them banned.' In the same way, 'Much of American business has run to government and said, "Let's change the rules. We don't want competition, we don't want pressure against regulation" . . . If you can deny other people capital, you can also prevent yourself from having a competitor.'

Especially galling to him were the attempts to restrict institutional investors from investing in high yield bonds. Beneath the surface this bureaucracy was financial racism: 'There are 306 black mayors today in the United States, and it's somewhat ironic . . . that nearly all of those cities' pension funds for their workers have restrictions which do not allow them to invest in the debt of non-investment grade companies. These are companies that make up 95 per cent of all companies in the US . . . So indirectly they are saying that we cannot invest in any company headed by a black since there's not one company in the US that's investment grade where the CEO is a black American.'

On another occasion, 'new legislation has recently been passed that prohibits US Savings & Loans institutions from investing in non-investment grade debt. That means that 95 per cent of all the companies in America are out of bounds for the Savings & Loans; that means that the companies which have created most of the jobs in this country during the past two years have been red-lined; that means that black Americans and hispanics, as well as many Asians and women, are being told that they don't have companies deemed worthy of loaning money to because they are too risky. We ought to think seriously about what such policies mean to a city like Los Angeles, in which 60 per cent of the school age population is hispanic.'

Milken likened this abundance of regulation to communism: 'As we look around the world today we see country after country that's moving towards privatization, that's moving towards capitalism, that tried other systems, that's giving people the right to succeed and the right to fail. Unfortunately, we're moving to a society . . . that appears to eliminate all the risk in our life and . . . when you eliminate risk you also eliminate the future.' Milken saw the abundance of regulation as a kind of communism and once sugested that the two world leaders, Bush, a man who has 'no new ideas', and Gorbachev, 'pushing for change, taking risks', might be more comfortable if they swapped countries.

The day that Milken made this observation he had gone, after the HELP luncheon honouring him, to pick up his son's driving licence. He was looking forward to it and had mentioned it at lunch (telling the story of his own rapid accumulation of parking tickets within the first few hours of being able to drive). But when he got there he learned that they had failed to fill out a particular form that was part of the process. This was not a 'problem' since, Milken assumed, there was an 'opportunity' to fill one out on the spot. But to his chagrin he learned that this was not the case and that they would have to wait twenty-eight days before refiling. Milken was 'caught up in the system', to use his own words, and it rankled him. His son had to delay his dream and put his future on hold, albeit for only a month.

Much later, Milken's defenders would see in this regulatory frustration an explanation of how he came to be on the wrong side of the law, arguing that his crimes were in fact no more than technical violations, which, like parking tickets, were easy to get. Others would see, however, a pathologically criminal disregard for the laws of men from top to toe. But what Milken himself identified very early on was that the great Washington debt debate had little to do with debt. Debt wasn't good or bad no matter how high emotions ran. As a tool it could either be used as a lever or a bludgeon: 'What the whole concern with debt comes down to, in a way, is who should make the judgement about what the right capital structure is for a company. Should it be the management and the investors, or someone from the outside like regulators, or bond raters? It seems to me that if investors feel safe loaning money to a company, they should be granted the right to do so. And hopefully they are charging a rate commensurate with the risk that they are taking.'

Maybe so. But Milken's perception did not square with the reality of government, and, with its predominance of lawyers, its preoccupation with regulation. Ultimately, the great debt debate was a squabble about power.

8

INSIDER TRADERS

EVEN if Congress had passed all the legislation it proposed, regulation alone could not stop the junk bond revolution. As a remedy it was a defensive reaction, and invariably short-lived as agile minds skirted the edges, maximized vagaries, and found loopholes to duck through, turning a statute's limitations into opportunities. But if regulation itself was not the answer, enforcement was. Just as market forces could neutralize legislation by creatively dancing around it, so it was possible to creatively enforce regulation. A law's lack of clarity, far from being a problem, could be used to prosecute a wide range of possible offences. As was often said, a prosecutor could, if he so desired, indict a ham sandwich. It all depended on the prosecutor and his desire. In Rudolph Giuliani the Establishment found an enforcer with an eighties-sized appetite.

'How much do we really know about the corporate takeover game and the complex network of information that circulates among investment bankers, takeover lawyers, corporate raiders, arbitrageurs, stockbrokers, junk bond investors, and public relations specialists?' asked the Senate Banking Committee chairman William Proxmire in April 1987. This question was directed to Rudolph Giuliani, the United States Prosecutor who had made his name as a zealous crusader in mafia and police corruption cases, and to Gary Lynch, the director of the SEC's enforcement division. 'Mr Lynch and Mr Giuliani,' said Proxmire, getting to the point, 'You are the Ferdinand Pecoras of the 1980s. Through your vigilance, Wall Street is being rid of some of its criminals whose greed has cut a sorry path through our American system.'

The comparison was both charged and significant. Wall Street, considering itself above reproach and regulation, was only brought to its knees by Pecora's smear campaign which excited public outrage against yesteryear's business magnates and which in turn led to reforms such as the creation of the Securities and Exchange Commission.

Ferdinand Pecora was a native Sicilian and assistant New York attorney who took on tough cases and boasted an 80 per cent conviction rate. He was recruited by the Senate in 1933 to revitalize it's investigation into banking practices and the causes of the 1929 crash. Faith in Wall Street was at an all-time low, and as one senator remarked, 'The best way to restore confidence in the banks would be to take these crooked presidents out of the banks and treat them the same way we treated Al Capone.' Pecora revived the lacklustre hearings by dragging America's premier financier before the Senate for a grilling. He used the occasion to reveal that the legendary billionaire financier J.P. Morgan had not paid any taxes between 1930 and 1932. Although neither relevant to the hearings nor illegal, this did not play well in the context of the Depression. Pecora also revealed routine wash or pseudo sales of securities to generate tax losses, and a list of inner track preferred clients consisting of America's most rich and powerful with whom the house of Morgan would curry favour by selling them issues of new shares at an insider's price that was well below market value, almost guaranteeing them an instant profit. Again, although not illegal this favouritism did not pass the smell test.

In short order, the hearings became a circus. 'The only things lacking now are peanuts and coloured lemonade,' snorted one of the few senators disgusted by the charade. The next day a Ringling Brothers press agent brought a midget to the hearings and dumped her in Morgan's lap. Pictures appeared in the next day's papers, and while this early 'photo opportunity' gave the financier a humanizing gloss, it reinforced the atmospherics. That there were any hearings at all and that Morgan was at them defending his integrity was sufficient indication of guilt. 'As a result of these hearings bankers would henceforth become known as "banksters,"' wrote Ron Chernow in *The House of Morgan*. 'The political movement to punish Wall Street . . . [became] a juggernaut . . . Pecora's sensational findings pressured the Roosevelt administration to take action against Wall Street.' In Pecora's own words, were it not for the fact that 'public indignation had been deeply aroused by the conclusive evidence of wrong doing', he doubted that Wall Street's vehement opposition to reform would have been overcome.

Together with the creation of the Securities and Exchange Commission, one of the results was a table of regulations outlawing certain business practices. Rule 10B prohibited insider trading, which was defined as trading on material non- public information. The underlying assumption was that the stock market, as a public institution, depended upon the all-round perception that it was fair, and offered to all investors a level playing field of equal opportunity. But what may have been a romantic idyll then, with the small investor playing the market, had become obsolete by the time the flow of information had become a roaring Niagara, demanding a specialized approach from investors in order to get an edge. Thus the idea that Joe Six Pack from Anytown USA could enjoy the same level of knowledge as Mr Arbitrageur of Wall Street was an absurd concept, and as Lester Thurow from the MIT management school further argued, 'to maintain this fantasy through the insider trading rules is to perpetrate fraud at a very high level, luring the public on to a playing field that is not only uneven but strewn with mines.'

Be that as it may, the concept of insider trading as a crime prevailed. When John Shad (the man who gave Fred Joseph his first job on Wall Street, and who would see the favour reciprocated when he became Fred's boss once again as chairman of Drexel Burnham) was named chairman of the SEC, he announced that he would 'come down on insider-trading with hob nailed boots'. In support of this feisty talk his colleagues actually gave him a pair of hob nailed boots and urged him to wear them to Capitol Hill, to reinforce his message. He chickened out. While this may be symbolic of his own lack of resolve, nevertheless, he did ask Congress in 1984 to 'give teeth' to the insider trading rules which hitherto only demanded disgorgement of ill-gotten gains. Congress obliged with triple reparations and a maximum prison sentence of ten years.

In spite of this added bite, Shad's hobnailed boots pronouncement was all bark. For a long time it was popular wisdom on Wall Street that Ivan Boesky was 'playing with a marked deck', as author Michael Thomas put it, and he actually confronted SEC head John Shad about it when he met him in Washington. In the summer of 1984 *Fortune* ran a generally flattering piece on Boesky but also added, 'Boesky's competitors whisper darkly about his omniscient timing and rumours abound that he looks for deals involving Kidder Peabody and First Boston.' A year later, an article in *American Lawyer* by the magazine's editor Steve Brill questioned Boesky's role in Boone Pickens's takeover bid for Phillips Petroleum, suggesting that he had used inside information to protect himself when the deal fell apart. But nothing happened.

It wasn't just that Boesky was doing it, everybody was doing it. In April 1985 *Business Week*, in a study of all takeovers, mergers and LBOs in 1984, found that in 72 per cent of the cases the stock price rose prior to a public announcement of the transaction (the assumption being that the rise reflected a flurry of people trading on inside information about the imminent transaction). Giuliani had been US Attorney since 1983, and his office had prosecuted twenty-nine people for insider trading compared to forty in the entire previous history of the Attorney's office.

Congress, galled by its own inertia, berated the SEC for its slowness and heavy-handedness. After one congressional grilling in the spring of 1986, the SEC team huddled in a taxi on their way back to their office 'groping for the hearing's greater meaning', as Greg Jarrell, who was at the time the SEC's chief economist (and a defender of junk bonds and takeovers), later related to *The New York Times*. 'Almost tongue-in-cheek, someone said, "Look, here's how we can bring them good will. The SEC has to bring three heads on platters; a major arbitrageur, a major takeover entrepreneur, and a major investment banker or financier." It was clear to everyone that Ivan Boesky was the arbitrageur, Carl Icahn was the takeover entrepreneur, and Michael

Milken was the financier.' Joke or not, this spelt out the truth with a cartoon-like simplicity, namely that something had to be done, sooner rather than later.

'When you have a case built on circumstantial evidence it's hard to prove,' Shad argued. But once the SEC had received a copy of the following letter sent to Merill Lynch's Manhattan Headquarters from Venezuela, they no longer had the excuse of not having the smoking gun that they said they lacked. Anonymous, and written in pigeon English, it was thought to come from a jilted lover.

'Please be informed that two of your executives from the Caracas office are trading with inside information. A copie with description of ther trades so far has been submitet to the SEC by separate mail. As is mantion on that letter, if us customers do not benefit from their knoleg, we wonder who surveils the trades done by account executives. Upon you investigating to the last consequecies we will provide with the names of the insider on their owne hand writing.'

The two traders whose signatures were copied at the bottom of the letter had been copycatting buy and sell orders issued by the Bahamian branch of the Swiss bank, Bank Leu. In its turn Bank Leu had been copycatting trades ordered by 'Mr Diamond'. Mr Diamond, it would turn out, was none other than Dennis Levine, a rising star in the mergers and Acquisitions department of Drexel Burnham Lambert.

'I'm not a banker, I'm a thespian,' Dennis B. Levine once chortled, and, overcoming the disability of a non-Ivy League background, he had learnt how to play the part of the charming and sophisticated investment banker to perfection. He announced that he wanted to be a millionaire by the time he was 30 and embodied the values of the age. 'Dennis describes himself as a person who truly loves to do two things: do deals and make money,' read his headhunters' résumé. For a $250,000 fee they placed Levine with Drexel, where he was on an annual million plus salary. When, at the end of his first year, they doubled his bonus to $1.5 million, his reaction was not gratitude, but outrage. He was insulted. And instead of being fired for insolence and ingratitude, they rewarded his rapacity with more. Even his costume was perfect. Gone were the days when he poured himself into tight suits that made him, in the words of a friend, look like a pimp. When he came to DBL he bought a wardrobe of monogrammed shirts embroidered with his initials – DBL.

But what he also meant by the thespian remark was that he was excellent at playing a double role. He could play the sophisticated banker and the crude con artist. 'I can out con any con on any game,' he once boasted to one of his circle of fellow insider traders. 'I grew up selling aluminium siding to niggers on welfare' (as quoted in Douglas Frantz's *Levine and Co*). Between 1980 and 1985 his insider trading earned him $11.5 million. Even while the investigation was going on, he flew to Washington at the invitation of John Shad to participate in a roundtable discussion on insider trading.

Both to himself and to those he persuaded to join his insiders' circle, Levine rationalized his actions as standard Wall Street stuff. 'Everybody does it,' he was supposed to have told one of his first victims. He too had noticed the run-up in a company's stocks prior to a public announcement, and in some ways he was probably right. 'It's no different from working . . . at a deli. You take home pastrami every night for free. It's the same with information on Wall Street.'

But Levine took home too many pastramis, and with the almost $3 million he made on the RJ Reynolds and Nabisco merger he seemed to be making off with the whole enchilada, throwing caution to the winds even as the investigative net closed in on him.

On 12 May the trap closed. He remembered his last day; 'Waking early in my Park Avenue apartment on 12 May 1986, I read the morning papers, checked on the European securities markets, and ate breakfast with my wife, Laurie, then six weeks pregnant, and my son, Adam, who was 4. By 8 a.m. I was in downtown Manhattan, meeting with my staff at Drexel Burnham Lambert. At 33 I was a leading merger specialist and a partner in one of the most powerful investment banks on Wall Street. Among the many appointments on my calendar that day were meetings with two CEOs, including Revlon's Ronald Perelman, to discuss multibillion-dollar takeovers. I was a happy man.

'In mid-afternoon two strangers, one tall and one short, came looking for me at Drexel. They didn't identify themselves, but the receptionist said that they weren't dressed like clients . . . I knew something was wrong and I fled. While the authorities searched for me, I drove around New York in my BMW, making anxious calls on the car phone to my wife, my father, my boss. Before leaving the car, I hired a legal team headed by superstar lawyer Arthur Liman.' After leaving his car he was arrested, spent the night in a holding cell of drug dealers ('whose odour I won't soon forget'), and watched his story on television the next morning, eating cornflakes in the cafeteria.

Levine was nothing if not persuasive, and he seems to have been protean in his ability to play any role he set his mind to. Today he is a professional repentant, all contrition when he teaches ethics at New York University or writes about his experiences for *Fortune* magazine. 'These were the 1980s, remember, the decade of excess, greed, and materialism. I became a go-go guy, consumed by the high pressure, ultra-competitive world of investment banking. I was helping my clients make tens and even hundreds of millions of dollars. I served as the lead banker on Perelman's nearly $2 billion takeover of Revlon, four months of work that enabled Drexel to earn $60 million in fees. The daily exposures to such deals, the pursuit of larger and larger transactions, and the numbing effect of 60-100 hour work weeks helped erode my values and distort my judgement . . . At the root of my compulsive trading was an inability to set limits. Perhaps it's worth noting that my legitimate success stemmed from the same root. My ambition was so strong it went beyond rationality, and I gradually lost sight of what constitutes ethical behaviour. At each new level of success I set higher goals, imprisoning myself in a cycle from which I saw no escape.'

Although Levine has learnt his lines well, beneath the plausible gloss of the competition junkie one gets the chill of the sociopath who would sell anyone his wretched aluminium siding - even his own mother. Which is essentially what he did. In return for a reduced sentence he agreed to co-operate, and, furthermore, try and entrap his co-conspirators by calling them up from pay phones to draw them out about their part in his scheme. Although the automated voice of the operator asking for additional cents would occasionally cut in and be followed by the sound of more coins being deposited, Levine wasn't calling from a public pay phone at all but a specially rigged phone in the basement of the US Attorney's office.

In return for his enthusiastic co-operation, Levine received a sentence of two years at a minimum security prison (he was released for good behaviour after seventeen months) and fined $11.6 million. It is doubtful that Levine would have got off so lightly had he not fingered, in addition to his four henchmen, the celebrity arbitrageur Ivan Boesky. During his sojourn at Club Fed (as minimum security prisons are derisively known), Levine's wife sent him a copy of *Bonfire of the Vanities*. 'I never felt quite like a master of the universe, but I saw parallels.' Levine was a junior master of the universe, and although the SEC dubbed him Moby Dick, he was a small fish compared to Boesky.

Like Levine, Boesky was a thespian banker. In *The New Crowd*, Ehrlich and Rehfeld commented that although Boesky had appeared in an off-Broadway production *Abie's Irish Rose* in 1975, 'despite what some reviewers praised as an apparent talent for acting, he never pursued it'. But that same year Boesky launched his own off-Broadway production, an arbitrage company.

Boesky played the role of risk arbitrageur to the hilt. He worked his humour and charisma relentlessly. Boone Pickens noted of him, 'He always smiled, no matter what he happened to be saying . . . then I realized that only his mouth was smiling – his eyes were unaffected. The smile was probably an indication of his self-control.' Consequently he was a popular speaker on the college circuit. Speaking at Berkeley in 1986 he uttered the memorable lines, 'Greed is all right by the way. I want you to know that I think greed is healthy. You can be greedy and still feel good about yourself.' The lines were of course immortalized by Michael Douglas playing the character of Gordon Gekko in *Wall Street* as 'Greed is good, greed works'. Although Gekko contained trace elements of Icahn and Pickens, the vicious lizard was based more than anyone else on Boesky, whose prominent features bore a distinctly reptilian streak.

But until he became an arbitrage star little in Boesky's life had worked out. As a boy he had been removed from one boarding school under what are described as 'mysterious circumstances'. He attended four colleges before he obtained his law degree, thereafter co-managing a disco that went bankrupt, then bouncing around Wall Street, unable to hold down a job permanently and spending much of the time between work sitting on a bench in Central Park. But despite these false starts, Boesky was not a loser. He had managed to marry into money and lived in modest luxury with his wife on Park Avenue. But his father-in-law, a real estate magnate who owned the Beverly Hills Hotel, had called Boesky's number from the beginning. He called him 'Ivan the bum'.

As luck would have it, it was with money his wife had inherited when her mother died that Boesky was able to launch himself on the world, having discovered that arbitrage was his calling. On the face of it, it was an unlikely choice. As he would declare in his bestseller *Merger Mania*, risk arbitrage was 'Wall Street's best kept money-making secret'.

Although fraught with risk it was in essence fairly simple. After the announcement of a takeover an arbitrageur would snap up as much stock as possible hoping that he would be able to sell it off at a higher price to the raider if the deal went through. A much more profitable variation was to buy up the stock before a takeover was announced, on the strength of a rumour. But in this high stakes game the arbitrageur was walking an impossible tightrope. On the one side there was the sheer risk of betting millions on mere rumour, while on the other, if he did the logical thing and tried to limit the risk by substantiating the rumour, he was likely to come into possession of inside information or material non public information on which he was forbidden to trade.

Naturally such risk-taking was not for the faint-hearted. Icahn, who had been an arbitrageur, told his wife that if he ever needed to have a heart transplant she should get him the heart of an arb because it had never been used. However, for those that dared and won, the rewards were huge and because it was so profitable to the few that dared to dabble in its arcaneries, the arb clan set a premium on maintaining their air of mystery. They forged almost masonic bonds, cloaked themselves in anonymity, and bought into blocks of stock in groups which offset the risk and strengthened the *esprit de corps*.

Broadway Boesky changed all that. Shut out of almost everything he had tried to get his hand in (except the family cookie jar), he decided to risk everything on an all-or-nothing play. He would take the hurrah of the wee arbitrageurs – all for one and one for all – and make it all for one and all for him, by taking a huge position rather than spreading the risk and sharing the rewards among his colleagues. Boesky's rivals called him 'Piggy'.

Boesky was also nicknamed 'Ivan the Terrible', for lashing his employees with his demands and paying them a pittance as though they were on a slave ship. He was no less ruthless with the family that had given him quarter. In 1983 he wrested control of the Beverly Hills Hotel from his wife's family, and turned it into a vehicle for his business by spinning off the aptly named Vagabond Hotels chain and taking it public (through Milken of course), raising almost $100 million, a third of which was for his arbitrage ventures.

He brought a blaze of unwelcome publicity to the business. He hired a PR person and invested hundreds of thousands in self-promotion and advertisements for investment partners in *The Wall Street Journal* (the terms of which make an interesting comparison with those Milken offered his early investors. Whereas Milken took 50 per cent of the profits and 100 per cent of the losses, Boesky took 55 per cent of the profits, and stuck his investors with 95 per cent of the losses).

Boesky cultivated a buccaneer image. He liked to tell the story of how he had bought with the $400 he got from his Bar Mitzvah an old truck, and, even though he did not have his driving licence, drove around Detroit making between $100 and $150 a week selling ice-creams. His budding career as an ice-cream salesman came to an end when he was apprehended by the police as an under-age unlicensed driver.

He allowed himself to be filmed in his hi-tech space age office. Standing behind his desk (the black marble top alone cost $10,000), he would monitor his business and flight crew by watching a video wall of TV screens. He would speak with them via intercom, and presumably beam them up from time to time for an old-fashioned earthling-style meeting. Chain-smoking and drinking black coffee by the quart, Boesky worked his 160 lines with 300 buttons living on a diet of fruit salad and cottage cheese. In a sexy twist the space age Fifth Avenue offices belonged to the commodities trader Marc Rich who fled the States in 1983 to evade tax evasion charges. Fear of a jinx might have given others pause, but not riskbuster Boesky, who wasn't afraid of no ghost. He commuted by stretch limousine (with three phones) to his seigneurial 160-acre Connecticut estate which was in the village next door to Carl Icahn and Nelson Peltz. At the peak of his fame he planned to add a dome that would make the Georgian mansion more resemble Jefferson's neo-Palladian Monticello, but it was never built. The estate housed his collection of vintage cars, and like Lady Penelope in 'Thunderbirds', he was fond of fooling around in a pink Rolls Royce. Boesky loved putting on the glitz because, like the junk bond jillionaires, he was a status-seeking missile. Although his alma mater was a small school in Detroit, he gave lavishly to Harvard, which won him entrance to the Harvard Club, the exclusive alumni-only club.

But things were not as they seemed. Boesky first met Levine at the 1985 Predator's Ball, and he offered him a ride home on his jet. Each found the other extremely useful: 'Like the CIA, Ivan Boesky seemed to have sources everywhere, and his intelligence was extremely valuable.' In turn Boesky was an infomaniac. 'He had such an insatiable desire for information he would call me up to a dozen times a day,' recalled Levine. 'My home phone would ring well before 6 a.m.; Laurie would answer and hand me the receiver, saying, "It's Ivan," rolling her eyes.' This was the trademark of his style. In this way he could flesh out rumours, and get a grasp to the parameters underlying speculation. Of course he could also pry out of his network of contacts material non-public information, confirming the illegality of this by paying for it – in several instances with cash-filled suitcases handed out by henchmen in dark alleys to recipients who knew the password.

The pinnacle of his success came with his bestseller *Merger Mania*. At book signings he would joke, 'There's no sex in it, but read it anyway,' and people did. This was Boesky at his best. Charming charismatic, entertaining and, like a true thespian, loving every minute of it. With sex and shopping novels like Krantz's *I'll Take Manhattan* and Trump's *Art Of The Deal* topping the bestseller lists, it was a shame that *Merger Mania* was not more autobiographical. As one rival arbitrageur said after his fall, what Boesky had to tell the US Attorney's office would read 'like a whore's diary'. Sadly the book did not live up to all these tantalizing possibilities. The contents themselves all but copied a 1982 monograph called *Risk Arbitrage 2* written by the rival arbitrageur who had nicknamed Boesky 'Piggy'.

Another arb suggested that Boesky's Vagabond Corporation would have been much more successful if he had been marketing a perfume. Although said in jest, the observation revealed the key to Boesky's personality. A well-seasoned actor, he excelled, like Trump, in the show business of business, staging his own personal 'Dynasty'. And *Vagabond* really could have been the perfect vehicle to sell his lifestyle no less successfully than Ralph Lauren sold his: the Wall Street arbitrageur, space-age office, international twenty-four-hour schedule, Gulf Stream jets, sleek stretch limos, and country estates. Vagabond – 'Ah, the smell of it!'.

The eighties buzz commodities were business and perfume, dollars and scents. The very brand names of the perfumes thrilled in the illicit and the maniacal. Joan Collins's 'Scoundrel', Elizabeth Taylor's 'Passion' and Calvin Klein's 'Obsession'. The adrenalous rush of *Koyaanasqatsi*, where everyone rushed round in a stop frame frenzy, was the way to be. If your life wasn't 'out of balance' (the literal meaning of the hopi 'Koyaanasqatsi') there was something wrong with you. Boesky on a permanent caffeine high, a workaholic and sleepophobe (two to three hours max), with his self-confessed addiction to making money, was – in spite of the scorn that has been heaped upon him subsequently – the perfect man of the moment, and really no more than a creation of his age.

Much has been made of what drives white collar-workers to commit greed crimes, and many, including the criminals themselves, have confessed that they became addicted to making money. 'I don't know why Ivan engaged in illegal activities when he had a fortune estimated at over $200 million,' Levine mused. When he himself was asked why, somebody making over $1 million a year would start trading inside information, he claimed that that was the wrong question, arguing instead that he was addicted to the mad glamour of it all. Boesky made the same plea. After his fall, he explained his behaviour as 'a sickness I have in the face of which I am helpless'. Of course by this time no one was laughing, because the mood had changed from champagne wishes and caviar dreams to sermons and soda water. Meanwhile Boesky was still the same old Boesky. The Gary Glitter of his day, Boesky was a creature of fad that was 'in' one moment and 'out' the next.

When Boesky learned that Levine had been arrested, he did the dishonourable thing and, like Levine before him, made the most successful deal of his career. It would be his ultimate − but not final − insider trade. But this time, instead of buying inside information, he was selling it, trading every scrap of information about his ring of insiders. As a result, in spite of the scope of his criminal activity, Boesky had to plead guilty to only one minor count of conspiring to make false statements to the SEC. Of course in reality it was precisely because of the broad scope of his activity that his lawyer Arthur Pitt was able to negotiate with the government for such a light plea. In addition to passing on everything he knew Boesky was also willing to entrap his co-conspirators by wearing a wire. Suddenly the workaholic who never left his desk developed a desire to lunch with his colleagues and clients.

Although Boesky would also have to pay a $100 million fine (which broke the record that had been set by Dennis Levine's fine) and serve three years in a minimum security facility (he was released for good behaviour after serving two-thirds), he nevertheless did extremely well. He was not, for example, obliged to tell the government about all his crimes, only the ones they asked him about. Finally, he was also allowed to conduct his final insider trade, cutting his liabilities by $1.32 billion and selling off $440 million of securities, in the weeks prior to the announcement of his agreement. In the uproar that followed John Shad argued that they had done this fearing a collapse in the market, insisting that Boesky had not benefited financially from the trades. Nevertheless the money realized from the trades went towards the payment of his fine. Thus was created a notion of 'good' insider trading to pay the penalties for 'bad' insider trading. There was no inherent difference between the two, only the SEC's arbitrary say so.

Were it not for Rudolph Giuliani, Boesky could not have negotiated such a sweetheart deal. As he later explained, 'That deal with the government was very, very valuable because if the government had not been able to work that out with Boesky, it then would have taken two to three years to prosecute him. And at the end of the road you might not have been able to prove all the things that he did. And a lot of the value of his co-operation would have been lost with the delay.'

The deal was worked out in total secrecy, beginning in the summer when Boesky had thrown in, or rather played, his hand. And on 14 November 1986, which would come to be remembered as Boesky Day, it was announced to an utterly unsuspecting world. That day it was business as usual in the high yield bond department. Terren Peizer was sitting as usual on Milken's left when he noticed across the Dow Jones wire service 'something to the effect that Ivan Boesky pleads guilty to insider trading'. According to Peizer, Milken 'was on the phone . . . and he read the tape and he was staring into the quotron and he lost his train of thought and concentration and started going "uh, uh, uh" and that was it.' Soon afterwards, 'He got up and went into Lowell's office.' Lowell was supposed to have come out and met him halfway where they exchanged a few words with concerned expressions before going on inside. (James Dahl, another eye-witness, contradicted this account and testified that Milken did nothing.)

Meanwhile on the East Coast Drexel was amusing itself by dreaming about global domination. Fred Joseph was up on the 38th floor, in the executive suite where Drexel was holding a series of management meetings in which, in the words of one present, 'they were plotting how they were gonna takeover the world.' To this end they had made up slides of Fred Joseph and Mike Milken with slit eyes to look like their Japanese rivals on whom they would soon be stomping. Unfortunately Fred was pulled from the session by the news of Boesky's plea, before he got to see the joke slides. This cocky snook at the land of the rising sun would mark the high point of Drexel's aspirations. Fred Joseph's dream of using Milken's junk bond empire as the foundation on which to build something as significant as Goldman Sachs, so tantalizingly within his grasp, would gradually fade.

THE ENFORCER

When Proxmire had hailed US Attorney Rudolph Giuliani as the new Pecora, back in April 1987, he was speaking with the benefit of hindsight since by this stage the largest and most expensive investigation into securities fraud was well under way. When he asked 'how much do we really know about the complex network of information' that circulates among the various players of what Proxmire called 'the takeover game', he was raising what writer Jay Epstein described as 'the spectre of a vast criminal conspiracy behind the battle for corporate control'. Even in his choice of words he was suggesting that the activities of Wall Street more resembled those of an illicit casino than a legitimate business. He also knew that Giuliani agreed with him. He had argued at his frequent press conferences that corruption was systemic on Wall Street, and that he was laying bare the whole ugly conspiracy. Giuliani also knew by this stage that Milken was his target. 'I'm going to get that guy!' Giuliani was supposed to have said after a speech at the City Athletic Club long before Milken's indictment.

In many ways Giuliani and Milken were very much alike. Virtually the same age (he was born in 1945, one year before Milken), Giuliani had a boyish look that made him look much younger. Like Milken he had tremendous drive and energy. As a baby he would fight off sleep for two days and as an adult would stay up two nights in a row writing a brief that he would then go and argue in court. As a kid Giuliani was also drawn to being a doctor and he even considered the role of priest. It could be Milken speaking when he said, 'I wanted to do something that made me feel like I was helping people. It's important to me to feel that I'm doing something bigger than just supporting myself.' In the end, where Milken was drawn to Wall Street, Giuliani was drawn to the US Attorney's Office, and for the same reasons: 'It seemed like it would be . . . a wonderful way to contribute, which of course was a very big concept in the sixties.' As with Milken, the turmoil of the sixties did not carry him along with it: 'All the years in college and law school nobody offered me a drug of any kind.' Giuliani also had legendary powers of total recall, matching Milken's encyclopaedic knowledge of bond prices with an ability, if a colleague were to hum six bars from an obscure aria, not only to name it, but also to say when it was last performed and to name the singer.

Like Milken, Giuliani liked hands-on work in the thick of things. Having been number three in the Justice Department, he took what many saw as a demotion to return to the field as US District Attorney in 1983. When Reagan offered him the post of chairman of the SEC he turned it down, and he rejected himself as a candidate to be director of the FBI.

Also like Milken, he saw himself as an artist: 'I could spend an entire Saturday writing a brief and at the end I felt I had created something, the way an artist might feel when he's just painted a picture.' Like Milken, Giuliani also took a moral view of his work. He felt that he could help people caught in the web of crime, and, believing that people were basically good, could eke that little bit of goodness out of people who had, until they fell into his hands, chosen evil. Like Milken he was extraordinarily successful at what he did. During his five years as Assistant US Attorney he had a 100 per cent batting average, with forty prosecutions and no losses. Most notable among them was a cross-examination that so unnerved the defendant that he interrupted proceedings to change his plea from 'Not Guilty' to 'Guilty'.

But his greatest coup was the role he played in the Knapp Commission, the massive investigation into corruption in the New York City Police Department. In the first round Giuliani was essentially an observer, but once he became head of the corruption unit he could play a more active role. The case was largely based upon the confessions of one police officer, Robert Leuci, and despite the convictions they had won up to that point Giuliani suspected that this was just the tip of the iceberg and that Leuci was protecting himself and his colleagues. Like Milken, Giuliani radiated a sense of security that enabled Leuci to put his trust in him, 'There is a sense of security around Rudy when you sense you are on his team, that it's going to be okay, that he can handle it.' In brother Giuliani's care Leuci unburdened himself and enabled Giuliani to chalk up eighteen more indictments. The case was also made into a film, *Prince Of The City*, in which Giuliani was one of the characters.

The same sense of protection that both Milken and Guliani could put out stemmed from a shared supreme confidence in their own abilities. Milken felt that if he could only meet with people he could persuade them to see things his way. Giuliani was no different. Speaking to an armed mob of workers, who had gone on strike after he had become CEO of a bankrupt company defrauded by its prior management, Giuliani thought to himself, 'I could convince them about anything . . . I am going to convince them like a big jury.' He won the day and set about restructuring the bankrupt company as effectively as any raider, cutting costs in half, trimming personnel, and dispensing with perks like the company helicopter. Eventually the company was sold for a large profit.

Little different from an LBO restructuring, one would have thought that this would have given Giuliani a respect for Milken's junk bond revolution, but three key differences overshadowed the common ground they shared, and made them irreconcilable opponents.

Where Milken directed his energy into a full range of activities as a superboy, Giuliani, also hyper-energized, didn't know what to do with himself. 'I couldn't sit still. I remember standing in the back of the room and getting hit with rulers.' Where Milken was encouraged to excel, Rudy was taught to conform. For all his rebelliousness Giuliani accepted, through an internal process of rationalization, the rules and regulations. He never resented being hit with rulers because 'I could never think of a situation where I didn't deserve it'. He told *New York* magazine, 'Once I got accused of doing something I hadn't done. I was outraged until I rationalized it and realized there were plenty of times I'd gotten away with things, so it probably only evened the score.' (The same kind of give and take attitude in trading pleas with his Wall Street indictees would characterize his style as US Attorney.) One was brought up living in the future of limitless possibilities, the other was brought up with a respect for the past and tradition. Milken didn't care what he looked like and rarely bothered with the traditional Wall Street uniform. But Giuliani wore uniforms at parochial school, and jacket and tie as a student. Returning to New York University three years after graduating and seeing kids 'dressed in sloppy jeans' was 'a shocking experience,' he once said in an interview. 'Coats and ties added a certain decorum and respect.'

Whereas history for Milken was something to be transcended, and disproved (history is bunk, the future is junk!), inbred into Giuliani was that sense of history that separated the East Coast from the wild untramelled West. According to *Vanity Fair*, Giuliani took Leuci's confession, lamenting, 'I wish I could change your history. I wish beyond anything that we could start now. But there's a yesterday, and we have to get it straightened out.' History must be obeyed, and the rules are the rules. The reason Giuliani decided against becoming a priest was because of the rules of celibacy, which he didn't think that he could abide by. It was on a retreat in a Trappist monastery that he said to himself, 'You know these are the rules; and you're going to have difficulty with them your whole life, so this is not the life for you.'

The second deciding difference between the two was that in both his work and his private life Giuliani was married to the media. Milken married his childhood sweetheart and burrowed down with her near where he grew up. To him the media was as sunlight to a vampire. But Giuliani, more like the junk bond jillionaires, divorced his first wife and found, in Donna Hanover – an anchorwoman on WPIX Channel 11 – something of a trophy, and a million-dollar earner in her own right. 'Rudy discovered his dick ten years too late,' Leuci volunteered to one magazine while another oozed that his wife 'looked like a delicious summer drink'. Even here Giuliani managed to abide by the church's rules, avoiding excommunication from the Catholic church by getting an annulment, because although his first wife was his second cousin he had failed to get the proper dispensation from the Catholic church permitting such a union in the first place (interestingly this sounds like precisely the kind of technical lapse that Giuliani would later delight in persecuting as full-blown crime).

Giuliani's literal marriage to the media symbolized his close working relationship with it. The reason his colleagues presented him with a conduc-tor's baton may have ostensibly been to save him from having to conduct the opera he liked to play in his office with a pencil. But it also symbolized his ability to orchestrate cases by playing on the media. In so far as it related to the great insider trading case, he was fortunate in his timing and playing to the changing spirit of the times. The supposed trickle down of Reaganomics was proving a long time coming, with the promised oasis of the greed decade turning out to be no more than a watering hole for the rich and a mirage for everyone else. This perhaps explains why he found the media such a willing instrument and eager to play his righteous symphony, as people began to tire of the excesses of the rich and famous.

But the final difference between the two men is the most revealing of all. Milken often said that it was important to remember 'who you are and where you came from and not to hold yourself above anyone else'. Since all people were equal he would not sit in judgement on them. Everyone in Milken's eyes had unlimited positive potential, so if he noticed the negatives he ignored them (blind of course to the consequences of this). Giuliani took a different tactic: 'In order to protect society, you have to understand that there's a portion of human nature that's evil.' He believed in goodies and baddies, and, unlike Milken, believed not only could he sort the wheat from the chaff, but that he was absolutely right. Leuci remembers an odd moment in which Giuliani warned him not to cross him because 'if you cross me, that means I've been mistaken and I'm never mistaken'. Instead of saying if you cross me I'll break your balls or something suitably human and mafioso, he turned it round into a kind of loony puritanism: if you cross me, it means that I am wrong, but I am so right that I cannot even comprehend the concept of being wrong. Given human fallibility such rectitude is truly chilling. If he was wrong, what then?

9

THE WALL STREET THREE

SUCH an occasion was the arrest of the Wall Street Three, which after Levine and Boesky was the third episode in the Great Insider Trading Scandal.

The story began with Martin Siegel. On Boesky Day Siegel was subpoenaed on the basis of Boesky's testimony and he immediately began co-operating secretly with the government. Siegel was a takeover defence specialist who had, unfortunately for Drexel, been lured there from Kidder Peabody as part of their aggressive hiring campaign. He had only been there a few months when Dennis Levine, whose office was next door to his, was arrested. Drexel hastily recalled the annual report that had just gone out and had a picture of Siegel pasted over Levine's.

Siegel went to Drexel to start a new life after four years of insider trading. He had not always been corrupt. For the most of his working life Siegel had lived modestly within his means, a bachelor divorcee saving most of his salary. But once he remarried he built himself a luxurious cedar and glass Connecticut home overlooking Long Island Sound and began commuting to New York (where he also maintained an apartment) by helicopter. Soon, with child (and nanny) he was living well beyond his means and eating into his savings.

Boesky proved to be a timely windfall. Siegel had been awed by Boesky's Westchester County estate, and seduced by his capitalist tool, Boesky's pink Rolls Royce, which he would drive over to Siegel's when the two got together for tennis. Without too much difficulty Boesky inducted him into his insider trading ring one night at the Harvard Club in 1982.

The mutual exchange of information proved hugely profitable to Boesky and turned Siegel into a rising star. Kidder Peabody began having their annual summer party at his home. The message was 'that if you come to Kidder and work hard, you're going to be like Marty – a beautiful home, a beautiful wife, beautiful kids,' one awe-struck attendee told *The Wall Street Journal*. 'It was like a stage set for *The Great Gatsby*.'

The fact that he was riddled with guilt and paranoia about his secret life didn't diminish his hunger for the money, and in a gangster-style arrangement he took suitcases full of it from Boesky henchmen (whom he increasingly feared were hitmen). Several times Siegel tried to end the arrangement in their coffee shop assignations when they tallied on paper napkins Siegel's profits from sold and stolen information. 'Don't you love me any more?' cooed Boesky.

Siegel did not, and soon after Boesky Day began a new insider trading relationship, swopping information about his deals for a reduced sentence. His information led to the famous arrests of the Giuliani Three.

Towards the end of the day on 12 February 1987 Timothy Tabor from Kidder Peabody was arrested at his East Side apartment on charges of insider trading. It was too late for him to be formally arraigned that night since there was no magistrate available, and Tabor did not yet have a criminal lawyer. Since he wasn't going to be processed, that meant he could not arrange bail and that meant he could not be released. He would spend the night in jail. When government prosecutors told him that he could go home if he agreed, according to his lawyers, to 'secretly record . . . telephone conversations which he [would] initiate' with other Wall Street executives, it was clear that they were putting a squeeze play on him. But Tabor refused, and so there was no remedy for him but to take his punishment, spending the night in the Metropolitan Correction facility.

The next day Richard Wigton, Tabor's colleague and head of the arbitrage department at Kidder Peabody, and Robert Freeman, head of arbitrage at Goldman Sachs, were arrested at their offices. Wigton was so surprised at the arrest that he initially threw the prosecutors out of his office, since he thought they were from some mail-o-gram company playing a practical joke. For an encore they threw him against a wall, frisked him and then led him away in full view of his colleagues, in tears and in handcuffs. Later that day Giuliani held a press conference to trumpet the arrests.

The use of these strong-arm tactics was much remarked upon at the time. After all, these white-collar suspects were not the same as homicidal criminals who were a danger to society, and yet they were pointedly being treated no differently. When asked at the press conference about the unusual nature of the arrests Giuliani disingenuously replied, 'It's not at all unusual for us to arrest people for federal felonies.' In a later interview he expanded on this: 'Almost everyone who gets charged with a complaint involving postal crimes, mail fraud, and the postal authorities gets arrested. And when they do, they're handcuffed. It is an unvarying rule of the US postal authorities. There's no way I would've said change the rules for these people. If we're going to change the rules, we're not going to change them for guys who make a million dollars a year because they're going to be a little offended about having handcuffs on them.'

But behind the mask of this disinterested application of the law were two distinct motives. As one of the lawyers 'close to the investigation of insider trading' told *The New York Times*, 'Put yourself in the role of a young investment banker at Goldman Sachs who sees one of your mentors led away by Federal marshals. It will have a very powerful effect on you and perhaps make you realize that insider trading is just as serious as armed robbery.'

General deterrence was one motive, and the other, Giuliani told *Manhattan Lawyer*, was to 'give the person the opportunity to co-operate with the government'.

Although he insisted on arresting them as though they were just the same as ordinary mobsters, Giuliani knew all too well that the two were as different as chalk from cheese. He told Congress, for example, that white collars 'roll easier', meaning that they were more likely to cop a plea and implicate others in order to save themselves hard time in regular prison, and reduce to a minimum soft time in a minimum security facility. In one of his many interviews he elaborated: 'In white collar situations, they don't think of themselves as thoroughgoing criminals, so when they get caught, there's a level of guilt involved. Suddenly there's a conflict between what they appear to families, friends, co-workers, and what they're doing in the secret part of their life. It tends to move them toward confessing, putting it all behind them. They haven't acquired the ethics of organized crime, which is that you never help the government [and] constantly try to frustrate it.'

Unlike hardened criminals, white-collar softees had a fear of incarceration. Giuliani's strategy, therefore, was to capitalize on this with orchestrated displays of government might spelling out what would happen if people didn't co-operate. Handcuffs and no bail. As he explained to the *Los Angeles Times* 'If you can present people with the distinct possibility . . . that they could be caught and that they can be held up to public shame, ridicule and possible prison sentences, you're going to be able to affect their behaviour.' Had he gone too far with the Giuliani Three? 'This isn't an invitation to a tea party,' he snapped in *Vanity Fair*. 'People are arrested in the hope that they are going to tell you everything that happened.'

With the spectacle of the Giuliani Three, Giuliani was sending a message to the Wall Street community, essentially no different from the way underworld heads send messages to one another by strategically dumping bodies. Perhaps this is what he meant when he once told the press, 'It's about time law enforcement got as organized as organized crime.'

This was typical of the overall approach of a US Attorney who was married to the media in every sense of the word. Believing, like Pecora before him, that the only way to effect change was to stir up public opinion, he led his office on a trailblazing campaign to fight crime in Gotham city. More showman than Boesky, a better thespian than Levine, Giuliani came in as a caped crusader, Batman for real. Bam! Thirty-eight indictments ripping apart the Sicilian mafia in the Pizza Connection case. Biff! $200 million in from fugitive commodities broker Marc Rich, record winnings for tax fraud. Unk! Giuliani ripped open Mayor Koch's Big Apple administration in the Parking Violations

Bureau scandal. Kersplatt! After an exhaustive seven hour summation Giuliani personally put away Bronx boss Stanley Friedman.

Instead of quietly notching up these achievements and moving on, each was celebrated as a great victory in the war on crime. At press conferences Giuliani would pose behind tables groaning with booty – dollars, drugs and guns. He would go on the popular daily news programme *Nightline* and announce that the mafia would be crushed in four or five years. In fact he appeared so many times on the show that, the story goes, a prospective juror had to be excused because she said she had heard all about the case she was about to be selected as a juror for 'on Giuliani's TV show'. On another famous occasion he went with then ally Alfonse D'Amato (who had recommended Giuliani for the job of US Attorney) on an 'undercover' crack-buying expedition to the Bronx, trailed by a media posse who lapped up the 'undercover' photo opportunity.

From Giuliani's point of view the method to this media madness was that it served the wider purpose of discouraging crime in general. 'We get a lot of our deterrent effect out of publicity,' he once told his staff. He also maintained that the Giuliani Three was not a media circus: 'If that had been planned as a media circus there would've been cameras there. And I would've made a big deal of it at the 12 February press conference that followed.' That there was a press conference at all suggests otherwise.

But others saw a very different motive. When Giuliani made the claim in his mayoral campaign that he had been the best US Attorney, a number of former prosecutors banded together and publicly denounced him, accusing him of 'ignoring traditional standards while using his office to publicize himself.' Giuliani, they continued, 'held televised press conferences for otherwise routine cases, engaged in publicity "stunts" . . . appeared on more television talk shows than all of his predecessors put together and travelled all over the state and country giving speeches on his theories of law enforcement.' 'I can't imagine how I could possibly have a lower profile,' Giuliani would counter in his defence, 'given the cases we've done in the last four years . . . they're historic cases.'

'Still,' pressed one interviewer, 'in your televised press conferences, for instance, you're always the one who seems to make the announcements. It seems as if all the cases are yours.' (Indeed the entire insider trading scandal began with the SEC and then, when the Attorney's office decided to muscle in by taking a civil case criminal, it was Bruce Carberry who was handling the investigations. But once they reached a critical mass, Giuliani stepped up to the microphone.) 'Sometimes I stand in the background,' Giuliani replied. Later in the same interview he maintained, 'I don't conduct myself frivolously to seek publicity . . . I like going out on walks by myself and not being recognized.' This did not stop him proudly displaying in another interview the departments press clippings which sat in huge albums in his office, nor, for another article, posing for photographs sitting on the bed with his newscaster wife wearing a baseball glove and tossing a Cabbage Patch doll in the air. Within his own office Giuliani was regarded as such a press whore that they even made a spoof video to celebrate his first year in office. The joke of the clip was that nobody knew who he was, except for a hooker who said he was fantastic. Some of the people they asked on the street responded, 'Is he the candidate for governor?' Close. In the end Giuliani's protestations that he was not using publicity for personal purposes all fell rather flat when he announced that he would resign and run for mayor.

'I have absolutely no ambition to be mayor of New York' declared Giuliani's successor Otto Obermaier, whose appointment Giuliani had himself opposed. 'I would prefer to blend quietly into the woodwork.' His low-key approach and the absence of press pyrotechnics was the most eloquent illustration of Giuliani's style. 'I have no message to deliver and I will have no message to deliver,' he announced.

Righteousness, a love of rules and a passion for the media differentiated Giuliani from Milken. And money. On the face of it would appear that they shared the same disregard for money. Not only did Giuliani appear to take a demotion when he became US Attorney, he also took a 50 per cent pay cut to $77,500 a year. 'I don't have a single basis to complain about my salary,' he said. However, unlike Milken he seemed to carry a moral sensibility about the amount one should earn. Of his private practice salary he commented, 'That was a tremendous amount of money – more than I ever thought anybody should be allowed to make for anything.' (Now that Giuliani is back in private practice and reported to be earning over $1 million a year, with his wife pulling down another mill, one can only speculate how he has learned to live with himself.)

Giuliani could understand financial need but not greed. 'I understand why – when somebody put $1000 in a detective's hand and said, "This is your take from the arrest" – that was tempting to him . . . he and his wife were trying to figure out how to get two or three thousand dollars as a down payment on a little house on Long Island. And here he had the down payment in his hand, plus some dollars for the kids. I can understand how those things tempt a human being and he falls. What I cannot understand is how a guy who's already got a million dollars defrauds for another hundred thousand . . . that I do not understand at all.'

In a way the real crime was not that people were cheating for an extra few grand, it was really that they were allowed to make the kind of money they were making in the first place. Time and again Giuliani would harp on about other people's multi-million dollar salaries as though he were obsessed. Milken's $550 million salary would be a key issue of the indictment, the hook on which Giuliani would hang Milken, rightly confident that popular opinion would share his money morality. Giuliani also delighted in keeping the score of the investigation. 'We came out ahead on that one and paid for the entire investigation!' he exulted about the $650 million fine he got from Drexel, which exceeded the profits from their biggest year. Add to that the $200 million from Rich, $12 million from Levine, $100 million from Boesky, $25 million from Kidder Peabody, and $600 million from Milken, and you get a grand total of around $1.5 billion. This string of multi-million dollar deals led one writer to comment, 'Giuliani is in the forfeiture business.' This illustrates how pervasive deal-making became in the eighties, the business of justice enjoying a boom no differently than the stock market or the art market. Indeed, Giuliani's Wall Street jihad was one of the most profitable businesses of the eighties.

Money was one of the reasons why Wall Streeters ranked so high in his criminal hierarchy, but there was another. He would normally beg off when asked for psychological insights into what made an insider trade, saying 'I'm not in the touchy feely business' or 'I'm the US Attorney not the US psychiatrist', but on the occasions that he would be drawn his answers were truly revealing. 'It involves the desire for power, status, to have yourself featured in *The Wall Street Journal*, *Business Week*, as the top trader, the guy who makes the firm operate. Just greed wouldn't explain why someone who's making $1 million a year – and already has ten million – gets engaged in insider trading to make another couple of hundred thousand.'

'Inside traders and white-collar criminals are not total criminals, but almost always they are leading two dramatically different lives,' argued Giuliani plausibly in *Vanity Fair*, as if to posit some theory of the schizoid criminal persona. But then he took a radically different line: 'How many of the people we've convicted were featured in big magazine articles?' For someone who answered 'I think I have a relevant mind' when asked if he thought he was intelligent, this was utterly irrelevant. How can someone who was himself featured in big magazine articles have used it as a basis of criminality? But instead of challenging the lack of a necessary connection between the two, Gail Sheehy, the writer of the piece added her own ludicrous gloss: 'His comment brought to mind the unctuous *Business Week* piece that only nine months earlier had canonized Mike Milken as the most important trans-formative figure in American business since J.P. Morgan.'

Sheehy had been seduced. Not by a heady introduction to takeovers on a ride in Boone's or Boesky's jet, but by a rather more down-to-earth joyride in Giuliani's car. What it lacked in the mile-high department it more than made up for in sexiness. Here was Giuliani forsaking the sanctuary of his bullet-proof office and tooling round Little Italy – the headquarters of the under-world – without any body guards and there was she, breathless, 'riding shotgun beside him'.

' "We're right near the Ravenite Social Club now . . . which is Gotti's club in Little Italy."

'I was just beginning to feel like a redneck driving through Beverly Hills with a map to the Homes of the Stars when we pulled alongside the next

Italian restaurant, a sidewalk café. And there, sitting out in the sun, brazen as pigeons in the park, was an assortment of the Boys . . .

' "There's Gotti!" I gasped. "Right there, John Gotti!" '

So remarkable and so thrilling is this whole interlude that we forget, as does she, that if media coverage is a necessary indication of a double life, of a life of crime that lurks beneath the gloss, then Giuliani is equally affected by his own weird logic.

Excited, Giuliani analysed the encounter: 'Didn't he look terrific? What Gotti was doing there is very subtle, a form of charisma and leadership. Like General MacArthur. "The bullets don't hit me," '. Giuliani was utterly starstruck. While Gail Sheehy grovelled before 'heaven's hit man' submitting that Giuliani's ambition was to be no less than 'a messenger of God', I would submit that above all else Giuliani's desire was to be rich and famous. But because his puritan ethics didn't allow that, he went after those whose ethics he thought did, ironically attaining in the process (for such is the nature of our celebrity culture) the wealth and the fame that he secretly always craved.

We have left the Giuliani Three twisting in the wind, which is exactly what Giuliani did to them. Although they were arrested on charges of insider trading the indictment detailing those charges did not come for a further two months. However, instead of copping a plea the three stood firm and insisted on a speedy trial as was their right. The judge upheld their stance and squeezed Giuliani; go to trial now or withdraw the charges. Giuliani dropped the charges. Maintaining that this was 'the tip of the iceberg' he promised a superseding indictment 'in record breaking time'. The fact that Giuliani did not hold the standard press conference suggests that this was more posture than proof. Indeed, two and a half years later all charges against Wigton and Tabor were dropped. In what would come to be remembered as the 'bunny caper' Freeman pleaded guilty to a single count of mail fraud that was almost comic.

'The iceberg turned out to be an ice cube, and even it melts under close scrutiny,' wrote *The Wall Street Journal* in its editorial on the bunny caper. This is what happened; following the announcement of an LBO of Beatrice led by Kohlberg, Kravis & Roberts, arbitrageur Robert Freeman invested heavily in Beatrice stock. But then rumours began to circulate that the deal was in trouble and so Freeman got on the phone and began fishing for information. After speaking with fellow arbitrageur Bernard 'Bunny' Lasker who echoed these rumours, Freeman placed an order to sell his stock. Seeking more confirmation, he next called Henry Kravis at KKR who appropriately refused to comment, but seemed, in their brief conversation, anxious. Then Freeman called Martin Siegel at Kidder Peabody who was working on the deal. When asked by Freeman if the Beatrice deal was in trouble he did not answer directly, but asked who his source was. When Freeman told him that it was Lasker he said, 'Your bunny has a good nose.' He did not disclose any more information and Freeman did not ask him to.

But does the bunny's good nose constitute 'material information' as required by SEC regulations? According to the Supreme Court, materiality is determined by the 'substantial likelihood that the disclosure of the omitted fact would have been viewed by the reasonable investor as having significantly altered the "total mix" of information'. But with the rumours circulating, the bunny's nose was already in the mix. And, quite apart from the immateriality of the rumour's vague confirmation, it turned out to be an inaccurate one at that, since the deal was not in trouble, it was just being tweaked. Neither should we forget that Siegel did not even act on this cryptic tip, since he had already placed his sell order (technically this does not count since possession alone of inside information is against the SEC rules). However, to extricate himself from the crime of acquiescing to inside information after the fact, Freeman should have cancelled his sell order, thus divorcing his actions from the rumours, determinedly making himself an outsider (ironically had he done this and held on to his stock he would have ultimately reaped a greater profit).

Moreover, unlike the clearcut cases of Levine, Boesky and Siegel, there was no quid pro quo arrangement where suitcases of cash were exchanged as payment for information. The helpful thing about such compensation schemes was that they signalled complicity and sealed a defendant's guilt. Boesky paid Levine for the information he bought, indicating that he was aware of its value as inside information as opposed to dross and rumour. Had Freeman been a participant in such a scheme he would not have needed to go fishing for information. In calling round he was really only doing his job. 'By definition arbitrageurs exist to pursue information that is not wholly public in the economic sense of being fully reflected in the price,' *The Wall Street Journal* once explained. 'They trade information as furiously as they trade stocks, forever calling raiders, investment bankers, and takeover lawyers to get the slightest informational edge on their competitors. They walk up to the legal line the SEC has drawn and then lean as far over it as they can.'

But this was not the fault of the arbs, who were the creatures of a market in which 'inside' information was at a premium; as convicted insider trader Foster Winans wrote, 'Wall Street, after all, is about secrets – especially trading secrets . . . Knowledge can be converted on Wall Street into money. The value of knowledge is inversely diminished by the number of people who have access to it. In other words the only reason to invest in the market is because you think you know something others don't. . . . This is the central psychology of the market.'

Small wonder, then, that the judge on Freeman's case found the way the arbitrage market functioned was almost criminal (the judge admitted that with Freeman he was unable to find much in the way of premeditated criminality).

More specifically the arbs were the Frankenstein creations of the regulators, of Harrison Williams who sponsored the Williams Act and who, shortly thereafter, was exposed as a criminal (in an interesting coincidence Brady took his place). Because a raider had to declare his holdings and his intentions within ten days of crossing the 5 per cent line, arbs came in to play as friendly share gatherers who, because they were only in it for the money, could be relied upon to sell their shares to the raider at the right time and for the right price. Given this origin of the species, the arbs were as vulnerable to criminal temptation as they were to the regulators who abhorred their bastard progeny. As *The Wall Street Journal* explained, arbs were in a precarious position with the SEC who 'in recent years . . . seem to think that anyone who had any more information than anyone else is a criminal.' As *Fortune* put it, 'The SEC keeps moving the line.'

The problem was that insider trading is one of the most ill-defined crimes on record. In fact it is not even on the statute books, since Congress has never passed a law specifically prohibiting it, much less defining it. However, at the SEC's request it gave teeth to the punishment of the offence on two occasions. In 1984 the Insider Trading Sanctions Act increased the civil penalty to triple profits (or triple the loss avoided) and a criminal fine of up to $100,000. Then, in 1988, they doubled the maximum jail term to ten years, increased to $1 million the maximum fine and authorized the SEC to reward informers.

Passing laws specifying the punishment to fit the crime, when Congress has not first defined the crime, seemed surreal. But what seemed like madness at first blush was cool calculation. As Senator Tim Wirth explained, 'Congress has been wrestling with this for three or four years. Many of us have wanted to leave this area deliberately ambiguous . . . I'd rather live in a situation where that ambiguity is out there and management of companies and raiders of companies are a little bit afraid of that, afraid that there may be an ambitious District Attorney out there in some way shape or form, so therefore they are going to stay within that ambiguity.' This would appear to be the regulators' answer to the way Wall Street managed to run around its clear cut rules.

Those who dared, like the arbs, could venture into this mined no-man's land at their own risk. But they had only the SEC regulations to guide them, and they were an inaccurate map of where the mines were in the field at any one moment. Three cautionary tales will illustrate the treacherous quirkiness of the rules.

On a tip-off investment analyst Ray Dirks came into possession of inside information about Equity Funding, an insurance company that was cooking the books, concocting bogus policies and making mafia-like threats to anyone who threatened to expose the fraud. Dirks reported this to the SEC but was hauled into court because he first alerted his clients who traded on this inside information.

Then there was *Wall Street Journal* writer Foster Winans who wrote a business gossip column called 'Heard on the Street'. Although the column contained no material inside information that was not accessible to anyone with initiative and a telephone, the column did have an impact on the stocks included in it. Unlike the column's first writer back in the twenties who turned a $2,500 loan into $3 million, Winans never invested in any of the stocks he wrote about, and earned a measly $28,000 a year for writing the column. Seduced by the line 'Wouldn't you like to be millionaire?' he would sometimes, in return for a small share of the profits, disclose the column's contents to a Kidder Peabody broker prior to publication. Although Winans was defrauding the *Journal* by retailing information that belonged to them because they had paid him to gather it, he was hardly insider trading. But thanks to a fresh look at the rules which had been expanded to include trading on misappropriated or stolen information (regardless of whether it was inside or outside information), he was convicted.

Or take football coach Barry Switzer who overheard an oil executive talking with his wife about a takeover at a race meeting. Switzer was the target of rule 14e-3, which made it illegal for anyone with inside information about a takeover to trade stock. To be in violation of this rule they didn't even have to get the information directly from an insider. They simply had to 'know or have reason to know' that it came from an insider.

'Where do you stop the criminal process in the tippee chain?' someone once asked Giuliani at a seminar on insider trading. Jokingly Giuliani had opened the event by observing that the Chinese had cut crime in half by doubling the number of executions. When asked if the hairdresser of the mistress of the chairman who traded on a tip was an insider trader (and who therefore deserved to be beheaded), Giuliani again joked that he thought it would make a good book but that he wasn't sure it would make a good criminal case.

For all the banter, clearly the lack of clarity gave the SEC unlimited reach. As Shad once put it bluntly, 'We are the judge, jury and prosecutor.' Giuliani was right behind this prosecutorial omnipotence. In support of Tim Wirth's championing of the vagaries of the rules Giuliani, who was obviously 'the ambitious DA out there' (especially since he was at the time sitting only a few feet away from Wirth in a television studio), quipped 'If you guess wrong you'll get sued, and if you deliberately guess wrong you'll get indicted.' And, if Giuliani had his way, maybe you got your head chopped off too.

Taking the rules in concert with the creativity with which they were enforced, it is small wonder that not many people knew – least of all the so-called market professionals who were supposed to know – what insider trading was. Of 121 stockbrokers surveyed in 1988, 84 per cent erroneously believed that it was defined by Federal law. The general public fared little better. In 1986, at the beginning of the entire scandal, an opinion poll asked people if they would trade on an inside tip that the company they worked for was going to be taken over, only 39 per cent said that they would not. Of this group only just over half thought that it would be wrong, illegal or that they would get caught. The rest only decided not to because they feared that the tip might be wrong. One law firm that prepared a memo for its staff on insider trading laws consisted of four pages of illegal activities as against twenty-five pages of indeterminables.

Even the courts seem confused. As Judge Sweet, who sentenced one of Levine's co-conspirators to a year and a day in jail for insider trading (even though he never took a dime for the information he passed on), later explained to *Esquire* magazine, 'Right now the laws on the books say that the public has to believe that the markets are fair, and in order to sustain that faith, there has to be no information passed on that is not yet public information . . . somewhere there is a line over which we do not cross.' Precisely what laws or where that line might be he did not care to specify. However he did offer, in this portentous vagary, that the accused had been seduced and 'confused illusion and reality', and in the courtroom he rhapsodized on what he saw as 'the crux of the matter', namely, 'that element in the world that has abandoned all that we used to cherish – integrity and honesty – an element that ignores reality and the law of the land, an element which exalts form and discards substance, which is only for apearance, and the appearance is success'. No need, then, for precise definitions. Insider trading was the shibboleth for the cultural revolution that was the transition from the industrial age to the information age. Sweet came down on the West Coast dream-based spectacle and futurism, and instead harked back to good old-fashioned East-Coast values of history, reality and substance.

PLEAS PLEASE

But in the case of Freeman this does not explain why a man convinced of his innocence would plead guilty.

All an investment banker has is his reputation for integrity in the eyes of the public. Mob figures don't have that reputation and don't care. They trade in a different kind of respectability. In fact they expect to be arrested, indicted, and called gangsters. But for an investment banker to be so treated is to destroy him. When Giuliani claimed that he would not change the handcuff rules for people who thought they were too rich or too important, he was in fact making a special example out of them, and drastically changing the spirit while technically keeping within the letter of the rules. He knew that headlines that would make a mobster smirk would destroy an investment banker's most precious asset, his reputation. Showmen like Boesky were exceptions. To most people on Wall Street (and the public in general), publicity – especially adverse publicity – was like a stake through the heart. If Giuliani cared more about making headlines than making cases (as *The Wall Street Journal* accused), it was because headlines were more effective than cases. Within this context pleading guilty was to be preferred to guaranteeing more destructive headlines by insisting on a trial that would be excruciatingly public, and a trial which even if it ended in acquittal could not reverse the taint of conviction from the trial by media.

The same factors that most likely swayed Freeman could usually be counted on to yield a great deal more. 'Insider traders are just another set of hoodlums. With one difference – they roll much easier,' said Giuliani. In Giulianispeak rolling didn't mean just giving in, it meant co-operation – making tapped phone calls to their friends like Levine, wearing a wire like Boesky, or incriminating their colleagues like Siegel. Rolling was doubly humiliating because no one was forced to roll. Rollers only did so to save themselves. It was a tawdry transaction of self-prostitution that finally robbed the roller of any remnant of integrity. In the eyes of the public it was, where trading crimes are complex abstracts lacking any kind of moral dimension, an act of such self-incrimination that nothing more condemning was needed. 'By and large people do not co-operate with my office because they're good citizens and want to further democracy and an ethical marketplace. People co-operate with my office because they have to in order to benefit themselves. Therefore, it has to be known that you get certain benefits for co-operating,' explained Giuliani. What he was really saying, when we strip away the politesse, is that 'rollers are scum, because they roll. Reluctantly we have to pay these whores because of our larger agenda.' This was the core of the plea bargaining arrangement.

But in terms of a pure – if romantically naive – notion of justice, it was a deeply flawed system. It unfairly privileged the people who least deserved it, at the expense of marginal offenders who most qualified for mercy. The guiltiest had both the greatest motivation to try and protect themselves from the consequences of their crimes and the most material with which to trade in order to soften the effect of the law. The people they traded in were often those less guilty than themselves, and who had little with which to shield themselves from the full brunt of the law. In the case of Foster Winans, the *Wall Street Journal* reporter, it was Kidder Peabody broker Peter Brant who profited more than Winans (reported to have got less than 5 per cent of the booty). But Brant became the government's star witness and was never indicted. Siegel, who would appear to have had the least to offer, gained the most. He only got two months. In contrast Freeman, whom Siegel shopped, got four. Thus plea bargaining as a system is also vulnerable to exploitation. Since white-collar criminals would do anything to keep themselves out of jail, it is not too hard to imagine someone selling third-rate information to the government as prime stuff to try and extricate himself from the ghastly web of the criminal system. Siegel in his desperation to reduce his sentence may have sold the Justice Department a bill of goods when it came to the Giuliani Three. It certainly looks that way.

But more than this, the cornucopia of information provided by Levine and Boesky led the government to believe and declare that they had uncovered a Wall Street-wide conspiracy of corruption. The dynamics of a plea leading to further convictions gave the impression of a row of falling dominoes, each more important than the last, leading to the kingpin. But the fact that Levine and Boesky could provide such a wealth of material signified that they were the kingpins of their respective conspiracies.

Later, much later, Michael Armstrong, who was Milken's brother's lawyer, confronted one of the government's attorneys with the theory that Boesky was the kingpin who had conned the government into believing that Milken was Mr Big. According to *Esquire* magazine, instead of a direct answer Armstrong was told, sheepishly, 'Well, have you ever known anyone to lie about everything?' However, there was no recourse for the government here since they had already made their deals with Boesky and Levine, who were thus virtually immunized from further prosecution. But at the same time, as *Business Week* so delicately put it, the government had 'invested mammoth resources' and had its prestige on the line as a result of having gone public with their 'inflated idée fixe' and 'richly limned image' of Wall Street malpractice. Thus the government 'had to go forward even when its findings didn't fully bear out its preconceptions.' This meant that the investigation was in the back-to-front position of having to go out and find the villains of the piece even though they already had them under lock and key. (This would lead to the criticism that the prosecution was 'a criminal case in search of a crime. To call the Milken matter a "fishing expedition" defames fishermen, who, Captain Ahab aside, do not usually seek one specific fish,' wrote the Dean of the George Mason law school.)

Nevertheless the government was utterly dependent on this deal-making. For the ease with which they could get a nice white-collar defendant to roll was in inverse proportion to the ease of winning a conviction in court. The effort and expense of a trial were tremendous and the outcome was far from certain. It was much easier to persuade a suspect to deny his own constitutional right of a free trial than it was meet the burden of proof that a trial would demand. 'There's a realistic chance that Boesky never would've been convicted had he not agreed to plead guilty,' Giuliani once admitted. 'I believe we would have made a good case on him, but I can't tell you how good the case would've been.'

The slow pace of the legal system within the six-year time frame of the statute of limitations was an additional reason for preferring the plea bargaining short-cut. 'If he was convicted it would've happened two years from now. Many of the leads the government had to obtain for other convictions would've evaporated.' The ability to move on these leads was absolutely vital to fulfill the government's announced agenda of rooting out the 'systemic corruption that undermines the financial world'. With every roller and each new deal they gave the impression of exposing the grand conspiracy as they had said they would.

In this context Freeman's plea can be seen as a face-saving compromise on both sides. That Freeman should have been allowed to plead guilty to only one minor count must have sugared the pill. It also shows that the government could not let him plead guilty to anything less. After all the braggadocio about icebergs, the fact that they had only been able to pull one bunny count out of the hat was humiliating enough. But having given Siegel a sweetheart deal, they needed to win a conviction based on his testimony to justify their leniency with him. A conviction, however slight, was also necessary in the wider agenda of the vast conspiracy that they had vowed publicly to uncover. So far the dominoes, from Levine to Boesky to Siegel, had kept falling. But they couldn't stop now. They did their level best to win as stiff a conviction as possible, going so far as to present to the judge, after Freeman's plea, a hundred-page pre-sentencing memo supposedly packed with details of other crimes. The judge refused to take it into consideration.

So much for Freeman. Aside from their reputations Wigton and Tabor both lost their jobs. 'I will certainly never again read about someone being prosecuted and assume the government is right and they are guilty,' said Wigton. Reminded of the debacle at the time he was runing for mayor, Giuliani conceded, 'It was a mistake to use the handcuffs.' Wigton responded, 'I hear he has said he regrets the arrest, but that wasn't on the front page, I was on the front page.'

Generally, Giuliani's strategy was remarkably effective. As Leuci, the corrupt cop turned whistle-blower, commended him, 'He knows what he's doing is a close call, but it works. By the time Rudy is ready to move, he is 100 per cent sure. It's his ball, his bat, he sells the pop corn, the ball game is about over. All you have left to do is dance off to prison.'

With its plea-bargaining pressures, trophy-oriented press conferences and multi-million dollar fines, Giuliani's office promoted its own brand of justice that didn't seem to care about being presumed innocent until you were proven guilty. Justice was a deal. When as a child Giuliani had been falsely accused he was outraged until he rationalized that it probably made up for all the times he hadn't been caught. No matter that the lives of these three people had been irrevocably damaged, these Wall Street millionaires probably got what they deserved. If the Wall Street Three had been falsely accused this time, it probably made up for all the other times they had gotten away with it, even if all 'it' was was being guilty of earning too much money or being featured in glossy magazines. Cross-examined about the Boesky deal, Giuliani had said, 'The end result will make a great deal of sense once it becomes public.' With this assurance, that the ends would justify the means, his department had become as organized as organized crime. It was a giant rolling machine which, once its dynamics had been perfected, would lumber on virtually unstoppable.

In the meantime there were other fish to fry, other deals to make.

Although Kidder's chairman had wanted to fight the government's charges, even offering to contribute to the cost of their defence himself, he had assured General Electric (Kidder Peabody's new owner) that they had nothing to fear from Giuliani's industry-wide purge. As one might expect of one of America's biggest corporations, GE wanted no embarrassment, and in a kind of judicial greenmail, they bought protection from an indictment of the entire firm of Kidder Peabody by paying a $25 million fine. The chairman was reshuffled into obscurity. A month before this settlement Gail Sheehy asked Giuliani if he'd made the choice not to indict Kidder or Goldman Sachs as companies because he had a larger agenda in mind. 'He hesitated but finally answered "Yes"'.

All this was just a taste of things to come.

10

THE RICOTEERS

THE US Attorney's office, who had promised that the Handcuff Three was just the tip of the iceberg, thought they had found the rest of the underwater morass in Princeton Newport Trading Partners, a relatively small trading firm based in Princeton, New Jersey, and Newport Beach, California. It was run by Jay Regan and Edward Thorp. Thorp, a friend of Milken's and an investor in several of his partnerships, was also a former MIT maths professor and had found a way, as the title of his book *Beat The Dealer* suggested, to do just that. 'All those guys at the casino counting cards, we found an even better way,' he told Jesse Kornbluth. Having read the book, Jay Regan (who had been Freeman's roommate in college) persuaded Thorp to turn his academic ideas into a money-making reality. Through a complex pattern of computer-developed trading patterns, Princeton Newthorp created an effective market hedge where the potential for profit was protected from the risk of loss. By trading in bulk they turned microscopic opportunities into handsome profits, giving their investors a consistent 20 per cent return, and Regan alone taking home $4 million a year.

Since 1984 strategic tax trades had also become a part of the winning formula. In this arrangement securities were sold to a willing participant who, after the necessary thirty-one-day period had elapsed for bookkeeping purposes, sold them back to Princeton Newport. By doing this they avoided holding stocks over a long-term position, which gave them a tax advantage. There was nothing furtive about these trades, they were a part of company policy. In the unlikely event the SEC decided that these trades constituted the offence of stock 'parking', where a holding party held securities in order to hide true ownership, they would simply recalculate Princeton Newport's tax bill, and maybe throw in a fine to discourage them from doing it again. This was what they had done in the past, when they had decided that certain trades were 'sham' or 'wash' trades. Indeed stock parking had never before been prosecuted as a criminal offence. Regan, who kept an annotated volume of the tax code in his office, didn't think he was violating the law, just working with the tax code.

But based on the grand jury testimony of William Hale, who had executed the trades at Princeton Newport, the Attorney's office took a different view. On 17 December 1987, armed and wearing bullet-proof vests, fifty Federal marshals raided the offices of Princeton Newport Partners, carting away boxes of tapes containing routine recordings of trades.

That same evening in the Sherman Oaks suburb of Los Angeles, a criminal investigator for the US Attorney's office waited for Lisa Jones to get home. Jones, then 24, was a junior assistant trader for Bruce Newberg who worked on the 'X' in Drexel's high yield bond department. Newberg reported directly to Milken. Hence their interest in Jones who had been deputized to handle the tax trades with William Hale at Princeton Newthorp. Nervously she began to answer the investigator's questions, before clamming up and insisting on speaking with her lawyer. Taking his leave the investigator handed her a grand jury sub-poena. 'We were hoping you would be willing to co-operate with us in this investigation,' he said, 'I know you're just an Indian like me. The government is just interested in the people who told you to do this.' And then he left. After he had gone, and convinced that her place was bugged, she hopped in her car and called the only lawyer she knew, Kevin Madigan, Milken's hand-picked compliance officer. He calmed her down, told her to go home and write down everything that had happened. This she did, staying up all night.

William Hale and Lisa Jones were similar in that they were both small fry that Giuliani's office wanted to roll in order to get to 'Mr Big'. There the similarity ends, although both their stories are sad.

William Hale was born William Turner and changed his name to William Warm for a brief spell before settling with Hale. He was as unable to settle on a job as he was on a name. By the time he had been recruited by the government as a star witness in their rolling campaign, he had worked for five securities firms, the last with Salomon Brothers in London where Michael Lewis, author of *Liar's Poker*, remembered him as a Big Swinging Dick Wannabee. He seemed to have the chutzpah. In the box where he was supposed to fill in his desired salary on one application form he simply wrote 'The Sky'. And he certainly had the mouth. 'How do you tell the difference between a Jew and an Ethiopian Jew? The Ethiopian Jew wears his Rolex round his waist' was supposed to have been a favourite. When challenged in court about his language he replied, 'That's Wall Street,' but it was too blue even for the Street where he bounced from firm to firm, ending up at Princeton Newport where Regan gave him the no-talent job of making the tax trades. But even there 'He couldn't get along with people. He had fights with his superiors.' As the firm's defence lawyers argued in court, 'He used obscene foul language that he was warned about. He just couldn't develop the kind of relationships necessary for this business, and so after fourteen months he was fired.'

When contacted by the US Attorney's office in London the Big Swinging

Dick was once again unemployed and hanging loose. He hired as a lawyer a good friend of Giuliani's and struck a deal granting him immunity. He then claimed that he had been let go by Princeton Newport because he was 'not comfortable with a lot of the things they were involved in'. He also claimed to have complained about the tax trades to his boss at the time.

The other part of his Grand Jury testimony concerned his Drexel partner in these trades, Lisa Jones, and was instrumental in winning the government their first conviction by trial in the insider trading case. However, Jones was not convicted for insider trading, stock parking or tax fraud. She was convicted of perjury. Given that Jones's troubled background had made her as compulsive a liar as Hale was a swearer, this was a pyrrhic victory.

Lisa Jones had grown up in New Jersey, but ran away from home when she was 14. In LA she got a job as a bank teller by lying about her age. Her mother advertised her disappearance on television. When she was 17 she started work at Drexel, claiming that she had graduated from Fernlyn Prep, a school she invented, and that she was enrolled at Pierce College (which does exist but where she only completed one course on Philosophy and the Occult). But although Lisa Jones lied to survive in her new world and escape her past, she did not, like Ivan Boesky, thrive on outrageous self-invention. When asked why, having failed her licensing exam three times, she had lied on her tax form by claiming that she was a stockbroker she said, 'I just wanted to be like everybody else.' Pushed to be more precise in a television interview she began to cry and mumbled through the tears, 'People who come from supportive families, who graduate from high school, and go to college and have husbands and a car and everything, those were the things I didn't have.'

In her boyfriend's parents she found an adoptive family.She was engaged to be married to him but he was a PCP addict, and when he emerged from a detoxification clinic he broke off the engagement. Thereafter Drexel became her family. Her boss Bruce Newberg she saw as a surrogate father-figure and she adored Milken. When she bumped into him in an Encino restaurant she proudly introduced him to everyone. Although colleagues remembered her as shy and difficult to get to know, she would often perform kindnesses such as cooking and babysitting for the divorced men in the department.

She also dedicated herself to her work, performing meticulously under pressure. Because of this Newberg put her in charge of supervising what he called some special 'programmed trading' with Hale at Princeton Newport. Her salary was $13,000 in her first year. By 1986 she was making over $100,000 a year. In 1987 Drexel sent her to London to help open a trading desk and train trading assistants.

With this background it was less surprising that she should lie to protect both the people she worked for and the life that she had made for herself. In her Grand Jury testimony, unaware that Hale was a co-operating witness who had already told them all about the trades, and unaware that they also had their daily conversations on tape, she perjured herself by denying that she ever made the trades in question, and was supposed to have lied 150 times. (Although she could never deny doing the trades or using the term 'parking' it was quite possible she had no idea that it was illegal. When she was hired as a trading assistant she didn't even know what a trading assistant did. And as she later claimed, 'No one pulled me aside and said this is an illegal activity . . . it was just part of everyday trading.')

The government was offering her their standard deal of immunity from prosecution, but only if she told the truth. However, from the evening the prosecutor came to visit her, the entire investigation threw her into a blind panic, making her all but incapable of rational thought. The life she had built for herself, albeit on lies, was everything to her, and like a child she clung to it, even when it was foolish to continue to do so instead of taking the government's offer.

In this she may have been ill-advised by her lawyers who were provided by Drexel, and who first and foremost represented Drexel's interests. Whether or not they encouraged her in this she naively believed that Drexel, in whom she had placed her all emotionally, would reciprocate by rescuing her. But even though Drexel continued to pay her salary and bonus and even hired a ballroom in which they held trial trials, they could not legally provide her with the emotional rescue she felt she deserved.

But was she 'an innocent working girl too young and too confused to save herself from going to prison, or . . . a greedy opportunist who refused to confess to the crimes of her bosses', as television personality Connie Chung tantalizingly put it in her exclusive on the story. The government thought the latter. 'She was up to her eyeballs in illegal conduct,' said prosecutor Mark Hansen who said that all she was asked to do was 'tell us the truth and you'll walk away. But it meant giving up things that meant too much to her and unfortunately, as we told the jury, those things amounted to money and luxury.' Although Giuliani's rolling machine had managed to make their case against Princeton Newport and Bruce Newberg without Jones's help, they decided, nevertheless, to make her an example of what happened to people who didn't co-operate. Lisa Jones's subsequent trial for perjury was a public hanging.

'There's a place for big fish and a place for little fish,' said Hansen who relished gutting this guppy. In his prosecution he vivisected Jones's life of lies so mercilessly that one laywer who witnessed the examination said that it made him sick to his stomach.

On the stand Jones's voice was barely audible and she seemed disoriented, almost paralysed with the terror that paralyses rabbits when caught in the headlights of a car. She drifted towards perjury and seemed not to know even the simplest of things.

'Do you have a recollection of whether you ever went to California State University at Northridge?'

'I don't know,' she replied.

'You can't recall whether you ever went there?' sneered the incredulous Hansen.

She claimed she had been to school there, but when Hansen produced a record from the school indicating the contrary she finally backed down. When then asked, somewhat rhetorically, if she had known whether she had been there when she had told the Grand Jury that she had, she answered, 'I guess I thought I did. I don't know.'

As the government investigator, who sub-poenaed every single document pertaining to Jones's life especially for this character assassination, exulted, 'It was like taking each layer of her personality apart.' Jones herself afterwards said that she felt that Hansen was trying to murder her. When later confronted by Connie Chung who asked him if he had not been out for blood instead of justice, 'Sometimes in the search for justice blood gets spilled,' Hansen shrugged with characteristic warmth.

But sometimes in the search for press people get fired. By the time of the trial in March 1989 Giuliani had left and the Attorney's office, under Obermaier, was no longer a press whore's paradise. Unmindful of the change Hansen neglected to ask his boss for permission to give the interview. 'It was not excellent judgement on the young man's part,' said Obermaier, and Hansen was fired. Lisa Jones was sentenced to eighteen months (later reduced to ten) which was half Boesky's sentence and four times that of her boss Bruce Newberg, who had instructed her to do the trades.

At Princeton Newport the man who had delegated the controversial trades to Hale was called Paul Berkman. In a meeting in early 1988 Assistant US Attorney Bruce Baird was supposed to have told his lawyer, 'We have no real interest in Princeton Newport, but through Berkman we can get Regan, and through Regan we can get Drexel Burnham and others. We have bigger fish to fry and we will roll over you to get where we want to go.' In an interview with Jesse Kornbluth Baird later denied the comment, although he did add as clarification that 'There's no point in forcing a trial no one wants' and expressed surprise at the lack of negotiational dialogue that would normally have led to a mutually beneficial settlement. Under normal circumstances the government would have won its trophy conviction and multi-million dollar pay-off to add to its collection, while Princeton Newport, although tarnished, would have lived to fight another day. But Princeton Newport, convinced that the tax trades were legitimate, were unapologetic. 'The defence said, "The hell with the government,"' said Baird. In response the government said the hell with Princeton Newport and added new meaning to 'roll over', which they did to Princeton Newport with a steamroller.

The steamroller they rolled out was a law called RICO, the Racketeer Influenced and Corrupt Organizations Act.

Milken was just starting out on Wall Street in 1970 when, as part of Nixon's law and order package, a senator sponsored a bill that he promised would be 'a major new tool in extirpating the baleful influence of organized crime in our economic life'. It was designed to root out the weeds of illegitimate business from the field of legitimate business. As the preamble stated, 'The Congress finds that (1) organized crime in the United States is a highly sophisticated, diversified and widespread activity that annually drains billions of dollars from America's economy by unlawful conduct and the illegal use of force, fraud, corruption; (2) organized crime derives a major portion of its power through money obtained from such illegal endeavours as syndicated gambling, loan sharking, the theft and fencing of property, the importation and distribution of narcotics and other dangerous drugs, and other forms of social exploitation; (3) this money and power are increasingly used to infiltrate and corrupt legal businesses and labour unions and to subvert and corrupt our democratic processes.' The piece concluded that 'organized crime continues to grow because ... the sanctions and remedies available to the government are unnecessarily limited in scope and impact.'

To remedy this, RICO provided stiff prison sentences and penalties for people found to be racketeers. A conviction on each RICO count carried a ten-year jail sentence. In terms of penalties the government could exact triple damages, recover legal fees from attorneys defending racketeers, and seize any property connected with the convicted, no matter how remotely. Neither did it have to wait until after a trial to take them. On the assumption that organized crime infiltrated legitimate business merely as a front, it seemed prudent to provide for a pre-trial seizure of assets to prevent their overnight disappearance, so that once there was a conviction there would be money to pay the fines. Wall Street, innocently believing that the law would only ever be used against the influence of illegitimate business, on its own legitimate business was particularly enthusiastic.

But how do you define a racketeer? RICO identified a racketeer as someone who engaged in 'a pattern of racketeering activity'. Racketeering activities ran the gamut from murder, kidnapping and drug dealing to mail fraud, wire fraud and securities fraud. A pattern of racketeering could be almost as long as a piece of string. Anything from a hail of bullets fired over a ten-second period to a phone call one day and a letter a decade later could be deemed to constitute a racketeering pattern.

The inclusion of mail fraud and wire fraud as possible predicate acts was fateful. As one former prosecutor has observed, 'To Federal prosecutors of white collar-crime, the mail fraud statute is our Stradivarius, our Colt 45, our Louisville Slugger, our Cuisinart – and our true love.' Since the intent to deceive can constitute fraud and since virtually no business is done in America today without using the wire or mail services of the United States government (phone, fax, letter, telex, modem), one need not even commit a crime in order to have committed the predicate acts necessary to trigger a RICO indictment. Securities fraud was added only at the last minute in the final passage of the bill, and was done so to cover the increasing presence of the mafia in the financial markets.

At the time there were a few dissenting voices. If RICO was broadly written in the innocent assumption that it would be responsibly used, the then director of the American Civil Liberties Union complained of 'a serious danger that the government's zeal in the pursuit of organized crime may result in a pervasive undermining of important civil liberties . . . to the detriment of us all', and he imagined cases 'in areas far removed from what we know as organized crime'. Dismissed at the time, his remarks have since proved to be prophetic.

Giuliani defiantly defended RICO's powers: 'It is a needed weapon because it allows the government to deal with enterprise crime, as an enterprise. In other words, in the past if you were going to have to deal with this criminal cartel you would have to deal with it on a piecemeal basis, prosecute Al Capone for tax evasion . . . prosecute somebody for dealing in prostitution. You can do that forever and you are still not attacking organized crime . . . as a business and trying to roll it back . . . I think it has been very effective in dealing with organized criminal activity, including financial fraud.' By quietly changing the specific noun of organized crime into the broader adjective of organized criminal activity, he deftly opened an umbrella under which he could include financial fraud.

By this subtle shift he demonstrated how the wording of RICO allowed for a rainbow of interpretations and applications. 'There aren't two consecutive words in the RICO statute that aren't under some sort of dispute. You feel like you're back in the seventeenth century,' complained one critic of Robert Blakey, the law professor who wrote RICO. 'Blakey is knowledgeable about a lot of things, but he is not a person who believes you solve a problem by simplifying things.' Blakey did not appreciate the attacks, muttering darkly about vampires trying to grab the virginal throat of his statute. But if he was unrepentant about his ambiguities it was perhaps because he made a nice living as the foremost expert on RICO, providing expert testimony on its true meaning and arguing civil suits from both sides. Maintaining that 'I have no real ambition . . . most of what I've done has been on the merits,' Blakey threw up a smokescreen when probed about his on-the-side earnings, telling one journalist, 'If I remembered [how much I made] I would probably tell you. No, I probably wouldn't tell you. But I wouldn't try to hide it from you.' In another law case he once argued that he had mastered a theory of language predicated upon 'eight universal constraints of discourse' from which he could deduce the 'intrinsic' from the 'extrinsic' context and thus divine the true meaning of someone's words, even if the utterer thought they were saying something completely different.

This serene faith in his eccentric abilities was an appropriate frame for his comments on RICO, which, he claimed, was always intended to be used above and beyond organized crime. 'The remarkable thing about the Drexel-related cases is not that they were conceptualized as RICO but that similar cases have not been brought in the past.' Making the popular equation

between mobsters and investment bankers he once wrote, 'Victims of crime
. . . rightly care little that their life savings are stolen by mobsters wearing
black shirts and white ties or by accountants while dressed in Brooks Brothers
suits and white collars.' Of Milken he said, 'Mike Milken made $550 million
in one year . . . nobody else made that much in the history of the country
except Al Capone. What did he do? He cheated. What was Milken doing? He
cheated. Of course Capone stole and killed to do it.' Capone's murderous
habits are acknowledged as an afterthought, as mere nuance.

It speaks volumes that the name of the act, RICO, was an acronym of the
character played by Edward G. Robinson in the classic gangster movie *Little
Caesar*. Talking about the movie, Blakey warmed to his theme: 'If you look at
Little Caesar as an effort to understand the rise of organized crime in the
United States,' he said as though we should, 'you see that it perceives only
half the problem . . . but in his rise to the top of organized crime, Rico
Bendello apes the techniques of legitimate business. In an important scene,
he's fitted for his first formal suit, the one he'll wear when he sees "Mr Big",
the businessman who lives in the beautiful house on the hill.'

Giuliani's department may also have been watching too many gangster
movies, – they nicknamed Milken 'Mr Big'. More than this, Giuliani's
'Securities Fraud Unit was so woefully neglected and understaffed that major
responsibility for the new cases developed upon people recently transferred
from the narcotics unit who, by their own admission, "did not know a stock
from a bond," ' complained a group of former prosecutors who banded
together to denounce Giuliani's rule. Giuliani himself had attended Blakey's
seminars on RICO and, having used it with tremendous success to scalp the
mafia (and commodities broker Marc Rich), now turned it on Wall Street,
choosing to make an example out of an unco-operative Princeton Newport.

Given the fact that RICO allowed for the pre-trial seizure of assets, the
threat of the law could be extremely persuasive in encouraging recalcitrant
businesses to co-operate. After all, the primary asset of an investment bank or
securities firm was its capital, which it needed to keep liquid in order to be
able to function and do business on a day-to-day basis. To freeze this capital
in a RICO attack would be the equivalent of a pre-strike nuclear burst, and
would knock the company out in an instant.

Even the mere threat of a RICO indictment without an asset freeze could
prove fatal. Given that most of a financial house's capital is borrowed, it is
utterly dependent upon its reputation for legitimacy and integrity to maintain
those loans. To be branded a racketeer by the government's application of a
law usually reserved for the mob inevitably undermines that reputation. In
such an eventuality investors (who are known for being nervous about their
money) could be understood for taking their funds elsewhere.

This is but one more example of how the prosecutors who did not know a
stock from a bond also cared not to know the difference between a mobster

and a trader, and that the purpose of this patently false equation was to persecute the latter.

Indeed the mob, which was in no way dependent upon these niceties of perception to do its business, revelled in the thought that because RICO was concerned with the presence of organized crime in legitimate business, it did not apply to them. Law writer Gordon Crovitz quoted this one hilarious instance:

Gangster 1 'Our argument is we're illegitimate business,'
Gangster 2 'We're a shylock.'
Gangster 1 'We're a shylock.'
Gangster 2 'Yeah.'
Gangster 1 'We're a [expletive] bookmaker.'
Gangster 2 'Bookmaker.'
Gangster 1 'We're selling marijuana.'
Gangster 2 'We're not infiltrating.'
Gangster 1 'We're illegal here, illegal there . . . we're every [expletive] thing.'
Gangster 2 'Pimps.'
Gangster 1 'So what?'
Gangster 2 'Prostitutes.'
Gangster 1 'The law does not cover us, is that right?'
Gangster 2 'We're not infiltrating legitimate businesses.'
Gangster 1 'I wouldn't be in a legitimate business for all the [expletive] money in the world.'

Aware that RICO could be used by one zealot as another might use a nuclear bomb in a holy war, the Justice Department had published in 1981 a four-hundred-page volume of guidelines for Federal prosecutors thinking of unleashing RICO. Creative uses of RICO were expressly argued against. 'It is not the policy of the Criminal Division to approve "imaginative" prosecutions under RICO which are far afield from the congressional purpose of the statute.' There were other restrictions too, recommending that it should not be used to encourage a plea bargain, to coerce testimony, or be used in mail fraud, tax fraud, or securities cases, and that the pre-trial forfeiture of assets should be strictly limited to cases where their disappearance was likely.

In addition to these guidelines each application of RICO had to be cleared by the Justice Department. Although Giuliani made much ado about this, claiming that it was no rubber stamp, he obviously knew how to petition them.

'I have always prided myself on the imaginative qualities Federal prosecutors have brought to their tasks,' Attorney General Dick Thornburgh once announced at a press conference with Rudy Giuliani present. As well he might. Giuliani's use of RICO had discomfited Thornburgh's predecessor, Attorney General Edward Meese. As part of the Wedtech investigation, Giuliani had ricoed lawyer Robert Wallach, who was one of Meese's closest friends. He used as predicate acts two letters Wallach had mailed to a company that purported to be bills for legal services when they were in fact for services rendered in lobbying his friend Meese. Not that lobbying, or billing for it, is illegal. Nevertheless, Wallach's RICO indictment and conviction (which was overturned on appeal), as well as the Wedtech investigation as a whole, contributed to Meese's resignation.

What could stand in Giuliani's way? He was swept along with such huge public support (rumours were rife that he would run for mayor and the feeling was that it was his for the taking), who was going to risk political suicide by taking a stand?

THE WORLD OF SLEAZE

On 4 August 1988 the five partners of Princeton Newport and Bruce Newberg from Drexel were indicted on RICO charges. The predicate acts originally were the mail fraud and wire fraud involved in the 'parking' of stocks. When asked by the judge to produce a victim of these acts, and when the prosecutors could not, these charges were discounted, leaving alleged tax violations as the necessary predicate acts. Seeing a glimmer of hope to derail the RICO bandwagon, the defendants invoked the guidelines. But the prosecution simply brushed them aside, arguing that 'internal Department of Justice policies provide no substantive rights to defendants' and that 'even the violation of such internal guidelines would provide no basis for dismissal of otherwise valid charges.'

On the day of the indictment the prosecutors moved to seize all $1 billion of Princeton Newport's assets. 'There was a corny paragraph saying the business would be able to operate normally,' Regan's lawyer recalled. Finally, after a full day's wrangling and in the early hours of the following morning, agreement was reached that Princeton Newport would post a $14 million bond. The prosecution also let it be known that there would be a superseding indictment with more charges and, possibly, more forfeitures. The spectre of this hanging over the firm caused the firm's credit to be cut by $500 million, and for investors to withdraw their funds.

When the superseding indictment finally came it contained little that was new, but by this stage it was too late. In the first week of December 1988 Princeton Newport collapsed. A bitter press release read, 'The government has now accomplished the goal it set out to achieve when it commenced the investigation – co- operate or be destroyed.' It had taken twenty years to build up the firm and it employed seventy-five people. When it came to break up bust up shut down, RICO was vastly more efficient than junk bonds. It also made a mockery of the fundamental idea of being presumed innocent until proven guilty since the pre-trial liquidation of Princeton Newport was the punishment before conviction.

The case did not come to trial until almost a year later. The central issue were fifty-nine end-of-year tax trades that the partners of the now defunct

Princeton Newport maintained were perfectly legal. Contrary to the prosecution's assertion that these were part of a racketeering pattern of fraud, the defendants maintained that these were real trades and not wash sales. Princeton Newport openly engaged in the trades with a variety of partners in addition to Drexel. It was further testimony to Giuliani's precision-guided agenda that none of these other parties were indicted. Testifying at the trial one trader from S.G. Warburg asserted that the trades were legitimate, and that, although they bought the securities back, they did so at the market price without locking in any special fixed price (which would have been illegal). 'It was always in my mind that if you bought and sold the securities within the context of the market it was okay,' Regan told *The Wall Street Journal.*

In support of their claims they had planned to call two tax experts who would testify that the trades had real economic substance and that they were a standard year-end practice, as the existence of a number of how-to publications with exciting titles like *Year End Tax Tactics* reinforced. But they were blind-sided in this attempt by the prosecution who stuck with the mafia-busting techniques they were comfortable with. Acting on the assumption that the defendants were guilty of a broad raft of violations, as with most mafia suspects, the prosecution's strategy was to find one offence, no matter how technical, as a hook on which to hang all the other presumed but unproven misdemeanours (in this way Al Capone was successfully put away for tax evasion). From this point of view a technical analysis of the technical offence was seen by the prosecution as an attempt to split hairs and to use complexity as a foil to the real issue, which, in their eyes, was racketeering. As Giuliani himself once said, 'Certain kinds of white-collar criminals use complexity in the same way that organized crime uses omerta to conceal what they are doing.'

But as the defence countered, 'As our world becomes more complex, our prosecuting authorities have decided to really create new types of regulatory offences which create more complexity such that we get away from old-fashioned types of crimes that everybody can understand.' In this regard they were right. 'Conspiracy to park stock' was also a novel crime, since parking had generally in the past been treated as a civil offence rather than a criminal conspiracy. But to the prosecution it might as well have been conspiracy to park one's car. The conspiracy was the thing, which, no matter how trivial, was nevertheless interpreted as being the tip – no matter how tiny – of a titanic iceberg of conspiracy. As the former lawyer and prosecutorially minded journalist James Stewart commented after Milken's conviction, it was not that he said, ' "Oh, I'm going to stock park today." Stock parking and these other crimes are only a means to a larger end, which was the complete domination of a huge and lucrative market.'

Fortunately for the prosecution's line of argument, the judge had refused the defence's motion to throw out the RICO charges and proceed instead with just the predicating tax charges allegations. Thus, officially, the charges were fraud and not tax evasion, even if the fraud hinged upon tax evasion. Thus they were able to prevent the defence from calling its tax expert witnesses, arguing that they 'are going to provide almost an alternative charge'. Mark Hansen told the jury in his summation, 'You don't need a fancy tax law expert because common sense tells you it's fraudulent, it's phony.'

Instead the prosecution's case rested on a piece of local colour, a tape of a telephone call in which two Wall Streeters pal around:

'You're a sleazebag,' Bruce Newberg told a Princeton Newport trader.

'You taught me, man,' the trader rejoined.

Newberg laughed.

'Hey, listen, turkey . . . ' the trader began to protest

'Welcome to the world of being a sleaze,' Newberg interrupted.

Even though 'That's Wall Street', as foul-mouthed government witness William Hale explained, sleaze-busting prosecutor Mark Hansen (who was still riding high and had yet to give his fateful television interview about Lisa Jones) was having none of it. In his summation Hansen concluded, 'Doesn't it sound sleazy? If its sounds sleazy, it's because it is sleazy. Your common sense tells you that.' He then pointed out that the defendants were wealthy (a code word in the US Attorney's vocabulary for sleazy and guilty) and finished up with a brilliant flourish: 'In the world of being a sleaze, ladies and gentlemen, these defendants made their own rules.' Jurors interviewed afterwards said it was the sleaze factor more than any consideration of the tax code that had made them find Princeton Newport guilty on all but one of the sixty-four counts of racketeering, conspiracy, and securities, wire and mail fraud.

It was certainly hard to see anything appropriate in a court refusing to allow testimony that the 'crimes' on which racketeering charges were based were not crimes at all. As an additional irony the defendants were told that instead of defrauding the government of a measly $96,000 in taxes, they had in fact overpaid on their taxes by over $1 million. Instead of awarding the $22 million the prosecution was seeking to prop up and pay for its grand folly with another trophy penalty, the judge awarded them $1.8 million and even encouraged the defendants to appeal to him to lower this amount. Mark Hansen was dismayed. 'This cannot be good for prosecutors,' he said. A significant part of the case has been thrown out on appeal.

Although it would not be made public until after the trial, both the tax division and the criminal division of the Justice Department would issue rare blue sheet amendments to the US Attorney's Manual which, although they did not name the Princeton Newport case by name, would insure that its like never happened again. 'Tax offences are not predicates for RICO offences – a deliberate congressional decision – and charging a tax offence as a mail fraud charge could be viewed as circumventing congressional intent,' read the first. The second memo spoke of 'some highly publicized cases involving RICO' that 'have been the subject of considerable criticism in the press, because of the perception that pre-trial freezing of assets is tantamount to a seizure of property without due process,' and insisted that in future the prosecutor must first attempt to use 'less intrusive remedies'. But as with all guidelines it was up to the Justice Department to insist that they were observed, and some departments – such as the Tax Department – simply did not have the 'bureaucratic clout' to stand up to the US Attorney for the Southern District of New York, which was generally recognized as the most powerful of all ninety-three districts.

Furthermore, in 1989 a finding by a number of judges argued that RICO might even be unconstitutional and that it offered about as much direction as saying 'life is a fountain'. It continued, 'That the highest Court in the land has been unable to derive from this statute anything more than today's meager guidance bodes ill for the day when that challenge is presented.'

However, the responsibility for reform lay with Congress. 'I'll be damned if I let big fat cats rip off the American people,' snorted one senator of the 1989 RICO Reform Act, expressing the prejudice of many. The reluctance to reform RICO had everything to do with those whom it has threatened. Investment bankers were like mobsters in that they commanded little public sympathy. Outside Wall Street examples of RICO's misues abounded; in one RICO case a chain of bookstores were seized for selling six videos and four soft porn magazines worth $105.30. In another case a family were evicted from their home because they lived over a pizza parlour that was suspected of dealing in drugs. The family has since disintegrated, and the mother had a nervous breakdown. These evident abuses commanded little media attention and solicited no outcry because of the perception that they concerned undesirable and non-sympathetic groups, such as pornographers and drug dealers, whose right to due process did not demand vigorous defence.

So powerful would RICO prove to be that even when turned on Wall Street's most profitable bank, Drexel could not, in spite of their resources, resist its threat.

11

LEAKY BUSINESS AND
THE TRIAL BY MEDIA

UNTIL it witnessed the death of Princeton Newport at the hands of RICO, Drexel bumped through the two years following Boesky Day roughed up but defiant. Using at one point as many as 115 lawyers, it would spend over $105 million in 1989 on legal fees alone, and $46 million in xeroxing and collating the 1.5 million documents that the government sub-poenaed.

The fact that both Dennis Levine and Martin Siegel worked at Drexel compounded in the eyes of many its reputation as the Libya of investment banking. But to add insult to injury CEO Fred Joseph also had to contend with two other Drexelites (Senior Vice President Antonio Gebauer and securities analyst Robert Salsbury) being charged with securities fraud in two cases unrelated to the Boesky scandal.

Since all those concerned had been with the firm for roughly a year, Fred Joseph could plausibly attribute this misfortune to Drexel's rapid expansion. 'We think it's a coincidence,' he said in a candid talk-style advertisement. 'We've just hired our ten thousandth employee.' Using the magical flow of money from the West Coast Joseph had expanded rapidly. He maintained that in their scramble for new staff they had been tirelessly vigilant. True, the lie detectors were only used for hiring back office staff, while professionals were courted in a rather more civilized though no less thorough way (it supposedly took him over six months to hire Levine). But if this was the case how could he have missed the fact that Siegel was rumoured to be in bed with Boesky? Given that Joseph had not missed the fact that Beck was known as a habitual fantasist it is possible that he was aware of the rumours, but must have been satisfied that they had no substance. But then again, what kind of scrutiny could have been effected on these stellar recruits?

Joseph also liked to warn hirelings of the horrors of prison, scaring them into sticking to the straight and narrow. 'I tell them, "What happens is you go to jail. You really do. They put you in a cell, and they take your shoelaces away . . . " I do a much more gruesome thing . . . I really try to get kids turning green around the mouth,' he told *Manhattan Inc.*

In his remarks after Boesky Day Joseph appeared consistently upbeat. Publicly he leapt to Milken's defence, while internally he moved quickly to cement morale, and addressed the firm regularly on its internal communications system known as the Drexel Line. He projected as ever his trademark brand of candour, and his confidence brought a ring of brightness to every situation.

He supported coming down on the arbs: 'I regret having acted as Ivan Boesky's investment banker. Credibility is critical . . . the arbs have perfected the technique of obtaining inside information, and to the extent that leaves a public perception that they have an unfair advantage we ought to take that unfair advantage away from them.' But aside from the slight credibility smudge that having Boesky on their books represented, Joseph felt that they had nothing to fear: 'The public's perception of the markets is critical, all a securities firm has to offer its clients is a perception of integrity and honesty, no one's gonna deal with a securities firm if they don't think it's honest,' he proclaimed, obviously highly confident that Drexel would not fall under the shadow of such a perception. 'You don't sink the ship because a few rats have got on board.' But for all his bravado, his ship was beginning to settle in the water.

Immediately after the Boesky announcement paranoia had descended on the high yield department like an LA smog. Fearful that Giuliani's frightful gaze was about to turn in their direction – if it hadn't already done so – people walked round speaking in low tones and turning on faucets assuming that they were being bugged. Four days later the SEC issued a formal – but not public – order of investigation to Drexel and that same day chairman Bob Linton was pushed to make a public statement that Milken had not – as was wildly rumoured – resigned: 'It's like the presidential asassination stories,' said Linton. That same day the first of many leaks concerning the SEC and the government's investigation began to appear in the press. 'According to lawyers familiar with the government's investigation,' began *The Wall Street Journal*, using one of the many formulas that would become all too familar to Drexel and Milken over the next four years.

Although Giuliani held a strong legal hand with all sorts of magic laws that could be turned into any kind of weapon with which to entrap any kind of victim almost at whim, his real strength was his ability to use the media. We have already seen how his office became the centre of a media circus, and when it came to busting Milken and Drexel, an info-war of unprecedented barbarity broke out as the defendants attempted to fortify themselves against a barrage of public opprobrium. Most attritional of all the weapons arrayed against them were the flow of mysterious leaks that provided the media with material on which to base their torrent of criticisms. Alvin Toffler called them 'guided leaks' – informational missiles consciously launched and precision. targeted. By the time Milken entered his plea *The Wall Street Journal* had made 326 references (twice a week on average) to unidentified sources in connection with the investigation. Over the same period the *Washington Post* quoted unnamed sources in 450 instances.

Before becoming District Attorney Giuliani had in private practice represented *The Wall Street Journal* on First Amendment matters. He said that this gave him an insight into how the press works: 'I have a sense of how quickly things have to be done in the media,' and that this was why he favoured openness. But the same awareness may well have made him aware of how vulnerable the press was to the powers of suggestion. The demand for a scoop coupled with the pressure of deadlines made newspapers all but sit up and beg for scraps of information. And none more so than *The Wall Street Journal*, which had been going through a metamorphosis throughout the eighties that went into turbo gear when Norman Pearlstine became editor in 1983. Befitting the model of eighties man, Pearlstine had a clinically proven photographic memory and a penchant for turning up to work at 4 a.m. He also loved rock 'n' roll, blasting Motown greats in his office in the privacy of the pre-dawn hours. After moving into the post-modern and Bonfire-lavish headquarters in the Pelli designed towers of the World Financial Center, the *Journal* continued to splinter into additional sections, a process that had begun at the beginning of the decade. One of the first things Pearlstine did was hire an additional hundred reporters.

These changes were a snug fit with the change in the times. The media explosion created a huge potential void of blank magazine pages, dead airwaves and empty television screens that somehow had to be filled. It was what it was filled with that surprised so many. Instead of dry and disinterested data, the kind of material that sold was infotainment, trivial details about the ins and outs of people's personal lives. Just as the Nouvelles found themselves the stars of a glossy new media, so business people suddenly found themselves the attention of a gossipy new business press.

Also in the spirit of the age, what justice was supposed to be to prosecutors and what truth was supposed to be to journalists was passed over in favour of the universal urge to compete, and more importantly, to win. The more victories Giuliani won the more likely he would win the mayoral election. Meanwhile the media, while mediating between all sides, wanted to win too – win the scoop, win ratings, win sales. After all, journalism was a business too, specifically the art of buying paper at two cents a pound and then selling it at ten cents a pound, as it was once famously defined. In the deal-making eighties winning the journalism game became just as important as winning the justice game and winning the investment banking game.

It was in this environment that business news, which used to be 'the sorry sister of news publications' according to former *Wall Street Journal* reporter Dean Rotbart, came into its own. As deal-making became the decade's buzz activity readers wanted a different kind of business reporting, more reflective of the speculative blaze of the tearaway stock market. The dull and dry financial analysis of old-style reporting, with its worthy sobriety, was 'out'. 'In' was a new go-go and gossipy excitability. Traditional business reporters disdained this trivialization, where mastery of difficult detail was passed over in pursuit of 'sexier' copy. 'There was a lot of good tipping, but not a lot of good digging,' said one senior Drexel executive.

'What the public wanted was people who could get inside information before inside information became the latest gossip,' said Rotbart. Suddenly business journalists, who now 'began to think of themselves as celebrities, and as doing much more important work than they had done before', were moved to boost their status and fuel their egos by being first with the kind of inside information that the popular craze for business was creating a seemingly insatiable demand for. 'They felt', said Dean Rotbart, 'an intense pressure to fuel the speculative fire.' If knowing the difference between a stock and a bond was the old yardstick, dishing the dirt was the demand of the new.

It was this sea change that brought a new importance to columns like 'Heard on the Street', which were the financial equivalents of Suzy's society columns in the *New York Post* and were no less eagerly devoured. As a result 'Heard' would often make the stocks it wrote about giddy with excitement and drive them wild, up or down the chart.

It was this – and his own modest salary – that led 'Heard' writer Winans to sell ahead the contents of his columns. When Winans was finally caught the *Journal*'s reaction was most telling about the spirit of the age and the new journalism. Instead of being shamed by the episode, the *Journal* did not look a gift scoop in the mouth. It was the perfect opportunity to prove that instead of being the second newspaper it was known as, they too could compete and have their fingers on the button. Taking advantage of some twenty-four thousand pages of notes that Winans had left behind and his supposedly confidential file procured from the personnel department, their coverage led the way.

The savagery with which *The Wall Street Journal* devoured its own kind, was but one example of the advocacy created by the media hothouse climate. The animus it bore Milken and Drexel was another. 'We at the *Journal* think the Drexel story is going to be the major story on our beat and we're gonna cover it extensively and extremely aggressively,' Pearlstine was supposed to have intimated to a senior executive at Drexel in the beginning. (Joseph was supposed to have initially made himself open to 'Norm' but became less inclined to chat once it was clear to him that Pearlstine would cherry pick from their conversations to support his basically anti-Drexel position.) 'The *Journal* stuck its neck out a real long way to say he [Milken] was a crook. If he had gone to trial and been acquitted, the damage to that paper's credibility would have been tremendous,' said Rotbart. This was more than mere advocacy. One of the *Journal*'s star reporters, James Stewart, was a trained lawyer whose style was spiked with a prosecutorial zeal (and as the author of the book *The Prosecutors* he clearly had a fascination with the species). As *Newsday* writer John Riley commented, he imagined the *Journal* thought that 'The way to play this story is as a detective story, and the detective is gonna solve the crime.' The consequence of this, intended or not, was that 'The assumption was that there was a crime to be solved. It colours the water.' And in their pursuit of the truth the journalists enjoyed unparalleled powers. Their right to protect the secrecy of their sources remains as sacred as motherhood.

Taken together the gossip and the advocacy created the real villain of the piece, the unnamed source. To get the *plat du jour*, journalists needed to get good and intimate with their sources. Such intimacy could only be won with trust, and, as far as their deep throats were concerned, that trust was dependent on their not being embarrassed by seeing what they had said attributed in print. In return for the information, anonymity had to be guaranteed.

But with the nameless source (expressed in a variety of ways as 'sources close to' or 'people familiar with'), one enters a twilight zone of relative truths, in which things in print were not what they seemed.

'I was guilty of striving to be close to my sources to bestow upon me their secrets' admitted Dean Rotbart, who took over 'Heard on the Street' after Winans's disgrace. And all around him at the *Journal* he saw people that were even closer. 'Two of the greatest anonymous sources of all time were arbitrageur Ivan Boesky and investment banker Martin Siegel,' according to Rotbart. 'Why the business press never bothered to tell its readers about its close association with Boesky and Siegel . . . says an awful lot about how far reporters and editors will go to protect those sources, even when those sources turn out to be scoundrels of the highest order.' According to one unnamed source, every time Siegel was on the phone James Stewart would come running. But there was no mention of this special relationship in the otherwise comprehensive piece 'The Wall Street career of Martin Siegel was a dream gone wrong', which was cited in winning *Journal* writer James Stewart his Pullitzer Prize in 1988. In his preamble Stewart told us that Siegel's story 'is a vivid chronicle of how systemic the abuse of inside information had become on Wall Street'.

A righteous eye might say that the *Journal*, however unwittingly, was part of this systemic abuse. As an unnamed source, and therefore protected from verification, both Siegel and Boesky could use any degree of truth or untruth in an attempt to shift the market wheresoever they would like it to go. And why would they behave altruistically in talking to the press when deceit and self-interest informed their every other move? Even when the *Journal* called them for quotes they could deduce inside information from what the unnamed journalists might divulge to them by way of necessary background to pose their question. Had Giuliani seen matters from this perspective, he might not have had too much difficulty finding the predicate acts of a racketeering enterprise necessary for a RICO indictment against the *Journal*..

Still in the twilight zone of the unnamed source, there was the spice that it added to the total mix of information. More often than not 'sources close to Ivan Boesky' meant Boesky himself. But to the reader they were not one and the same. 'If I read "Sources close to Ivan Boesky say he's buying this stock" you might think that I had dug around and uncovered some valuable information that might influence your decision to copy his trading,' said Dean Rotbart. 'If on the other hand Ivan is telling the whole world instead of just two or three friends you may be less inclined to ride his coat tails for what might be a bumpier ride.' The analogy worked just as well with unnamed source leaks about the investigation. What in naked truth might not have borne much scrutiny took on a much more authoritative aura under the objectivity of a supposed third party. The basic interpretation was that 'sources close to the investigation' were neither too close to be compromised nor too far away to be uninformed. The secrecy was a tissue paper wrapping that gave authenticity and value to the information. After all, if it was worthless why would the purveyor seek to protect himself with anonymity? It had to be important, and it had to be true.

And there are more nuances still. Into this spectrum of relative truths we must add 'the complete fabrication'. In a survey of more than 150 top business journalists 15 per cent admitted that they had, at least once, made up sources. In this they were virtually unchecked.

At the same time the unnamed sources built up a reservoir of goodwill with the journalists who compromised themselves for their contacts. As early as 1984, 'We sat around and heard a rumour about some sort of improper relationship between Boesky and Kidder Peabody [Siegel's old haunt]. We may have made some small effort to track it down, but it wasn't really in our interests to do some confrontational reporting to find out if it was true. He was an extremely important source to *The Wall Street Journal* at that time in its history, and you don't bite the hand that feeds you.' And to make up for it you raven down the hand, arm and torso of the fool who doesn't feed you. Milken, who had generally avoided the press, had no comparable reservoir on which to draw. Instead of going soft on him, they had every reason to go extremely hard.

No matter how routine the leaks themselves became they were not a routine part of any investigation. In the cases of both Boesky and Levine the investigations proceeded with watertight secrecy. When the announcements finally came, everyone was taken by surprise. In stark contrast, hardly a week passed without an article claiming that the indictment of Drexel and Milken was coming soon. And yet, while virtually all other aspects of the case were leaked, Milken's record-breaking salary and the enormous dollar amount sought by the government as compensation were kept under wraps until they were revealed as part of the indictment itself. The day after his indictment, the leaks began again announcing that Milken would soon be faced with a superseding indictment.

The negative impact these leaks had on Milken cannot be overestimated. The mere suspicion of investigation cast him as villain, and the relentless repetition of the imminence of criminal charges added a further sinister dimension to the man, who, to be the focus of this much attention, had to be guilty of everything he was being investigated for and probably a lot more besides. Some of the leaks even took the government unawares. When, in January 1989, *The Wall Street Journal* disclosed the contents of a confidential SEC memo, Gary Lynch, head of the SEC, called the paper directly and harangued them: 'I think you ought to put it high up in your story that you were provided with non-public documents by a committee of Congress,' he said, and then, before hanging up, abruptly added, 'The whole thing stinks.'

The thirty-three page single-spaced document was dated October 1983 and was the report of an SEC attorney who argued that Drexel had 'a major supervision problem', and that Milken ran 'a trading scheme . . . to warehouse and manipulate securities for the benefit of certain high yield department clients'. The *Journal* also maintained that Milken, when questioned on Hallowe'en a year earlier, had ducked questions about his relationship with Boesky and had been singularly cocky with the investigators, commenting on the people he was being asked about: 'Are these potential customers that we should be taking their names down?' The article also added, in parentheses, that Norman Pearlstine, the paper's managing editor, refused to disclose the sources for the story. Another significant leak, also directed to *The Wall Street Journal* and concerning an SEC memo, detailed two secret meetings Milken had with Boesky, who was wired at the time by the government.

In general Arthur Liman observed that the most serious offences prosecuted by the SEC were 'the misuse of inside information,' he told *Institutional Investor*, 'yet the SEC has been in this case the greatest abuser of confidential information. And I don't see how they'll ever get the moral legitimacy to discipline others for [the same offence].' In a motion filed with Judge Kimba Wood, Liman further argued, 'The transformation of these proceedings into a spectator sport is no accident. . . . These leaks resulted from decisions by some in government to use publicity as a prosecutorial weapon, carefully timing the disclosures to "pressure" defendants. . . . This stategy – which has apparently become commonplace in "high profile" cases brought in the past few years . . . has threatened the ability of Michael Milken and Lowell Milken to receive a fair trial. . . . The leakers have timed these disclosures for optimal effect. . . . These leaks sent – and continue to send – an unmistakable message to defendants and potentially co-operating witnesses that "the boat is leaving" and the time is running out to "strike a deal".' As soon as two months after the investigation but fully two years before Milken's indictment, *The Wall Street Journal* published what the defence called an 'exhaustive summary' of the government's theory arguing that this was the first of many innumerable attempts to coerce co-operation.

Giuliani has always denied leaking information – and even went so far as to maintain that it was the defence who were making prejudicial leaks. But his knowledge of the value of publicity is clear. In the famous Bess Mess, the trial of former Miss America Bess Myerson, Giuliani moved to have the judge removed after he insisted that an order restricting publicity by the prosecution be enforced. In the 'Queen of Mean' Helmsley trial the judge despaired that 'leaks of pending indictments have become so commonplace as to make a mockery of the secrecy provisions of the Grand Jury'. While violation of this secrecy was a crime, people were seldom prosecuted for it, and it was generally left to self-regulating investigations which rarely yielded more than token results.

Meanwhile Drexel was floundering around in the dark. The very notion of a criminal investigation baffled Joseph. A close colleague claimed that Joseph didn't even know what a US Attorney was. He soon found out. His immediate reaction was typically candid. He went straight to the SEC to find out what was going on. 'They stonewalled him. They said he knew what had happened and whether he co-operated fully or not they were going to complete their investigation. Thereafter he learnt almost more through the leaks to the *Journal* and the *Washington Post* than any other way', reported the same source. In their video department Drexel installed a bank of video recorders pre-programmed to record every newscast on every channel. Compilation tapes were edited and distributed to key players on a daily basis. In this way they hoped to learn the latest moves against them and keep abreast in the information war.

On more than one occasion, however, Giuliani hinted that he himself was on the defensive, countering a massive and unprecedented PR campaign. After Milken's sentence he told *Barrons*, 'This was a defence in which millions and millions were spent for what was done in court. But as many, if not more, millions were spent in public relations . . . I have never seen such an attempt to use so many of the levers that are available to exert pressure in one's favour . . . it was like a major political campaign rather than a criminal case.'

Drexel, not atypically for a major corporation, did have an advertising budget and an active image campaign which, also not unusually, was affected by their being the focus of the investigation, as they assumed from reading the papers. Drexel began to backpeddle on the aggressiveness that had characterized its glory days. Caring was more important than winning. Their initial response was to go for a team image and pull together. When they hired their ten thousandth employee they commemorated this with a series of ads listing all the employees alphabetically by name in a solid block under the headline 'Ten thousand strong.' The ad was a message to its workers, a call to stick together through whatever lay ahead. It was remarkably effective and within the company there was an *esprit de corps*, a feeling that the investigation was an unwarranted hostility from outsiders and a rap that could be beaten.

In 1987 and 1988 they spent, according to one estimate, $20 million each year on a series of glossy television advertisements. Bob Giraldi – famous for directing Michael Jackson's videos – directed some of the spots, while the others were done by fashion photographer David Bailey. The theme of the six spots was 'Helping people manage change'. In each of the advertisements some financing miracle takes place thanks to Drexel: a power plant is built, a playground filled with children. The only problem was that the set-up of these two ads – the abandoned site against a louring backdrop, and the child's swing creaking eerily in the breeze – was so potently sinister that it threw shade on the happy ending. This creeping unease was fine if you were making the video for *Thriller*, but not if you were trying to paint junk bonds as mom and apple pie.

'The challenge facing Drexel was to let America know that we were the creative financiers', recalled one Drexelite working in Corporate Communications, 'but in finance "creative" means crooked, cooking the books, so how could we say that without sounding criminal?' In the past the adoption of a feisty image had done the trick, but now, with the investigation, the perception was that that would count against them and would not work as it had before. But as more than one person observed, it was even harder to change direction. 'Once you've represented yourself as a buccaneer it's very difficult to turn around and say, "We didn't mean it, we're nice people" '. Drexel's new-found gentleness clashed with their inherently tart image. Like a smooth door-to-door salesman, the ads were trying to force their way into people's homes. Drexel seemed insincere.

Especially after the scandal surrounding the Vidalia advertisement. 'In 1985 over 16 per cent of the population of Vidalia were unemployed,' claimed the voiceover. 'In December 1986, the Catalyst Energy Corp. began construction on the Vidalia Hydroelectric plant, financed with the help of high yield bonds provided by Drexel Burnham. Today this project has helped reduce unemployment by over 20 per cent – proof that high yield bonds are not just good for business, but good for everyone.' Trouble was, as Laurie Cohen gleefully reported in *The Wall Street Journal*, the quaint town in the ad with the Main Street and dixie cinema wasn't Vidalia, but a small town over three hundred miles away in Arkansas. Vidalia, less picturesquely, had a two-lane highway instead of a Main Street and only ever had a drive-in picture show that blew down in a hurricane. Laurie Cohen then went on to maintain that unemployment was never that high and that the power plant didn't reduce it by that much anyway.

Truth in advertising is of course a fiction, but woe betide the company that gets caught on its hook. For Drexel the Laurie Cohen article could not have come at a worse time. Fudging the facts in their ads while under the shadow of investigation was all that the public needed to nail Drexel as crooks in their minds. The ad debacle seemed to give the general public a personal taste of the fraud alleged by Giuliani and his men. Where the parking and insider trading charges were beyond their ken, a phony ad on the television set in their living room was well within their grasp. No matter how minor the inaccuracies, and no matter how standard such techniques were in the advertising industry, people took away from reading the piece in the *Journal* that the ad was taking them for a ride. As Drexel's market research confirmed, the article had an abiding negative impact: '10 per cent of the people we polled said they remembered the piece. People would spontaneously make reference to this article,' remembered one Drexelite involved in the project, concluding that, 'It just shows how powerful *The Wall Street Journal* really is.'

The ads backfired in other ways. In Washington the reaction to Drexel's ads peddling the palliative powers of junk was so negative that they pulled the campaign fearing that they would be counterproductive. Some even questioned the wisdom of trying to educate America about junk bonds in the first place, since the average Joe wasn't ever going to have a use for them. However, once Drexel had implanted junk bonds in the public consciousness this still but dimly understood piece of Wall Street chicanery (as it was so perceived) became the perfect scapegoat for all economic ills, and thanks to its own ads, Drexel had made itself virtuously synonymous with the dastardly bonds.

In addition to the advertisements, Drexel retained a 'battery of spin control experts who were paid millions of dollars to come up with brilliant ideas that sounded like they would do good but couldn't,' remarked one Vice President drily. Many of PR's greatest stars were on the pay roll, providing a corporate security blanket while fleecing the firm with their astronomical fees. 'There is a certain comfort in having people who did spin control on the Exxon spill and the poisoned Tylenol cases.' But as these examples so graphically illustrate, there is no such thing as damage control, and retaining such experts merely illustrates how much damage has been done.

For 1989, Drexel's last year in business, the ad budget was cut to $12 million, but none of it was ever spent. At a certain point, 'The advertising was a band-aid, but the firm was haemorrhaging,' said one, arguing that it was better to save on the price of the band-aid. 'There's no advertising budget that can fight ten billion dollars worth of negative publicity,' said another senior executive.

A significant part of that $10 billion came from the Washington hearings. In April 1988, not to be outdone by the investigations of the US Attorney and the SEC, John Dingell, chairman of the House Ways and Means Committee, decided to get in on the action by holding his own hearings. Having been condescended to by Wall Street and bamboozled with bogus studies, Washington was finally getting its own back.

Dingell's concern, as he spelled it out in his introduction, was the familiar junk bond bust up of America. 'Companies which have existed for decades which have carried the blunt [sic] of national defence through two World Wars, which have provided employment in the heartland of America, no longer exist. They have been the victims of takeovers, financed through the junk bond market.' In other words, companies that could resist the Nazis could not resist Drexel Burnham, the leading manufacturer of junk bombs.

The House Ways and Means Committee enjoyed the broadest powers. As his press aide joked, 'if it moves, burns or is sold' it fell under Dingell's jurisdiction, and Dingell was nothing if not adept at exploiting this to the maximum.

Issuing Milken with a sub-poena would oblige him to appear to testify before the House. But because of the investigation he would be obliged to take the Fifth Amendment, which gave him the right to remain silent and not answer questions or otherwise incriminate himself by saying things that could be used as evidence against him in the investigation. Routinely in such circumstances an affidavit was acceptable in lieu of an actual appearance. There was little point in insisting on a personal appearance, since the person would just invoke their right and remain silent. According to the *Washington Post*, Dingell had made such an agreement with Milken, but then he changed his mind. The promise of the photo opportunity of the reclusive publicity-shunning Milken being sworn in, and then looking like a cheap crook as he refused to answer any questions, must have been too good for the publicity-loving Dingell to miss. With Milken standing there with his right arm raised as he took the oath, it would have looked as if the Junk Bond King had finally been brought to justice, and by Dingell. It would be – and turned out to be – the modern equivalent of the midget in Morgan's lap at the Pecora hearings, and it would make Dingell look like a hero. 'It's a joke in Washington that they measure hearings by how many cameras there'll be there. It was said that they thought that this would be a six camera-hearing . . . he certainly got his six cameras,' said a colleague close to Fred Joseph.

Fred Joseph, who had testified voluntarily, took a beating at the hearings. He had been tutored for the session by John Kraushar, the right hand man of media guru Roger Ailes, and had also had the benefit of an elaborate dress rehearsal, with bright lights shining in his eyes, mock senators asking hostile questions, tape loops of general hubbub, and even light flashes and the sound of motor drives simulating a wall of cameras. For some of the more technical questions about securities law he had hoped to rely on one of his lawyers for answers. But Dingell, invoking committee rules that would have forced Joseph's legal expert to waive the usual attorney-client privilege that protected the confidentiality of their deliberations, managed to deprive Joseph of his aide. Joseph was grilled for some seven hours, riddled with hostile questions and ridiculed for his answers which were peppered with I-don't-knows and I-don't-think-sos.

At issue were the dealings of thirty-three 'insider accounts' identified by the investigation, which were investment partnerships owned by approximately 135 Drexel employees. Drexel defended these accounts as a way for employees to practise what they preached daily to their clients by risking their own money in deals. The theory went that with these accounts they would not be distracted from their daily work as they might if the accounts were at an outside house. The accusation was that these groups were self-dealing in hot new issues at preferred prices before they were offered to outside clients. 'We cannot have investment bankers secretly taking the juiciest parts of the best deals themselves,' said Dingell.

The nub of the matter was SEC rule 10B6 (not to be confused with 10B5, the insider trading law) which dealt with fraud in the distribution of new issues. Fred Joseph maintained that the rule only applied to shares and not to bonds. But in a 1983 ruling an exception was made for 'non-convertible investment grade debt and preferred securities', the preamble for which stated that 'historically, 10B6 has applied to distributions of all securities'. Bereft of his expert counsel and pressed on this point, Joseph said, 'I think I'm confused.' However honest an answer, he was subsequently much ridiculed for it.

It is not certain if there was anything illegal about any of these dealings, but as one Congressman told Joseph, 'the public perception is that what you have done doesn't pass the smell test.' The following month Drexel suspended partnerships from buying into new issues. 'We're in a business where appearances of fairness are very important,' said Joseph. The only down-side of bowing to 'public perception' in this case was that no matter how carefully they crafted it, it looked like an admission of guilt.

But the real impact of the hearings was on morale at Drexel. Many people at Drexel first heard about these partnerships as a result of the hearings. 'The question was "Don't we all work for the same place?" and the answer was, "obviously not." There was a lot of dismay among the good smart people in New York,' said one. Instead of the commune of the ten thousand there was an elite on a fast inside track. Where the message of the advertising and the exhortation of the frequent internal memos went along the lines of 'together we stand and divided we fall', the partnerships would drive the first wedge between the East and the West Coast. It can only have been a boon for an investigation that knew that to a large extent its chances of success lay in breaking Drexel's united front and separating the company from Miken, its profit engine.

THE PREDATOR'S BALL – THE BOOK

Drexel and Milken were under fire from all sides. On either side of the hearings it had been leaked that the SEC had first resolved to file civil charges and then that it would wait on the US Attorney's office until they had fulminated their criminal investigation. But even pre-empting the filing of any charges, Drexel and Milken would be tried and found guilty in Connie Bruck's book *The Predator's Ball*, which was tantamount to another few billion dollars of bad publicity.

A few days after the disastrous hearings Fred Joseph fired off a letter to the publishers Simon & Schuster. 'Only the press of other matters has delayed this response to your April 11th letter, the contents of which I find quite remarkable . . . in no sense have I been given "every opportunity to read, review and comment on the manuscript".' His letter referred to what Connie Bruck herself described as 'rather an unusual offer (which I hope you will keep confidential)', in which she offered Fred Joseph, in return for his co-operation, 'the right to read any portion of the manuscript that involves Drexel specifically'. She would give him the opportunity to suggest corrections and in the event that they differed over a point of fact, would allow him to include a comment in the book. It was on this understanding that he gave her access and co-operation in February 1986, nine months before Boesky Day.

But once Fred Joseph read the manuscript of what he hoped would be a favourable treatment of Drexel, the agreement rapidly broke down. 'It is sufficient to say that the manuscript is permeated with factual errors and falsities, a specific listing of which would make a book in itself,' railed Joseph.

Drexel claimed they were only allowed to read the manuscript for six hours over a two-day period. Simon & Schuster retorted that the manuscript was available for review at the publishers' offices on a rather improbable 'twenty-four hour a day, seven days a week basis', and that Drexel spent more than thirty hours reviewing the manuscript and making changes in numerous subsequent meetings. Bruck did agree to change the fact that instead of owning 67 per cent of Drexel, Milken only owned 6 per cent (which still left him the largest shareholder). 'They kept saying there were mistakes, then they would wait two weeks and write us a letter,' said the publishers, describing what they saw as a deliberate paper trail left by Drexel to prove that their efforts to make changes were ignored.

The core of the book was a consideration of some half dozen deals and transactions, some of which would later resurface in the SEC's complaint and in the indictment. In several instances she surmised that Milken used raiders, arbs and other active investor clients as a club to bully companies into doing his bidding. For example, a company called Wickes had already decided to do a bond offering with hated rival Salomon Brothers and the prospectus had even been printed up. But when Milken learned of this he was supposed to have orchestrated an accumulation of shares that gave him virtual control of the company. The company then supposedly dumped Salomon for Drexel. Wickes denied any extortion and happily continued to do business with Drexel.

In 1985, according to Bruck, a company called Green Tree Acceptance did a large offering of stocks and bonds through Drexel but stipulated that the offering should be broadly distributed so as not to give control to any of Milken's favoured raiders. However, Bruck says Steinberg ended up with just under 10 per cent of the stock, although he seemed to be a passive investor not interested in taking control. But then when Green Tree had passed on a number of investment opportunities offered by one of Milken's pet traders, James Dahl, Steinberg began to get aggressive. For refusing to play the game, suggested Bruck, they were threatened with takeover terror tactics.

In 1987 a company called Staley claimed in a lawsuit that Drexel had made an 'extortionate attempt to force Staley to use it as an investment banker'. This they had done by simultaneously buying stock and, via James Dahl, making overtures to Staley. When Staley resisted Drexel's approaches and instead decided to do a public stock offering with another investment banker, Dahl was supposed to have driven the share price down by heavy selling which necessitated rethinking the offering. 'It is very important for us to sit down and talk before you do something that hurts me and before I do something that hurts you,' Dahl was supposed to have threatened.

Beverly Hills Savings & Loans was another unhappy customer, a thrift that also sued Drexel after it had gorged itself on junk and sustained heavy losses. They claimed they had been insufficiently informed about certain junk bonds they had bought. Perhaps. But as with so many S&Ls, their junk losses would be dwarfed by losses from other disastrous investments in, for example, real estate.

Bruck also reviewed the Caesar's World issue, which the SEC had previously but inconclusively investigated. In Milken's Fatico hearing the charge would be revisited yet again. The accusation was that Milken, having attended a meeting about the casino's finances, afterwards traded on inside information when he bought Caesar's bonds (as did a number of other favoured clients such as Princeton Newport, First Executive and Columbia Savings) in anticipation of what would come of the meeting. This would not have made Milken an inside trader. But it was not even sure when he bought the bonds, since the ticket was stamped the day after the meeting and yet written in by hand is 'as of June 29th', the day of the meeting. The bond trader recalled selling the bonds to Milken on that day and in the morning before the afternoon meeting. In Milken's deposition Bruck noted that he was 'full of certitude about details that would help him, but aphasic on those which would not'. For someone with a photographic memory, he was, she argued, suspiciously selective.

It was a measure of the sieve-like nature of the government's case that although the SEC did not file its complaint until September 1988, its contents were in fact known in sufficient detail well in advance for Bruck, thanks to the investigative reporting of James Stewart teamed with Daniel Hertzberg, to be able to preview them in her book.

In the Fishbach allegation, for example, Boesky was supposed to have been used as a player to help free up another Milken client, Victor Posner, who had been stalemated by Fishbach in his long-running takeover bid. Posner had tied his hands by signing a standstill agreement in which he agreed not to acquire 25 per cent of the company unless a third party acquired more than 10 per cent. With that Milken was supposed to have persuaded Boesky to go in and cross the 10 per cent line, thus breaking the chains of the standstill agreement so that Posner could reactivate his takeover bid (with money raised by Drexel). This was not in itself criminal, just good business sense. However, Boesky told the government he had been assured that he would be made whole on any losses incurred performing this service. This under-the-counter arrangement supposedly confirmed that Boesky's role was a sham designed to conceal the intent and identity of the interested parties. As it turned out it was a sour deal for Posner. No sooner had he acquired the firm than its profits plummeted.

At the heart of all the accusations was the Boesky-Milken relationship, according to Boesky's confessions. Soon after Boesky Day it emerged that there was a $5.3 million payment from Boesky to Drexel, which, the government maintained, was an end tally of the profits and losses incurred by both sides in their illicit parking scheme. Stock parking is when one party parks securities by making a sale and agreeing to buy them back at a certain point in time. The purpose of this is to conceal the identity of the true owner. Parking became illegal if the two sides had some kind of compensation scheme whereby the pseudo-owner of the securities was protected from any losses he might incur as a result of holding the securities (if, for example, their price dropped) but would also share in the profits. The government argued that this was what the $5.3 million represented. Drexel maintained that the amount was an invoice of 'soft dollar' services, courtesy services that have a value but which were not generally charged for. In the Boesky case Drexel argued that this was courtesy research they had done for deals that never got done. Against this it has been argued that Boesky prided himself on his own research and was unlikely to go out of house. Overriding this was the fact that for Boesky there was no such thing as too much information, and, as was consistent with his insider trading and life philosophy, the more he could get in return for the least in outlay – be it in risk or dollars – the happier 'Ivan The Bum' was.

Bruck admitted that when she set out to write the book she suspected 'that this stunning success story might well have some unholy if not illegal underpinnings', and she did not feel that she was disappointed in this. 'Indeed, it seems plain to this writer if . . . Milken's and, by extension, Drexel's actions are not worth prosecuting, then the securities laws were not worth passing.' If she was unsure exactly what laws he broke, and what crimes he was guilty of committing – as she later admitted she was – she was sure that the break up of the offences into technical accounts was a deliberate attempt to trivialize them. Whatever they were, the individual counts had to be 'seen in concert . . . if the true sense of Milken's machine is to be grasped'. In her mind there was no doubt that Milken's machine was 'the brass-knuckles, threatening, market-manipulating Cosa Nostra of the securities world'. Indeed it is not hard to see in Bruck's writing the feeling that the machine's very existence aped organized crime, consisting of a tightly knit group fiercely loyal to a godfather-type figure to whom they were all bound in some way, either through blood ties, lifelong friendships or other bonds such as indebtedness.

To try and look at Milken's machine from the other side, as a normal business with the normal networks and relationships that go to make up any enterprise was equally futile. It was immediately different from most businesses because it was so much more intense. It was more efficient, it performed better, it was more productive, it worked harder, it made much more money, and so it was not surprising that the relationships that bound it together were much closer.

Quite apart from this, so quickly and so completely did the issue become polarized that anyone who argued this case was discredited as an insider, camp follower, cult junkie. Indeed many of those who defended Milken's activities as legitimate business suffered from the disadvantage of being made by him. He had made many of them far richer, far more successful than they ever could have been under their own mediocre steam. And those writers, academics and politicians who leapt into the breach as disinterested parties were laughed off the stage, as bought and paid for, either through financing studies, such as Glenn Yago's research into high yield bonds, or through speaking fees at the junk bond conference – as in the cases of historian Robert Sobel and economist George Gilder, both vocal defenders of Milken. However, as Sobel has pointed out, these people were not hired as patsies – they had taken their positions before Milken invited them to the Junk Bond Conference. Sobel remembered telling Milken at the conference in 1988 that junk bonds had reached the end of the line. One of Milken's colleagues turned on Sobel for his audacity, but Milken just replied: 'You know, I think you're right.' To him the conference was supposed to be an ideas bazaar, a free-for-all, not the predator's ball it was increasingly characterized as. But to the outside world, this was really all it was, for the credible and legitimate side of the proceedings had been thoroughly obscured. Only to corrupted insiders could Milken's network look like a normal interconnectedness and mutuality of interests. To everyone else it was a sinister cabal with nothing but fraud on its mind.

But was this really the truth of the matter or did the dynamics of this no-win situation indicate a rather different set up? To be sure market domination was the goal of Milken's X, but was this goal or even its achievement a necessary evil? America's record of trust-busting and anti-monopoly activity comes out of a fear of domination or totalitarianism. And in America's history we have plenty of examples that this fear – fear of domination by Satan, fear of being invaded by communism – has been intense enough to express itself as paranoia and hysteria, resulting in the excesses of the Salem witch-hunts and McCarthyism.

In abstracting 'the basic elements of the paranoid style in American politics', Richard Hofstadter wrote, 'The central image is that of a vast and sinister conspiracy, a gigantic and yet subtle machinery of influence set in motion to undermine and destroy a way of life.' This would not be an unfair paraphrase of Bruck's argument.

Hofstadter then went on to expand on paranoid scholarship which starts with 'a careful accumulation of facts, or at least what appear to be facts, and [goes on] to marshal these facts towards an overwhelming "proof" of the particular conspiracy that is to be established . . . what distinguishes the paranoid style is not, then, the absence of verifiable facts . . . but rather the curious leap in imagination that is always made at some critical point in the recital of events.' Instead of hysterics, Bruck gives us exhaustive research and punishing detail, all served up with a slice-and-dice ninja articulacy. But a mass of facts do not necessarily make crimes. In the book the curious leap of the imagination from the data to a mafia-style cult run by a weirdo workaholic was established in the book's bookends, which act as a frame for the reader.

Chapter 1 began with Milken 'the braino-nerd', as another hostile mythographer portrayed him, boarding a pre-dawn bus in New Jersey with a miner's headlamp strapped to his head. 'I never wore a miner's helmet,' protested Milken in vain. But overall the book both began and ended with a bang. The bang at the beginning was quite literal, with a description of high yield raiders living it up in Bungalow 8 in Boesky's Beverly Hilton, which, to hear Bruck tell it, was the best little whorehouse in Beverly Hills. Ironically it was in a side bar written by the editors of *Manhattan Inc* to accompany a feature of Epstein's on Milken that the question of junk babes was first raised. In their account they rather more genteely speak of 'would-be actresses and fashion models brought in to cozy up the event'.

Although Bruck maintained that her conclusions were merely the inevitable results of her reporting, it is hard to imagine a more prejudicial or irrelevant frame for an evaluation of Milken. Although Bruck generally kept a tight reign on her emotions, which she hid behind the mask of a professional journalist, her contempt for the Bungalow 8 antics peeked through. To read her evaluation of Don Engel, the man who arranged many of the festivities, he was no more than a procurer of girls for Drexel's high-rollers. But even if this was the case and even if the events in Bungalow 8 really were as lurid as she described them, such behaviour was not unusual in the male-dominated business world. More goes on at a furniture convention in Vegas. While there can be no gainsaying that Wall Street was a fundamentally unpleasant, insensitive and sexist environment, it had nothing to do with Milken. However, Bruck's set-up provides a wash over the whole book.

The end was no less inflammatory, with a hilarious description of a Godfather-like Milken trying to dissuade her from doing the book: 'He asked me a few questions about its genesis and then he declared, "I do not want it to be done." When he was told that it was already in progress, he reiterated that he did not want it done. He seemed surprised, almost, by the assurance that it would be done. Then he said, "I was saying to Fred, why don't we pay you the commitment fee that your publisher would have paid you – except we'll pay it to you not to write the book?" . . . "Or," he went on, as though he had not heard the response, "why don't we pay you for all the copies you would have sold if you had written it?" ' In response to this account Milken's spokesperson Ken Lerer said, 'If he said that I think it was an off-the-cuff comment not made in a serious tone and she knew it and she added her spin to the story which [she] then converted it into "I'll pay for your book." '

His suggestion early on in the project about buying the book – however it was meant, it was clear how it was taken – cannot have helped predispose her to her subject, and throughout she seems to have accorded him little sympathy. Perception versus reality to her was 'how he could see what most of the world could not'. Another reason was that Milken was 'inaccessible or accessible on only fairly horrendous terms', in the words of one senior East Coaster. At the same time her expectations were wound to a pitch by those who worked around him mythicizing him as a messiah. Such expectations were bound to be disappointed. When she met him she found him transparent. Instead of a myth she found a man. 'If Drexel officials were hoping for magic as Milken went public they would be disappointed,' wrote Bruck.

In the end, for all her smarts and articulacy, Bruck's book was founded on one prejudicial premise that came out later. In a television interview given after his indictment she commented that she thought there was something obscene about making $550 million a year: 'Personally, I do not think that anyone should make that kind of money,' she said, admitting she had a problem with it. The thinking is how could such a basic moral wrong be committed without illegality? This does not disqualify the contents of Bruck's book, but it gives us a clearer idea of what Milken's real problems were. For she was not alone in this prejudice. Few really believe in the American Dream of limitless success. There has to be a ceiling. It was the single most important thing in the downfall of Milken, and it was to be the focus of the Prosecutor's Ball.

12

THE PROSECUTOR'S BALL

IN the exchange of letters between Joseph and Simon & Schuster it was possible to discern a certain amount of posturing on Joseph's part. Having made every effort to 'correct' the text (which some say he did not do until the eleventh hour), there was little more he could do. Colleagues indicate that Joseph did not think there was any point in going to war over the book, and that publicly the less said the better. Denouncing it would only make it a bestseller, and indeed it did appear briefly on *The New York Times* bestseller list, perhaps because Robinson, Lake & Lerer, Milken's PR firm who were retained separately to Drexel, alerted journalists to alleged factual errors. At any rate, the print run of the book was doubled, and increased media coverage was the result.

These two different approaches to *The Predator's Ball* illustrate that Milken on the West Coast and Drexel on the East had two different agendas. Ken Lerer, who handled Milken's PR on a day-to-day basis, was aware of this from the day he was hired in March 1988, merely because he was hired. For while their interests seemed mutual and proceeded along parallel tracks, Lerer soon started dropping out of the weekly crisis committee meetings (sources at Drexel say he was uninvited). Quite apart from anything else the meetings were, in the words of one present, 'pretty much a waste of time. They were a lot of smart people who knew nothing about communications . . . it was a bunch of guys talking to each other basically . . . and then the few times that they did have a strategy, it didn't strike me as particularly intelligent.'

Originally Joseph came out vigorously defending Milken: 'I see every trade Michael does for his own account, every trade he does for the firm, and I can guarantee that not only is Michael straight but he bends over backwards to be straight,' he told one magazine. 'What I knew changed,' he has subsequently maintained. 'We had to be careful and play by the rules, but the assumption was that we were gonna play by the rules and that would immunize us. I didn't realize that we had a soft underbelly and that we weren't playing by the rules,' said another on the crisis committee. Joseph's re-education about Milken began with hearing the Princeton Newport tape in the summer and climaxed on 10 December when Giuliani took Joseph downstairs to a secure room with bullet-proof steel doors and showed him an assortment of records and spreadsheets of suspect trades. For Joseph this was the end of the road. 'What we hoped was Boesky bullshit was not,' said one Drexel insider.

Joseph himself said he was guilty of 'surprising naivety' and that he was 'appalled and surprised by the organized nature of the crime wave,' as *Fortune* put it. 'Michael had the best business in the world' said another East Coast executive close to Joseph. 'He was making five hundred million a year on zero risk. He could have been Secretary of the Treasury, there was unlimited social and economic upside. He did not have to cheat to win.' Meanwhile, as far as Joseph was concerned it was merely a matter of playing by the rules. But the rules were as confusing as they were irrelevant. Joseph floundered about in Washington trying to figure out just what they meant, but it seemed that he had not in fact been summoned there for breaking them. As Dingell made clear in his introduction, he was there to answer for the 'junk bond bust up break up shut down' of corporate America. What the rules said was irrelevant in the face of this financial revolution.

But what is extraordinary is the way Joseph, after the epiphany of the spreadsheets, should have swung from one extreme to the other, from protesting that Milken was absolutely innocent to an equally strong conviction that he was absolutely guilty. Those on Milken's side argue that this story of a revelation is a convenient apocryphal construct to get Joseph out of an embarrassing situation. While denying this, Joseph has taken the opportunity to clarify the nature of their relationship. In between telling one reporter in a post-settlement fireside chat how 'working with red-hot iron sure needs one hundred per cent concentration' (he likes to make things in the iron forge on his New Jersey farm), Fred underscored the distance between the two men: 'We never had dinner with our wives, that sort of thing. And as far as I recall we never even had lunch alone together. But Michael and I did talk on the telephone.' The message is clear. Interdependence was not intimacy or complicity. But they did talk on the phone a lot, sometimes fifteen times a day. Others argue that their relationship was as intimate as marriage. 'When you get divorced you've got nothing good to say about your ex, and you only remember the bad times,' said one of Milken's team.

Almost wilfully, the East Coast had blinded itself to any possible reversal of fortune. When asked shortly after Boesky Day what impact it would have on the firm if Milken were forced to resign, Joseph preferred instead to fantasize about the possibility of Milken being run over by a bus. The $4 billion in revenues that he represented was, as Joseph said, 'not chopped liver', it was the whole enchilada. When they launched an in-house investigation it was dainty and cursory. Instead of sitting down face to face with Milken, his lawyers spoke to their lawyers. When the East asked the West if they had anything to worry about, the answer came back from Milken's lawyers, no, they had nothing to worry about. For some odd reason this was considered sufficient. At the time the joke around the company was that if Michael was asked a question he didn't feel comfortable answering, then they took that as their answer. Joseph has confided to close colleagues that, with hindsight, he should have sat him down in the office, looked him in the eye, and asked him if he had done anything wrong – though he did not believe that had he done so he would have got a different answer.

This reluctance to probe has been read as a sure sign of Milken's guilt, although it merely illustrates the East Coast's refusal to get to grips with the realities of the situation. Preventative action in good time could have prevented this politically motivated crisis altogether. Harry Horowitz says he saw it coming as early as December 1984, when *Forbes* magazine printed their merry-go-round cover story. Instead of being worried by the accusation that they were 'Taking in each other's laundry', as the article was titled, 'the people at Drexel were thrilled,' fumed Harry; 'it put them on the map, made them look like real players. Corporate finance took that magazine into every company in America and said "look at this."' Harry, meanwhile warned Michael that he had to get out there and tell his side of the story.

Ken Lerer maintained that the East Coast should have done more than sit back while the money rolled in from the West. 'I think Drexel did him an enormous disservice. They had Michael Milken out in California working away sixteen, seventeen hours a day . . . And I think they used him. I think they realized that he was going to be attacked and they didn't knock on the door and say "Michael, you've got to get out there. You've got to go to Washington, you've got to give interviews, you've got to talk to the media, you've got to tell people what you're doing." I think they were so taken with the amount of business he was bringing into the firm that they made him into this mad genius and I think that was an enormous disservice.'

Meanwhile the government began to tighten the pressure on Drexel, with the publication of the SEC's charges in September. They were tired of waiting on the criminal investigation to file their charges, and they needed a press tonic to re-enthuse the investigation with some brio. Gazumping the criminal department instead of patiently waiting in their shadow gave them just the kind of lift they needed, although there was no getting round the fact that as a sequel to Bruck's book the SEC's 184-page complaint was a damp squib. Nineteen of the twenty-one counts (or 632 of the 712 paragraphs) dealt with the same alleged scam, whereby Milken would manipulate companies to do his bidding by using Boesky as a sort of securities goon. At Milken's direction he would buy into companies and then sell out, threatening a takeover or driving their stock down to ensure that they did whatever Milken wanted them to do. After all the ballyhoo about insider trading it was significant that only two counts (or fifty out of 712 paragraphs) dealt with insider trading.

At the time the charges were generally regarded as weak, and that this was the tenor of the civil charges did not bode well for the criminal charges, compounding rumours that the reason for their continual delay was that the prosecutors were having a hard time making a case that would stick. However, the SEC scored a coup by circumventing the usual lottery-style method of case assignment and getting Judge Pollack, considered to be a pro-government lawyer, assigned to the case. The afternoon that the complaint was filed at the clerk's window in the Federal courthouse, the judge's assistant, possibly tipped off by the SEC, was waiting near the filing clerk to snatch up the case and carry it back to the judge's chambers. There was almost a scuffle as Drexel's lawyers tried to prevent this sleight of hand, with Michael Armstrong, Lowell Milken's lawyer, allegedly towering over the SEC paralegals.

Pollack had a conflict of interest in that his wife was the chairman and major shareholder of a retail company that one of Drexel's clients was acquiring in a leveraged junk bond buyout. She stood to gain some $30 million if the deal went through. When it comes to judicial conflicts, a husband and wife are considered one and the same person, and so the logical thing would have been for the judge to recuse himself. But he refused, and the SEC lawyers even went so far as to suggest that Drexel had perpetrated the larger fraud of deliberately engineering the deal in the first place to create the conflict of interest. 'With these people you just don't believe in coincidences,' one of them told Steven Brill (editor and publisher of *American Lawyer*, which was also co-publisher of *The Predator's Ball*). Although there was little else they could have done, in pursuing the recusal of Pollack, it is hard to imagine that Drexel endeared itself to the Judge.

Other pressures were mounting, too. In October it was leaked that James Dahl, one of Milken's most favoured traders, had testified before the Grand Jury after a compulsion order. This was a popular technique used against mob suspects, where, by giving them immunity whether they liked it or not, the prosecution deprived them of their constitutional right to take the Fifth Amendment, since it was impossible for them to incriminate themselves because they could not be charged on account of their immunity. If they still refused to talk they could be charged with obstruction of justice, or if they talked but didn't tell the truth they could be charged with perjury (as happened to Lisa Jones in November). On 7 December news was leaked that Cary Maultasch, Milken's key New York trader, had also agreed to cooperate. Two days later, the day after Princeton Newport had announced that it was liquidating under RICO pressure, news was leaked that Terren Peizer, a Milken trader, had also rolled. Another particularly aggressive pressure tactic was to sub-poena Drexel's own lawyers for their papers. Usually these materials were protected from investigation and attorney/client privilege was upheld. On 10 December Joseph was shown the books by Giuliani.

'I want to bring you up to date on the status of the investigation,' Joseph wrote in one of his regular staff memos dated 12 December 1988, two days afterwards. 'In recent weeks we have had discussions with the government which are now reaching a crucial stage. If we do not agree to settle with the US Attorney, we believe that he intends to indict the firm . . . and to include in such an indictment so-called 'racketeering charges ("RICO"). We expect that one of these two alternative scenarios will unfold within a short time.' Reprinted in *The Wall Street Journal* under the headline, 'Guilty plea by Drexel appears more likely,' the memo made none of the usual mention of the firm's innocence. 'An indictment will put pressure on the firm and its businesses. We will also face a long drawn out battle in the courts (and unfortunately in the press) before any final resolution of the matter . . . if we settle we can put this constant attack on the firm behind us. But to do so will require a guilty plea . . . we believe Drexel has lost some $1.5 billion of potential revenues, and has spent over $175 million in direct expenses.' Finally Joseph closed with the usual rousing chorus: 'Throughout the past two years of the trial of Drexel and our employees by leak, rumour and innuendo, the employees of Drexel have stood together with our loyal clients and the results have been sensational. Over the next weeks and months, almost regardless of the alternative, as we have in the past, we will all need to pull together and to call upon our internal resources and the loyalty of our clients.'

On 19 December the board unanimously rejected the government's settlement offer. The sticking point was that Giuliani was still insisting that Drexel waived their attorney/client privilege (so he could pore over the firm's usually confidential legal strategies for evidence of more crimes). 'At the present time discussions may be winding down,' Joseph announced over the hoot and holler. 'We could be indicted at any time . . . it's very clear that the firm didn't do anything wrong, and couldn't really know.'

It was Drexel's finest hour. That night at the firm's corporate finance party Joseph was greeted like a hero. In a skit former CEO Bob Linton sang Fred a song, 'Rudy the Brown-Nosed Litigator', wearing a policeman's hat and handcuffs. Greeted with deafening whoops, cheers and applause, Fred made a rousing speech, something to the effect that after all the uncertainty and hesitation Drexel was going to take a stand and be damned. Many in the audience broke down and cried.

The moment was short-lived. Within forty eight-hours Drexel had settled with the government, agreeing to fire Milken, and pay a $650 million fine. Myth has it that the day after the party Joseph had left at 10 p.m. for a private meeting with Giuliani in which the final details of the settlement were hashed out. 'Don't worry,' he was supposed to have reasured his colleagues on the board, 'Rudy likes me.' The notion that a zealous prosecutor would have a soft spot for a juicy investment banker – even if he did brush his hair like Edward Kennedy – was much ridiculed at Drexel. Joseph didn't deny he made the remark but says that it was taken out of context. The statement was Joseph's ironic way of saying that he didn't think he had any cards in his hand or any real hope of relief at the hands of Giuliani. Having negotiated the deal with Giuliani, Joseph was then supposed to have cast his vote against it, a token gesture for which Joseph also received much criticism.

A significant detail of the settlement was that Drexel did not technically plead guilty to the six counts, it was simply 'unable to contest' them. 'We aren't saying these things happened,' Joseph announced over the Drexel line. 'We don't know whether these things happened or not. But we can't disprove them and we want to get on with things.' This was of course true. With RICO hanging over their heads, they were literally unable to contest the charges, since to do so would invoke the RICO indictment that would collapse investor confidence in the firm, irrespective of any pre-trial seizure, and thus bankrupt them. However, niceties of phrasing could not alter the fact that as a company Drexel was a convicted felon. When after the settlement Congressman Markey announced, 'We now know that the single most successful firm on Wall Street during the 1980s largely built its fortune on a foundation of criminality,' he spoke for public perception at large. From this point on Drexel's business would gradually begin to diminish.

Donald Trump, riding high before his own crash, was, as ever, on hand for a quotation: 'I think the government totally beat Drexel . . . I can't imagine how Drexel could be happy with this deal.' Privately Joseph let it be known that he thought the settlement was onerous and that they had a fifty/fifty chance of survival. Publicly he said, 'We ended up with a settlement that is less unfair than the one we rejected. But it is one that allows us to continue in business.'

In reaction Milken picked his words carefully: 'I spent a lifetime helping to build a firm. I don't think I'm going to be doing that much longer. That's just not an uplifting experience.' According to Ralph Ingersoll II, chairman of Ingersoll Publications, who was both a client and friend of Milken's, Milken apparently felt that 'the firm put the interest of the commercial institution ahead of the interests of its employees'. Milken of course thought that the real capital of any company was its people, and therefore Drexel had made a mistake. Unlike Joseph, Milken was convinced the firm wasn't going to be around much longer. Other close allies like Steve Wynn said that Milken felt 'bewildered' and 'betrayed'.

As part of the settlement Drexel agreed to restructure itself, incorporating a bureaucracy to replace its buccaneering spirit. The unprecedented degree of government involvement virtually turned Drexel into a nationalized firm. Drexel agreed to hire a compliance director, three compliance officials in the junk bond department, create a senior trading official, appoint a new general counsel to the firm and an ombudsman to whom employees could express their concerns in confidence about any possible wrongdoing. All these people would be SEC-approved stooges, and would report to the new oversight committee consisting of three outside directors, also SEC-approved. Perhaps not surprisingly, two of these new directors came from the SEC and one had been president of the American Stock Exchange. In addition Drexel would appoint the SEC's chosen accounting firm of Peat Marwick. Their twelve-strong team would not only review each and every junk bond trade, but would also review trades from the last three years.

Drexel also agreed to move certain of its operations back to New York from Beverly Hills (but not the junk bond department), and hire at its own expense an SEC approved law firm to conduct a review of Drexel's operations and make recommendations, in addition to reporting monthly to the SEC. The firm also revised its policies concerning employee investment partnerships, and promised to further restrict them from investing in Drexel's own issues. In sum, these changes would make Drexel 'as pure as Caesar's wife' as Joseph put it.

In one of the most outrageous ironies of all, Drexel appointed John Shad chairman of Drexel. Shad had been head of the SEC when it launched the insider trading investigation that began it all. Shad was brought in along with another regulator from the SEC and a former president of the stock exchange as outside directors, to give Drexel a squeaky clean image. Many questioned the appropriateness of regulators coming on board to run the ship. The Establishment was clearly showing its might, for not only were they 'the judge, jury and prosecutor', as Shad announced when head of the SEC, they were also, through Shad's very example, chairman as well. Granted, Shad did earmark his $3 million annual salary to Harvard Business School, so he couldn't be accused of cashing in on his regulatory responsibilities. He said he viewed his appointment to Drexel as another form of public service. But he was naturally Joseph's preferred choice since he had given Joseph his first job on Wall Street, and it would be under his figurehead leadership that Joseph would be able to continue to run the firm as he had done in the past.

This begged one of the great unanswered questions about the settlement, how Joseph managed to remain CEO and escape any kind of censure for failure to supervise the company in his charge. 'Like many of his outraged colleagues, Beck suspected that Joseph had cut a deal to save his own neck. Joseph denied it,' wrote Anthony Bianco in *Rainmaker*. One of those working on Milken's side said: 'Joseph was the guy with the neat hair and always buttoned up and always had a smile on his face and tried to make a lot of friends with the media and politicians while he had Michael in the back working away. Fred doesn't have any legal problems now partly because of that.'

After an indecisive and confused performance, the sudden settlement represented a new, and not improved, Fred Joseph. 'It was like 1984,' said one Drexelite disgusted with the doublespeak. 'You would listen for two years to Fred and the attorneys saying, "Drexel is wonderful, we're innocent, everyone else is the bad guy" . . . then the latest message was, "Once this is all settled we'll be the cleanest firm on the Street." ' There would be other volte-face, and he would by turns appear to be both helpless and unable. Instead of

Dr Feelgood, Joseph's new nickname would be Fred Isuzu, named after a fast-talking Japanese car salesman featured in television advertisements.

In addition to ripping out the entrepreneurial heart of the firm, the settlement also required that Drexel behead itself. Drexel agreed no longer to employ Milken, and to withhold his salary and bonus for 1988. Where Drexel had stood firm and made the government back down on so many points, this was a deal breaker. Even if they were forced into it, it was still a betrayal of the man who had made them everything they were. In the new year Joseph was summoned out to face a fuming high yield bond department on the West Coast. 'He made a fifteen minute speech,' recalled one person present. 'At the end of his presentation we felt that all he really did was turn our hides over to the Federal government and save his own, and we told him that.' However, as Joseph reasoned in his defence, he did have a duty to ten thousand employees, and when it came down to it, it was his duty to preserve those jobs even if it meant ditching the man who had created their jobs in the first place.

The settlement left Milken to fight alone, and in March, on the eve of the high yield bond conference, Milken was served with a massive ninety-eight-count indictment. The core of the indictment consisted of two RICO counts, namely the creation of a racketeering conspiracy and participation in a racketeering conspiracy. The individual charges, after the two RICO counts, consisted of fifty-four counts of mail and wire fraud (i.e. using an envelope and a telephone in the process of committing an offence), thirty-three counts of securities fraud, five counts of false filings and one count of assisting to prepare a false tax return. If convicted each count carried five years in jail, and if convicted on the two RICO counts Milken would face between ten and twenty years on each. All told – and as was much reported – Milken faced a possible 520 years in jail. But the massive number of counts and multiple life sentence in jail were misleading when it came down to an analysis of the charges, which added little to the SEC complaint.

The SEC complaint focused on the Boesky/Milken 'arrangement', and many of the same supposedly illicit trades were revisited in the indictment. In the case of Diamond Shamrock's merger with Occidental Petroleum, KKR's takeover of Storer Communications, Maxxam's takeover of Pacific Lumber and Ted Turner's acquisition of MGM/UA, Milken was supposed to have passed on inside information to Boesky who traded on that information, on the secret understanding that they would share profits or losses. In the case of Posner's takeover of Fishbach, the acquisition of Harris Graphics and Golden Nugget's sale of MCA stock, Milken and Boesky were supposed to have parked stock with one another, with the same shared loss/profit arrangement. In the case of Wickes and Stone Container, Milken was supposed to have directed Boesky to buy stock – once again indemnifying him for any losses – for the purpose of driving the stock up or down according to Milken's wider agenda. Milken was also supposed to have accommodated

Boesky's desire to do similar sham transactions, buying shares from Boesky just before the payment of a dividend, and then reselling them to him after the dividend had been paid (which usually caused the share price to drop). In this way Boesky could create tax losses. The $5.3 million payment also remained in the indictment cited as illegal compensation on illegal deals. The two deals that didn't include Boesky were also in the SEC complaint. In the merger of Lorimar Pictures and Telepictures, and in the leveraged buyout of Viacom, Milken was supposed not to have bothered to use Boesky as a screen, directly instructing people on the X to trade (no proof of any such instruction was included in the indictment).

Those charges not included in the SEC complaint came from Princeton Newport in a smaller but similar selection to those above; Mattel concerned a convoluted bit of stock parking, there were also the tax loss trades that Princeton Newport had believed were perfectly legal, and, in the case of US Home Shares and COMB shares, stock manipulation. In the entire indictment, the most compelling piece of evidence was a taped extract of a telephone conversation between Newberg and his counterpart at Princeton Newport (the pair whose infamous 'world of sleaze banter' got Princeton Newport convicted). Newberg wanted to drive the stock in question down 'And um . . . , you're indemnified, uh, you know, my –, it's, y –, you know what I'm saying.' The world of sleaze had struck again.

When one considers the years of work that had gone into the investigation (one investigator with the Inland Revenue service spent the better part of three years examining the tax aspects of one count), the millions of documents that had been sub-poenaed, and the number of transactions that Milken and the department engaged in over the period (by some counts estimated to be in excess of thirty million), this handful of examples hardly does justice to the repeated assertion of a massive conspiracy headed by Michael Milken, who, according to the indictment outline, 'established its criminal purposes and supervised its training'. As George Gilder observed, 'If you can't find an offence among those you're incompetent. He's guilty technically, as anyone who's gone through a tax audit knows you're really defenceless. Milken must have vigorously avoided insider trading.' Moreover Milken's direct connection with the events it described, most of which were carried out by his traders, was tentative at best.

But nevertheless the indictment was a masterpiece of orchestration.

'In America an indictment marks the beginning of the legal process, not the end. After almost two and a half year of leaks and distortions , I am now eager to present all the facts in an open and unbiased forum. I will plead not guilty to the charges and vigorously fight these accusations. I am confident that in the end I will be vindicated.'

Quite apart from the fact that Milken would have to eat his words, he could not have been more wrong. Although sub-poenas were supposed to be only requests for information, and although an indictment carried no burden of guilt, these legal formulations pre-dated the information age that Milken so proudly financed. In their new context they have become the symbols and shorthand of probable guilt. And in the world of ideas it is the perceived idea, running ahead of the physical reality, that counts for more than what we used to rely on as solid fact. As journalist Christopher Byron, who covered the Milken case for *New York* magazine, observed; 'The real event is the initial charge. . . . By the time you get to trial the man is already presumed guilty in the court of public opinion.' And that is all that really counts. With the battle for justice fought in the arena of the media, sub-poenas, indictments and pleas along the way are a kind of punctuation accompanying the trial in the people's court of the media. An eventual acquittal rebutting all the prejudiced speculation is merely a full-stop, that does not and cannot remove the taint of guilt.

What made Milken's indictment such a stunning condemnation was, in the absence of quality, the sheer quantity: 98 counts! 520 years in jail! These impressive statistics had the added advantage of futher convicting Milken in the court of public opinion. The presumption was that the government would never bring such a massive indictment unless he were massively guilty. Such a prejudice was only reinforced upon consideration of the chances of being acquitted of all the charges. (For example in another Boesky-related case where the accused was in court with a forty-two-count indictment, one juror, finding the defendant guilty, explained their reasoning: 'We've got to convict him on something – there are so many charges.') Giuliani's trial by press was dependent upon column inches for its success, and this compensated for the fact that the actual content of the indictment was a dry litany, too tedious and unsexy for mass media attention. Filed on the eve of the Predator's Ball, which ever since Bruck's book had become a legend, timing also helped the indictment make its mark.

Overall, however, the indictment depended upon one count that, while not technically a crime, was nonetheless seen as being bigger than all the rest combined: Milken's salary. It could be no coincidence that while virtually every other piece of relevant information was leaked, this jewel was not. As big as a rock, this jewel sat there twinkling on the page like the Koh Hi Nor diamond, implicating Milken as the magpie who thieved it: 'Nearly all of the unlawful proceeds from these racketeering activities allegedly were . . . passed on to the individual defendants, among others, in the form of extraordinary levels of compensation . . . Drexel is alleged to have paid Michael R. Milken, for example, $295 million in 1986 and $550 million in 1987,' read the outline. The indictment also revealed the salary of Lowell Milken which drew for Milken an additional round of criticism, in that he allowed there to be such disparity between brothers. (Lowell's indictment alongside his brother was a masterpiece of strategic hostage-taking. He was accused of being 'his brother's principal advisor in the conduct of the conspiracy' and in addition to managing and directing trading in 'certain investment partnerships' he 'also assisted in resolving disputes involving co-conspirators'.) All in all the deal the government was staking was $1.8 billion, the price of a modest buyout.

In addition to the government, Milken had also kept his salary a secret. When news of it finally went over the ticker it drew shocked gasps on the trading room floor at Drexel. Many who felt that Drexel had betrayed Milken now felt that Milken had betrayed them. 'People are so hung up on money,' Milken would complain many times, was this why he kept his record-breaking salary a secret from others, fearing that they would not be able to contain their envy? When finally revealed under such highly charged circumstances, it made Milken look twice as bad.

'Ill gotten or not, Mr Milken's whopping pay has captured the attention of the nation,' said *The Wall Street Journal* in a mocking front-page piece. 'Only Al Capone, according to the *Guinness Book Of World Records*, could sustain a claim to have exceeded Mr Milken's income – and he was self-employed.' The piece also included a 'How much is $550 Million' table that included the SEC's annual budget ($137 million), a stealth bomber ($280 million), a space shuttle launch ($350 million), and the gross national product of Guyana ($469 million) which was always a favourite statistical yardstick. Milken's pal Michael Jackson only made $60 million, and adjusted for inflation, Al Capone would, in his best year, have pulled down $600 million.

'Wages even Wall Street can't stomach,' snarled *The New York Times*. 'Such an extraordinary income inevitably raises questions as to whether there isn't something unbalanced in the structure of the way our financial sytem is working,' sniffed David Rockefeller, the blue cheese of Old Money who seemed oblivious to his own circumstances and in the privileged position of inheriting a fortune from his robber baron granddaddy who, after adjustments for inflation, only earned $100 million less than Milken in his best years. Donald Trump proclaimed, 'You can be happy on a lot less money.' Any irony was clearly lost on this millionaire's son who boasted a fortune in excess of $1 billion (ultimately, of course, he would have to be happy on a lot less than he led everyone to believe).

The sum was configured every which way for even greater effect. He earned $1,046 a minute according to one account and $107,000 an hour (computed on a fourteen-hour day). Globally he was only eclipsed by the Sultan of Brunei (no comparison), and the earnings of McDonalds ($549 million). No one thought to mention that the Big Mac figure was after tax, whereas the Milken figure was before tax. (Interestingly, the fact that Milken had paid $750 million in taxes between 1984 and 1988 received considerably less attention.)

That the frame surrounding such statistics is more important than the statistics themselves is forcibly brought home by the fact that a number of Americans earned more than Milken. The simple difference was that Milken was a salaried employee, whereas the likes of Sam Walton, and the

Newhouse Brothers were owner-managers. Walton, the supermarket king, reaped $4 billion in appreciation, while the Newhouse brothers of Condé Nast took in $2.4 billion apiece. The Sultan of Brunei earns $155 million a day. 'People don't mind when David Geffen made $800 million because he has his own firm that he sold. People do mind if you're an employee and you make that money . . . if he had sold that company for $550 million that year everybody would have said he was a genius,' argued Lerer.

13

MR NICE GUY OR
TWO-LEGGED DEMON

A number of people argue that that's what Milken should have done. He was responsible for turning the second-tier investment bank into America's fifth largest but most profitable investment bank, and consistently accounted for the lion's share of the profits. According to the indictment, the high yield bond department accounted for 75 per cent of Drexel's profits in 1983 and 1984, and an average of 50 per cent between 1983 and 1987. Other insiders estimate those figures were as high as 90 per cent in some years. It was, in effect, his firm.

Extraordinarily, the man who preached about the joys and wisdom of owner-managers wanted neither to own nor to manage Drexel. Only after he was persuaded that it might be tactical did Milken invest in Drexel stock, and even then only in a tailor-made special issue (the largest individual shareholder, he only ever held 6 per cent). 'He would criticize something,' said a senior Drexelite, 'and I'd say Michael why don't you get involved, and he'd say nope, I don't want to.' As Harry explained, 'Michael had his head in the sand. He said "I'm just an employee, I'm not an officer. I keep my nose to the grindstone."' 'In 1984, 1985, when he saw things going on in the firm that he didn't like, instead of rolling over he would have been far better off just leaving the firm and starting his own firm,' said Lerer without elaborating on just what it was he did not like. There was even talk on the West Coast, before it became clear that the investigation would be the ruination of Drexel, of buying the high yield bond department from the company.

'Drexel is the only company I've worked for since graduating from college, and it's the only one I ever expected to work for,' Milken said of his betrayal. In spite of being painted as scheming and duplicitous, he had displayed a dogged loyalty in only ever working for one firm. He struck a deal with Tubby Burnham and it never changed. In the teeth of criticism that the formula should have been shaved as time went on, Drexel argued that it was precisely the lack of such an incentive that caused Bear Stearns to miss out when

Kohlberg, Kravis and Roberts left to set up KKR (paying Milken's extraordinary salary as salary was also to their advantage from a tax point of view). 'Remember,' former CEO Bob Linton added, 'for every dollar that Mike Milken got paid, the firm got paid two. The arithmetic is pretty simple.'

But for Milken the timing was bad. Until this point Ivan Boesky, with his 'greed works' credo, had embodied the spirit of the age. Come 1989 the popular wisdom was that the roaring eighties were over. First titillated by glossy magazine profiles of profligacy but now sated, the public were beginning to look around for someone to pay for the party. And when the music stopped Milken was caught in the spotlight holding $550 million. At a stroke the government made Milken the living breathing symbol of the greed decade. At a stroke they also pre-empted the need for a trial and with this revelation 'proved' him guilty in the eyes of the public. With just less than one year for every million, Milken's prospect of 520 years in jail would be just punishment for his crime of earning $550 million dollars.

Somewhat quietly, Milken's PR people tried to limit the spill by letting it be known that he had paid 50 per cent in taxes and given away another 30 per cent, and argued that he did not lead a life of glittery excess. Milken, no doubt sincerely, consistently argued that money was unimportant, 'a fleeting emotion'. 'You guys are so hung up on money,' he had complained to a journalist. But these arguments did not wash. For while Milken may have believed that capital was not the scarce resource, it was a scarce enough resource in most of the lives of the general public. Milken's argument that personal wealth was not important to him was somewhat undercut by the fact that he had it, lots of it. Most people do not have wealth, lack wealth and thirst for wealth. They also tend to envy and resent those that do have it. Milken's attempts to downplay his billions, far from bridging the gulf between him and the have-not public, only seemed to make matters worse.

For while people envied the wealth of the junk bond jillionaires, they drooled over – and even demanded – the spectacle. They watched 'Lifestyles of the Rich and Famous' (even the sanctimonious David Rockefeller, according to the show's host Robin Leach, would have people over for dinner to watch the show every week). For Milken not to spend it lavishly, and live it up Trump-style, was more reprehensible than the crime of earning it. People expected the well-monied to be splashed across the pages of glossy magazines in larger-than-life pop-ups, living cartoon lives of glam and glitz. Milken was excoriated for using cheap paper napkins. His indifference to his wealth was not laudable, it was 'chilling.' In *Playboy*, across the page from a glowing portrait of Milken-made Ted Turner, 'Money Mad Mike' was lambasted for his 'unwillingness to enjoy his wealth' which was, the piece concluded, his least endearing quality and why everybody hated him.

A few days after the indictment Milken was arraigned in New York. In previous years he would of course have been at his high yield bond conference which was in full swing at the Beverly Hills Hilton. When asked how he pleaded he answered, 'I plead not guilty.' Outside he was cheered by a large group of colleagues and supporters, some wearing T-shirts and baseball caps declaring, 'Mike Milken We Believe In You.'

This was also the message of a series of full-page ads that had been taken out only a week earlier in national newspapers at a cost of $175,000. Led by Sig Zises of Integrated Resources, some ninety business clients put their names to the ads, including some of the high-roller raiders like Nelson Peltz, John Kluge, Merv Adelson and Bennett LeBow. But generally the list was filled out by the CEOs of many of the medium-sized growth companies such as Bernard Salick (Healthcare), Ralph Ingersoll (Ingersoll publications), William McGowan (MCI), Richard Grassgreen (Kinder Care), Don Liddle (Unimar), Hank Greenspun (Las Vegas Sun), Oz Mutz (Forum Group), Roger Stangland (Vons) . Conspicuously absent were the first-tier raiders, such as Boone Pickens, Ron Perelman of Revlon and Henry Kravis of KKR.

'You won't find the ghost of Michael Milken here,' Drexel's spokesman Steven Anreder told Marie Brenner snappishly, something that was flatly contradicted by former Drexel CEO Bob Linton who announced, 'There's a presence hanging over this conference and that, of course, is the aura of our long-time friend and associate, Mike Milken.' The few speakers who did not make a tribute to Milken were the exception rather than the norm. The most outspoken was Lorraine Spurge, Milken's syndicate manager: 'We have received a great deal of criticism from some so-called authorities for what they call playing with large sums of money and creating nothing. Allegedly that is our offence. It is ironic, indeed, that Michael and Drexel have come under such intense attack for allegedly producing and inventing and manu-facturing nothing.'

Futhermore, at the precise time of his arraignment, there was a feisty demonstration in the lobby of the hotel, co-ordinated by friends of the family. Joni, Milken's kid sister, had had printed up T-shirts that read De Lorean, Myerson, Milken & Milken. It was a significant selection of names. De Lorean was the entrepreneurial car maker whose attempt to introduce a sporty new car to the market crashed and burned amidst charges of fraud and cocaine dealing. De Lorean was acquitted once it was learnt that the cocaine deal in which he had been caught red handed was a government sting and entrapment.

The case of Bess Myerson was no less bizarre. The former Miss America was also Mayor Koch's close friend and cultural affairs advisor. She was indicted on corruption charges after supposedly having given the daughter of Judge Gable, who was presiding over her lover's divorce case (and who was also indicted), a job in the attempt to speed the divorce and win a favourable settlement. However, the principle government witness was Sukrheet Gable, the judge's daughter, an eccentric who admitted on the witness stand that she had a memory 'like a Swiss cheese' (because it was so full of holes). Generally considered to be a bit soft, she had taped her mother's telephone calls at the US Attorney's behest. 'When prosecutors start using children to tape their parents secretly as Giuliani had done in the Bess Myerson case,' said Arthur Liman, 'well, this is Nazi Germany type stuff.' The farce ended with the acquittal of both Myerson and Judge Hortense Gable (who was 75 and virtually blind), and some sideways glances at Giuliani's motivation for hounding such a weak case that was nevertheless embarrassing to Ed Koch.

'On the other side of this country a great injustice is being done,' said Charlie Sarkis, addressing the thirty-odd family friends and dozen colleagues who had gathered in the lobby. 'We have a challenge to tell people the true story of Michael Milken and what he has done for people. Take a minute to take the positive thoughts that we have – and I know Michael believes in this – and send that energy to New York City. They will feel it.'

And there was more. As was usual for the conference, there was the typical assortment of gifts and keepsakes, but one lunchtime each person found a book on his plate called *Tom Smith and His Incredible Bread Machine*. Written in 1964 by R. W. Grant, an aerospace engineer, it told in verse the story of Tom Smith who invented a machine that could make bread for a penny a loaf, and as a result feed the world.

But after a price rise of one cent because of an increase in business tax, Tom's woes began. First he was condemned by the intellectuals at their International Conference on Inhumanity and Greed, and then he was attacked in the media:

> Comments in the Nation's press
> Now scorned Smith and his plunder:
> 'What right had he to get so rich
> On other people's hunger?'

And by the business establishment:

> The people now should realize
> It's time to cut Smith down to size,
> For he's betrayed his public trust
> (And taken all that bread from us).

And summoned to Washington where he was told:

> You must compete – but not too much,
> For, if you do, you see,
> Then the market would be yours – And that's monopoly!
> Yes don't you dare monopolize!
> We'd raise an awful fuss!
> For that's the greatest crime of all!
> (Unless it's done by us!)

Smith then asked what he had done wrong, and the lawyers in Congress gleefully told him how in their lives they had avoided risk and entrepreneurialism, and how because they had never ventured they had also never lost, and so with an unblemished record they had found their niche as bureaucrats who were uniquely qualified (because they never failed in business) to run everybody else's.

Tom was then indicted:

> 'The rule of law, in complex times,
> Has proved itself deficient.
> We much prefer the rule of men!
> It's vastly more efficient!

And found guilty:

> Guilty! Guilty! We agree!
> He's guilty of this plunder!
> He had no right to get so rich
> On other people's hunger!

Then bundled off to prison:

> 'Five years in jail!' the judge then said.
> 'You're lucky it's not worse!
> Robber Barons must be taught
> Society Comes First!

The book ends with the government baking all the bread, which sells for a dollar a loaf.

Rumours that Milken would make an appearance at the conference circulated all the time, one even reaching the US Attorney's office. As part of the settlement, Drexel had agreed to sever all ties with Milken and help the government prosecute him. However, the settlement had not yet been signed into effect, and Milken was on a leave of absence. The firm had been seriously reprimanded for issuing a sympathetic statement when Milken was indicted. Any more public displays of support, Drexel were warned, could threaten the settlement. On hearing that Milken was scheduled to speak that evening at a small dinner for selected clients, the US Attorney's office called Fred Joseph, and Milken was cancelled.

The Milken tribute tape put Fred Joseph in a similarly awkward position. The two-minute music video had been commissioned by a core group of loyalists in the high yield bond department, and messianized Milken. It consisted of a pumping disco backing track with snippets of his speeches spliced in and intercut with a montage of high yield industries. 'Perception . . . Reality . . . to accept change . . . to resist change . . . high yield bonds,' it began, ending with Milken saying, 'No amount of money, no matter how great, is worth the sacrifice of our reputations, our principles and our beliefs.' When Joseph learned of the plan to show the tape at lunch, he put his foot down, arguing that it could jeopardize the settlement. But he was shouted down and had little choice but to let the screening go ahead. Afterwards Lorraine Spurge was supposed to have leaked the tape to CNN.

A few days before the SEC settlement went into effect in June, Milken resigned and announced the launch of his new company, The Alliance For Capital Access, which would focus on 'the creation of ownership opportunities for employees, minorities, and unions'. Located in his old office, there was no X, but a long rectangular table consisting of eighteen wooden desks pushed together and cluttered with quotrons. The company, a venture capital concern, would invest amounts between $100,000 and $20 million. In one deal the firm leased $2.5 million of barges and equipment to help Unimar, one of his pet ESOP companies from his days at Drexel, to clean up the Exxon Valdez oil spill. In another Wolfgang Puck, chef and owner of the celebrity watering hole Spago's, had hoped to fund a frozen pizza venture with Milken money. But the deal fell through. Milken also indicated that he might be interested in helping companies restructure their finances by swapping high yield debt for less expensive stock.

But no matter what Milken did, it was seen as imageering. 'I try to help people and even this reporters twist and think I'm doing for public relations,' he said of the press reports disparaging this latest venture as part of Robinson, Lake & Lerer's campaign for a kindler, gentler Milken.

Before the investigation it had not been possible to interest anyone in Milken's charitable activities. Although the press were invited to the Educator Award presentations, no one showed up, as a West Coast anchorman who had been drafted to host the 1987 LA presentation complained in his opening remarks. But once the investigation gathered momentum, the press, according to Lerer, mistook their own growing interest in his every move as a change in Milken's behaviour.

There was, for example, the baseball fiasco, which took place a week after SEC charges were filed in September 1988. At a breakfast meeting on education Drexel chairman Bob Linton let slip that Milken was taking 1,700 underprivileged children to a New York Mets baseball game at Shea Stadium that afternoon (this was part of Drexel's interaction with the Variety children's charity). Thus alerted, the event was inundated with press. Complained Milken, 'Then I have to read how my taking kids to a ball game is a publicity stunt. It is so ridiculous.'

Then in April 1989 he was invited to the Old Timers' annual dinner at Quincy Shipyard in Rockland, Massachusetts. The yard had been closed for the past three years, but since the previous autumn Milken had been trying to organize the financing so it could re-open employee-owned. Everything was in place. Milken told the fraternal gathering that 'by 30 June the money will be lined up for the yard', and he said he looked forward to returning to see the first ship launched. But it was not to be. The story crossed over from the local to the national press and the authorities were concerned that Drexel was violating its agreement by doing business with Milken. Although Milken insisted that he was only acting as a cheerleader, the brouhaha stymied the necessary government approval for the loan which was withheld, and the deal fell through. The president was convinced the refusal was 'politically motivated'.

Another occasion was the HELP luncheon honouring Milken in May. Milken claimed that he had been deluged with invitations for similar events, but had turned most of them down. He agreed to do this one 'for the children'. Reluctantly he agreed to let the press attend. 'What you see here is reality,' he told one reporter, but some took issue with the stage-managed event. While Milken cried quietly at his table handicapped children were led through their paces by actress Kristy McNichol in testimonials to Milken. One child, when asked how he felt when Milken gave him a stuffed animal on Valentine's Day, said, 'I felt proud, happy and excited. I think Mr Milken is a very nice and generous and giving person.'

But although the children who were up on stage and being led through their paces were clearly tutored in their roles, it would be presumptuous to dismiss this as contrived. The children were thrilled to be on stage and proud to be able to perform their parts, and Milken in turn may well have found support in their unconditional love which provided a shelter from the relentless investigation.

Vanity Fair writer Marie Brenner was also there: 'The tragedy of this contrived effort,' she commented, 'is that it takes away from a dimension of the man's real persona. At the lunch, I observed Milken with one of the children, a piano prodigy who had performed on the programme. Milken was unaware I was listening to his conversation. He said to the boy, "I want to come visit you later. I want to hear the new piece." No one was around, and the child, clearly used to Milken's attention, was casual. "OK, Mike, but I'm kind of busy. I have a lot of homework." Milken backed off immediately, with no impatience "Sure," he said. "I understand." '

In May he was in Oakland, California, a guest of the National Conference of Black Mayors. He was asked to come up with a model plan to rebuild urban inner-city areas. There he teamed up with Jesse Jackson who said, 'Banks, S&Ls, and insurance companies have abandoned not just blacks but urban America. Mike Milken has a genuine interest in making capital accessible to to people with ideas' (for a short while Jesse Jackson's son worked in the junk bond department at Drexel, until the deluge of press inquiries drove him out). In June he was honored by the business group '100 Black Men'. Reginald Lewis, the man whom Milken had financed to the tune of $985 million dollars for his purchase of Beatrice Foods (making him the first black CEO in the *Fortune* 500), presented him with an award.

The activities were derided by Robinson, Lake & Lerer's PR rivals as an orchestrated Mr Nice Guy campaign. 'I was turned off by the cynical attempt to characterize Michael Milligan as a Boy Scout. To me this was an arrogant, unprofessionally conceived campaign that underscored the superficiality of the advisors,' sniped a rival PR executive, getting Milken's name wrong and revealing the depth of his knowledge about the issue. Another called it 'The Al Capone defence; let's hand out candy to children and nobody will dislike us.' Still others felt it was relevant to point out that Saddam Hussein liked children too. Complained Lerer, 'It's a damned if you do, damned if you don't situation,' and denied that he had orchestrated Milken's schedule and said that Milken was behaving no differently than he had always done. 'This is a legal case that's going to court, and not a public relations issue.' They argued that they weren't trying to sell a political candidate or a bar of soap, which was why they tried to do as little as possible. All that had changed was the press's level of interest. 'We never tried to ignite any stories. All we did was try to extinguish them for four years. It was a successful day when Michael's name didn't appear in the newspaper.' But generally it did, and in some ways Lerer was pissing in the wind at best.

On some occasions he was able to keep some of these events out of the press, such as the occasion he took a bunch of Milken scholars (high school children whose college fees the Milken Foundation had agreed to pay) to the Apollo theatre with the Reverend Jesse Jackson. But more often than not word got out, such as when he taught the math club to the 102nd Street school in the Watts District in LA, bringing along vegetables, calculators, and Michael Jackson.

There is no doubt that Milken did attend more of these events, but forced out of Drexel he also had more time on his hands. He also spent time in West Philadelphia and speaking at his alma mater, handing out cheques for the Educator Awards programme from state to state, and teaching his Math Club. Such events and trips were probably a welcome alternative to the increased amount of time he said he spent making spaghetti and taking out the garbage. And brooding.

What Milken's PR people saw as a do-nothing policy others saw as stealth, and rather damagingly some of those came from inside the firm. Mary Gotschall worked in the Washington office of Robinson, Lake & Lerer. Fired from the firm, Gotschall sought to even the score by going public. She claimed that the company designed and disseminated a glossy appointments calendar to tout the Family Foundation's contributions. She also claimed that the firm retained a minorities expert to woo members of the congressional Black Caucus, and that she had ghost-written op-ed pieces for, among others, Reginald Lewis. 'We organized a fan club of Milken's better-known friends who, under our tutelage, signed full-page ads in his praise and loaned their names to op-eds on his behalf. We furtively planned letters to the editor in major papers. We left no fingerprints,' she claimed.

Gotschall began her account by describing her lifestyle when she was sent out to Los Angeles to work on a coffee table book about high yield bonds that Milken wanted to publish. She boasted how she gorged herself on Godiva chocolates and champagne – when not eating out at Spago's and Chez Hélène – in her pool- side room at the Beverly Hilton, and running up (in the six weeks she was there on assignment) $7,000 in room service. 'I charged it all to Mike Milken. Hey, you only live once,' she said, unabashed. It was not surprising that she was fired.

When not gorging herself greed-decade style she seemed to have spent her time with her feet propped up on the desk in Milken's offices, idling away on the junk book. Of course Milken didn't take offence at her casual approach. He told her he did his best thinking with his feet up on the desk. She was disappointed, not to say a little resentful, at this spectacle of unaffected ordinariness and humility. She had expected a walking-talking Gordon Gekko, 'someone decked out in a $3,000 suit, a Hermes tie, and cuff links as big as quail's eggs. He was, after all, worth about $1.3 billion at the time.' Instead of that she described how he would go around gathering up all the pizza boxes, paper plates and styrofoam cups after long twelve hour meetings.

The book she had been sent out to work on was intended to showcase 150 high yield companies, and was tentatively titled *The American Spirit*. She said that Milken intended to distribute the book free to every school in the country and sell it to the featured companies who would then use it as a promotional item. 'It was a measure of Milken's näiveté and obstinacy – as well as his lack of perspective – that he persisted with the idea in the face of common sense,' said Gotschall in between mouthfuls of free Milken lunch, the details of which are faithfully recited: guacamole, blue corn chips, fajitas, wild rice, kiwi lime sparklers – one of her favourites – chocolate cakes, petits fours, and raspberry iced tea. 'He could no longer appreciate how the man on the street viewed his junk-bond empire,' she commented. Finally the book was published as *Portraits of the American Dream* by Lorraine Spurge's company Knowledge Exchange Inc. The coffee-table format volume features most of Milken's pet junk bond companies. Dedicated to Michael Milken, the book includes an artificial-looking picture of him surrounded by children. 'It is no apologia,' reads the jacket blurb, 'it is an evocative clarion call of affirmation.'

One thing Lerer did admit to doing was releasing the Ben Stein letter to the public. Ben Stein was perhaps Milken's most vociferous critic, and according to Lerer had turned Milken-bashing into a cottage industry. His indictments of Milken as 'the betrayer of capitalism' had appeared principally in *Barrons* where his byline listed him as a writer, lawyer and economist.

In his writings, with increasing abandon he portrayed Milken's junk bond business as a giant ponzi scheme, criminally conceived by a 'cheerleader' pretending to be a 'braino-nerd'. It was a 'something-for-nothing', 'get-rich-quick' scam. The 'daisy-chain' of Milken clients created the illusion of a genuine market where there was none, while they went about dismembering and plundering corporate America with their chainsaw leveraged buyouts, junking S&Ls by loading them up to the hilt with bad debt all the while indulging in a frenzy of insider trading.

In this way, according to Stein, he looted small investors of $75 billion through the sale of worthless bonds, and bribed and corrupted academics and journalists to keep the whole thing afloat. 'He is even now engaged in a large PR effort to mislead Americans about who he is,' he wrote in a letter to Judge Wood.

He also maintained that many of Milken's clients were 'organized crime honchos' ('Drexel Burnham was also the preferred financing entity for the casino industry'), and that *in toto* Milken's 'gleaming marble cube on Rodeo Drive' was the HQ of 'the new organized crime' and made the real thing look like a joke. In one article, 'drug abuse may have contributed to Drexel mayhem,' he concluded. 'It may well be that the use of drugs among top daisy-chain players . . . explains much about the willful refusal of the whole gang to see that the scam had to come to a bad end.' On television he called him 'the bomb-throwing anarchist of the ordinary investor' and 'the premier financial swindler of our time.' In short, 'The idea that he is a friend of the free market is like saying that Bluebeard was a friend of women.' Or that Ben Stein was a friend of Milken's.

But there is some evidence that Stein would have liked to have been. They once met in the elevator of Milken's Century City headquarters and Milken gave him 'a little pep talk about them' remembered Stein. 'But it seemed kind of scammy to me and I left.' In November 1988 Stein wrote a letter to Milken basically asking him for a job. Stein proposed that he act as an 'in-house vetter of deals from a fairness to stockholder's standpoint, and teacher of ethics to your young and bright colleagues.'

In full, the tone of the letter was somewhat flip. 'Isn't it amazing that both you and Michael Ovitz went to Birmingham High School . . . both come from the Val, both have built buildings in Beverly Hills and both dominate your respective fields? What can they be putting in the water at Birmingham High School?' Before signing off he said, 'None of this means that I will stop writing about deals,' and he added, as a P.S., 'I enclose a collection of my articles. I do not expect you to read them.' Nevertheless the putative relationship was a fantasy that he cherished. 'Tomorrow Michael Eisner will call from Disney and tell me they can't live without me, Michael Milken will call from Drexel and tell me they will fail without my insight,' he wrote in his novel *Hollywood Days, Hollywood Nights*, subtitled 'Diary of a mad screenwriter'.

Stein claimed he wrote the letter after receiving death threats from someone at Drexel, and instead of calling the police he called Drexel's lawyers who suggested Milken and Stein should sit down together and discuss their differences. It was in response to this that Stein wrote the letter. He also claimed that he wrote to Drexel's representative Steven Anreder making it clear that he never expected to be paid.

Milken never responded to the letter, and according to Lerer it was after this perceived slight that Stein's writings against Milken became more virulent. Before the letter they could only identify two pieces Stein had written. In the first, written in 1985, Stein hailed the new business heroes with ambiguous feelings. Unlike sports heroes, business stars did not make people's hearts 'swell with pride' he wrote, 'instead they make us feel diminished, smaller, weaker.' He confessed to 'red surges of envy' at Milken's purported $25 million annual salary for 1984 (in fact it was $123 million). In the second piece he praised Milken's work ethic and encouraged graduating students to develop their human capital.

But some of Stein's prior activities raised their own questions. In 1988 he was sued by Joan Rivers for $50 million. Under the pseudonym Bert Hacker in *GQ*, Stein had written that he knew Rivers and that he had heard her joke about her husband's suicide. Stein later admitted that he had never met Rivers and they settled out of court.

An engaging interviewee in the documentary *Fallen Angel*, Stein himself was no stranger to the screen, since he also moonlighted as a bit-part player in the movies. Screen credits included *Ghostbusters II* and *Ferris Bueller's Day Off*, and he was a regular in *The Wonder Years*, a popular comedy television series. He had also done ads and jingles for junk bond companies like Western Union and Fox Television.

Once the letter was published in *Spy* magazine Stein said that he regretted the awkwardness of some of the wording and added, 'I regret having made a sincere offer to help, on a volunteer basis . . . and then having that [effort] turned against me by a group of sadistic and unethical publicists.'

Generally Lerer also made Milken marginally more accessible to the press. Deluged with requests for, by his estimate, over 500 interviews, he estimated Milken gave no more than a dozen. Not that there was that much he could say. All the press really wanted to know about was the investigation, which was the one thing he was unable to talk about. That might not have been so bad if Milken had been able to give good interviews, but Milken didn't believe in revealing any more about his private life than he absolutely had to. Neither did he answer questions with sound bytes. Instead he would talk about what he wanted to talk about, and went off on long convoluted monologues about finance. This gave the press very little with which to work.

When asked, for example, how he felt about the nightmare his life had become, Milken wanted to know how exactly one defined a nightmare. *Newsday*'s John Riley remembered him picking away at his dry breakfast muffin and picking at the semantics of the question, exploring 'its nuances and subtleties, before deciding whether he was living in one'. While he turned the concept over in his mind for what seemed an eternity, Riley worried about whether he was ever going to get the answers to the rest of his questions for this portrait of a man in crisis. 'Suffocating, stifling and painful are not necessarily the same as a nightmare, sometimes a nightmare is over. Sometimes I think this is never going to be over,' he finally answered.

On other occasions his answers were Delphic meets Haiku. 'Oftentimes when things are at their worst you have the seeds of great improvement,' he told *Time* magazine. 'The sun still comes up and the sun still goes down,' he told *The New York Times*. 'I'm still allowed to sleep like other people, I'm still allowed to eat like other people. I spend more time with lawyers than the guy walking down the street does.' At the other extreme his answers were sad, vulnerable comparisons to the mirage world of movies and television: 'I'd like this family to be as much like Ozzie and Harriet as possible. Unfortunately times have changed and circumstances have changed.' Or, 'It's like the movie *Star Wars* when Princess Leia's planet blows up and Obi-Wan Kenobi feels the force of all these voices calling for help.' With lines like these Milken was more alienating than simpatico.

He just doesn't know how to relate to reporters,' said Riley. In what way? 'In every way you can imagine.' They would shrink from his informal style and mocked the sentimental privacies he brought to share. This is an extract from a page 1 *Wall Street Journal* article after one of these awkward press encounters.

' "I'm probably one of the first people to cry at a sad movie," Mr Milken volunteers, his eyes downcast, his hands thrust deep in his pockets. "I was probably crying," he says, "during the credits of Camelot."

'Between mentions of old movies and his days as a high-school cheerleader and prom king, the 42-year-old financier urges everyone to "Call me Mike. . . . When I hear one of you call me Mr Milken," he tells the assembled press, "it sounds strange." After all he works in Southern California, where everybody goes by first names.

'What is wrong with this picture? Well, to begin with, Mr Milken isn't running for office, or for Mr Congeniality.' The article continues, 'To those who have followed his career, the most notable thing about "Mike" these days may be the spectacle of an unregenerate publicity-hater taking needy children to a baseball game.'

Another factor counting against Milken's press initiative was his timing. 'He's learning to say hello when he should have been saying goodbye,' observed one. Once the shadow of suspicion had fallen over Milken with the investigation, any kind of action looked like a reaction, a defensive manoeuvre, yet another attempt to manipulate things in his favour. The time to have been accessible to the media would have been before Boesky Day when he could have explained his work and ideas to the public.

But Milken did nothing. 'You can't make a dime off publicity,' Wynn said to Milken, according to Bruck. In doing nothing he wasted his greatest asset, himself. Roger Ailes was the media guru who shepherded George Bush into the White House and almost got Giuliani voted mayor. *You Are the Message* was the title – and message – of his book. Milken had not built the high yield department through spokespeople. He did it through the sheer force of his personality which was accessible and led by example. He knew how to persuade people one on one, and how to win an audience. But having done this to great effect in his business and social life he stumbled when it came to the media.

But why? On the eve of the nineteen eighties Milken was celebrating New Year's Eve over at his neighbours', the Sandlers. They spent the time videotaping one another about their hopes and dreams, and one of Milken's fantasies was to do some kind of public service. But then he added that 'my aversion to public, the desire for privacy is so great that it will always be a fantasy'. Although he was a confident public speaker, and although he was aware of the influence of the media (as was apparent in his use of his own private media at the high yield bond conferences), he simply could not bear the exposure, which triggered such a phobic reaction that he even balked at pinning it down when he tried to speak of his 'aversion to public'.

'Since when was the Donald Trump style the only way of doing things?' challenged Lerer. Trump's love and use of publicity was in inverse proportion to Milken's abhorrence. 'Michael believed, rightly or wrongly, that he could do his business and do it properly without playing to the press . . . and he chose not to live a public life. Only in the 1980s would that be ridiculed. Kind of crazy, you know?' Crazy, but true. And it was more than ridiculed. Since Watergate the media had come to be seen as the agent of truth. It dragged out into the open all dark secrets. In this way a new moral axis had evolved. What was private was bad and suspicious, and only what was public and open was good. In this context the very desire for privacy and the slightest hint of secrecy was cause for suspicion of wrongdoing. In *You Are the Message* Ailes etched out the new agenda, arguing that television had 'changed the rules', making people 'guilty till proven innocent' and that the new challenge was 'communicate or die', especially in business: 'Journalists tell me that they are sometimes tough on business because business hides from them and they figure there must be something to hide . . . many people in business still wait until news coverage escalates to kangaroo-court proportions before they finally defend themselves.' In the electronic Eden of media rule, the people hiding behind the bushes with the fig leaves must be dragged out into the open to face their maker. As David Vyse of the *Washington Post* said, 'Milken was really hurt by the decision not to talk to the press until it was too late. It fuelled the basic journalist instinct that if people refuse to talk they must have something significant to hide.' Of course this is not an 'instinct' at all, merely arrogance and prejudice.

For a long time Milken refused to come on down into the media arena and allow his life to become a part of the infotainment circus. He saw the media not as an instrument of truth but one of distortion. As he told Jesse Kornbluth, 'Media notoriety changes things; when I was at Berkeley a film crew came to shoot a fraternity party. We were eating spaghetti. Within half an hour there was a huge food fight. It seemed to me that people acted unusual in front of the camera.' In this he was quite correct. The media was not interested in the ordinary, mundane or unremarkable. As a medium – print or electronic – it intensifies experience, making it more colourful, more compact, and more exciting than it really is in ordinary life. It thus seeks out the miraculous, the extraordinary, the intense, hyping every experience and glossing all it touches. But Milken would not – just as he had refused to play the Wall Street game which he had abandoned for his West Coast idyll – play the media celebrity game. But he was mistaken if he thought he could sidestep the process. The consequence of failing to shape his own cartoon and myth was that one was shaped for him. His followers made him a messiah, his enemies a demon. As the saying goes, 'If the hat fits, wear it.' But Milken refused to wear a hat. He didn't see that he would be made to wear a hat and that if that hat didn't fit, it could be made to fit. In Milken's case the hat in question was even literal, a miner's hat. 'But I never wore a miner's headlamp,' Milken protested. 'A retail salesman gave me a doctor's lamp – maybe I wore it once.' Too bad.

Significantly this detail appeared in Jesse Kornbluth's piece in *The Trentonian*, which was a medium-sized New Jersey newspaper. The feature had been originally commissioned by *Vanity Fair* who rejected it as a whitewash. In its place they recruited Marie Brenner whose masterpiece of psycho-surgery appeared almost a year later. However, the warmth of Kornbluth's piece did not compromise the intimacy of the portrait it provided, and it was a perfectly serviceable piece and considerably less sycophantic than many of the magazine's frequent celebrity snow jobs. Far from being hypocritical, *Vanity Fair* was being utterly consistent. The magazine prided itself on its edge, but was never over the edge. It wanted to stand apart, but it never took a stand. That this vanguard magazine, for all its derring-do, never went against the grain of the prevalent moral journalistic tone but merely polished it to new heights, succinctly demonstrates how, once the Milken myth was cast, the man was poured into a mould as rock solid as one of the mafia's famous concrete overcoats. From this no media would save him. That *The Trentonian* printed Kornbluth's piece is the exception that proves the rule since this newspaper was owned by Ralph Ingersoll, a Milken client and supporter.

By this stage it was too late to go out there and tell his own story. No matter how subtle Robinson, Lake & Lerer were, their efforts to fashion an image for Milken would only reinforce the very myth that they were trying to dispel. Meanwhile the tragedy was that Milken had yet another layer of interpreters and spokespeople speaking on his behalf, and using the talisman of his name. Some reporters, frustrated in their access to the man himself, reacted by peddling to the public the easy notion that the very fact of hiring a PR firm indicated that he was trying to manipulate them, though with press calls flooding in it was hard to see what else he could have done.

Milken didn't hire just any PR firm. Founding partner Linda Robinson was, as per the times, X-ray slim and a workaholic, described variously as a 'water canon' and 'fireball'. She was the trophy wife of American Express chairman James Robinson, although he would seem to be her trophy. She once asked a reporter from *The Wall Street Journal* to feel his biceps. One stunned friend, who also copped a feel, let it be known that she hadn't seen muscles on a man like it. He did nine hundred sit-ups daily and worked out to an exercise video called *Buns of Steel*. These titbits of information were gathered from *Vanity Fair*, and when the feature ran in the magazine Robinson was supposed to have pulled American Express's advertising. With a $250 million annual advertising budget to spread around, Robinson enjoyed fair weather in the media and 'The American family Robinson' have been described as the most powerful couple in America, second only to the couple in the White House.

Daughter of Amos of the 'Amos 'n' Andy' show – a classic American comedy radio show of negro dialects done by white men – Linda Robinson started out working on Reagan's press campaign for election in 1980. Six years later Robinson, Lake & Lerer would open for business and became a powerhouse, representing clients such as Boone Pickens, Ron Perelman from Revlon (she also sat on the board and recruited Kissinger from her husband's board to boost the line-up), and Ross Johnson, the CEO of RJR Nabisco.

But her tangible successes were somewhat patchy. Their strategy brought more attention to the 'Predator's Ball' than it might otherwise have been afforded. In the battle for RJR Nabisco she played a key role trying to get her husband and Kravis to buddy up and share the deal instead of competing. The initiative failed and Johnson and American Express were trounced by Kravis. Johnson was also badly hurt by a *Time* cover story that Robinson had shepherded along which was titled 'A game of greed'. An article about Milken was also included in the piece for good measure. Although Milken was out of the picture and had nothing to do with the deal he nevertheless got tarred with its brush. However, beyond a little work at the beginning, Linda Robinson did not take on Milken's account. In return for Robinson, Lake & Lerer's Services, Milken was supposed to pay a monthly retainer of $50,000 and bills that went as high as $100,000 per month.

However, there were those – mostly opponents of Milken – who thought the campaign was a great success. Thomas, who once wrote a piece on the interior of the Robinson's thirty-six acre Connecticut estate for *Architectural Digest*, believed that she was especially successful at persuading journalists to forget about their responsibilities, while seducing them with access and contacts – from the White House to American Express and a host of high-powered media friendships in between – reducing bloodhound journalists to the equivalent of a bunch of groupies clamouring for a back-stage pass. Ben Stein even argued that Linda Robinson was so powerfully connected that she was responsible for what he saw as a bargain basement plea deal with the government for Milken, instead of the two-to-three-hundred- count super-seding indictment that he believed should have followed. Ken Lerer rejects these opinions as utter falsities.

In my own experience of working on the television documentary *Fallen Angel*, access to Milken was frustratingly tightly controlled and never materialized until well past the eleventh hour. When finally Milken agreed to give an interview for the documentary, Richard Sandler and Ken Lerer were present to control proceedings. Milken had wanted to be filmed against a backdrop of children, which might have been almost as bad as the flat brown backdrop that was chosen instead. Where all other interviews in the film were shot from the side, interestingly framed with interviewees directed not to look into the camera, Milken somehow was filmed head on looking straight down the barrel of the lens. As a result he looked like he was some kind of madman already in prison or a padded cell.

Although the film's director thought the interview was rubbish, there was little – because of the investigation – that Milken could say. When asked if he knew how big his high yield bond business would become he did not answer, but looked straight ahead into the camera, and shifted in his seat. Instead of answering questions he looped a prepared spiel that was extremely repetitive and, under analysis, devoid of much real content. All in all it was a powerful illustration of all the problems Milken had with the media, and how in spite of his good intentions, there was little that he could do.

Nevertheless the interview did contain two truly revealing moments. Setting up the interview, everyone was tense and the room was hot. The cameraman had had his assistant, whose name was Mike, place a cup of ice and water by the tripod. Milken had been brought into the room and they were almost ready to shoot, but in making a final adjustment the cameraman knocked over the cup of water. 'Oh, for God's sake Mike clean it up,' the cameraman snapped to his assistant. Without a word, and to everyone's horror, Milken leapt out of his chair, pulled his handkerchief from his pocket and began mopping up the water. He also picked up the ice cubes and put them back in the styrofoam cup. Everyone in the room was transfixed. At another point Catherine Bailey got a further glimpse of the real man. Stuck on the phrasing of a question they had stopped filming and were working it out with Lerer and Sandler when Milken turned to her and said, 'If I had my way I would say an awful lot more, but I'm not allowed to.' (Similarly Milken would want to testify at his hearing but submitted to his lawyer's advice not to do so.)

However, neither moment was caught on film. When completed the documentary argued that in addition to building a house of cards Milken had, when indicted, redirected his PR and marketing machine to save himself. This supposed plan served as reinforcing proof of Milken's original conspiracy to destabilize corporate America. Such an argument is wrong-headed. The purpose of PR is to impact public opinion (Milken would not – at least one would hope not – have retained a PR firm and paid their considerable fees if he didn't want them to do anything). But while Robinson, Lake & Lerer undoubtedly sought to manipulate Milken's image, this does not mean that PR by definition promotes lies and is the kind of dishonest pursuit or immoral last resort of the desperate. What the documentary played up to was this very prejudice, the paranoid fear that in the electronic and information age the simple truth will be manipulated and corrupted by Big Brother types.

This was a popular anxiety, based on a puritanical clinging to the romantic but fictitious notion of 'the simple truth'. In today's media world, where we are bombarded with a kaleidoscope of variable truths, where spectacle and reality and fact and fiction intermingle, we are constantly challenged to balance more variables, and be comfortable with complex truths that often contain many contradictory elements. If there ever was a simple truth it no longer exists. The conservative reaction to this informational deluge was to try and sort the true from the untrue, the junk from the valuable, and to evaluate the surface versus the substance. This traditional prejudice militates against advertising and PR which are seen as surface arts and glosses that are at best superficial and at worst duplicitous.

Just as the documentary's two truly unique insights into the character of Michael Milken did not even make it onto film, so by extension fundamental truths about the man eluded the mainstream media and the public awareness. The reason for this has already been indicated. The media takes raw material and kneads it into myth. As some kind of hybrid of truth, a cartoon or caricature of reality, whether the picture drawn is true or untrue is really beside the point, which is, simply, whether it is a sufficient spectacle that will sell. Milken, for refusing to position himself, found himself packaged and mythicized in what he complained was an untrue way. But truth had nothing to do with it.

Giuliani, Milken's nemesis, makes for an illuminating contrast. Media guru Roger Ailes maintained that PR is rarely able to reverse the tide of public opinion. 'Your guy is a surfer . . . you've got to ride the wave,' he once said. Significantly Milken wasn't his client, Rudy Giuliani was, and while Milken floundered in the water Giuliani sought to ride the wave of his popularity as far as it would take him, which he hoped would be all the way into office as the mayor of New York City. When he set out on the campaign trail in May 1989 it looked like nothing could stop him.

But then his ratings began to sag as the overzealousness with which he had held office was held up to closer scrutiny. *The New York Times* reported on Judge Sprizzo's dismissal, six months earlier, of charges against drug dealers and quoted his decision which the angry judge delivered to the Assistant Attorney prosecuting the case: 'There is in your office - I notice it not only in this case but in other cases – a kind of overkill, a kind of overzealousness which is not even – from my point of view as a person who has been a prosecutor – rationally related to any legitimate prosecutive objective.' Bill Tatum's *Amsterdam News* printed the judges remarks in greater detail: 'Your natural assumption is that we will go in all or nothing because in every case we have gotten away with it. I am telling you that in this case you didn't get away with it. If you had been a competent prosecutor, which you are not, you would have hedged against the possibility that maybe the judge would disagree with you. But it never occurs in the mind of you or anyone in your office that any trial judge will ever disagree with you on the law.'

Giuliani finally apologized for the Handcuff Three, but there were two other incidents, unrelated to Wall Street, that were also highly embarrassing and illustrated the zeal of his tenure. It was also under his stewardship that the Grand Jury reportedly investigating John Gotti, the most powerful mobster in America, were caught according to writer Christopher Byron, 'cavorting like extras on *Night Court*'. One morning in November 1988 a witness who turned up to testify on an unrelated case was greeted by Grand Jurors wearing blue sweatshirts depicting kangaroos dangling from a hangman's noose underneath the slogan 'We hang 'em on Thursday'. The Grand Jurors also drank from coffee mugs bearing the same design. In another less frivolous instance Simon Berger, a 62-year-old survivor of Auschwitz, was dragged from his bed in a dawn raid and taken, in handcuffs, for questioning and sat in a room where, written on the blackboard in German, was the motto 'Work Will Set You Free'. The words had also been written on the gates at the entrance of Auschwitz. When confronted on the campaign trail about the incident Giuliani initially denied all knowledge of it, later admitting that he had in fact been told about it at the time, but had not followed it up personally.

Giuliani's zealous prosecutorial style was the trademark of a campaign that increasingly focused on the supposed criminality of his opponent. He attacked Dinkins for being a multi-millionaire and living in subsidized housing. 'I think the people of this town want a mayor who has nothing to fear from a prosecutor,' said Giuliani in the last few days of the campaign. After an allusion to the Parking Violations Bureau scandal (which the Republican Giuliani had proudly and personally prosecuted with the conviction of one Democrat leader, Stanley Friedman, and the suicide of another, Donald Manes), Giuliani announced, 'With David Dinkins we're going to go through a scandal over the parking of stock.' He was referring to the cable television stock that Dinkins had sold to his son for what was not considered to be a proper market price.

This was a deliberate strategy. As Ailes said on the eve of the election, 'The question is whether David Dinkins can drag himself across the finish line with his integrity around his ankles.' To this end they scored a coup when they discovered that Dinkins had not disclosed that he had taken a vacation to France paid for in part by a friend. This minor detail became in the hands of Giuliani's campaign manager proof that he had 'stomped on the code of ethics' and concealed the trip 'until he was forced in a bathroom to reveal it'. Reviewing Giuliani's performance in the two televised mayoral debates *The New York Times* wrote that he made 'aggressive assertions based on wisps of evidence'.

Following the racial murder of Yusef Hawkins, a black, in the white Italian neighbourhood of Bensonhurst by a gang of youths, racial tension was high.

'It's wrong for David Dinkins to expect the voters to choose him because he is black, if that's what he believes, just as it would be wrong for me to expect the voters to choose me because I am white,' said Giuliani, ingeniously injecting race into the campaign by suggesting that that was not what it should be about. On the final weekend he released a television ad attacking 'the crowd', as it referred to Dinkins's team, and attacking one of his functionaries for his anti-white stance, identifying him as 'the man who led a riot which injured over twenty New York City Cops'. (The Brooklyn Bridge demonstration had been held to protest against the Bensonhurst murder.)

The strategy was effective, in that Giuliani lost the November 1989 election by only a narrow margin. Where Giuliani rode his wave of righteousness by stoking popular paranoia, playing on people's suspicions of yuppies on Wall Street or blacks in power, Milken, bereft of almost all the guile and cunning he was accused of having, was unable to get out of the way as the tidal inquisition came crashing down on him. Although he liked Wall Street no better than Giuliani and had left it years ago, he made the perfect scapegoat.

In his campaign against Milken, Giuliani – the people's puritan – made great play on the fact of Milken's PR. 'You have to remember there was a component to this case that was, for all intents and purposes, unprecedented,' he reflected afterwards. 'It was a major political campaign rather than a criminal case.' But Giuliani didn't think the opposition's enterprise worked: 'In the long run it isn't the public that decides a case on the publicity. It is the jury or the judge who decides a case and they do so on the facts.' Be that as it may, the fact is that few jurors, due to the omnipresence of the media, are clean slates about the high-profile cases they sit on. In the case of Milken, the pre-trial info war had effectively poisoned the air with prejudicial publicity, that, given Milken's all but invisible counter-image, did not have too much difficulty fixing itself in the public mind. This was the single most significant reason why Milken's case never made it to trial by jury. From Milken's point of view, what was the point of appearing before a publicity-contaminated jury to whom 'the facts' were already writ in stone? Giuliani may have championed jury trial as the one true course of justice, but circumstances had effectively put it beyond Milken's reach. He'd already been hanged in the kangaroo court of public opinion.

The following is a perfect popular press description of how Milken was perceived:

> This enemy is clearly delineated: he is a perfect model of malice, a kind of amoral superman: sinister, ubiquitous, powerful. . . . Unlike the rest of us, the enemy is not caught in the toils of the vast mechanism of history, himself a victim of his past, his desires, his limitations. He is a free, active, demonic agent. He wills, indeed he manufactures the mechanism of history himself, or deflects the normal course of history in an evil way. He makes crises, starts runs on banks, causes depres-

sions, manufactures disasters, and then enjoys and profits from the misery he has produced . . . very often the enemy is held to possess some especially effective source of power: he controls the press; he directs the public mind through "managed news"; he has unlimited funds; he has a new secret for influencing the mind (brainwashing); . . . he is gaining a stranglehold on the educational system.

This reads like a tailor-made description of Milken the myth. The junk genie who slept only a few hours a night working superhuman hours. The man who moved to the West to escape the history of tradition in the East and told students at his old business school, 'The past is only important in so far as it relates to the future.' The Reverend Moon of Wall Street, the betrayer of capitalism whose evil junk bond empire sowed chaos and financial ruin while reaping record profits. The would-be goody-two-shoes who hired – no expense spared – one of the most powerful public relations firms in the country, appearing at orchestrated events such as the Educator Awards. The weirdo workaholic who wore a bizarre array of headgear; a toupée, a miner's headlamp, and even, as depicted in some magazines, devil's horns. In short, Milken was the two-legged demon. But this extract, from Hofstadter's *The Paranoid Style in American Politics* also shows that this image, although satisfying the media's demand for myth and not reality, was a deranged construct, and not the reality of the man.

14

DREXEL BURN 'EM

NOT everyone at Drexel was sad to see Milken go. The revelations of Milken's half-billion dollar salary had had a divisive effect. 'Michael was a pig,' said one, summing it up. 'The King is dead!' another East Coaster told a reporter at the 1989 conference. There was also both the determination and the delusion that it could all be done without him: 'There's a kind of pride here that, goddamn it, we can do it without Michael.'

With the removal of Milken other Drexel characters stepped forward into the limelight. Their presence conveniently dramatizes how different Drexel was without Milken, or rather, how apart from Drexel and even from his own department Milken had been all along. His departure from his magic kingdom left no natural successor. Reluctantly John Kissick stepped up to the plate. Milken's shoes were impossible to fill, and just how impossible became clear when Kissick made his keynote address at the conference. However weird Milken's presence, it was nonetheless compelling and he was a good speaker. In contrast Kissick lacked charisma and one of his previous speeches had been considered so bad that a videotape of it was used internally at the company as an example of how not to give a speech. For this important occasion Kissick had obviously been given some basic training, and it showed. Like an actor who has no understanding of the lines he was reciting, Kissick trudged through the speech, which was a consommé of Milkenspeak, trying to give exciting emphasis to key words while dolefully moving his head from side to side.

Kissick's management style also drew flak. Instead of being autocratic he ruled by committee, instead of being quick and decisive he liked to deliberate and, instead of sitting on the X he ran the department from an office off to the side. Old-timers chafed under this new bureaucratic style, especially when there was even a committee meeting to decide whether the former trader turned government informer should be allowed back on the trading desk. However, Kissick's intentions were good and his bravery commendable. In terms of what lay ahead, there was little he could do. In both Milken's management style and his knowledge of the market he was absolutely indispensable to his set-up. Joseph had not exaggerated when he said at the conference that Milken's brain power was irreplaceable. He was the keystone of the arch, the hub of the wheel. Once removed from the structure, the centre could not hold and it would implode.

The collapse would not happen immediately. As in a cartoon when some unlucky toon runs over a cliff and keeps on cutting through the air, feet pedalling furiously, so it was with Drexel. For a while everything looked fine. In spite of Milken's ghostly presence 'Last week's High Yield Bond Department conference had a record attendance of over 3,000 issuers and investors,' read an internal memo, launching '16 new public issues representing over $6 billion in securities.' There was also the RJR Nabisco deal in which Drexel, in classic style, set out to place $3 billion in bonds and went on to increase the issue to $5 billion, earning itself a $100 million fee. For a while it looked like they really could do it without Milken. But then suddenly the toon looked down and realized that it was suspended in the air. It hung there a moment, then plummeted.

Sheena Easton performed at the conference, and 'Back to the Future' was the optimistic theme. It was designed to be a morale-raising corral. As one employee put it in one of the videotaped testimonials; 'There's no stopping us, this investigation is behind us, we're a rocket ship, we're moving on.'

The music video that year was a re-working of Bobby McFerrin's 'Don't Worry, Be Happy', and was supposed to be a lighthearted look back on Drexel's troubles.

> Another firm took your accounts
> Your commission checks begin to bounce
> Don't worry, be happy.

Drexelites clowned in their offices, in grass skirts, on surf boards. To illustrate the lines

> The banker club you want to greet
> Lompoc's where we gonna meet
> Don't worry, be happy

three Drexel executives in prison stripes and with balls and chains round their ankles (Lompoc was the local prison) clowned around in the 'emergency suite' that had been specially constructed during the crisis so Joseph could tape videostatements that could be beamed out to all the stations. But in spite of the risqué humour, the overall effect somehow failed to capture the laid-back and carefree spirit of the song. A tired-looking Fred Joseph pushed down the word 'worry', and up sprang the word 'happy'. This attempt to banish care was in sync with the flat and dispirited nature of the entire piece.

> For 25 months we've had some trouble

> Get back to the future on the double
> Don't worry, be happy.

Exactly what management meant by the future became clear ten days after the conference, and five days after the company signed its agreement with the SEC. With the agreement in place Shad officially became chairman. The man who eight years earlier had promised to come down on insider trading with hobnailed boots, spoke again and no less fatefully: 'It won't be business as usual. This is going to mark a turning point in the terms of the future prospects of the firm.' On 18 April, a mere two days later, Fred Joseph came on the Drexel line and made the announcement that Drexel would be getting out of the business of retailing stocks for individual investors and sundry other activities. With 350,000 accounts, this was the original core of the firm. However, it had never been the money spinner that high yield bonds had been, and it was this – and related activities such as corporate finance and arbitrage – that the firm decided to focus on in getting back to the future, as it rather fondly misconceived it.

After all the exhortations to remain loyal and pull together as a team, exhortations that had largely been heeded, this was seen as a far greater betrayal than the settlement with the SEC and the ditching of Milken, who was, after all, only one man.

'Don't you have a moral liability to us?' asked one.

'We don't have enough Vaseline,' jeered another. In the background on the two-way line could be heard the sound of toy bombs and the exterminator sounds that are available on cheap key rings. In the past Fred Joseph had patiently answered all questions, but as the mood turned ugly he moved to cut the meeting short.

'Today you're in a hurry,' another could be heard in the mounting chaos before the line went dead.

It was the wrong decision, and one that earned him the undying enmity of a firm that had been bound together rather than torn apart by the siege mentality. With the settlement and now the downsizing, Joseph was seen as betraying the firm. 'I hope he gets anally raped by his least favourite minority,' one trader said bluntly.

Cutting off four and a half thousand people who had stuck with the firm through thick and thin was bad for the morale of those who remained. When a new slim in-house phone directory was published, morale dropped further. Drexel had gone from being ten thousand strong to being one of the smallest firms on Wall Street in very little time. And the problem of Drexel putting all its eggs in the high yield basket was that the market was about to go to hell.

Remembered as the Junk Bond King, Milken had in fact always preached the need for a flexible capital structure. As early as 1973 Milken argued in a paper he wrote with his professor James Walter, towards the completion of his business degree, that the financial structure of a company should be 'subject to modifications as conditions warrant' and that 'neglect of such matters is patently inconsistent with rational behaviour'.

As early as March 1987 the *High Yield Newsletter* had said, 'The by-word is equitize.' In an interview in 1989 Milken said, 'The capital structure, like the individual, is constantly changing.' He made the same point in speeches: 'How each company should be financed is different for everyone . . . so you can't use the same blueprint, you can't xerox deals any more than you can xerox money and think it's money.' To this end Milken made use of a wide variety of hybrid bonds – commodity indexed bonds, floating rate bonds (where the interest payment fluctuated), zero-coupon and split-coupon bonds, payment in kind bonds, exchangeable preferreds, high-premium convertibles, currency hedge bonds, increasing rate notes, asset-backed securities – as well as exchange offers where he exchanged debt for equity or equity for debt as the company's economic circumstances and needs changed.

But xeroxing deals, maintained Milken, was exactly what people were doing. In their eagerness to get in on the junk bond jamboree, competitors were xeroxing deals done in 1985 without heed to the changes in the market by 1989. Furthermore, in their eagerness to compete with Drexel's 'highly confident' letter, which was no more than an assurance that Drexel could raise the money, firms were pledging their own capital in bridge loans. In such arrangements the bank lent the money to the raider until such time as it placed the junk bonds it said it could. Instead of just being 'highly confident' in the words of the famous Drexel letter, competitors were putting their money where their mouth was. A result of this was that deals were getting done that shouldn't be done. Specifically, for example, the *High Yield Newsletter* warned 'cautious investors should avoid' Robert Campeau's takeover of Federated Stores in October 1988. The next year the deal went belly-up. Campeau blamed his sorry state on a case of 'junk bond fever'.

Without Milken the tempest-tossed firm drifted towards the rocks of the junk bond market. As a Drexel managing director said, 'I don't think Fred ever understood the financial dynamics of the firm. He [just] didn't comprehend the risks of trading and owning securities.' Another frustrated executive told *Business Week*, 'Joseph didn't understand any of this . . . we tried to tell him, but he was listening to Leon Black and Peter Ackerman.'

Known as 'the dark twins' Black and Ackerman embodied the new Drexel. They had both threatened to quit when Drexel abandoned Milken. But they didn't, and although their discontent was much publicized, what quieted them was not. Generally it was assumed that superbonuses were the pacifier, but it was also suggested that maybe in return for Milken's head, Drexel promised these two big-timers that it would give up the other departments that the junk bond and corporate finance departments both felt they had been carrying for too long as excess baggage.

Ackerman was the mystery man, a stealth banker who kept such a low profile that he managed to keep clear of the journalists' radar. He was supposed to have been the designer of the tiers of hybrid securities that made the RJR Nabisco buyout possible, and yet his name did not even appear in the index of *Barbarians At The Gate*. Marie Brenner discovered that Drexel did not even have a picture of him on file. Nevertheless she gleaned some first hand observation and afforded us this tantalizing glimpse of the real man: 'He was the kind of person who, on a six-hour Los Angeles New York flight, would command the first-class flight attendants, laden with rare fillets, cheese, shrimp, and ice cream, to give him two tiny salads of naked lettuce leaves and seltzer water and "absolutely nothing else", as I once observed him do.' We get a chill thrill from such an account. Sinister, rigorous, tall, lean, and mercilessly focussed.

Perhaps. Other accounts describe him as an absent-minded professor with a fondness for ropey old cardigans and wrinkled chinos. This portrait fits with the fact that as the summer of Drexel's discontent turned into its winter of despair, he seemed increasingly eager to put as great a distance between him and Drexel as possible. Asked to succeed Milken, one of his colleagues said that he refused because 'he's a very able guy who doesn't have the patience to deal with human foibles or people'. To persuade him to stay Joseph had created for him his own West Coast department. Once he announced his intention to move to London and write a sequel to his doctorate thesis on non-violent resistance, Joseph, rather than let him go, put him in charge of Drexel's worldwide capital market services.

In addition to being the 'funny money' man, the creator of all the wampum that Theodore Forstman so reviled, he also brought in a number of bad deals that burdened Drexel's books. Paramount Petroleum needed just $43 million to re-open a bankrupt petroleum company north of LA. When there were no takers for the issue of junk bonds, Drexel ended up being obliged to lend the money to the group themselves in the form of a bridge loan. The refinery re-opened and began losing money immediately. They tried to sell it, but even an Indonesian group backed off. The refinery closed and went back into bankruptcy. There were also Odyssey Partners' flop buyout of JPS Textiles (Drexel had to swallow half of the $385 million issue) and the Memorex offering. Immediately after this the company's profits tumbled by 66 per cent, tanking the bonds and leaving many unhappy clients, with the exception of foreign investors who had, unfortunately for Drexel, the right to sell the bonds back to them. Drexel also ended up with about $70 million worth of junk issued for the buyout of Edgcomb Metals (in an interesting twist Ackerman owned a stake in the company for which he received an estimated $6-7 million).

Black brought in his fair share of turkeys too. Together with Ackerman he overcame Kissick's reluctance to do a $1 billion deal to complete underwear king Farley's acquisition of Westpoint Pepperrell. Unable to sell $250 million of the bonds, Drexel had to inventory the stuff on its own account.

Black was variously known as 'the Teddy Bear despot' and 'Pizza the Hut'. Where Milken and Joseph had worked well together, when Joseph moved on from head of Corporate Finance up to CEO he left in his wake a duopoly consisting of Dennis Kay and Leon Black. Kay was the administrator, Black was the action man. Milken was supposed to have been suspicious of Black because he was always interested in the one shot, the hit and run of the fee. Milken's network was based on relationships instead of transactions. If a client wished to unload their bonds, he would be there. True, they might pay some kind of premium for the service, and that premium might vary accordingly, but they could depend on the fact that Milken was there to support them. And when the regulations changed or when the market changed, making a capital structure too onerous, Milken would be there to fix it. Puritans take this to mean that the concept – or rather the fraud – was to keep the game going. But Milken was not being cynical when he compared himself to a doctor.'There's no fixed capital structure that's always right,' he said. 'Some days it should be debt, some days equity. You have to look at the markets every day.'

However, according to Connie Bruck, it was Black who had changed the whole feel of the game by including a paragraph on the first page of every deal memo detailing what Drexel's compensation would be. And so the fee charged won out over the value created. Black enjoyed a reputation. His M&A partners were known as the 'Hitler Youth' and he managed to push aside the elders and get some young blood on the executive committee. With the oldest member only 47, the new line-up was called 'the student council'.

But Black was the most aggressive when it came to money, his money. He was a key player in demanding that Drexel indemnify Drexel employees who had invested in the controversial partnerships that the company had since discontinued. Because these were general partnerships, the wealth of the individual members was personally liable, and since the settlement a number of people who had happily glutted themselves on the unlimited upside now wanted protection from the downside, which, coming in the form of civil suits seeking damages, could be equally unlimited. Fearing mass defection if he didn't, Joseph agreed to indemnify all participants who came forward with all the details of their investments.

Apart from the bum deals, the funniest money around Drexel in its demise was the vast amount the dying firm paid out in superbonuses to Ackerman and Black. It was reported that Ackerman told Joseph that Milken had agreed to pay him $75 million in 1988. Joseph agreed to honour the supposed arrangement (although at the time it still owed Milken $100 million for his stock and $200 million for his 1988 bonus and salary), and as an added inducement to persuade him to stay was supposed to have agreed to pay him the same again for 1989. Through an intermediary – remember, Ackerman did not talk to journalists – he made it known that this was not in fact the case and several months later *The Wall Street Journal* reported that he had earned only $45 million in 1988. Anyway in April 1989 he was supposed to have received a cheque for $107 million – payment for the previous year and an advance upon the current year (Ackerman's wife, a novelist, was supposed to have abhorred Drexel's materialism). When Black heard that his bonus was only to be $12 million, he went, in a scene reminiscent of Levine's tantrum, bananas. He was insulted. Through the RJR Nabisco deal he had brought the firm $270 million dollars. If he had had the same deal as Milken, his bonus would have been in the order of $100 million. Joseph eventually capitulated and tossed him an extra $3 million (Kissick got $11 million). Temporarily sated, Black returned after a Christmas holiday in Acapulco with his family to Joseph's office and demanded that henceforward his bonus be paid on a quarterly basis. Joseph apparently also capitulated to this outrageous demand.

Drexel had always been known for its outsized compensation. 'Bonus' had originally meant in the Drexel lexicon 'a generous slice of the bounty', but by the time those profits evaporated, bonus had long since ceased to mean 'bonus'. Joseph felt obliged to maintain the largesse even if the wherewithal was lacking. He also argued that he was contractually obliged to make many of the outsize payments. In both 1988 and 1989 Drexel had suffered significant losses and yet the bonuses went on, as they paid out $506 million and $260 million respectively. In fact the bonuses were really more like bribes to try and get the employees to remain loyal to the firm. As an added inducement Joseph guaranteed that bonuses for 1989 would be no less than 75 per cent of 1988 bonuses, irrespective of whether or not any new business was brought in. Every inch Joseph gave his greedy colleagues took a mile. In December he was besieged in his office by partners demanding more. When he finally announced that enough was enough, thirty quit within a week. Setting an example that no one seemed interested in following, he took his relatively modest $2.5 million bonus all in stock (generally people took between 20 and 25 per cent in stock).

Milken's presence had kept the firm in check. Once he had gone the firm lost its head literally and figuratively. Many Drexel diehards noticed the change. 'The firm lost its soul. Fine young investment bankers subconsciously knew it was the last inning and, without Milken's review, began printing tickets to collect fees . . . in the face of a declining market, with badly underwritten credits, top management had to prove the firm could sell securities without Mike Milken . . . even if the "sale" was, after failing to persuade buyers around the world, to itself,' said Fred McCarthy, a senior East Coast Drexelite.

Many in the high yield bond department noticed the change too. 'His understanding of what Drexel's franchise was – creating value for and protecting the investor – went out the door with him,' said Finneran who worked with Milken on the DBL Americas fund. Said Dahl's assistant, 'Too many greedy misguided chiefs and not enough Indians. Deals were cranked out solely for the almighty fee,' and another commented, 'People began thinking only of themselves.'

Kissick, the head of the junk bond department, all but acknowledged that he was out of his depth. 'From a personal point of view, I know that I could have greatly benefited from being able to further access Mike's judgement and vision during this difficult time in the high yield market. I am certain that the performance of . . . the entire high yield market would have been immeasurably improved with greater insight and direction from Mike Milken during this time.'

The bankruptcy of Integrated Resources, for example, an event that was equally critical in the erosion of junk bonds and Drexel, would never have happened. In 1986 Integrated's main line of business, the sale of real estate partnerships as tax shelters, came to an abrupt end with tax reform. But Drexel continued financing Integrated's expansion into other areas such as insurance and money management, piling up almost $2 billion in debt. In June 1989 Integrated was caught in a squeeze, unable to service its short-term debt, and looked to Drexel to carry the shortfall on its books until something could be worked out.

In Milken days this would have been done in a second, but 'Milken was the money', as one Integrated executive put it, and Milken was gone. As a consequence Drexel's books were choking on buybacks and bad issues (in order to shift the massive RJR Nabisco bundle, for example, traders had agreed to swap bad bonds for the new RJR bonds that were in demand). By the end of September 1989 Drexel would have $1 billion on its books in junk bonds and bridge loans. Had Milken been around he would have been able with his irreplaceable brainpower to place the junk in any number of ways.

With no more room on its books, Drexel could not provide the 'added value' service that had enabled it to build its junk bond franchise and loyal roster of clients. Integrated turned to its Establishment banking partners who took the line that if Drexel weren't there for them, things at Integrated must be bad, so they would not make the loan either. Integrated defaulted on its debt, but did not file for bankruptcy. 'We're not selling shoes, we're selling confidence,' said founder Arthur Goldberg. But once it had evaporated, confidence was harder to sell than shoes, and Integrated would wind up filing for bankruptcy the following February (coincidentally on the same day that Drexel would file).

When Drexel allowed Integrated to default it all but threw away its franchise, since other junk bond companies knew that they could no longer look to Drexel like they had in the good old days of Milken to keep them on their feet. Ultimately it would have been cheaper to provide Integrated with the money they needed, since, given the nature of the Milken network, a number of Integrated creditors were valued Drexel customers and they demanded from Drexel – and got – guarantees that they would be made whole on their investment. Perelman was in for $24 million, First Executive for $49 million and even Drexel itself for $41 million.

But there were some things that Milken could have done nothing about. In August, as part of the Federal Institutional Reform Recovery and Enforcement Act, Savings & Loans were prohibited from investing junk bonds and required to divest their holdings by 1994. Savings & Loans were also required, in the meantime, to reflect the current market value of their junk bonds on their balance sheets.

The provision was something of an afterthought, and was supposed to have been added by Richard Breeden while he was still in the White House, and before he became the tough new chairman of the SEC. Breeden's legislative gambits vis-à-vis the S&L crisis are widely regarded as turning a $50 billion problem into a $500 billion problem (and the price tag has even been put as high as between $1 and 2 trillion).

The measure was draconian given the fact that junk bonds 'have not been a factor in the failure of thrift institutions,' according to the Government Accounting Office's report published only months before. Only 198 banks of the nation's almost 3,000 thrifts held junk bonds, which represented about 2 per cent of their total assets, and a negligible 0.7 per cent of all thrift's total assets. Since one of the thrifts, Columbia Savings & Loans, held almost half of all the S&L junk, Breeden's addition could be seen as a deliberate move to get to Milken (for whom he was supposed to have had a special antipathy), since Columbia was one of Milken's closest customers.

But since Savings & Loans held about 7 per cent of all junk, the impact on the junk bond market was sudden and dramatic. There was no reason for the thrifts to hold onto their high yield bonds and they scrambled to offload their junk portfolios, further driving down the price and weakening the market. As writer Paul Craig Roberts explained, 'The value of any security can be destroyed by arbitrarily proscribing it as a legitimate investment [as happened when the savings and loans were deregulated and allowed to diversify in their investment policies] and then forcing investors to market it during adverse conditions.'

At the same time the jittery junk bond market was further battered by the unravelling of a number of the foolhardy deals that the *High Yield Newsletter* had warned against. In addition to First Boston's massive $11 billion Campeau crash there was the $3 billion Ohio Mattress fiasco, which was dubbed 'the burning bed', and Goldman Sachs's $800 million issue for Southland.

Towards the end of 1989 Drexel faced a long laundry list of other woes. In September Drexel had to pay out $500 million as part of its settlement, and its legal bills were a runaway expense. Running at over $10 million a month in 1988 and 1989, Milken's bills alone ran as high as $2 million. Drexel, which had agreed to pay his legal fees, put his posse of lawyers on a strict budget of $1.25 million a month, forbidding them to fly first class or take deluxe hotel suites. Earlier in the year when Drexel had downsized, it cashed out almost $300 million of Drexel stock within ninety days. In September the firm announced that henceforward Drexel stock could only be cashed out over a period of ten years instead of five. To beat the new rule over two dozen quit. The collapse of the UAL takeover in October cost Drexel $25 million in arbitrage losses, and although Goldsmith had retained Drexel for his BAT takeover, the deal was stumbling.

Now that Drexel was an admitted felon there were one or two regulatory consequences crimping its business. New Jersey had banned it from casino financing, and New York State had suspended Drexel from doing Municipal issues. But the number of companies that wanted to do business with an admitted felon – especially the blue chip clients Drexel craved in its bid to join the Establishment – diminished. Meanwhile rival firms picked off Drexel clients.

And there was more. In November the ratings agencies that Drexel had so berated showed their true power. When S&P downgraded Drexel's short-term debt some lenders cut them off. In December founder Tubby Burnham quit, voicing his discontent. Burnham was anti-Shad (who reportedly dozed off in meetings) anti-bridge loans ('our bridge loans have become piers,' moaned one executive), anti-junk madness ('I tried to limit the junk bond deals several years ago . . . I got tired of objecting to everything they wanted to do' said Burnham), and sick of what he called 'the piggishness of Wall Street' and the craving for instant wealth. John Phelan, chairman of the New York Stock Exchange, announced that he would be seeking a fine in the tens of millions to punish Drexel for its regulatory transgressions. In December Drexel lost $86 million and in January it lost $60 million. It also paid out its $260 million in bonuses. 'Nobody was shovelling money out of the door because they felt the roof was caving in,' said ex-SEC turned Drexel director Roderick Hills, suggesting that that was exactly what they were doing.

Meanwhile John Shad, who had spoken out against junk bond leverage in 1985, was touring the Middle East trying to sell some of the junk on Drexel's books. The firm's Chief Financial Officer was in Paris trying to persuade Groupe Bruxelles Lambert (Drexel's largest shareholder and owner of Radio Luxembourg) to put up more money. Neither attempt was successful. So great was the fear of lawsuits resulting from the settlement that on the home front none of the usual role call of raiders – Perelman, Kravis, Icahn – could be persuaded to snaffle up the firm.

'Only wimps get tired,' Fred Joseph told *The Wall Street Journal* in early February. The former boxer tried to keep up the firm's fighting spirit by giving employees key chains with miniature boxing gloves. 'The tone was supposed to be, "Let's hang tough." But to some of us the tiny boxing gloves were a symbol of Drexel's tiny clout in the marketplace,' commented one under-whelmed recipient. The following week, Joseph was out for the count, in bed at his New Jersey farm with an ear infection.

On Friday he got a call from his Chief Financial Officer. Like Integrated before them, they had a short term $30 million loan coming due on Monday, but no way to refinance it. Up until this point they had been paying off the short-term loans when they came due by dipping into the $2 billion excess regulatory capital that Fred Joseph had always referenced as a guarantee of the firm's financial health. But now that pot was down to $300 million and the SEC moved to stop them from withdrawing any more.

When Black reached Ackerman with the news, he was delivering a paper at Harvard. When he spoke to Joseph he was supposed to have resigned on the spot. Other accounts tell of Ackerman and others writing out cheques in a desperate attempt to try and cover the loan. On Monday afternoon Joseph led an eight hour meeting to try and persuade bankers to make the loan, but there were no takers. After midnight they packed it in. 'It looks 80 per cent certain we'll get the money,' Joseph was supposed to have told a colleague, before heading back in to huddle with his Chief Financial Officer.

And then came the call. Joseph was instructed to call the switchboard at the US Treasury Department to hook up a conference call between the Federal Reserve Bank President Gerald Corrigan and SEC head Richard Breeden. Wrote Christopher Byron, 'Was this the call that would bring the news that would save Drexel? Were the Feds about to step in and help? . . . hadn't he done everything they'd asked of him? He'd fired his key employee, pleaded his company guilty to felony crimes, paid a fine of more than half a billion dollars. He'd done all these things because he was sure they were right, and he'd paid a terrible price. Was he at last about to be vindicated . . . were Fred and his firm about to join the Establishment?'

When he hung up Joseph said, 'I've just been told by the most powerful men in America to put this company into bankruptcy – immediately.' Instead of joining the Establishment, Drexel was about to move into the hereafter. The executive committee met at 6 a.m. the next morning and voted on the plan that was announced to employees over the Drexel line later that morning.

Joseph maintained that Nick Brady, Drexel's old enemy and Secretary of the Treasury, was listening in on the call. There was no valid reason why Joseph was asked to arrange the conference call with the Federal Reserve Bank and the SEC through the Treasury switchboard. In denying the accusation, an official claimed that Brady had attended a state dinner and then gone straight home. But both Breeden and Corrigan were at home, so the explanation was irrelevant.

Whether he was listening in or not, the absence of a bailout for Drexel smacked of conspiracy. 'They were investment bankers for heaven's sake. They knew the risks of what they were doing. The taxpayers weren't going to assume it for them,' said one official. But when E.F. Hutton nearly went under in 1987 the banks, at the government's prompting, tided the firm over until it could be sold. Others argued that the impediment was Drexel's criminal record, although E.F. Hutton suffered from the same thing (they pleaded guilty in 1985 to a check-kiting scam). As the author of the Brady report which proposed keeping banks afloat that were staggering from Third World defaults on their loans, Brady appeared to be in favour of propping up troubled concerns.

It was also unnecessary for Drexel to go out of business. As more than one person observed, the firm had $2.1 billion of assets, $1.1 billion of liabilities leaving a net worth of $1 billion. After filing for bankruptcy it was pursued by ludicrous claims to a total of $30 billion in all from claims from the New York Stock Exchange ($25 million), the government ($11 billion), and individual Savings & Loans.

There was a gleeful vengeance in the air. *The Wall Street Journal* quoted a 'Bush administration official monitoring the situation' as saying, 'The old Drexel Burnham that everyone knew and hated for the last ten years is gone.' 'I don't think it's sad for these jerks on Wall Street,' said the wampum man Forstmann, finally vindicated at last. John Phelan, chairman of the New York Stock Exchange was supposed to have told Drexel before Christmas of Wall Street's desire to 'dance on Drexel's grave'. Perhaps conspiracy is too paranoid a word; a communal determination not to help Drexel in its hour of need might be a more sober description. As one Drexel executive told *Fortune*, 'We were tough on the way up. We never made any friends. We stole business from other firms. We made the banks look silly. This was payback time. The Establishment finally got us.'

A media mêlée awaited Drexelites as they left the office on 13 February 1990. They were only allowed out after guards had inspected the cardboard boxes that contained their possessions. In the middle of June Drexel held a five-day liquidation sale. On the first day a motley crew of two thousand milled around the trading room floor picking over modems and quotrons. One man found a three-inch thick tome packed with the financial details of a Farley takeover. Leon Black's name was printed in gold leaf on the bottom right-hand corner. When it was found it was being used as a doorstop in the men's room.

Meanwhile in Beverly Hills a delighted Ben Stein got his second tour of Milken's junk bond department. In the parking lot Stein eyed the reserved parking spaces for Drexel, Columbia Savings, EII holdings (one of the companies involved in the leveraged buyout of Beatrice) and Rapid American (headed by Meshulam Riklis, the man who gave junk its name). 'Some parts of the building . . . were literally never finished. They have concrete floors, exposed wiring. . . . 'They were making so much money that the loss of 10,000 square feet of rental didn't mean a thing,' said a guide. On the corporate finance floor the picture boards of the department's picnics were still there, taken down from the walls and lying on a table. The floor that housed the X had been turned into a litigation defence file room. At the centre, where Milken used to sit, Stein said there was a shredder and a large plastic trash barrel, with 'for shredded material only' written in magic marker.

It is testimony to how far business and particularly Milken, Drexel and junk bonds had moved into the realm of pop culture, that one month after the bankruptcy 180 ex-employees appeared on the Phil Donahue show, one of America's classic afternoon talk shows. They had heard about the show through word of mouth and mobbed the studio.

Donahue began the bizarre encounter on an aggressive tact; 'You all drive BMWs . . . all the men look alike . . . you all make at least $100,000 a-year. I saw you in the movie *Wall Street*, and all across America people think you are the yuppies who embody the greed that caused the destruction of America's sound financial system.' But within a few minutes he was romping around the studio wearing a 'Mike Milken we believe in you' baseball cap and singing a different tune: 'You're the sons and daughters that we want our sons and daughters to bring home . . . you're the smart people, you did your homework . . . you're very good-looking nerds, and here you are, you're out of work. This is terrible.'

Identifying themselves in defiance of Donahue's stereotyping as non-BMW-driving ethnic mix of regular Joes who 'eat Nathan's hot dogs, like anybody else', the Drexel congregation wasted no time in pinning Giuliani to the wall: 'We are here because Rudy Giuliani decided to make it his project to gain votes by going after Drexel with RICO.' When Donahue said that Giuliani 'puts the gun on the table, and says, "Now you either shoot yourself, or I'm going to shoot you," ' one audience member snapped, 'If he had walked into Drexel, we all would have shot him.' During the break Donahue called Giuliani and invited him to come on down. Although his offices were only a few blocks away he said he could not get there in time, and covered himself by offering a re-match on another occasion, an offer that Donahue could easily refuse. As for Brady, he got just as short shrift from the audience who dismissed him as the water-carrier for white shoe Wall Street: 'Drexel Burnham was a small mom-and-pop shop at some time and big powerhouses saw us getting too big too fast. We made too much money too quickly.' The moral, they concluded was, 'Once the government, Giuliani and Nicholas Brady, once they want to get you, they get you.'

There was one other revealing moment. 'What good is a system that relies on the genius of an individual who – what would we do if he gets a cold? . . . there's something wrong with a trillion dollar system that collapses when you lose one person. I don't want to work for a company that's that dependent on – '

'What's Donahue without you?' interrupted David Dreyfuss, the head of Broad Street Productions, Drexel's former video department.

'What's Donahue – well now you're talking. What's Donahue without me? . . . This is a different matter, entirely.'

But was it?

Whatever else the programme illustrated, it was that the firm was bonded by a uniquely fierce energy. It would be hard to imagine the bankruptcy of any other company producing such a turn out, nor even making such good television. The 'us against them' mentality that had been the rocket fuel of Drexel's assent had only been intensified by the two-year siege mentality. Three months after the firm went out of business they held their first reunion and over 500 people turned up. 'Shit Happens' read the invitation. In stark contrast to the gratis luxuries of the Predator's Ball, attendees had to pay $5 entrance fee and jostle at a cash bar. But Tequila Willies, a five-storey club where the party was held, was jammed to the gills.

15

JUNK JUSTICE

THE conspiracy, cheered on by the roar of the junk bond market collapsing all around it, was now on its final triumphant lap. Milken himself was all that remained.

Whatever Drexel had thought of their chances of survival, Milken knew that without him Drexel was doomed. One Vice President who visited him was interested in spinning off his particular department. 'What's this?' asked Milken, pointing to something on his business plan. He answered that that was the amount of business he expected to continue to get from Drexel. Milken was supposed to have replied that there wasn't going to be a Drexel for very much longer.

With one exception Milken would not be drawn on the demise of the firm he had built. Reached at his home by the persistent Marie Brenner (who, according to Lerer, had managed to persuade Milken to return her call by leaving a message to the effect that she was interested in making a charitable contribution), Milken said, 'I had long discussions with Drexel in 1988, when I made many, many suggestions of what they should do in the company. How do you think it feels when I am being blamed for the very things I warned them not to do?'

As the months passed Milken began to feel the heat. Later he would write in his letter to Judge Wood: 'Lori and I have often wished that there was a way to turn back the clock . . . we often reminisce about the time when our life was quiet and peaceful . . . there were no reporters at the end of the driveway, no helicopters over the house . . . in July 1989 I attended a funeral for a close friend . . . As they lowered his casket and we shovelled dirt into his grave to say our final goodbyes, a camera crew came up to me, shoving their microphone and camera in front of my face, asking me what I thought about the government's activities, and did I think the government was fair. There is no respite. There is no day off.' On the advice of his lawyer Milken had taken to reading the sports pages in the newspapers first, explaining, 'It talks more about mankind's successes, while other parts talk about mankind's problems or failures.'

In the letter he continued, 'It's hard for our 9-year-old daughter to turn on her TV without a newsbreak, political ad or commentary being shown, causing one of her friends to call her and tell her her daddy is on TV. My sons don't verbalize the pressures they feel, even though Lori and I attempt to talk about it.'

When they went to see *The Witches*, starring Anjelica Huston, Milken's youngest daughter Bari burst out crying and ran from the theatre. The witches in the movie were hideous old hags who put on nice faces and masqueraded as child-loving do-gooders. When asked by Jesse Kornbluth how Lori explained Milken's plight to her kids she said, 'I've told them "your father is a genius and has totally revolutionized the finance industry. People don't like change, and they're trying to get rid of your father, and if you look in your history books, you'll see that people who have tried to make change have had this happen."' 'Do they believe it?' asked Kornbluth. 'They believe it,' said Lori.

They have also screened clips for their kids of the McCarthy era, and shown their children the film *Tucker*. Starring Jeff Bridges, the film tells the true story of the man who launched an innovative new car while Big Cars managed to squeeze out the competition by getting him indicted and busting up his operation. The film was not entirely dissimilar to the story of De Lorean and his dream car.

'Visitors to Milken's home these days can find themselves listening awkwardly as their host discusses the persecuted figures of history, from Christ to Galileo,' wrote Christopher Byron. He described the household as one where entropy had taken hold. One of the gates hung off its hinges, the tennis court saw infrequent use, and the government laid claim to the property (which was part of the $700 million bond he had to post to remain free on bail). 'As his guests depart, Milken may make them a gift of a favoured book that somehow captures the tragedy of his time, either a copy of a children's book called *The Giving Tree* in which a boy makes friends with a tree only to chop it down or a 1915 Cadillac advertisement with a blurb on the penalty of leadership.'

In addition to this relentless exposure it was the character assassinations that Milken found the hardest to take: 'What I have not been able to accept, and what has been the most painful during the past four years, has been the assault on the sincerity of my beliefs, my moral system, and my basic inner being. It has been very difficult for me to cope with. I have been forced to face the challenge that not only am I portrayed as a fraud, but everything my life stood for is called a fraud and all the principles I have spoken about my whole life are hollow. At times this has been almost too difficult to bear.'

Giuliani knew exactly what this was like and knew that used against Milken it would be the most effective pressure tactic. Not that Milken was vain, it was just that he had an unquestioning faith in the value of his work. Contemplating running for Mayor Giuliani had once remarked, 'When you see how vicious it all gets, it has to give you a little pause. You get the impression that the theory about people in public – particularly political – life is, "Do anything you can to destroy them" . . . It means that everyone in public life – at some point – is going to be painted a failure. Everybody makes mistakes. But if you exaggerate those mistakes beyond the context in which they should be viewed, you can destroy anyone in public office.'

True, Milken was not in public office, nor was he in political life. But the saga had long sinced moved from the personal into the realms of symbol and metaphor, making Milken and his junk bonds hot political entities. Indeed, because he lacked the official stamp of public office, the venom directed against him was all the stronger. Here was someone revolutionizing finance and corporate America, an impostor acting as a shadow Secretary to the Treasury. His lack of Establishment tenure made him an easier figure to scapegoat, and they loaded him up with all the baggage.

Once Giuliani twigged Milken's twofold love of anonymity and family, he had found his Achilles' heel. In this, the indictment of his younger brother was key. If, as he said, he lay awake at night worrying about the effect it was all having on his children, the guilt Milken felt about his brother was all that more intense. The promise of an acquittal for Lowell was one of the strongest inducements they had to make Milken cop a plea. There was also the undercover visit FBI agents paid to his 92-year-old grandfather Louis Zax, who has two hearing aids, to quiz him about stock transactions. Learning of the visit, Milken was supposed to have remarked, 'This is never going to stop is it? I can't take it anymore.'

The plea was so much more effective than a trial. Not only was it quicker and less expensive, but its outcome was certain. A plea was a plea, but a jury could never be counted on to be so certain. Furthermore, in terms of public credibility, a plea was preferable to a conviction. As Giuliani explained, 'In a conviction after the trial he could have continued to maintain "I didn't do it, it was unfair." But having him actually stand up and plead guilty obviated that possibility.'

To this end the drumbeat of leaks kept up, and Laurie Cohen of *The Wall Street Journal* wrote no less than eighteen stories that anticipated a new expanded and superseding indictment coming soon, consisting of between 160 and 300 additional counts. Although it would have eventually come, the superseding indictment, as in the Princeton Newport case, was primarily a psychological device designed to terrify its targets into submission. With Laurie Cohen predicting events rather than reporting them, the government maximized the leverage to be had from this threat.

To further persuade Milken to roll he was threatened with prosecution in almost every state for his supposed part in the Savings & Loans crisis. In short, if Milken resisted he would become a professional defendant for the rest of his life, fighting legal battles that would be debilitating whether he won or lost.

The government also had a dozen additional government witnesses. To corral a dozen to testify against Milken the government administered cram-down immunity – the kind that coerces people unwilling to testify to do so or face charges of perjury or obstruction of justice. If not actually coerced Milken's former colleagues were certainly very reluctant to testify against their boss and mentor (as the government reminded Judge Wood).

The tactical significance of these witnesses lay in the fact that much of the scandal had depended on the testimony of Ivan Boesky, who was supposed to be the government's star witness. Boesky had disappeared from public view once he had begun to serve his three-year prison sentence in a minimum security prison in California. But in late November 1989 he made a dramatic reappearance when, late one Sunday night, a *New York Post* photographer acting on a tip off snapped him as he emerged from a local grocery in Stamford, Connecticut, with a bag of groceries. Instead of the lean and elegant figure, Boesky more resembled a bum. His hair was dishevelled and he had allowed his beard to grow the length of his chest. Some compared him to Howard Hughes.

But Boesky lacked credibility as the government's star witness for reasons other than his appearance. One of the people he traded in for his sweetheart deal with the government was the godfather of his children, John Mulheren, a manic depressive who, at Boesky's behest, did illegal favours for him such as park and manipulate stock. Mulheren was a colourful character. He had once brought a dixieland band onto the trading floor of Merrill Lynch, and on another occasion, a chimpanzee on roller skates. He was also stopped leaving his home with a semi-automatic rifle with the intention of shooting Boesky.

In this, the one case in which the government was actually forced to put Boesky on the witness stand, the former arbitrageur showed his true colours. He admitted that he was no stranger to lying under oath. When pressed on how many times he had so lied Boesky snapped, 'I cannot tell you the number.' No surprise, then, that on the stand he could not be sure he ever said that greed was healthy, avoided a direct answer to whether he had told the government about all of his insider trading activities (even though he was asked the question twelve times and ultimately could only say, 'It's not a yes-or-no question I believe. But the answer to your question really is, that I believe the answer is yes'), and could not recall what he had done with all his assets. Part of his plea agreement was that he would no longer break the law, but he also admitted that he had done so by bribing inmates with a few quarters to do his laundry when in Lompoc minimum security prison.

Neither could the government expect Boesky to fare well in Liman's hands. Liman had also been Dennis Levine's lawyer and thus might well have been party to 'inside' information about Boesky (who was engaged, remember, in an illegal relationship with Levine) which he could have used in the courtroom to discredit Boesky as a witness. Moreover Liman was good generally at discrediting government stooges. In another Boesky spin-off case Liman had exposed Boyd Jefferies, a co-operating government witness, as a rather dubious character who had fraudulently altered documents that were a key part of the case and won from the government in exchange for his co-operation a 'sentence' that consisted of teaching golf to handicapped kids near his home in the swank ski resort of Aspen. Liman did not fail to emphasize that such circumstances underlined how fraught with moral dubiousness were Jefferies' status and testimony. And indeed it was his lack of credibility as a witness that caused the case to be overturned on appeal.

In short, the government's case – in so far as it involved Boesky – lacked moral grounds and credibility, problems that would only be spotlighted if they had to put Boesky on the witness stand, especially after the fiasco of the Mulheren trial. He was sentenced to a year and a day, but this case too was thrown out on appeal.

Finally, a little over a year after he had been indicted, Milken cratered and copped a plea on the afternoon that the Grand Jury in New York was supposed to vote on the superseding indictment. The following Tuesday he appeared in court and pleaded guilty on six counts, facing a twenty-eight-year sentence and a $600 million fine. It was three years and one day after Boesky had made the same appearance and only twenty minutes after Adnan Khashoggi, the once famed arms dealer and richest man in the world, had made the same entrance. As Milken ran the gauntlet of the seventeen steps through the media throng he told the marshalls, 'It never ceases to amaze me.'

Inside, when asked if he was aware of the maximum possible sentence, if he was on drugs or in the care of a psychiatrist, Milken answered without hesitation. When asked if he was making his plea under any force or threats he paused a few seconds, as if unsure, before answering that he was not. Then Milken read his allocution: 'I am here today because in connection with some transactions, I transgressed certain of the laws and regulations that govern our industry. I was wrong in doing so and knew that at the time.' His wife cried quietly.

In detailing the six transgressions he sought to distinguish himself from Boesky. 'We were not social friends and had little in common. His philosophy of business was different from mine.' Boesky would also call 'incessantly', pestering Milken about the losses that he was sustaining. Milken also defended the 'underlying soundness and integrity' of the junk bond market and said that 'our business was in no way dependent on these practises.'

At the end of the eleven page confession he began to choke up as he said, 'This long period has been extremely painful and difficult for my family and friends.' Milken's face flushed and his voice trembled when he added 'as well as myself'. Tears welled up in Milken's eyes as he placed his finger under his nose to try and keep in the emotion about to burst out. 'I realize that by my acts I have hurt those that are closest to me. I am truly sorry.' Liman put his lawyerly arm around Milken and motioned to the judge who allowed him to sit. After drinking a glass of water he was ready to continue.

'Mr Milken, how do you plead?'

'Guilty, Your Honour.'

On the the courthouse steps Liman added a postscript to Milken's confession, talking about 'instances in which Michael went too far in helping clients'. Speaking for Milken he said that it was his hope that 'history will see his violations in context and judge him not just on the basis of his lapses, but on the basis of the contributions that he made to the economy.'

Editorial after editorial named Milken as 'the living symbol' of greed and of the excesses of the roaring eighties. But in the headlines that followed it was Milken's tears rather than the details of his plea that received the gleeful scrutiny. There was unrestrained delight in seeing a master of the universe cry like a baby. One paper lambasted Milken as 'billionaire trash' unable, for all his money, to purchase enough self-dignity to prevent himself from betraying his social inferiority by crying in self-pity. Gangsters weren't supposed to cry, argued another, invoking Jimmy Cagney who would have taken it on the chin with a defiant smile. For this and other lapses 'he should be tied by the ankles to the rear bumper of a pick up truck and taken on a slow tour of a long gravel road. Then his head should be put on a spike and taken around to the nation's most prestigious business schools as a lesson in ethics,' wrote columnist Donald Kaul.

Ridiculed as a blubber baby, I think Milken cried out of rage and frustration at the impossible position he had been put in. Used to making the terms of the deal, he had had to make a deal he detested and brand himself a felon. The concept was an anathema to him. Used to winning, he had to admit the fact that he had lost. When he had refused to bend to the government, the government – which brooked no defiance – determined to break and humiliate him. When he cried in the courtroom Milken finally acknowledged his defeat. Milken – who may well not have committed any deliberate crimes (even the ones he confessed too) – had been broken for sinning against the social and bureaucratic order.

There was the usual rainbow of reactions, quotables from the usual notables, from the invited to the indicted. Celebrity Congressman Dingell claimed he thought that the list of transgressions that Milken had probably committed more resembled 2,500. Charles Keating, head of Lincoln Savings & Loans, and one of the symbols of the S&L folly, declared, 'You don't put Michelangelo or Da Vinci in jail. To lose that mind for even a day would be a tragedy.' It was a testimonial that Milken could have done without. Lowell Milken issued a terse and bitter statement: 'This is one of the saddest and most frustrating days of my life. I can take no satisfaction that the charges against me are being dropped. They never should have been brought in the first place because I have done nothing wrong.'

Crowing that this was yet another decisive victory against 'Crime in the suites', Breeden let it be known that he would be pushing for a 'substantial period of incarceration'. That evening the predatory prosecutors had a ball, with a knees-up in Harvey's, a restaurant in Chelsea. Giuliani could not attend, but the rest of the gang were all there. Bruce Baird even hopped on a train up from Washington to join the feast.

Milken was scheduled to be sentenced in October. Meanwhile over 500 of Milken's friends, colleagues and supporters wrote letters to Judge Wood pleading for a lenient sentence. Some of the letters were sickly sweet: 'Michael is a national treasure . . . we need him to balance the toxicity of a topsy-turvy world . . . we have polluted our environment, decimated our forests, neglected our children. Imprisoning Michael Milken is a waste of the same magnitude.' Some of them were moving. Judy Sherman Wolin wrote of how she was attending Milken's arraignment when a woman whom she did not know presented her with a shoe box tied with a bright red ribbon. 'These are for Michael,' said the stranger. 'They're cookies from Bea. Her husband, Lou, is critically ill, and she could not be here but they both wanted Michael to know how much they both love him.' Bea also wrote to the judge, describing Michael's final visit to his dying friend who was like a surrogate father. When just starting out at Drexel, both couples had lived across the hall in Cherry Hill, New Jersey. Lou, dying of cancer, got dressed for the first time in months for the special visit. He also gave Michael a piece of his metalwork sculpture, the only person he ever allowed to have a piece. Two days later he died. Other letters described Lori's helpless dependency on Milken when it came to the epilepsy of their children, or their youngest daughter Bari asking a family friend why she didn't get to see much of her dad any more.

The letters were from the full range of the people Milken came in contact with. Many of them were from former co-workers and painted a warm picture of a familial life on the X. One was a drawing from a 9-year-old of a stick Milken behind bars and shedding a tear. Others were from his bodyguards, drivers and trading assistants. One man wrote in because he knew the Milkens' plumber. Then there were the heavy hitters, CEOs like Revlon's Perelman, Safeway's Peter Magowan, CBS's Laurence Tisch, Time Warner's Steve Ross, Armand Hammer, John Kluge, Merv Adelson.

But it was impossible not to wonder if this wasn't an orchestrated effort, as an article in the *Los Angeles Times* which reviewed some of the letters suggested. Lerer denied organizing a campaign: 'I think it's normal for friends to call and say "How can I help?" if a friend is in trouble. And they called the law firm and the law firm said, "Well, one of the things you can do is, you can write a letter to the judge." And people did it on their own. You know Ivan Boesky got twenty letters, as a comparison.' The piece in the *LA Times* concluded by giving the readers Judge Wood's courthouse address if they wanted to write in, which Lerer condemned as irresponsible: 'The tone of the invitation was . . . if you want to write something negative, write it . . . that's the clear message of a newspaper affecting something, not reporting on something.'

The story flared up in the press and created a deluge of negative letters. Stored in eighteen large files in the bowels of the courthouse, the letters betrayed a skin-deep media-fed level of knowledge about the issue. Many misspelt his name as Milliken, and called for all sorts of sadistic punishments:

'My family and I are most interested in the future of Michael Milken, and wish to express our desire to see him hung by the balls until death.' A 'family of victims' wrote, 'we will only be happy when he is slowly executed.' Liman said of these and other no less gruesome demands that they 'would probably stagger the secret police of totalitarian regimes.'

There was only one letter from a co-worker who did not get on with him. He claimed that for a Christmas gift Milken gave him Drexel Burnham promotional towels and that his favourite saying was, 'I don't mind a little brown nose if I can get some green in my wallet.' Then there was Dianne de la Vega who Milken rear-ended on the freeway. 'People should know what kind of a crumb he is – when he hit me he was worth over a billion.' She got a $30,000 settlement and claimed that he told her over the phone, 'If I dared to bring legal action against him, "I would know what was good for me" . . . his tone was so threatening I didn't know whether my life was in danger or whether he was planning to overwhelm me in court.' She was, she said, a basket case for years afterwards. One writer was in despair over the fact that Yale would accept Milken's son (as it had), noting that Princeton's most prominent alumna was, he said, Brooke Shields who was in his estimation a child porn star.

Many of these letters were from bona fide loony tunes. Some were anti-Semitic, ranting against greedy kikes and exhorting the judge to 'burn them good', others were just insane. One person wrote in offering the services of his 'NATIONAL TRANSDUCER' which was 'a science and technology of routes of some 800 foot or so' to replace 'the mesmerized mercenary cult' of Wall Street.

In what looked like a setback for the government, part of the plea agreement did not require Milken to start co-operating with them until after his sentencing. But this gave the government five months to concoct a pre-sentencing memo in which they would cram all the additional offences they could, and thus try to get the judge to take into consideration crimes above and beyond the six that Milken had made his plea on.

'Few white collar-criminals have ever attracted as much public attention as Milken,' began the government's pre-sentencing memorandum. It was 132 pages long after the judge had ordered almost a hundred pages be redacted before unsealing it to the public view. It was the ultimate character assassination. His crimes of 'greed, arrogance and betrayal' were motivated by 'power and wealth' and were 'calculated and systematic'. It also, as the defence pointed out, made twenty-five references to 'greed' and 'wealth' in the first twenty-five pages. As the man atop 'the Drexel colossus' (not strictly true, that was Fred Joseph), Milken was also culpable for fathering 'excesses in Drexel's corporate culture', and he was blamed for destroying the firm he had built because of the bonuses it paid out in its last few months.

But in their argument Milken deserved additional punishment because he was 'unreconstructed and unapologetic' and had plied the probation inspector with 'self-serving rationalizations'. He should also be penalized, argued the government, for resisting them for so long and insisting that they prosecute them. This had necessitated granting immunity to a number of people against whom the government had hoped to win prosecutions. His intransigence had so drawn matters out that those he could incriminate were now protected by the statute of limitations. They argued that he should be made to pay for these additional collateral costs and inconveniences.

But this was just window dressing to the litany of additional crimes with which the memorandum preoccupied itself. If there had been any substance to the superseding indictment this would have been the time to display its wares. As it was it largely contented itself with rehashing the now familiar charges of the SEC complaint and the original indictment, adding in details of two meetings between Boesky and Milken (that had already been leaked to the press). The defence shot back on all these counts, accusing the government of 'sneaking in through the back door evidence regarding the very offences for which it has foresworn prosecution', and adding that 'Mr Milken would not have entered into the plea agreement . . . if it was regarded, not as the final curtain in this complex case, but only as the first act in a protracted process.'

They pointed out that the government remained obsessed with the *de facto* criminality of Milken's wealth, which made him guilty of greed. Ignoring all the letters that had been written, the government instead chose to include in their memorandum only one unattributed quote from a Milken co-worker: 'Milken never let go of a nickel except to get a better grip.'

Blaming Milken for the bankruptcy of Drexel was an especially low shot. 'It is unfair for the government to accuse Michael Milken of being responsible for Drexel's downfall after forcing him to sit on the sidelines unable to help in any way the downfall of the institution he helped to build.' Milken had no say in the final round of bonuses. Up until the time he had been forced out of Drexel as required by the settlement, the high yield bond department had been the firm's profit engine, and at the time that he left the firm was in healthy financial shape. It was without his advice – not because of it – that Drexel then did a run of bad deals causing it to choke on its own junk.

Far from being intransigent, Milken's lawyers argued they had been interested in co-operating from the beginning. 'Both Edward Bennett Williams and members of this firm attempted to initiate discussions with prosecutors at an early stage, only to be told in no uncertain terms that the government was unwilling to have such discussions until its investigation was completed. By the time the government was willing to explore settlement it had already granted immunity to most of its witnesses and had committed itself to an unprecedented use of RICO, which further inhibited settlement.'

As for the details of the Boesky/Milken relationship upon which so much continued to hang, Liman argued that the score-keeping, or the tallying of gains and losses on an account, was not in itself illegal, and common practice.

He also pointed out that in any bartering relationship reminders about losing money on transactions and appeals to a consequent indebtedness are stock in trade, and a staple of the trader/client relationship; 'Boesky thus used score-keeping to try to extract concessions from Mr Milken – as any savvy professional would have done.' In the case of Milken this score-keeping ended in March 1986, when the financing of Boesky's limited partnership was complete: 'Boesky no longer needed it and Mr Milken no longer wanted to hear Boesky's complaints.' As Charles Thurner recalled Milken telling him the month before, 'He told me to forget it – that it was all a bunch of [expletive] anyway and he didn't care.'

Because there was no reconciling the two contradictory accounts, Judge Kimba Wood decided to hold a Fatico hearing, so called after the Fatico brothers who were convicted after hijacking a van in 1979. Prior to their sentencing it became known that the Faticos were a part of the Gambino crime family, which would have merited a stiffer sentence. It was therefore decided to have a pre-sentencing hearing that was in effect a mini-trial, in order for the judge to get as full a picture as possible of the true character of the defendants. Held before a judge, the key differences between a Fatico and a full trial was that there was no jury and that the burden of proof, instead of having to be 'beyond a reasonable doubt', was lessened to a 'preponderance of evidence'. Wood imposed her own house rules on the hearing which she said would last for two weeks, limiting each side to twenty hours apiece to make their case.

Although not happy that Milken was once again in the grip of procedures used against the mafia, the plea agreement did not restrict the government from presenting additional charges, and so there was little Milken could do to protest the hearing. The government let it be known that they would need an additional room behind the courtroom in which to store a mass of documents.

In the otherwise mundane appearance held to deliberate this matter there was one revealing moment. Wood addressed the government's loaded reference to Milken's 'post-investigation social and charitable good works' and had asked the probation officer to look into this and see if they were of 'recent vintage and prompted by the sub-poena he received'. The report came back that Milken had been doing good works well in advance of the investigation against him (since 1982 the Milkens have endowed their family Foundations with some $370 million). Unheeded Milken's supporters had been saying this all along. But it was US Assistant Attorney John Carroll's response that was so revealing, utterly bare-faced in its dishonesty: 'If there was some suggestion in our papers questioning when Mr Milken began working with disadvantaged children, that was not intended.' To this writer this is a self-evident and bold-faced lie.

In spite of the thirteen hundred pages of testimony that the Fatico produced, it was essentially a big yawn. There was no Ivan Boesky on the stand, and Milken's lawyers refused to let their clients testify without immunity, more worried about the potential civil lawsuits than the sentencing. Milken followed their advice, but later wrote to the judge about his frustration at not being able to speak out. Prosecutors waded through the technicalities as if through a bog. 'No, you have the wrong preferred,' a witness had to answer after detailed questioning in which it turned out that the government had the wrong end of the stock.

It was the recounting of atmospherics that roused a courtroom stupefied by both the tedious detail and the heat. The temperature in the crowded courtroom tweaked the eighties, while a solitary air conditioner huffed and puffed away. On several occasions the judge had to ask witnesses to speak up to overcome the background din. In the end, as had been typical throughout the case, it was this kind of thing that had most impact on the judge, and, in the absence of a jury, therefore most decided the outcome of the hearing.

The first third of the hearing was taken up with consideration of the manipulation of Wickes stock. At stake was a preferred stock that was paying out what was for Wickes a costly dividend. However, if this stock closed at a certain level on twenty out of thirty consecutive days, then Wickes could recall the preferred and thus save itself great expense. The government maintained that Milken was motivated to do this to win Wickes as a client and thus pull down significant banking fees.

The defence did not deny that there had been a manipulation of Wickes stock to achieve this, but said that Milken had had nothing to do with it. Gardiner, a trader on the high yield bond desk, maintained that Milken had asked him to do this. Pointing at his quotron Milken was supposed to have said 'Peter, Wickes, six and an eight,' indicating the price he wanted. But Gardiner had been sitting some forty feet away from Milken at the time of this supposed exchange, and it is unlikely that Gardiner would have heard him unless he had shouted over the hubbub of the X. But Milken, as one witness testified, did not shout.

Gardiner claimed that he confronted the department's in-house compliance officer and Milken buddy Kevin Madigan: 'I told him point blank that if he didn't think there was material use of non-public information going on on the floor, that he was crazy.' Madigan denied the conversation ever took place.

He also claimed that another X-er, Alan Rosenthal, had, shortly after Boesky Day, come over to his desk and huddled with him, saying 'Clean out your desks. Get rid of anything that isn't nailed down . . . and don't throw it in the company garbage.' When he asked him if he was serious Rosenthal was supposed to have added, 'Listen, I talked to Mike, you know, let's get rid of the stuff.'

Many were the times that people used Mike's name without necessarily having spoken to him. In the world of junk bonds the word 'Mike' was an abracadabra that worked a certain magic. People did what you wanted them to when you said that Mike had said it. And Gardiner was also an extremely unreliable witness. He admitted to having perjured himself before a Grand Jury. This is exactly what Lisa Jones did, and, by her example, Gardiner should have been tried and convicted for this. But instead he got immunity on the basis of what he had to offer concerning Milken. As Liman complained 'It wasn't supposed to be that people who committed rampant perjury were to get immunity in order to go and testify against him [Milken].'

In the end Maultasch, an ex-X-man on the East Coast, claimed he carried out the crucial manipulation by getting the Boesky organization to accumulate 1.9 million shares in the last nineteen minutes of trading and effecting the necessary price hike. He claimed he had his instructions from Gardiner. He also said that he thought Gardiner was a liar.

After this fiasco, which did more damage to the government's case than it did to Milken's, Liman tried to persuade the judge to abandon the hearings. But Wood, on a different tack, responded that the hearings were proving 'very helpful' and 'filling a void of a certain type of information that I did not have before'. This was the first indication that perhaps, no matter how much right the defence may have had on their side, things were not going to go their way. To make matters worse the chemistry between Liman and Wood soon went awry. As the hearing wore on Wood bothered less and less to hide her irritation with Liman. At one point she told Liman, 'You have a long way of telling me something that I already know is in your mind.' If she thought he was a pompous old windbag, Liman treated her with some condescension, as though she were a new kid on the block.

Given the lack of proof, lack even of preponderance of evidence, Judge Wood could only have been tuning into the atmospherics, such as the bizarre dawn meeting that Milken and Maultasch held in a conference room off to the side of the X. In that meeting no word was exchanged. Milken wrote questions on a yellow legal pad and Maultasch indicated the replies. Not only was there supposed to be an armed guard outside the conference room (although this did not stop Harry Horowitz from walking in and giving them both a start), but the security guard at the front desk was also supposed to have screwed up his visitor's slip and assured him that he had not been there.

But Maultasch – who had flown in fright to Beverly Hills and insisted on seeing Michael – was on the verge of a nervous breakdown and taking medication to calm his nerves. He expressed concern that Milken had met with Boesky but Milken was supposed to have assured him that he assumed he was 'speaking for the record'. In the sentencing memo the government proudly revealed that indeed he had been, since they had taped the meeting in the Beverly Hills Hotel. The government also alleged that there had been a poolside meeting at Milken's home in May 1986. According to Boesky's account Milken had suggested cooling the relationship during the period of 'increased law enforcement'.

Liman made every effort to put this in the proper context. In the reply sentencing memoranda he pointed out that, 'Much of what the government characterizes as "obstruction" is not obstruction at all. During the immediate aftermath of the service of the Grand Jury and SEC sub-poenas at Drexel there was unquestionably confusion, fear and paranoia. But confusion, fear and paranoia are hardly illegal and were surely justifiable under the circumstances.' Cross-examining Dahl he asked if there wasn't a sense that 'Big Brother was bugging everyone at Drexel', and throughout the hearing Liman underlined the paranoia in the air. But even though he may have framed this as blameless, his emphasis may only have reinforced Wood's impression to the contrary.

Indeed, in the Fatico findings the atmospherics were pre-eminent, while the crimes themselves languished in the background. Wood too found Gardiner unconvincing. Most compelling she found Peizer's account of being asked to give a blue ledger book to Lorraine Spurge. According to Wood this 'young former protégé' testified 'forthrightly, carefully, and credibly'. She waived aside the fact that Peizer had traded his testimony for protection against prosecution, had squirrelled sub-poenaed documents away at home until he had made his deal with the government (possibly to use them as a bargaining chip), had incorrectly identified incriminating records in someone else's handwriting, and had seen Milken and his brother on an occasion when Lowell was not even in the office.

Instead she went with the account of the exchange which took place in the kitchenette off the trading room floor. Instead of just handing it over, 'I turned on the faucet in case anyone was listening,' testified Peizer, adding, 'I had seen everyone talking while faucets were on.' The blue ledger, supposedly a running tally of the score on illicit dealings with ex-Drexelite David Solomon, has never been seen since. Spurge, who testified before a Grand Jury, denied that Peizer gave her the book. But Judge Wood found her testimony lacking in credibility, owing to her considerable compensation and close working and personal relationship with Milken.

The second item on her list of examples to obstruct justice took place in the men's room on the trading room floor, again with faucets running. Milken had called James Dahl, another of Milken's closest traders, into the office on a Sunday. 'I did some work at my desk and after about two hours I was getting a little impatient and wanted to go home. I said, "Mike, if there is something you want to talk to me about, let's do it because I am out of here soon." And he got up from his desk and walked out of the trading room by the elevator banks and walked into the men's room and he went over to the sink, turned on the water, started washing his hands, and he leaned over and he said, "There haven't been any sub-poenas issued and whatever you need to do, do it." He turned off the water. He looked at me for a response and I said, "Okay," and I walked out and I went home.' Further examination revealed that Milken said this 'in hushed tones with his head down near the running water, which is not what I was expecting when we walked into the men's room.' It was this testimony that provided the anti-climactic hearing, numbing in detail, with its dramatic finale.

The third example of obstruction of justice in the judge's eyes was an exchange between Peizer and Milken. Looking through his desk for sub-poenaed documents, Milken asked him what he was doing. When Peizer told him Milken opened an empty drawer and said in an apparently glib manner, 'If you don't have them, you can't provide them.'

And it is here that we come to the nub of the hearing.

In their post-hearing memorandum Milken's lawyers pointed out, cor-rectly, that, 'No witness was asked by Mr Milken to destroy a document; no witness was asked to give false testimony; no witness was asked to withhold evidence from the government; no witness was ever intimidated.'

But Judge Wood interpreted things differently. 'The court took note of the fact that by their demeanour and manner of responding to the questions, both witnesses appeared to be deeply reluctant to testify against Michael Milken, and testified to only that which the facts forced them to. Their reticence in responding to these questions appeared to stem more from an attempt to do whatever they could to avoid drawing inferences that could hurt their former mentor and benefactor, rather than from confusion about what Milken was communicating. I believe they were both bending over backward during their testimony to avoid testifying to drawing the only reasonable conclusion that can be drawn from these events.' Instead of taking the evidence at face value this interpretative spin could also transform a paucity of evidence into a cornucopia.

The paucity of evidence concerned the charges themselves. She concluded that there was scant evidence linking Milken to the Wickes manipulation, or to insider trading on Caesar's World. The only remaining charge was the disposal of warrants in KKR's acquisition of Storer, the cable television concern, in what was, at the time, the largest buyout ever.

Initially KKR had proposed to acquire Storer, and to that end Drexel had committed itself to raising $1.2 billion. But as a result of a competing bid, KKR raised its bid, and in so doing required Drexel to raise an additional $261 million. This they decided to do by issuing PIK preferred stock, a hybrid security that pays its interest or dividend in kind instead of in cash. The nature of the deal was such that Drexel needed to guarantee that if buyers could not be found it would buy all the PIK itself. Drexel was caught between a rock and hard place. On the one hand it had to maintain the virtual franchise and lock-up that it had created as a result of its 'highly confident' commitment letters, but on the other it was unwilling to commit itself to the risk of being the buyer of last resort, which, obviously, was the bedrock of what would otherwise be an idle boast and worthless assurance.

Although Bruck portrayed such situations as instances where Milken either bullied deals through or simply ignored the East Coast committee that approved deals, Milken was in fact extremely useful to the East Coast. For they could count on Milken, either alone or through an assortment of his investment partnerships, to take an initial critical position in a deal that others considered too risky. In the case of Storer, Drexel was unwilling to commit itself to buying the preferred. The use of PIKs for such a purpose and on such a scale was unprecedented. KKR did not yet have their track record and the cable business had its detractors. 'Drexel then asked Milken if he would commit to buy any . . . preferred that Drexel could not otherwise sell to the investing public (up to the full $261 million).' Unless Milken had agreed, 'exposing himself personally to hundreds of millions of dollars of risk', the deal could not have gone through. (On a number of other occasions Milken also supported Drexel by lending it large amounts of capital.)

Milken of course always intended to sell the preferred to his clients, and in order to sweeten the deal he asked KKR for warrants which when exercised at a certain future date for a certain price could be turned into stock. These 'equity kickers', as they were also known, had been evolved by Milken and Joseph some years earlier and had proved to be a good incentive for investors hesitant about risky bonds. The warrants were not necessarily a sure thing. If the company failed in the wake of the buyout, the stock price would be wiped out and so would the value of the warrants. But given that the warrants were bought for a token discount price (25 cents a share in the example of Storer, while KKR was offering $91 per share), they could also prove to be a bonanza for investors.

In November Milken's partnerships bought $154 million of the $261 million preferred and the warrants to go with them. Soon after they sold the preferred to a number of familiar clients, but retained the warrants. According to the government Milken 'nominally committed the High Yield Partnerships to buy substantial amounts of the PIK Preferred so that he and his associates could take down 82 per cent of the equity.'

One of the partnerships holding Storer equity was the MacPherson partnership. Investors in this partnership included Milken and his brother and a number of fund managers. The charge here was that Milken had offered these fund managers as individuals the chance to invest in this partnership, either to bribe them to get their institutions to buy the preferred or as a kind of illegal gratuity that was a reward for loyalty and an inducement for future business. But the one witness the government called who was an investor in MacPherson, Richard Grassgreen of Kinder-Care, testified that the MacPherson opportunity came after he had decided that Kinder-Care would invest in the preferred. He also testified that he had asked Milken whether the opportunity was for him personally or for his institution. Milken told him that it was for him personally. Once again, however, the government had struck out when it came to reliable witnesses. Grassgreen had just resigned from Kinder-Care for having stolen $600,000 in fees from the company.

The government also called Fred Joseph to testify against his former partner. As with the hearings in Washington, Joseph's candour was such that he could not remember the specifics of very much at all. As one reporter wrote, his appearance provided for 'a tiny jolt of electricity in a numbingly complex hearing'. But it was only a tiny jolt. Joseph, who on previous occasions had said he saw every trade that Milken did, claimed he did not know about the MacPherson partnership and that it was possible that it violated company policies. At a breakin proceedings Liman was overheard saying, 'How did he not know it? You know he has schizophrenic feelings, maybe worse.'

Out of all this, the only impropriety Judge Wood could find was that Milken had not told KKR that he intended to keep a large share of the equity for himself, his family, and Drexel associates. Had KKR known this they would have used this – as they later did – as a negotiating factor when it came to Drexel's fee. The judge also found that KKR had been falsely led to believe that the warrants were needed to sell the preferred. Judge Wood wrote in her Fatico findings, 'The court will take this conduct into consideration in assessing his character.'

In the absence of much drama inside the courtroom, one altercation that went on outside was both compelling and revealing. In court Liman had prefaced his approach to the allegation of a manipulation of Wickes stock by saying that he did not deny that there had been a manipulation, but that Milken had had nothing to do with it. Connie Bruck thought that this was absurd and, during a break outside in the hall, told *New York Times* reporter Kurt Eichenwald as much: 'I can't believe you'd be so naive as to think there would be a manipulation and Milken wouldn't be behind it,' she was reported to have said, according to *Esquire*. Whereupon Eichenwald rejoindered, 'I guess that's the difference between coming in with your mind made up and coming in and listening to the evidence.' Bruck was then supposed to have stalked off, but later exacted revenge by speaking to Page 6, the gossip column in the *New York Post*, where she was quoted as saying, 'Every time I read one of his stories I'm off for the rest of the day . . . his stories are like reading Arthur Liman's briefs.'

The incident reveals much about the climate of the Fatico hearing. Only in a fundamentally hostile environment would the essential fairness of Eichenwald's reporting be lampooned as no more than propaganda from someone in the pocket of the defence. By contrast the prosecutorial zeal that coloured *Wall Street Journal* reporters James Stewart and Laurie P. Cohen and the creatively foregone conclusions Bruck herself was so partial to escaped any and all criticism whatsoever. By extension the Fatico hearing itself was less of a hearing and more of a foregone conclusion. Literally by his own 'admission', and also by the tone of the press, Milken's guilt had already been established; this was not the purpose of the ritual which could only – no matter what the evidence – underline Milken's guilt.

For as Judge Wood observed in her sentencing, 'As has been the case with several other of the government's allegations during this hearing, the record contains little direct evidence linking Milken to wrongdoing.' Under normal, neutral circumstances this absence of direct evidence linking Milken to wrongdoing should have counted for a great deal. But it didn't. In fact it counted for the complete opposite. Instead of exonerating him it incriminated him and was where a famine became a feast.

'To the extent that your crimes benefited your clients, that is, of course, no excuse for violating the law. In addition there is no escaping that your crimes also benefited you, not necessarily by lining your pockets directly and immediately, but by increasing your clients' loyalty to you, hence, increasing your edge over competitors and increasing the likelihood that your clients would pay for your services in the future.

'It has also been argued that your violations were technical ones to be distinguished from accumulating profits through insider trading and that your conduct is not really criminal and that it is barely criminal.

'It was suggested that if you were truly disposed to criminal conduct, you could have made much more money by committing more blatant crimes such as repeatedly misusing insider information.

'These arguments fail to take into account the fact that you may have committed only subtle crimes, not because you were not disposed to any criminal behaviour but because you were willing to commit only crimes that were unlikely to be detected.

'We see often in this court individuals who would be unwilling to rob a bank, but who readily cash social security checks that are not theirs when checks come to them in the mail because they are not likely to be caught doing so. Your crimes show a pattern of skirting the law, stepping just over to the wrong side of the law in an apparent effort to get some of the benefits from violating the law without running a substantial risk of being caught.

'Michael Milken's pattern of wrongdoing, as shown in the crimes to which he pled guilty, is to step just over the lines into unlawful conduct, and to do so in a way that preserves his deniability; and minimizes the risk of detections . . . the court will not conclude that because Michael Milken chose to be subtle rather than blatant, no wrongdoing occurred.' On the contrary it was her conclusion that there was a great deal of misconduct, of which these bits and pieces were but fragments of a grand architecture.

This fit Giuliani's portrayal of Milken as 'the fellow sitting at the top', the evil mastermind. 'In a more traditional criminal operation,' he told *Barrons*, 'the people doing the money in the suitcases are basically middle-level guys. The people at the top stay miles away from that and get the benefits of it in other ways. Like having it pumped into legitimate businesses, or having it laundered, or having it affect your seemingly legitimate compensation. They enjoy some insulation against getting caught, rather than taking a million dollars in an envelope.' In other words, the less like a criminal you were and the less you behaved like one, the bigger a criminal you were likely to be, and the more your business aped legitimate business, the more of a criminal enterprise it was likely to be. Such thinking, so convenient for snaring the mafia, could easily tip over into paranoid delusion when inappropriately applied to legitimate business.

In the eruption of media babble that followed Milken's sentence, attention was focussed on the wisdom of Milken's legal strategy. As Liz Smith delighted in the *New York Post*, 'Consider this! The distinguished law firm of Paul Weiss Rifkind Wharton and Garrison with the Iran-Contra legal star Arthur Liman heading the defense is said to have earned anywhere from $60 to $100 million in fees... for this defense Milken received ten years in jail, a $600 million fine and [5,400] hours of community service when he gets out of jail someday. Maybe Milken would have done better with Legal Aid.' There were many who agreed with Smith, and felt that the key to Milken's problem had been a failure to co-operate at an early stage.

By all accounts Milken's lawyer Arthur Liman took the defeat personally, since this was a defeat over the very thing that had led him into the legal profession in the first place. Renowned for his absent-mindedness, popular apocryphal stories detailed him wearing mismatched socks and eating off someone else's plate at a restaurant. But beneath the intellectual distractedness, Liman was motivated by a profound passion that had been ignited when he had witnessed as a student at Harvard the red-hunting antics of McCarthy and his supersleaze lawyer Roy Cohn. Liman wrote his graduate thesis on the constitutional limits of congressional investigations, and, noting that the few who dared to stand up to McCarthy in those days were lawyers, went on to law school at Yale.

Although Liman did not absent himself from blame, he felt that his stunning defeat in the Milken case had more to do with larger socialized forces rather than legal specifics or tactics. 'I am convinced, and have always been convinced, that society needs a certain number of demons... and if somebody becomes a demon it is very hard for the process to operate the way it should on paper,' he told journalist Jennet Conant. 'The case took on some of the characteristics of a heresy trial.'

In the Middle Ages dunking suspected witches was considered to be an effective way of wringing confessions from them. Either they drowned – proving that they were a witch all along – or they begged for mercy and confessed that they were a witch. Whereupon they were drowned. This is a useful model for understanding Milken's fate. Having finally been bludgeoned into pleading guilty, Milken was then handed down an unprecedented ten-year sentence.

16

THE BATTLE FOR THE VERDICT
OF HISTORY

THE last thing Milken had expected was a ten-year sentence. But whatever the length of it, perhaps more than anything else Milken hoped that the sentence would at least be the end of it. Had he not finally done what they had always wanted, branded himself a felon and copped a plea that he detested? Now that he had confessed, recanted, and even cried real tears of remorse in public, surely he would be spared. Discarded as a symbol, he thought he would now be allowed to pick up the pieces of his private self and shuffle off into anonymity. At least that was the hope he expressed in a rambling and moving eleven-page letter that he wrote to Judge Wood on the eve of his sentencing. It was as pathetic and plaintive a plea as the misspelled note Michael Jackson once threw from his Tokyo hotel window. Besieged by fans below he begged them and the media to leave him alone. Needless to say this cry for help had exactly the opposite effect. And just as Jacko's note was splashed all over *People* magazine as proof that he was whacko, so Milken's letter earned him nothing but derision: 'Junk Bond King Begs for Mercy' was the headline in the *Daily News*.

Given the vestigial nature of the judicial process in our modern media-dominated culture, Milken's sentencing was less of an end and more of a beginning. It was not a sentence but a coronation, marking Milken's complete transformation from private Joe to public symbol, from mere man into werewolf. This was the mock crowning of the King of Junk, anointing him as the living, breathing symbol of the greed decade. For despite Woods' careful yet hollow words to the contrary, reporters outside on the courthouse steps did not hesitate to read the numerological significance of a ten-year sentence as a verdict on a decade of greed (one year for each year of the roaring eighties). And they were not shy in surmising that this was the end of an era.

And so with the legal chapter all but closed, the history of the greed decade was ripe to be written and the battle for the verdict of history could begin. Within a year of Milken's sentence Simon & Schuster, who had done so well with *The Predator's Ball*, published *Den of Thieves*, by *Wall Street Journal* reporter James Stewart. It would prove to be even more successful, climbing to the top of the bestseller lists within three weeks of its publication.

The book did not shrink from its title. 'Once upon a time,' the cover read promisingly, 'four men nearly destroyed Wall Street. Now a Pulitzer Prize-winning reporter tells their story, how they made billions and how they got caught.' The four men were, of course, Siegel ('the good guy who couldn't quite make it on $1 million a year'), Dennis Levine ('a man of limited talent and unlimited ambition'), Ivan Boesky ('the arbitrage master who arrived at parties in helicopters'), and Michael Milken ('the financial genius who turned junk bonds into gold'). In Stewart's argument this 'Milken-led conspiracy' was one that dwarfed all others, making Milken's crimes 'far more complex, imaginative and ambitious than mere insider-trading'. (As it turns out the book does not deliver on its promise that the conspiracy nearly wrecked Wall Street, with the exception of the bald assertion that 'more than any other single person, Milken had been behind the massive reevaluation of stocks that had carried the Dow Jones average above 2700'.)

Stewart's special task is to argue that Milken compounded his sinisterness by trying to pervert the course of justice and prevent the revelation of the truth: 'If money could buy justice in America, Milken and Drexel were prepared to spend it, and spend it they did. They hired the most expensive, sophisticated, and powerful lawyers and public-relations advisors, and they succeeded to a frightening degree at turning the public debate into a trial of government lawyers and prosecutors rather than of those accused of crimes.'

However, 'they failed, thanks to the sometimes heroic efforts of underpaid, overworked government lawyers who devoted much of their times to uncovering the scandal.' In support of this there are touching scenes of Frank Cannon-sized prosecutors drooling over hamburgers in the Beverly Hills Hotel, hamburgers that they could not afford on their meagre government allowances.

Thus in Stewart's moral universe there is on the one hand the evil Darth Vader of finance threatening the planet, and on the other the honest Harrison Fords fighting the good fight. It is their destiny to win because they can feel The Force. As Stewart explains, 'Morale in the U.S. attorney's and SEC offices is usually buoyed by two convictions: that the government's cause is just, and that the government will win.' And win they do. Good triumphs and evil is vanquished.

Stewart's Hollywood sense of morality is as strictly defined as it is mercilessly applied. Directly after learning of his sentence

'The blood drained from Milken's face. He took Lori's arm and the two disappeared into a small witness's waiting room off the corridor, closing the door behind them.

'Moments later, first Lori, and then Milken, emitted bloodcurdling screams. Sandler burst into the room as Milken collapsed into a chair, hyperventilating, struggling for breath. "Oxygen!" someone yelled, as a federal marshal raced for help.'

That's it. The End. Stewart adds no comment because the meaning is perfectly clear. Finally confronted, bound and tied by the forces of good, the forces of evil bare themselves in a horrid display of weeping and wailing and gnashing of teeth. And if Stewart expresses no pity as Milken all but melts, like the wicked witch of the East, it is simply because in his book none is deserved. As he explains in his acknowledgements, he learnt 'the moral lessons of this book' from his parents 'long before I knew anything about the riches and power of Wall Street.'

After graduating from Harvard Law School (where Stewart interviewed Dershowitz for the school paper), the young Indiana Jones joined the distinguished firm of Cravath, Swaine and Moore. After a not altogether happy three-year stint he left to join the start-up magazine *American Lawyer*, eventually becoming executive editor before moving on to the *Journal* as a reporter in 1983. One of his early front-page articles at the paper was about law professors who cheated on their students by moonlighting. The piece began with an example of a professor who avoided preparing for a class by playing a tape recording. The professor was Alan Dershowitz, who was stung into writing a letter of complaint.

Although Stewart had foresworn the law as a career, he dedicated his writing muse to it. *The Partners* was his first book, subtitled 'Inside America's Most Powerful Law Firms'. *The Prosecutors: Inside the Offices of the Government's Most Powerful Lawyers* was his second. It began, 'In popular American literature, it is always the criminal defense lawyer who is the hero. Who even remembers the name of the prosecutor in the Perry Mason television series? As I hope the tales in this book make clear, it is the prosecutor who wields the greatest power, undergoes the greater stress, is faced with the more intractable dilemmas, and, in the end is the keeper of the flame of both justice and order.' It was an unusual angle – traditionally the press regarded the government and its prosecutors with some skepticism. Although he portrayed them warts and all, and was particularly unflattering of Giuliani, Stewart's book was a giant step in kindling affection for this unloved species. And Alan Dershowitz gave the book an unfavourable review in the *American Bar Association Journal*.

At the *Journal*, Stewart is generally credited with the timely revitalisation of the paper's style. As business went pop in the eighties, turgid financial reporting needed to reinvent itself as something altogether more sexy. As *The New York Observer* reported in a fulsome piece headlined 'Daniel in the Lion's Den', 'Mr. Stewart has established a reputation as a journalist who...has transformed business writing into a narrative form that often wields the dramatic power of decent, if not good, fiction.' So vivid and dramatic were his pieces on the stock market crash and the wreck of Marty Siegel's career, that in 1988 he won a Pulitzer Prize, which proved to be a stepping stone to his becoming, in October of that year, the *Journal's* Page One editor. Under his stewardship Stewart also re-energised the paper's trademark whacky fourth column pieces, with pieces among other things on gangs of transvestite burglars in Florida.

The piece in *The Observer* continued, 'Mr. Stewart who advises journalism students to approach writing as if they were telling a story at a dinner party regarded the intrigues as manna: "So many things were more fascinating than fiction...you couldn't dream up characters like this".' And of course manna was what they would prove to be. In 1986, not long after Boesky Day, Stewart signed up – for an undisclosed sum – to write the book of the scandal that was yet to happen. And throughout Stewart's reporting there was a strong suggestion that Stewart felt that he had found in Milken one of those characters who are stranger than fiction. There are those who say that Stewart's portrait of the financier was fictional to the point of being willfully blind to the facts. 'My own concern is with the facts. I have no ideological axe to grind,' Stewart has said in his defence, but is this really the case? Both thanks to his reporting and then under his direction the front page of the *Journal* offered a continual sneak preview of the latest developments of the government's investigation. There were also at least two eyebrow-raising pieces about Milken; one was an apparently flip look at Milken's PR campaign that was a total character assassination, and the other – published on the eve of his sentencing – was an indictment of Milken's theories about the value of junk bonds. It was known that Milken always defended the soundness of his economic principles and this can only have been designed to pull that rug out from under his feet. In contrast to this there was no Page One coverage of the Fatico hearing, which Stewart rather extraordinarily deemed irrelevant.

In April of 1992, Stewart delivered an 800-page manuscript to his publishers, and almost from the beginning the story surrounding the book's publication was as exciting as its rumoured contents. On October 2nd *The Wall Street Journal* – which does not usually excerpt books – published a long adapted extract from the forthcoming book. 'What follows,' wrote Stewart under the headline SCENES FROM A SCANDAL, 'are major, newly revealed episodes from history's biggest insider trading scandal.' Leading the line-up was an account of Milken ordering Boesky to buy Diamond Shamrock at the same time as shorting Occidental Petroleum in what Stewart calls 'a brazen example of Mr. Milken's and Mr.

Boesky's joint insider trading'. Stewart's assertion, which he said was based on numerous interviews, eyewitnesses and sworn testimony, was compelling because none of the six crimes that Milken pleaded guilty to included insider trading. Furthermore, in the Fatico hearing the government had tried to prove – and failed – that Milken had engaged in insider trading. What made this so significant was that the government did not even have to prove that Milken had committed the crimes beyond 'reasonable doubt' as they would have had to in a regular trial by jury. All they had to show to win their point was 'a preponderance of evidence'. But once again, strangely, the Fatico cut no ice with Stewart.

The rest of the extract consisted of the juiciest details from his book: how one of Milken's traders, James Dahl, explained that he was leaving the office early one day to visit his mother, who had just been diagnosed with cancer and Milken's only response was 'When are you going to be back?'; how Milken once collapsed at his desk and Lowell merely looked at the unconscious body before returning to his office. 'The message was clear: Keep working'; how Gary Winnick, another of Milken's traders, remembered being asked by his boss, 'What do you think it'd cost to buy every building from here to the ocean?' He was, Stewart argued, 'Obsessed...with enhancing his wealth and power'.

The excerpt excited the usual flurry of letters to the *Journal* from friends and colleagues of Milken. Such letters had come to be expected whenever Milken was written about in the news. They were dutifully printed by the *Journal*; no one payed them much attention. Coming from inside the Milken camp they were easy to brush aside as lacking credibility when compared, say, with the objectivity of someone of Stewart's journalistic reputation. If anything, the letters gave credence to his withering attack. After all, they would say that, wouldn't they?

The matter might have ended there were it not for Alan Dershowitz, Stewart's old adversary. Dershowitz was hired one afternoon after Lori Milken had gone to see the film *Reversal of Fortune*. The film, a box office success produced by Dershowitz's son, tells the true story of how Alan Dershowitz (played by Ron Silver) led the appeal that overturned the verdict that Claus Von Bulow (played by Jeremy Irons) was guilty of attempting to murder his wife. In the movie Dershowitz and Bulow first meet over lunch at Delmonicos; 'You do have one thing in your favour,' an unfased Dershowitz tells the aristocratic Bulow. "Everybody hates you." The words must have sounded like music to Lori Milken, who cannot have been unaware that her husband was one of the most unpopular men in the country. Emerging from the darkness of the movie theatre into the California sunshine, she knew one thing; if anyone could reverse her husband's misfortune it would be Alan Dershowitz.

'I made it very clear to her that I'm not a miracle worker,' says

Dershowitz. 'I'm a hard worker and I try to leave no stones unturned, but it's very hard to reverse one's fortunes when there's already been a plea of guilty. I was a little reluctant to get involved, initially.'

Although he would later change his tune, Dershowitz was not predisposed to view Milken in a favourable light. He once told the *Washington Post* that he felt that Milken and Boesky had eroded public confidence in the nation's stock and bond markets, and in his syndicated column he wrote, 'I smell a rat in the Milken plea bargain,' arguing that 'Milken's entire career was premised on keeping the public in the dark about what was really going on in the junk bond market.' Milken, he felt, had finagled for himself 'a pretty good deal' and he was clearly not at all sure if it was deserved.

Asked by Jeannie Kasindorf in *New York* magazine to account for this reversal of opinion, Dershowitz responded:

'From what I read in the newspapers, I virtually expected to see a devil with horns and a tail, and here was this really sweet guy.... It was hard for me to understand that this was the guy I had formed a prejudgment about. I felt like a heel – that I had said something about somebody on the basis of what I had read in the newspaper. I think of myself as a fairly sophisticated reader of newspapers, and yet I fell for it. I really bought the party line on Milken.'

'A lot of people would say you've now bought the party line.'

'Well they're just wrong. I have now gotten to know Michael and Lori very very well. These are people I could really be friendly with. These are not, to me, Claus Von Bulow. These are really nice people.... The one thing Michael said to me at some point, I took it as high praise, he said, "Alan, the reason I like you as a lawyer is that I think you are to the legal system what I was to the investment-banking profession."'

What Milken meant of course was that they were both outsiders, contrarians who went against the grain and who weren't afraid to stand alone. At the mere age of twenty-eight Dershowitz became Harvard's youngest law professor, and although this put him on the inside of the establishment, he remained very much an outsider, if for no other reason than his choice of clients. Dershowitz says he could always assimilate himself completely and that he has had no lack of invitations. In spite of this he continues to pour scorn on the WASPy Old Boy Network, people who in his eyes prefer to use two books instead of the library law books: the address book and the cheque book (ironically one of these people is Dershowitz's sworn enemy, Michael Armstrong, who represented Milken's brother Lowell).

Dershowitz delights in taking on the legal equivalent of junk clients, bad-smell cases no one else wants to be bothered with. 'The more unpopular the client, the more likely it is I'm gonna want to take the case,' he once explained. (Sometimes he worries about the limits of such an approach. In his book *Chutzpah* he writes of a recurring nightmare in which Nazi war criminal Joseph Mengele calls him from South America demanding representation. When Dershowitz hesitates, Mengele taunts, 'I thought you were supposed to be this big-shot civil libertarian! Will you take my case, or are you the world's biggest phony?' In the dream Dershowitz reluctantly agrees to a meeting and cannot decide whether he will represent him or kill him with his bare hands.)

In addition to Claus Von Bulow, some of the more stellar clients Dershowitz has represented over the years include Hotel 'Queen of Mean' Leona Helmsley, fallen televangelist Jim Bakker, and car-of-the-future whiz John DeLorean – in other words, celebrities who are seen to be as guilty as they are wealthy. This roster has earned him opprobrium as a publicity maniac who is primarily interested in aggrandizing his own celebrity status through his high-profile clients. Others argued that he defends the undefendable not for the sake of Justice or Truth, but for his fee.

However, Dershowitz's choice of clients is not mere posturing but his very inspiration. 'Most of my cases involve poor, obscure people who nobody's ever heard of. Half of my cases are for free,' he says. 'But I also believe that if the government, the media can get away with victimizing the powerful how much easier it's going to be to victimize the powerless. So I don't apologize for representing some powerful and wealthy people...sometimes it takes wealth and power to expose the abuses and excesses of the government and media. Only if we're not worried about the budget, can we afford to fight back and leave no stone unturned.'

Contrary to the cynical assumption that people who can afford the best justice that money can buy are thus capable of buying the judicial result that they want, Dershowitz argues that these cases are crucial to showcasing cracks in the legal system. No matter how unpopular they may be, he points out that they are still entitled to justice: 'Instead of reducing the level of justice for the rich – we should increase the level of justice for the poor.... It's very important to use these kinds of cases to bring home to the American public a scepticism about our system of justice. Obviously there's more of an opportunity to make an impact with a public-interest case.'

To be sure, Dershowitz believes in the power of publicity and it is his views on this that most define his outsider status: 'Being a public lawyer today is an essential part of being a lawyer in America. Most of the cases I come into have already been publicised by the prosecution. Claus Von Bulow, Leona Helmsley and Jim Bakker were all tried in the press, and you have to fight back, you have to fight fire with fire.

'When I came into the Milken case, the playing field was so unlevel.

The prosecution had made its points unanswered. A book, by Connie Bruck, had already been published. The Stewart book was imminent. *The Wall Street Journal* had devoted its front pages to a mercilessly one-sided and false account of Michael Milken. And there had been no responses.

'Now I never go to the media first, but if the other side has so skewed the public perception that every juror, every judge, every fact finder, every journalist already knows the outcome, then it seems to me you're playing with one and a half hands tied behind your back. I would prefer to see the American legal system less focussed on a circus atmosphere, I would prefer to see prosecutors not hold press conferences in which they try defendants in the media, but that's not the country in which I live. It's very hard to litigate a case in the context of a one-sided media presentation. And I see, as part of the job of a lawyer, not only to defend his client in the courtroom, but also in the court of public opinion.'

His book *Reversal of Fortune* is a case in point. He says he only wrote it after Claus Von Bulow pleaded with him to do so after the publication of another overwhelmingly negative account (in an aside Dershowitz has expressed a desire to write what could be *Reversal of Fortune 2* – the Milken story). 'My clients don't only want to be legally acquitted – they want to be vindicated in the public mind.'

Needless to say, not only did the old-boy network disdain such limelight antics, but they also went against the grain of Milken's own defence team. Arthur Liman always maintained that the place for comment was in the courtroom and not in the press. But Dershowitz did not believe that the way to win the battle was to keep above the fray. As Milken's personal lawyer, Richard Sandler, told *The Wall Street Journal* in measured but hilarious tones of understatement, 'You don't ask Alan Dershowitz to join your team if you don't want to at least be more aggressive in certain areas.'

Just what those areas were became clear to the *Journal* when two weeks after they published 'Scenes From a Scandal,' a blistering Op Ed by Dershowitz appeared in the paper. What made it unusual was that it was accompanied by a reply by Stewart, which was then rebutted by Dershowitz and once more surrebutted by Stewart. But that's not all: 'When I asked for space to respond to Mr Stewart's final salvo,' wrote Dershowitz, 'I was told that the *Journal* insisted that Mr Stewart have the "last word." Fair enough. After all, freedom of the press belongs primarily to those who own a press.' Dershowitz then offered to buy the space to run his surrebuttal as a paid advertisement, but the paper 'refused to run an ad critical of its Page One editor', Dershowitz says. Michael Thomas claims that an editorial official at the paper told him the reason was because "We don't run false advertising."

Determined to be heard, the resourceful Dershowitz went to *The New York Times* and took out a half-page advertisement. It was headlined 'Here

Is the Paid Ad *The Wall Street Journal* Refused to Run' and which began: 'For several years, people have been talking about *The Wall Street Journal* and its dramatic shift in its Page One policy. Badly-researched, mean-spirited, sensationalistic hatchet-jobs are routinely published and have replaced classic workmanlike responsible reporting in the Dow Jones tradition. Victims of this new front page policy have been asking for some time when someone would say "enough is enough". The *Journal's* vendetta against one of my clients has prompted me to step up and say that, indeed, enough is enough.'

In his surrebuttal, as in his preceeding two pieces, Dershowitz continued to take issue with Stewart about his claim that the Diamond Shamrock/Occidental petroleum transaction was a clear-cut case of insider trading. The substance of Stewart's claim was that Milken, on the West Coast, had phoned Boesky on the East Coast and given him inside information about Diamond Shamrock, information that Boesky had then acted on. 'Mr Stewart's account contains a core of reality around which is woven a massive fantasy,' wrote Dershowitz. The core of reality was that Milken had in fact spoken with Boesky about the deal, but only given Boesky lawful advice and no inside information, which, Dershowitz argued, Milken simply did not have in order to impart. When Milken spoke to Boesky, it was only after a public announcement about the merger and only then that trading in the shares opened.

At the centre of the controversy was former Milken trader turned immunised government witness James Dahl, who was supposed to have overheard the illegal conversation. According to Dershowitz in his initial Op Ed piece, 'Dahl testified that he overheard Mr Milken advising Mr Boesky to sell Diamond after a public announcement...not that he had overheard Mr Milken tip Mr Boesky to purchase Diamond shares before the announcement of the proposed merger.' Then Dershowitz contacted Dahl's lawyer, who confirmed that Dahl had never told Stewart about such a phone call. To which Stewart responded, 'Mr Dahl's lawyer wasn't a witness to the conversations I described...others, including Mr Dahl, were, as the passage makes clear. Given the witch hunt under way within the Milken camp to identify and intimidate my sources, it isn't surprising that one of Mr Dahl's lawyers would have sought to deflect Mr Dershowitz or his colleagues.' Undeterred, Dershowitz shot back, 'Well, neither was Mr Stewart a witness. Dahl's lawyer was, however, speaking for Dahl.' And so on.

Dershowitz also took issue with Stewart's portrayal of Milken as being 'obsessed...with enhancing his wealth and power.' When Milken asked a colleague 'What do you think it'd cost to buy every building from here to the ocean?' Milken was, he said, making a favorite point about world finance:

'That story is a twisted retelling of a version of a standard speech that Mr

Milken liked to deliver concerning often-expressed fears in the 1970s that oil sheiks would soon own the entire country. The transcript of his speech shows that he said that after calculating the assets available to the sheiks "we discovered these Middle Eastern countried did not have enough money to buy all of Fifth Avenue, Michigan Avenue and Wilshire Boulevard. Therefore it was unlikely that they were going to be able to buy the whole country".'

Stewart's lame response to this was the remark wasn't part of a speech, but a spontaneous remark made to a colleague. However, those who know Milken know that he has a repertoire of stock ideas that he never tires of repeating, whether in speech or conversation, making it extremely unlikely that he would take a favourite illustration and twist its meaning. Most of Milken's conversations are like speeches anyway.

Dershowitz also took up Dahl's claim that Milken resented him leaving the office early the day his mother was diagnosed with cancer:
'Allegations of Mr Milken's insensitivity...run contrary to what just about anyone who knew Mr Milken would have told Mr Stewart had he asked. Mr Milken was obsessed with cancer's ravages, having lost a father, a stepfather, a mother in law and several aunts to the disease.

'In a typical situation, when a Drexel security guard developed acute myelogenous leukemia...Mr Milken told the employee to "just get well and I'll take care of any financial responsibilities". When the man was released from the hospital and visited Drexel "Mike saw [him and] he ran to him [and] hugged him and wept over him" according to the letter.'

Dershowitz then raised the question of why Stewart had brushed aside some 400 more glowing testimonials to Milken and why he also chose to ignore the fact that Milken had given $60 million to a cancer research institution. Stewart responded that he reviewed all the letters, reached his own conclusions, and that 'the much-touted charitable contributions' reveal 'surprisingly little generosity for a man of his extraordinary wealth' (in a television appearance Stewart went so far as to say, 'I'll gladly hold up my charitable contribution to the percentage of my income against his' – although so far he has not done so). He threw in the old – and discredited – chestnut that 'the sharp increase' that Dershowitz cited as marching in step with his income 'clearly coincides with the public relations campaign to portray Mr Milken as a "national treasure".' He also argued that their 'primary motivation' could have been tax considerations, which Dershowitz challenged by claiming that tax benefits decreased year after year during the period. He also pointed out that Milken gave generously with his personal time as well – 'Time is not tax deductible!'. And so on.

To some extent this crossfire was a comparative sideshow to the core dispute over the book – Stewart's sources. The most surprising aspect of *Den of Thieves* was that he decided to base much of it on Boesky's version of events as opposed to Milken's. 'He is an admitted felon, he has no credibility,' Stewart said of Milken, but the same could be said of Boesky. Stewart decides between the two by reasoning that 'after making his plea agreement, Boesky's only obligation was to tell the truth; indeed, his plea agreement could be revoked if he lied. . . . In contrast Milken didn't testify under oath, even at his sentencing hearing, and during the investigation he repeatedly invoked the Fifth Amendment.' Furthermore, according to Stewart, although Milken could be prosecuted for perjury if he gave false testimony, his plea agreement could not, unlike Boesky's, be revoked.

But the only problem with Boesky is that even the government despaired of his ever telling the truth. The one time he did testify in court he was such a disaster (and ultimately the conviction that Boesky's testimony was engineered to secure was thrown out) that the government realized that they could never get him to testify at Milken's Fatico hearing even though he was their star witness. Not that the government was interested in revoking Boesky's plea agreement anyway. Once the agreement had been made public, revoking it would have been a massive loss of face that might have jeopardised the entire securities fraud investigative jamboree. And as it happened, Boesky did admit that he had both lied and committed additional – albeit trivial – crimes after his plea agreement. But the government did not move to revoke his plea agreement. Perhaps they thought he was lying.

In his series of rebuttals Dershowitz attacked Stewart's accreditation of Boesky: 'Mr Stewart misunderstands the incentives facing Mr Boesky and the other witnesses. He fails to recognize the ready availability of people who were willing not just to sing, but to compose in order to win leniency for their own offenses. . . virtually every witness against Mr Milken had too much to lose by telling the truth and too much to gain by "cooperating".'

Nevertheless, Stewart props up Boesky, arguing that the one time he was on the witness stand nothing new was learned from his cross-examination, on the basis that it was already public knowledge that he was a complete liar, and that nothing was done to further damage Boesky's 'already shakey credibility'. But little could be done to damage it further, although the less than little credibility Boesky did have was utterly levelled. But this is not the point. For years now the public has been told, and taken it on good faith, that Boesky had been an exemplary witness and that his co-operation was unprecedented. But now, in this embarrassing spectacle, the public could see for themselves Boesky's true colors for the first time. Fortunately for the government, Boesky's bargain deal was sufficiently distant in the public memory so that this courtroom shambles did not incense the public that a deal had been made at all.

Boesky is the key to Stewart's thesis of a Milken-led conspiracy and, to make it look like Boesky was Milken's puppet, Stewart relates how the former off-Broadway actor 'recounted his dealings with an almost palpable sense of trepidation'. Boesky was afraid that Milken, 'who had close ties in the casino industry', might have him rubbed out. Over and over Boesky told the government lawyers that if 'Milken had told him to do something, he did it, because Milken could make him rich or destroy him'. Boesky's ability to put on a show should not be underestimated, but if his performance was perhaps inspired by sincere concerns they are much more likely to be a reflection of his own personality rather than an accurate assessment of Milken's. It was Boesky, after all, who claimed to have had a part in the CIA, and who employed the *noir* types who so terrified Siegel to make movie-style cash drops (in an interesting detail Stewart tells us that the cash was bundled in Caesars casino ribbons). If anyone was capable of rubbing someone out, it was Boesky, so it should come as no surprise that he would expect the same from others around him. The idea that Milken, in spite of his casino chums (and Boesky clearly had a few of his own), would attempt an assassination is an idea that should rather be ridiculed than entertained.

In the end Stewart's idea of a Milken-led conspiracy is belied by the fact that Judge Wood found that the financial value of Milken's crimes totalled just $318,000. This should be compared with the more than one hundred million dollar price tag put on Boesky's insider trading career. Had Milken seriously led Boesky in an insider trading conspiracy the profits would have been in the billions. And if Boesky was a money-making puppet for Milken, Boesky would not have needed Levine at Drexel grubbing around selling him inside information as well.

In short, Stewart's choice of Boesky over Milken seems illogical and needs more explanation. Former colleagues at *The Wall Street Journal* are of the opinion that Boesky had been an unnamed source for Stewart before the investigation even started and that the longevity of this relationship overrode other considerations. 'He first came to my attention in 1986 as the *Journal*'s mergers-and-acquisitions reporter.... Stewart drove the *Journal*'s competitor's crazy because he always seemed to get the big M&A stories before they did...how did he do it? Was his "Deep Throat" Ivan Boesky? Boesky was even then manipulating the *Journal* and the rest of the financial press for his profit,' wrote Jude Wanniski in *The National Review*. Dean Rotbart, another former colleague at the *Journal*, claims that Boesky was a very important source both to the *Journal*, and particularly to Stewart: 'We used to sit in cubicles so I sat six feet from where Jim Stewart sat, and people like Marty Siegel and people like Ivan Boesky would constantly be on the phone to him.' Rotbart says he knows this because often when Boesky called he would try and get on the phone as well. (Stewart denies that Rotbart and he ever sat that close, and that it was not possible for him to have been overheard.) Wanniski's thesis was that after Boesky Day, 'Stewart, stunned that his pal Boesky turned out to be a crook, was only too ready to believe Milken was the evil genius who led Boesky astray.'

What's the big deal? In *Thieves* Stewart relates an instance of how Levine and his partner in crime, using the guise of anonymous sources, tipped off the press with the express purpose of manipulating the market to their own ends. To be sure, this was not an isolated incident, and was something former *Wall Street Journal* writers are convinced Boesky and Siegel practised on their own paper. The point here is not whether Stewart was the unwitting mouthpiece for insider traders but whether or not his possible sources have similarly been able to manipulate the so-called 'verdict of history' to their own ends through the strength of their relationships. Siegel, a blatant insider trader, emerges as a hero. As Dershowitz wrote in his initial broadside against *Thieves*, 'It is much easier to be a source for an investigative reporter who is sometimes inclined to accept self-serving versions and even outright fantasies, than to be a government witness who has to be prepared to testify and subject himself to confrontation by documents and cross-examination by his intended victims.' It is also more than likely that a source is likely to be treated more sympathetically than someone who refuses to speak to a writer on or off the record. This source pay-off is simply a fact of life.

We can only speculate whether or not Boesky and Siegel were sources, since Stewart is not about to reveal who was. However, one thing we do know is that Michael Milken was not a source, and that compared with Boesky and Siegel's treatment, Milken got it in the neck. While denying any such source payoff, Stewart told me, 'I have discovered over many years of reporting that people who do co-operate have less to hide, and as a result may legitimately be treated somewhat more favorably than those who continue to stonewall and conceal.' Of Milken's own silence he said, 'The fact that Milken has remained a cipher at the centre of all this is very much by Milken's design. Based on my reporting I can only conclude that this is because if everything were known about Milken and his empire, the portrait that would emerge would be even less flattering than the one that has emerged as a product of his isolation.'

Contrary to Stewart's claim that he had met Milken, Milken denied either meeting or talking to him. It turned out that Stewart had only attended a High Yield Bond conference at which Milken was present, although in fairness to Stewart if he never met Milken it probably wasn't for lack of trying. Still Stewart likes to give a sinister spin to Milken's silence, but he would have learnt from Milken had he ever sat down with him that he found his inability to speak out utterly frustrating. He was upbraided, in his first interview since his imprisonment, by *Forbes* magazine for not being wise enough 'to know that if you don't explain what you are doing, people will mistrust you. You not only tried to keep a low profile, you tried to be invisible to the media.' To which Milken replied, 'You are absolutely right, I made a mistake. I should have opened up more. Then my legal problems began and my lawyers advised me not to do interviews.' As Milken wrote to Judge Wood prior to his sentencing, 'I accepted my lawyer's advice not to testify in the recent Fatico hearings, even though it was terribly difficult and frustrating sitting in the courtroom and not being able to speak.'

Milken also took the *Forbes* opportunity to speak out against the book and, finally, to defend himself for himself: 'The book's dust jacket says, "Once upon a time..." that's how you start a fairy tale, and the book is a fairy tale...despite what *Den* suggests, I've never traded our divulged inside information in my life.'

Another group of supposed sources have also garnered Stewart scrutiny and criticism. 'Jim Stewart is not a journalist, he's a bulletin board. All he does is put up notices that the United States Attorney, Justice Department and the SEC – the other side of litigation – give him...he was used, knowingly, by the other side. He was used to help to try to get people to plead guilty. He was used to leak information. He was used to help the other side make its case,' says Dershowitz.

This is a double accusation. On the one hand Dershowitz is satisfied that leaks were part of the strategy: 'Rudy has said over and over again – he said it in my class, he said it in a debate with me – he believes in using the press. He believes in using journalists to try to frighten witnesses to come on to his side. He believes very strongly that if the witnesses believe they're on a sinking ship, like rats they will abandon that ship.' It was all part of the way Giuliani shrink-wrapped complex securities violations as pop crimes that could be understood by all. Giuliani has always denied the crime of leaking information. But he has also sought to distance himself from Stewart. 'I get the sense Stewart would hold Mike Milken responsible for the Second World War,' he said.

Stewart, because of his committment to the confidentiality of his sources, cannot clear himself of the suspicion that he was on the receiving end of these leaks. Nevertheless, he denies that he received any leaks from the prosecutor's office. In what he frames as a hypothetical example, he points out that while prosecutors are legally precluded from revealing grand jury testimony, there are no such restrictions on grand jury witnesses who have a 'a first amendment right to disclose everything they learn in those proceedings'.

But wherever the information came from, there can be no disputing the material impact it had on the case. Stewart himself has countered the accusation that he was merely a mouthpiece of the prosecutors by arguing that 'I did a lot more work in many cases than the prosecutors did'. There are several occasions in the book when Stewart points out how far ahead of the government he and his colleagues at the *Journal* were; in other words, how their journalistic prosecution outstripped the official investigation.

For example, Stewart quotes the Page One *Journal* article 'Suspicious

Trading', which investigated the Freeman case 'in a level of detail,' he says, 'that startled the prosecutors', finding information that even the prosecutors had not uncovered, including the memorable quote 'your bunny has a good nose'. It would be on this one 'bunny count' (as the *Journal's* editorial pages ridiculed it) that Freeman would eventually plead guilty. The quip was supposedly crucial in proving inside trading. Although he only mentions it in an endnote, Stewart was co-author of the article. Is the argument, then, that he wasn't a noticeboard for the government, but – true to his legal training – a freelance prosecutor for the government? Stewart says he was not: 'I'm not a prosecutor, I'm a journalist. All good reporters are investigative reporters....I was simply doing my job.' He was, he said, interested but ultimately indifferent to the legal consequences of his findings. Be that as it may, his work was, as this example makes clear, instrumental at key points in the investigation. In another example, cited by Stewart of another article co-written by him that took the investigators by surprise, Stewart detailed, early on in the investigation, the $5.3 million payment that was the supposedly smoking gun at the core of the Boesky/Milken investigation. But in spite of these instances, Stewart asserts, 'There is absolutely no indication at any point that media coverage influenced the judicial process as it unfolded.'

Ironically enough, some of the strongest criticism of Stewart comes from within the *Journal* itself. For the editorial pages at the heart of the paper argued a very different line to Page One. Although they shared the same floor as the front page, that was all they shared beyond a bank of elevators and a tenuous corridor bridging the two sides. They are like two halves of a brain that have been separated and have no interconnection or mutual interest. Gordon Crovitz, a senior editorial writer at the paper (and author of the 'Rule of Law' column) recently made the general observation that 'day after day we had headlines before the indictment and after the indictment, about possible offenses that Michael Milken might have committed and this went on, actually, for some years. So it built up a kind of impression in the public that he was guilty of very serious offenses....There was, I think, what we might call prosecutorial journalism where the claims made by the prosecutors were repeated day after day without a really aggressive look behind some of these transactions to see what was really going on.' Crovitz is careful to keep his remarks general, while Stewart is almost blasé and applauds the Chinese wall that separates the editorial and news staff: 'I respect how lively and well phrased and how sharply pointed they are. Even when, in some cases, they're aimed at the very reporting that I have been working on.'

Although the popular wisdom is that when you buy the *Journal* you get two papers for the price of one, this is like saying that the good thing about schizophrenia is that you have two completely different people in one body. It may be good value for money, but it's not necessarily healthy. The *Journal's* lack of connected self-awareness was demonstrated to many in the publisher's annual letter to its readers in early 1992: 'Since the media appropriately hold other elements of society up to scrutiny and skepticism, perhaps this is an appropriate time and place to do the same to the media,' began Kahn, taking a moral high road that did everything but scrutinize the paper's own approach. Kahn criticised blurring the line between news and entertainment, the failure to see that every issue has more than one side, ethical puritanism and prosecutorial journalism: 'The prosecutorial press falls back on "appearances" – the anonymous perception of impropriety. The allegation becomes self-fulfilling and the subject is pilloried for a "perception" emanating largely from the media.' At the core of the piece was a recognition of the very real power of the media. 'CBS and "60 Minutes" are more powerful than most subjects they expose. A network anchorman or editor of a major newspaper can have more influence on public affairs than most congressmen. *The Wall Street Journal* probably has more influence on national economic policies and public views of them than most corporations.' More powerful than their subjects, more powerful than corporations and politicians, journalist have become supermen whose power is to make the news rather than report it. In short, 'We can't honestly claim to be little David's out smiting Goliath's and have the public believe it.'

But Stewart certainly believed that he was up against some kind of Goliath. His book is filled with accusations made against the Milken PR machine: the argument that Giuliani was recklessly zealous in his pursuit of Milken, that RICO was unfairly used to bludgeon Milken and others into submission, that Milken's admitted crimes were mere technicalities, these were all deranged PR constructs. In addition to the usual claims that they packed their client's calendar with goody goody charity events, Stewart also suggested that Milken's media cronies began recruiting black supporters because 'any Manhattan jury would likely have a large contingent of black jurors'. Then when the furore over the book erupted, Stewart blamed virtually everything in sight as a PR construct: the charges that he was a mouthpiece for the government, the idea that the media shaped the prosecution, the accusations that the book was anti-Semitic and so on. Stewart has said that he does not 'fault Mr Milken for embracing any avenue that was available to him', and that the more people who have access to the media the better, but that does not stop him from resenting Milken and his henchmen for what he sees as the desire to stifle any and all coverage of the case pending any legal investigation.

The sinisterness of these un-American activities and their attempt to twist the verdict of history in their favor is deservedly matched by the utter failure of their efforts: 'Don't you think the verdict of history was written when Milken pleaded guilty?' Stewart asks rhetorically. But just as *Journal* publisher Kahn made no link between his taking the moral high ground and the paper's own reporting, so Stewart sees no connection between Milken's plea and his role (both as reporter and editor) in the years that led up to – and may have contributed to – that plea. Others do not see the same degree of separation as Stewart. 'Milken might not be sitting in jail today if the true story of the media's involvement in his prosecution and ultimately his confession were known to the public,' says Dean Rotbart. As a *New Yorker* cartoon put it, 'Since the defendant has already been found guilty in the court of public opinion', argues a judge convening a case in court, 'let's dispense with the trial.'

Defending his book, Stewart said, 'This is the court of public opinion. This isn't some legal proceeding.' Stewart clearly prefers 'The Chase', as he calls the second half of his book. As a one-man judge and jury whose reporting pre-empted the need for a trial, Stewart is unlikely to have much use for the Fatico hearing, a vestigial mini-trial that followed Milken's white flag plea. Indeed Stewart believed it was 'a footnote to history', and so, logically enough, 'it ended up as a footnote to the book', banished from the body of the book to the endnotes, a desert of small print and detailia unvisited by the general reader, and traversed only by pedants. As Glen Kessler wrote in *New York Newsday*, 'Stewart, a lawyer turned journalist, acts as his own prosecutor, charging people with serious crimes for which they've never been tried....Stewart also acts as judge and jury. He decides who's telling the truth and who's committing perjury, burying any denials in twenty-two pages of footnotes.' But the Fatico hearing was genuinely important in that it was the first time that Milken's lawyers got to cross-examine the government's witnesses and Milken's accusers (though not, of course, his main accuser, Boesky). It was also important because the government's charges did not stand up.

Informed speculation about Stewart's links with Boesky and the government, the inside nature of much of his information and the prosecutorial style of his journalism add up to a peculiar combination of connection and circumstance that transformed Stewart from being merely a reporter into one of the main players in the drama. If ever a movie is made of this saga – as one surely should be – Stewart's character will have a starring role.

But if there are any movies going to be made, Dershowitz is not going to be shy about taking a starring role too. The day after the battle of rebuttals in *The Wall Street Journal*, Dershowitz declared war on another target, *The New York Times Book Review*, which had published a glowing review of Stewart's book that began, 'This is an absolutely splendid book and a tremendously important book, as good a book on Wall Street as I have ever read...it at long last gives a full and true record of systemic criminal behaviour in the financial markets.' The review, written by Michael Thomas, continued in the same vein without a single criticism.

Thomas had quit Wall Street for a writing career. He liked the old Wall Street, and viewed the new crowd with their workaholism, workouts and

Evian with disdain. He lived year round out in the Hamptons where he observed with acid bark the comings and goings of the rich and famous. In his columns in *Manhattan Inc* and *The New York Observer*, he vented his spleen on the excesses of the decade. Those in his cartoon menagerie of fools included Donald Trump "The Prince of Swine", Henry Kravis "The L'il King", Alan Dershowitz "The Don King of Law", and Ralph Lauren "The Wee Haberdasher".

And Michael Milken. Although Thomas did not have a favorite soubriquet for Milken, he had, variously, called him 'scum', 'a pig' and 'a beetle' (that needed squashing). 'Whatever Judge Wood gives Mr Milken won't be enough,' he wrote, and he hoped that life inside – and an introduction to buggery – would help him remember all the other crimes he had committed: 'The prospect of having one's sphincter enlarged to the circumference of the Holland Tunnel by the rigors of the prison social calendar often works wonders when it comes to refreshing memories.' Why did Thomas hate Milken so much? 'He looks like someone you'd like to hate,' he once told me. 'You don't have to know what a junk bond is to become infuriated by one.' Thomas even argued a connection between junk and crack:
'1983-4: A new product of unrivalled commercial appeal and unsurpassed power of cash generation hits the street; it's called "crack." 1984: The first billion dollar junk bond takeovers start getting done. 1985-88: The Milken glory years when for whatever he does he earns $1.2 billion total. 1985-88: A period during which surplus cash at the LA Fed rises from $165 million to $3.8 billion, we are now told, and the Drug Enforcement Agency now tells us that LA . . . is the drug money-laundering capital of the world.'

Thomas was also a writer of a number of financial novels, and no doubt had hoped that his latest, *Hanover Place*, would push him over the top. It was a bonfire-rich account of crooked dealing on Wall Street, in which corrupt new-crowd Jews turn an old fading bank into a go-go powerhouse. Not unlike Drexel Burnham – where Thomas had once worked. However, when their shenanigans are exposed, it precipitates an anti-Semitic backlash that evokes the horrors of Hitler's pre-war Germany. Unfortunately the book was somewhat overshadowed by the all-encompassing success of *Bonfire of the Vanities* but it was also killed, Thomas believes, by a review in *The New York Times Book Review* which began, 'Doing the author the courtesy of assuming that *Hanover Place* is intended only as a dramatization of Wall Street anti-Semitism from 1924 to 1990, rather than an example of it, is a strain.' The reviewer was Judith Martin, an etiquette columnist whom Thomas refers to as 'The Ralph Lauren of manners'.

The result of this was that Thomas fell out with the editor of *The New York Times Book Review*, Rebecca Sinkler, a woman he had known since the age of fifteen as a school friend. It was over lunch that she offered Thomas the chance to review *Thieves* as a conciliatory gesture. Thomas gladly took the commission, and set to work on the proofs. At a Hamptons garden party towards the end of the summer, he told Stewart's agent that he was going to give the book a review that would sell 500,000 copies. The tattle appeared in Liz Smith's gossip column, and Dershowitz immediately dashed off an eight-page single-spaced letter to Sinkler protesting her choice of Thomas as a reviewer. In the letter Dershowitz claimed that Thomas said he was a friend of Stewart's. However, the two had never met. Sinkler then went ahead with Thomas's review, brushing aside Dershowitz's request for space in which to answer the review.

Thomas's rave contained not one iota of criticism of Stewart's book. When *New York* magazine asked him about this, he answered: 'There's no question I might have tempered it. That's entirely true.... I'm not a lawyer; I didn't cover the story. When I used the words true record, I was probably thinking in terms of true as opposed to the false account that has been put about by the Milken publicity people. This was not something about which I had a powerful pre-existing knowledge. Most of this was news to me. I was not interested in the specifics.'

'You didn't follow the newspaper accounts of the legal proceedings?'

'No, no. The Fatico hearing. I didn't even know what that was. I knew there had been some kind of hearing. I knew the following things: I knew that Milken was a crook.... I knew that he had confessed; I knew how business was done on Wall Street... it's all winks and signals over the phone.'

Elsewhere Thomas compared this way of doing business with the Second World War. 'It's rather like the BBC in the last war, they would intone solemnly from London "it will be raining in Tours", and 67 Frenchmen would turn up in Nancy on Tuesday to shoot the local Gestapo commandant.'

Thomas's certainty about his gut instincts and dyed-in-the-wool hatred of Milken would have been familiar to Thomas readers, but were not acceptable to Dershowitz. 'That's not a review. The books are cooked when you get a reviewer like that to give his personal endorsement on the pages of *The New York Times*', he told me. After his letter to Sinkler fell on deaf ears he took out a full-page advertisement in *The New York Times* that was headlined 'An Open Letter from Alan Dershowitz concerning a conflict of interest hidden from the readers of *The New York Times Book Review*'. The ad repeated many of the charges in his letter, that Thomas was prejudiced against Milken and his old firm Drexel, and favorably disposed to Stewart. Thomas, for example, had admitted to dropping Stewart a line after he had written his review and before it was published asking 'if my review should make you as rich as Croesus' for a couple of copies of the book. Dershowitz did not mention it, but in the note Thomas said he wanted one of them to ram up Dershowitz's ass.

Dershowitz then opened the floodgates by criticizing *The New York*

Times for getting a writer its own pages had branded as anti-Semitic to review a book that he felt was also anti-Semitic. 'Its very title – *Den of Thieves* – comes from the New Testament story of Jesus chasing the Jewish moneylenders out of the Temple.' Stewart says he chose the title from *Bartlett's Familiar Quotations* and didn't give it a second thought until it became such an issue. After he 'looked into it a little more deeply' he came back with the rationale that it appealed to him because the Stock Exchange was deliberately designed to look like a temple 'to emphasize the fairness and integrity of the commercial process that was going on inside. And this was what was corrupted by insider traders. Not just Jewish insider traders, but Christian insider traders as well who are described in the book.' Although Stewart denies asserting any divinity on the part of Jesus – who was Jewish – and maintains that biblical scholars have told him that those who were driven out included Jews and non-Jews alike, the popular understanding of the saying is nevertheless that it was the Son of God who drove the Shylocks out of his father's temple.

Stewart, Dershowitz maintained, gratuitously invoked religious stereo-types: 'Every one of Stewart's good guys is a Methodist, an Episcopalian, an Irish-American. Every one of his bad guys was of Jewish background, of yeshiva background.' Stewart argues that he identified the religious background of all his major players, Jewish or non Jewish, for good or bad: 'There are good characters who are Jewish... there are bad characters who are Christian. The problem here was that... the bad guys lost sight of their religious upbringing, Christian or Jewish, and turned to crime. They weren't religious enough.' Although there are non-Jewish insider traders in Stewart's book, the four names on the cover – whom Stewart says he did not choose – were all Jewish. As one reviewer put it, Stewart had unintentionally written a book with 'subtle anti-Semitic undertones'.

Thomas, who happily pleads guilt to insensitivity but not anti-Semitism (his wife is Jewish), has little patience with the newfangled climate of political correctness. 'If I point out,' Thomas told the *Washington Post* in defence of his book, 'that nine out of ten people involved in street crime are black, that's an interesting sociological observation... if I point out that nine out of ten people involved in securities indictments are Jewish that is an anti-Semitic slur.' However, there is an unwritten rule practised by many journalists that skin color, religion and sexual preference are only mentioned when it is shown to be important, which it often is not. Alternatively it is best only to identify people in this way in a positive context. 'For instance,' wrote journalist Richard Cohen, 'Jewish Nobel prize winner is acceptable, "Jewish stock swindler" is not.'

Meanwhile, Dershowitz addressed this same question of why so many Jews were getting into trouble in *Chutzpah*, his follow-up to *Reversal of Fortune*. He reasoned that on the one hand this meant that they were less discriminated against, finally gaining the access and opportunities previously denied to them. But on the other hand it also meant that 'Jews are just like everyone else, and a certain small proportion of them will exploit their power and become corrupt.'

The thesis of his semi-autobiography was that American Jews needed more chutzpah in combatting subtle but pervasive anti-Semitism. Thomas has no time for such rarified arguments and sees Dershowitz as virtually delusional as a result of his bestseller and movie, thinking that he can walk on water. 'So you're walking on water and all of a sudden here comes the conning tower of this dreadful submarine called *Den of Thieves* firing torpedoes in every direction.' Dershowitz's response to this threat is to say, 'That's no submarine out there, that's a fishing boat.' For Thomas the bottom line is 'I think by and large that anti-Semitism is a stupid entropic contagion. . . . I'm not particularly interested in catching it, which is why I've avoided meeting Mr Dershowitz'! He also adds that by creating the controversy Dershowitz boosted flagging sales of *Chutzpah* (as *Den of Thieves* shot to the top spot in the bestsellers, *Chutzpah* was at number 14).

Dershowitz denies this, but did not win many accolades for running up the anti-Semitic flag, and even got into a scrap with the Anti-Defamation League: "The book is not anti-Jewish nor was the review of it. It does not serve the cause of fighting anti-Semitism to fill the air with baseless accusations and plant false suspicions in the minds of the community.' Dershowitz then infuriated the ADL by replying that they 'simply count the number of swastikas painted on synagogue walls and other gross acts of bigotry.'

With this kind of support, Stewart's argument that introducing the anti-Semitism issue was 'a blatant and consistent effort on the part of Milken and his entourage to deflect attention from the serious nature of his crimes onto a completely collateral issue' seemed to win the day. Dershowitz is unapologetic. 'I believe that the worst kinds of religious stereotyping in this country are the most subtle kinds.'

Dershowitz also drew muffled criticism from Milken's own legal team. All along Liman had announced that he did not believe that the place to try cases was in the media, and beyond reiterating this basic formula he refused to comment. However, approached by the *Journal* during the controversy, he did concede, 'We have our own ideas of how to try a case, and what is appropriate strategy, and what should not be used,' said Liman in a characteristically dry-as-a-bone response that seethed with meaning. 'Mr Liman also says he disagrees with Mr Dershowitz's decision to wage a public attack' on *Thieves*. He even interceded with friends at the paper: 'The last thing in the world I thought Michael needed was *The New York Times* as an enemy,' Liman was reported as saying.

Acknowledging their differences, Dershowitz continues to rail against Stewart: '*Den of Thieves* is a pack of lies and everybody knows it . . . what Stewart has done is just beneath contempt. He's just distorted the field of investigative journalism, destroyed the front page of *The Wall Street Journal*, made it into his own little plaything...to win his prizes and paper his pockets. If we're talking about one person in this society who is incredibly greedy and who has made a fortune of money off the misery of Michael Milken and his family, that's Jim Stewart.' Ill-fated or not, he has vowed to continue his campaign to discredit the handsome, successful Pulitzer Prize-winning journalist: 'Investigative journalists in this country have one target that they will not investigate. They'll investigate the president. They'll investigate the Supreme Court. But they will not investigage each other.... We accuse Jim Stewart of intellectual, scientific and economic fraud. We're issuing an indictment in the form of a chapter by chapter analysis. And we're challenging the investigative reporters of this country to read what we've written...and if they do Stewart will be exposed as a fraud.'

Already the resource book he is preparing – which has the working title *Pack of Lies* – has the thickness in manuscript form of two telephone directories. It consists of chapter-length repudiations of Stewart's accounts of eight key transactions that he used to establish Milken's criminality, and additional chapters on Stewart's mischaracterization of the High Yield Bond market and his techniques in assassinating Milken's character. It is as damning an indictment of Stewart as Stewart's book is of Milken, although whether or not it will ever be published remains to be seen. Months after the imminent publication of the resource pack was announced, only the research on one transaction, Harris Graphics, has been completed, and Milken is still tinkering with the final nuances of the finished draft. The reason for this, one of his lawyers explains with a sigh, is Milken's pursuit of perfection, or, as others would see it, his inability to make a final decision (something that characterised his direction of his legal campaign as a whole). Also to the frustration of his legal team, Milken is more interested in the broader financial canvas: "We have different goals, we're here to look at the book as a legal document, we're not here to propogate Michael Milken's theories of the universe.' But whatever the contents, if *Pack of Lies* is ever published, will people be bothered to read it? In the media age audiences have a short attention span and a limited capacity for detail. When it comes to selling lemonade, Stewart set his stall up in the right place at the right time, and it was the flavor everyone wanted. And he may well have slaked everyone's thirst. However unjust Stewart's book may turn out to be, it is hard to imagine *Pack of Lies* winning Milken the coveted verdict of history.

17

NEVER MIND THE REALITY,
FEEL THE MYTH

To carry away a meaningful understanding of what happened to Milken we need to look at the spirit of the times rather than dwell on the underwhelming details of his crimes.

What really happened in the roaring eighties? Little more than a year after Milken had decamped with his department back West, leaving Wall Street for Hollywood, Reagan, a fellow Californian, would take Hollywood to Washington. Reagan will always be remembered as the Mickey Mouse of the eighties, the decade's essential mascot and icon. Like Milken, Reagan was untramelled by history, unrestricted by the mercurial seasons of the eastern seaboard, and brought with him a sunny optimism and permanent good humor. Reagan wanted to cut through the Gordian knot of government and the dead hand of the past that prevented people from becoming all that they could be. 'Government is not the solution, government is the problem,' he announced in his inaugural speech. 'We have every right to dream heroic dreams,' he continued, cutting the ribbon on his movie-style presidency in which spectacle would rule. Reagan 'persuaded himself that all dreams do come true, and that the script of every American life is written by the kindly mythographers of Warner Brothers,' sniped one of his intellectual critics, Lewis Lapham. Whatever the case, Reagan gave the mythographers free reign in spending $8 million on an inauguration worthy of *Gone With the Wind*. As in the animated Disney corporate logo, when Peter Pan blazes a trail and sprinkles stardust over the castle of the magic kingdom, so Reagan, when he took possession of the White House, lit it up with an inaugural fireworks display of ten thousand rockets, transforming it into a lighthouse for the rich and famous. On the fourth day of celebrations there were nine inaugural balls, $400,000 of hors d'oeuvres were eaten and 14,400 bottles of champagne were drunk. Throughout his reign Reagan spent lavishly on spectacle from the $12 million spent on the Statue of Liberty bicentennial (replete with a cast of 12,000, including 200 Elvis impersonators) to the opening parade at the 1984 Olympics in Los Angeles.

In this programme Reagan was assisted by his wife Nancy, who, before she turned to fighting drugs, put the White House back on the hill. As author Dominick Dunne observed, 'The Reagan White House gave sort of a benediction to public spending, a public showing off.' Like many people he believed it all started with the china syndrome, in which Nancy ordered new china (with the presidential seal raised in gold in the centre) at a cost of $209,508. She also retained Ted Graber, the interior decorator who normally charged $50,000 per room and who referred to his clients as 'the merchant princes who are today's royalty'. Her extravagant style cut a swath through Washington society. 'I don't think there's been anyone in the White House since Jaqueline Kennedy Onassis who has her flair,' oozed designer Bill Blass. *The New York Times* went one better, naming an entire female type after her lead. Today's Nancy woman 'Does not want to look unobtrusive...she [has] a sensibility founded on buying power and an unabashed appreciation of luxury.' Encouraged by the Reagan line, private fortunes came out of the closet to flaunt their wares. 'We've worked hard for this,' said the wife of a Texas real estate developer at the inaugural ball. 'We're proud, and we're not afraid to show it.'

But it wasn't just a question of showing off: spectacle was an important dynamic of business in the eighties. Malcolm Forbes, the eccentric billionaire, nicknamed his personal jumbo jet 'The Capitalist Tool,' had sixty-eight motorbikes, and a collection of Faberge eggs – one of which he had reproduced on a giant hot-air balloon. Forbes used these toys as a promotional device for his magazine. He also spent $2 million on his seventieth birthday party in Morocco. In addition to flying one thousand guests to Tangier for a weekend of festivities, he provided for a press corp that numbered several hundred so that the spectacle of the event could be broadcast all over the world. He used pleasure for business, as was evident when it became known that Forbes intended to write off most of the bill for his party as a business expense.

Or take showman Donald Trump. At his peak he had buildings, hotels, casinos, an airline, a yacht, a board game and a bestselling autobiography, *The Art of the Deal*. Stamping his name on everything, Trump used his lifestyle to build a celebrity brand-name empire. Courting headlines, he used the media exposure as free advertising for his business, and to leverage bigger and bigger loans to finance his shopping spree. Exposure accreted the franchise value of his name which became collateral where the books would have cautioned less star-struck investors. 'The show is Trump and it is sold out everywhere,' he once crowed, agog at the media coverage news of his split with Ivana occasioned (which cheated Bush's trip to drug-torn Colombia, the bankruptcy of Drexel, and even the freedom of Nelson Mandela of their deserved headlines in the *New York Post*).

Illusion is often an important part of spectacle and the show does not create wonderment by revealing its backstage mechanics. Trump Tower, due to city zoning regulations, was in fact only fifty-eight stories high. But Trump created a sixty-eight story tower by having two banks of elevators and inserting phantom floors between the end of one and the beginning of the next. Moreover, in the soufflé of spectacle hard boundaries between fact and fiction blur, and it was hard to tell where reality ended and fantasy began. Donald Trump had a cameo role in which he played himself in the mini-series for Judith Krantz's bestseller *I'll Take Manhattan*, and Henry Kissinger appeared in 'Dynasty'. 'Dynasty's royal wedding in Moldavia was, on a scale of opulence, indistinguishable from Gloria Thurn and Taxis' costume ball in Moldavia. In a prelude on the Danube, as reported in *Vanity Fair*, the billionaire eccentric (a.k.a. Princess TNT) sang a song she had written for her husband accompanied by a bavarian folk rock band;

Forget JR, Blake Carrington and Alexis,
The only one who turns me on is Goldie Thurn and Taxis.

But Goldie Thurn and Taxis turned us all on. From the high moral ground of the nineties, Reagan and the extravagant follies of his billionaires make for easy targets. But they were really no more than the creations of their time, and if they hadn't existed, it would have been necessary to invent them. Obligingly they invented themselves, and flaunted it around the globe for our pleasure. As one economics student remarked as he watched Reagan's inauguration in January 1981: 'In the last inauguration Jimmy Carter fantasized the common man, walking down Pennsylvania Avenue, but Reagan fantasizes the business man, coming on strong in a limo...for my money we need a business man fantasy right now, so Reagan is right on time.' Boesky and Levine gave us that business fantasy, vogueing down Wall Street competing, with their red Ferraris and pink Rolls Royces, in the category of 'Executive Realness.' Everyone wanted in and to be a part of the business fantasy. The idealists of the sixties became the greed junkies of the eighties. *Rolling Stone* celebrated its twentieth anniversary with a series of perception versus reality ads. The perception was that the *Rolling Stone* reader was a free-wheeling non-material type, but the ads implied that the reality was that he was turned on and tuned in to making money. The hippies of yesteryear who basked in the summer of love now tooled around in red Porsches grooving out to the big chill of business. Sixties activist Jerry Rubin issued shares and went public, while Ben and Jerry, two kinder and gentler hippies from

Vermont, became model capitalists and multi-millionaires with their ice cream business. They even went so far as to turn Jerry Garcia, founder of the Grateful Dead and one of the gurus of the age, into one of their ice cream flavors – Cherry Garcia. When the singer sued, it was not because this icon of a revolutionary era had been turned into a yuppie consumable, but because the royalties were not sufficient.

That the affluenza of the eighties was epidemic is also evident in the popular consuming passions of the age, where the emphasis was on the conspicuousness of the consumption. In New York there was such a boom in the stretch limousine business that it was possible to hail one on the street for little more than the price of a cab. In both England and America champagne sales doubled, while chocolate truffles and designer Godiva chocolates came in vogue. The label was the thing and brand-name mania ruled like a psychosis. Chanel, Hermès, Gucci and Louis Vuitton all enjoyed a renaissance in the eighties. But the greed for wealth and its iconography was not restricted to a yuppie elite who could afford it. The logos of all four houses were appropriated for homeboy street fashions, and vinyl Vuitton baseball caps, and Gucci T-shirts abounded. It was the symbol, the trademark, that was the thing.

Also popular with the home boys was Ralph Lauren, whose line and lifestyle was one of the most flagrant and successful examples of this logo marketeering. His Polo range evoked a yesteryear of bespoke tailoring and an elegant country life that was part Brideshead, part Mar-A-Lago. But deciphering the Latin numerals embroidered in the regal seal of the Lauren logo yields 'Established 1969'. Born in the South Bronx and named Lipshitz, Ralph Lauren's business empire is brilliant neo-antiquery. On Madison Avenue he has recreated the Rhinelander mansion as a shopping environment. The advertisments read 'Ralph Lauren. A tradition becomes'. Becomes what? Traditionally a tradition evolves over the years, becoming encrusted with heritage. But in the eighties, with history no more than a fantasy theme park, a tradition could be as instantly and as easily acquired as the traditional rules of syntax could be transcended in the nonsensical but portentous announcement that 'A tradition becomes'. It was all a great pretend, very *Great Gatsby* (appropriately it was Lauren who did the costumes for the movie).

The eighties also saw the perfume wars, championed by Fred Hayman, whose Giorgio perfume was one of the best-selling scents of the eighties. Attractively packaged in yellow and white stripes with a regal-looking heraldic logo and tied with red ribbon, the scent became the rage, with demand for his shopping bags, especially, outstripping supply.

Brand-name mania also showed up as the literary style of many of the decade's bestselling 'sex and shopping' novels. Dominick Dunne's *People Like Us* and Judith Krantz's *I'll Take Manhattan*, to name but two, catalogued the lifestyles of the rich and famous in fetishistic detail and with unfailing attentiveness to designer labels. 'These books read like catalogues from Neiman-Marcus,' groused Lewis Lapham. 'Nobody goes anywhere without drinking from a glass of Roederer Cristal wearing a Cartier watch or picking up a Mont Blanc pen to write a check for the odd two or three million while sitting at a table by William Kent in a suite at Claridges.'

The popularity of these aphrodisiacs and sensual indulgences – champagne, chocolates, clothes, perfume and popular bestsellers – show how it was the symbols and tokens of wealth, the perks and the accessories, that were set at a premium and that it was everyone, and not just the rich and famous, who wanted them. Producers marketed lifestyles and consumers bought fantasies. Thus the eighties weren't really about greed, they were about the fantasy of business and the romance of wealth, which was fleshed out with these logos, symbols and brand-name props. The eighties was a simulated decade in which nothing was as it seemed and the show was all.

But just as Fred Hayman's quintessentially eighties store was at the opposite end of Rodeo Drive to Milken's office, so Milken stood in complete contrast to all this. To some extent he shared the vision. Like Reagan, for example, he peppered his discourse with references to movies as though they were real. *Star Wars* was a favourite. But beyond this, he was not interested in the extravagant spectacle and the symbols of wealth. He had no yachts, no palatial homes. Unlike Forbes he did not throw lavish parties, and unlike Trump did not seek out publicity. He was not interested in being a celebrity, in being featured in glossy magazines, or on 'Lifestyles of the Rich and Famous'. Milken instead was lost in his work, fascinated with the changes that were going on in society beneath the surface, in which many traditional and time-honored values were displaced by new values that were, in the eyes of many, junk.

To be sure there has been an inversion of value that adds up to a virtual cultural revolution. What had historically been valuable became worthless and what had hitherto been seen as worthless became valuable. Sand for microchips became more important than steel for skyscrapers, as the rust belt lost out to silicon valley and as the industrial economy gave way to the information age. As George Gilder wrote, 'This device [of putting entire computer central processing units on tiny slivers of the silicon in sand] overthrew all previous relations between material resources and real value.' The traditional moral superiority of material things that were seen as valuable and good because they were solid and of substance was superseded by a new system in which abstract ideas and their symbols ruled. Proliferating plastic credit cards continued to displace cash, as money became an electronic blip generated by a silicon chip. Or take Coca-Cola, which although no more than water with sugar and fizz, has become the symbol of 'the real thing', the authentic American experience of freedom and fun. As Coca-Cola Chairman Robert Goizueta pointed out, when people drink Coke they are drinking the trademark. Thanks to Coke anyone in the world can now enjoy the taste of freedom – even if they live in the most oppressive of regimes.

Thus sand and water, materials that were until recently considered worthless, are the building blocks of America's pop culture, just as oil and steel were the staples of America's industrial might. And today it is this Pop Culture – the combined might of celebrities, movies, pop music, merchandise, fashion, and fast food (from Michael Jackson to Madonna, from Mickey Mouse to Teenage Mutant Turtles, from Big Macs to Coca-Cola, and from Levi's to Fruit of the Loom) – that is America's number one export. Coca-Cola is called for over 480 million times a day and McDonalds have stopped boasting about how many billions of burgers they have served. 'The Japanese have a name for this so-called new media. They call it 'Omizu Shobai", or the "water business", meaning, in its most modern sense, tricky to get a hold on', claimed a recent cover-story in *Fortune* on the Pop business. The article also focused on the fact that, with Sony's purchase of CBS records and Columbia Pictures (from Coca-Cola) and Matsushita's purchase of MCA, Japanese investment in American entertainment has been $12 billion in the last three years.

But in spite of the proven financial value of this new junk culture, our prejudice against this reversal of value dies hard. That the Japanese should have invested so aggressively in this profound superficiality only rein-forces our prejudice against this junk culture. After all, 'Made in Japan', like 'Made in Taiwan' or 'Made in Korea', are the symbols of junk toys and junk electronics. In Japan they churn out chicket pot noddles, in Taiwan they churn out Walkman-wearing dancing Coke cans, and in Korea they spew out knockoffs of designer labels – fake Gucci, Vuitton and Rolexes. In short, it's all junk.

Milken was wise to this. When his high yield securities were derided as junk bonds he replied, 'Everything that we like is junk, junk food, junk clothes, junk records. Everything that seems to stand the test of time is junk. And particularly everything someone else thinks of is junk.' He argued that in the new environment his junk bonds were real money, and that people needed to overcome their resistance to change if they were going to survive, since in his view change was as inevitable a force as evolution, and the message was simple: 'Adapt or die'. But it was Milken himself who failed to adapt to some of the changes going on in society. Not only did he not participate in the spectacle of the decade, but he also refused to participate in the pageant of celebrity.

Milken saw that in the dawn of the information age telecommunications would be a growth area. With computers, televisions, telephones, and movies wiring the global village for sound and vision, he saw the huge potential for all these businesses. Milken financed CNN, for example, which from its unlikely beginnings looks set to become the televisual equivalent of Coca-Cola. As Andy Warhol pointed out, the Coke that the president drank in the White House was the same Coke that the bum drank on the street, the same Coke that people drank all across the world. Today CNN is a kind of electro-cola whose impact on world events and consumer choices has already been demonstrated.

But even though Milken saw that the media would become the lifeblood and nervous system of the information economy (just as manufacturing had been the backbone of the industrial economy), he did not anticipate what this supermedia would consist of. Now that the world is wired for sound and vision (by 1986 there were in the United States alone 1,220 television stations – not counting cable channels – 9,871 radio stations, 482 newspapers and 11,328 magazines), the media, to avoid the horror of dead airwaves or blank pages, needs an ever-increasing endless supply of material to pump out. Those who thought that the media would be a conduit of scholarly information and scientific data have been disappointed. There simply aren't enough facts to fill the void. But there are more than enough people, and our insatiable voyeurism has resulted in a media that is primarily a gossipy mixture of fact and fiction, of truth and lies all about other people's lives.

Thus, out of all of junk culture, Celebrity has become the biggest growth area feeding the new supermedia. As Deyan Sudjic wrote in *Cult Icons*, 'Celebrity has come to be as much of primary product as oil and steel once were'. To keep up with demand, celebrities have been recruited from all walks and warps of life. In the eighties, businessmen, bond traders, lawyers, and real estate magnates, were sucked into the media vortex and joined the all-star choir. Furthermore, this vortex is also collapsing traditional hierarchies and distinctions, dragging them down into the celebrity mix. As Toffler wrote in *Powershift*, 'For better or worse, the old lines between show business and politics, between leisure and work, news and entertainment, are all crashing.' The wall between public and private has also been demolished. Private people who were successful were dragged into the celebrity limelight while public people lost their right to their private lives, with political figures – to pick one obvious example – leading more by force of personality than by a grasp of the issues.

The new media also replaced many moral and ethical notions of privacy, truth and goodness with its own spectacular amorality. 'If you're invited you're indicted', wrote *The Wall Street Journal* about the rehabilitation and celebrity status of criminals. 'Sexy' became a buzz word in media circles and was the key criterion of the new media. You could be a sinner or you could be a saint, but were you 'sexy'? The one cardinal sin of the supermedia was to be boring. In the new media morality, good was sexy, bad was boring, and it didn't even matter if you were a serial killer. In this medium the rigid lines between fact and fiction blurred in the spectacle.

For the media does not exist as a clear glass window pane on basic truths, but is a magnifying lens or distorting mirror for many truths and many falsehoods. It is an infotainment in which mythical pearls are spun round grains of truth.

The darlings of this evolving supermedia were the Reagans, the Trumps, and all the other colourful, and larger-than-life figures that populated the eighties. They said outrageous things and there was a cartoonlike dimension to them. They gave good spectacle. But Milken did not. He resisted the limelight. He did not talk in sound bites and was not 'sexy'. He did not mythicize himself or cultivate his personality, but was instead obsessively private and had an almost physical aversion to being a public figure.

Meanwhile the confidence that had driven men and markets ebbed as it had flowed. What went up came crashing down, and the money that had come out to play jumped back into the closet. As Carolyn Roehm, the thinking person's Antoinette, told *Vogue*, 'I've been thinking about the fall of Michael Milken and the demise of Drexel Burnham, which stood for...quick money....I thought about Donald and Ivana's divorce and Malcolm Forbes' death. I thought about the nineties and the Bush administration. And I vowed to stay home.'

The crash had more to do with the mass psychology of the times than the specifics of junk bonds, leverage and debt. But instead of an enlightened and collective sharing of responsibility, there has been a benighted backlash. In a speech at the New York Public Library one week before Milken's sentencing, the banker-hero and self-appointed pseudo-statesman Felix Rohatyn indulged himself with this caricature of the eighties: 'We have just seen the end of the greatest decade of speculation and financial irresponsibility since the 1920s. Financial deregulation, easy credit and regulatory neglect combined with a degradation of our value system to create a religion of money and glamour. The achievement of instant wealth and instant fame became the ultimate standard to be achieved at any price. The most conservative and traditional professions such as the law and banking became the engines of contemporary behaviour that would have made the Great Gatsby...look like Little Lord Fauntleroy today. Beginning first in New York, but subsequently spreading to the rest of the country and to the world, the junk bond peddlers and the raiders, the speculators and the S&L hustlers, with their legions of consultants, lobbyists and their friendly politicians, turned this country into a vast casino and its value system into show business. As we now watch the indictments and the trials, as we hear the defence arguments about technical violations and innovative finance techniques, let us not forget that the basic crimes committed here were crimes against the entire nation. These will cost hundreds of billions of dollars. They have also undermined standards of confidence and conduct in our system which were built up over generations...the nation will need a lengthy period of recovery from this madness.' If Rohatyn does not mention Milken by name it is because he does not need to. It is abundantly clear who he believed to be responsible for the follies of the eighties – all of them.

This reaction, lamenting that society has gone to hell in a handbasket while simultaneously painting Milken as the enemy of the people who is to blame, and condemning Reagan's reign as a confidence trick of smoke and mirrors and debt, is typical of its kind, and hides the old and by now familiar prejudice of the East Coast towards the West. Californians are seen as shallow and superficial, as unable to distinguish the movies from real life. This is part of the historical puritan philosophy that distrusts surface and show, rejects what is new as worthless junk, resists all change and places its faith in good old-fashioned notions of value and substance. After all, 'Trumpery', as Michael Thomas once delighted in pointing out, is defined in the Oxford English Dictionary as 'something of less value than it seems'. But generally such prejudice is limiting as the information age propels us into an increasingly symbolic realm where the most valuable things are the most insubstantial (from Coca-Cola to silicon chips) and abstract (such as ideas and information).

Like most traditions, such entrenched ideas die hard. And so after a Wild West interregnum, in which California dreamers Reagan and Milken both sought to escape the constraints of history and look to the future (albeit in very different ways), the East Coast patricians regained control. After the glam and the glitz, Bush was touted as hailing from an authentic Wasp family. He was the real thing. After the greed, Bush announced a kinder, gentler America. But in spite of this reassertion of tradition and this discrediting of spectacle, little has changed. One television ad that ran during the 1988 campaign depicted a picnic at the Bush holiday home in Kennebunkport, Maine. With its chequered tablecloths, wicker baskets and young girls in white lace, it was indistinguishable from a Ralph Lauren advertisement. The man behind the advertisement was media medicine man Roger Ailes. In other words, although today the fantasy may be tradition and authenticity, it is no more than a fantasy, the latest creation of a media society in which spectacle continues – and will continue – to rule.

Making Milken a scapegoat for greed and spectacle – two things he neither comprehended nor represented – protects people from comprehending the roaring eighties and taking responsibility for the fact that it was something in which all of society, and not just a few, took part. Everyone wanted in in the eighties, from the $25 billion buyouts to the $15 knockoff Rolexes, and people kid themselves if they believe that they have exorcised greed merely because a man who has been daubed as greedy has been sent to prison. Just as spectacle continues to rule, greed endures, and the fact that it is by turns seen as a vice and then a virtue, in fashion and then out of fashion, suggests that this is a fact of life people have difficulty coming to terms with.

Every denunciator of Milken as the living breathing symbol of greed – and they are legion – fails to make the connection with the accuser's own greed. One writer, after trotting out the usual judgements about Milken's greed and criminality, revealed that he was the ghost writer hired to write Boesky's book *Risk Arbitrage*. Sensitive about this hack job, he explained that he could not say no to the money involved. Although his expediency somewhat undercuts his high moral tone, it is not too hard to feel compassion for his plight. But this same compassion – which everyone deserves – has been consistently denied Milken.

However, if Milken is a victim, he largely has only himself to blame. 'I'll tell you a cute story,' Milken told a management conference in 1989, going on to tell the story of a business student at Wharton who had wanted to open a sports shop. The Milken Foundation agreed to commit the $30,000 he needed to open his store, stipulating that he first work for six months in another sports shop. But after several months, this business school graduate had been unable to get a job. Milken paraphrased the student's explanation: 'I go to the store and tell them I'm planning to open a sporting goods store, I want some training, so I know everything about the business and I can compete with you.' As Milken concluded, 'All the intelligence and all the knowledge in the world doesn't necessarily get you common sense or a frame of reference.' Whether Milken realized it or not, this anecdote was a parable of his own predicament. On one simple level Milken's vision of the future for the business establishment was taken, by many of its executives, to mean no future for them. But on almost every other level, Milken, who was unacclimated to cultural norms, insensitive to political mores, and blind to media rule, utterly lacked a frame of reference when it came to understanding the consequences of his actions. Sometimes it is hard to imagine a man more uniquely unsuited to his times.

Meanwhile the man himself languishes in a federal prison work camp. Denied his request to be sent to a 'Club Fed' near Las Vegas (because a nearby hospital had special neurological facilities that his kids might need when visiting him), he was instead despatched farther away from home to a camp forty miles east of San Francisco. In contrast, Boesky's first choice of Lompoc was accepted. Lompoc – which has since closed – was also considered to be the most comfortable of all of America's thirty-four minimum security prisons. But the inappropriately named Pleasanton facility in which Milken is interred consists of a portion of incompletely renovated asbestos-contaminated army barracks that have been abandoned since 1959. Unlike Lompoc there is no library or tennis court, just a dirt track and some weight-lifting equipment. Unfinished at the time of opening, it has bare plasterboard walls and doors without handles. Milken and the other eighty-odd inmates are bused off for meals to the nearby medium security facility whose most famous inmate was Patty Hearst.

Four days before Milken was due to check in, the authorities, claiming that they had been deluged with requests, arranged a guided tour of the prison for the press. 'I can't tell you what it will be,' the warden's assistant announced to the twenty assembled journalists at the start of their tour, 'but he will be working.' The press reports delighted in the fact that the man who made $550 million in one year would instead be pulling down no more than $832 a year and be kept by the American taxpayer at an annual cost of $10,000. Where he had enjoyed an hourly salary of $57,000 an hour (twenty-four hours a day and 365 days a year), he now stood to earn between twelve and forty cents an hour doing menial tasks such as roofing, cooking or perhaps even tending the grounds of Alcatraz prison (where Al Capone spent his last few years and which has since become a tourist spot). His wages would be automatically credited to his prisoner ID card – number 16126-054 – enabling him to buy things at the prison store.

Milken had been due to begin his sentence on the Ides of March, March 4, but instead turned himself in at 6:30 p.m. on the previous evening. After spending the day with his family, he arrived on a commercial flight into San Francisco. While he would earn credit for the early appearance which would be applied towards his parole, part of his motivation was no doubt to avoid the media mêlée that would have awaited him. Once again Milken had cheated the press, who instead had to console themselves with the detail that in the television room there was a ragged paperback version of *Rich Man, Poor Man*, and that once inside he would not be able to wear his toupee. With so much time on his hands and so little else to do, Milken, who now wears a baseball cap all the time, no doubt wonders what happened to him. For an answer we have to turn to the long letter he wrote to Judge Wood a few weeks before his sentencing. Although redacted by the court, with certain portions kept under seal, it is nevertheless Milken's most intimate public utterance. A largely accurate analysis of his own situation, it is most revealing in its few but crucial misperceptions. Typed on plain notepaper it began, 'I crave your indulgence in reading this letter.... For the past twenty-five years, I have been more of a people person than a writer. I am more comfortable speaking since I have always felt that I could never write anything that would be perfect. I would always continue to edit it. However, in this world nothing is necessarily perfect, and particularly myself.

'All people, I am sure, have a fear of incarceration...and I, too, have those fears....When I made the decision to work in New York, I commuted to our home in Cherry Hill, New Jersey, every evening. Sometimes I had to go to meetings in the evening and didn't get home until midnight or 1:00 a.m. The next morning I got up and commuted back. The important thing was to be home with Lori, if it was only to sleep by her side a few hours or check on our children in their rooms. If I knew my family was fine, I could continue to meet the challenges of the next day.'

Milken then went on to write of how 'I never dreamed I could do anything that would result in being a felon. These words are hard for me to write and difficult to accept. . . . What I have not been able to accept, and what has been the most painful during the past four years, has been the assault on the sincerity of my beliefs, my moral systems, and my basic inner being. It has been very difficult for me to cope with. I have been forced to face the challenge that not only am I portrayed as a fraud, but everything my life stood for is called a fraud and all the principles I have spoken about my whole life are hollow. At times, this has been almost too difficult to bear.

'During the past four years while I have faced continued assaults on my life's work, in addition to constant character assassinations, looking at old pictures and reminiscing about past experiences has helped to remind me of who I am and what I believed in. I began to feel that it was someone else the newspapers were writing about, not myself. It was almost as if I had stepped outside of my body. Listening to the rhetoric. Interpreting one's motives. Defining how one had lived his life. It became like two lives. A life I thought I had been living and a life depicted in the newspaper.'

Like Peter Pan, distraught at the loss of his shadow, Milken is floored by his separation into the two opposing entities of his public perception and his private reality. Milken's injured incomprehension is all the more arresting when you consider that the difference between perception and reality was a favorite keynote of Milken's, and his success at both recognising and taking advantage of the difference between the two the basis of his business and 'life's work'.

Elsewhere in the letter one chances occasionally on what might be seeds of understanding: 'Success or notoriety brings with it a great deal of pressure and in some cases even potential threats to your children. In the 1970s I knew people whose lives were drastically changed forever by kidnappings or threats of kidnapping, and both Lori and I concluded that no success was worth the invasion of our home and family by the media. How naïve I was. By my own actions and failings I have subjected my loved ones to a lot of publicity and ridicule.

'To some it might sound ironic, but I have spent a lifetime trying to avoid publicity, even accolades. . . . For the entire time my family and I lived in New Jersey we were able to live a life of simple, quiet anonymity. I played with the neighbourhood kids on the weekends. After moving to California this anonymity continued until the mid-1980s. Then as I tried to avoid publicity, that fact alone received public attention.' As Milken,

possibly missing the connection, wrote earlier
have turned my shield into a reflector.'

But in spite of these fitful flickers, ⌐
illumination eludes him. Milken cannot squ⌐
his personal reality. He either failed to see or w⌐
that in the media age there is no difference b⌐
reality. Perception is reality.

'I do feel that much of my life during the past four year⌐
ping-pong ball with every cause on either side of the issues u⌐
symbol for their own uses. To every libertarian, to everyone who ⌐
felt that their privacy has been invaded by the government or unj⌐
accused, I have always asked please, "Don't use me as a symbol." To thos⌐
who I don't know, whom I've never met, who call me a symbol of the
1980s or a symbol of money and power, I say I've never sought notoriety.
I have asked both sides not to use me as a ping-pong ball. Let me return to
a life of anonymity if humanly possible for myself and my family . . . I am a
person not a symbol.' Milken could not be more wrong. The man was lost
to the myth years ago.

18

COLLECT CALL FROM MICHAEL MILKEN

'WELL, what I wanted to know was how you saw this final chapter—how are you going to present it?' The gentle sing song voice sounding far away down the other end of the phone was that of Michael Milken, calling collect from jail. We had just concluded the first of several lengthy phone interviews, and half an hour later he was back on the phone again.

I told him I intended to have him just speaking, adding what I hoped would be the appealing idea that this was his opportunity to speak out and have his say. 'But that's just it. This isn't my say.' I was choosing the questions, asking him about the things that I wanted to discuss, which were not necessarily the things that he wanted to talk about, he said. And when he had his say, he told me, he would be speaking for himself. 'I think you should present it as a conversation you had with me, that you happened to be out here in LA and—just as we did a few years ago—we sat down and talked about a bunch of things that were on our mind.'

This conversation took me back to the time I was at Robinson Lake and Lerer asking, for what seemed like the umpteenth time, for an interview with Milken. But this time, instead of the usual evasions like "Yes, but not right now', or 'Michael's not talking to anyone right now', I was asked if I was sure I wanted to talk to Milken. After all, it was suggested, the microscoping of every word and navel-grazing occasioned by every nuance might be more of a distraction than anything else. All I wanted, I said, with the weary clarity of saying the same thing over and over, was a simple interview with the guy. The baleful look I received for a reply suggested that there was no such thing as a simple interview.

And now, discussing the presentation of this the final chapter with Milken, I wondered if they weren't right. After all, as Jesse Kornbluth, who claims in his irresistible salesmanship to have spent over 400 hours talking to Milken, told me, whereas most journalists 'have total certainty about a man they've never met, I have uncertainty about someone I know quite well'. Was it worth all the time and effort just to get confused?

This writer also concluded that the five most terrifying and exhilarating words in the English language were 'collect call from Michael Milken'. Of course talking 12 hours a day for over a month would clock up a phone bill that could be terrifying enough. When I asked Milken what he thought Kornbluth had meant by the remark he said he had no idea.

As it turned out, in the course of writing my own book it did not take very long to understand that Milken was strangely irrelevant to what was supposed to be his own story. Yes, impenetrable mystery surrounded Milken and his secrecy excited the wildest of speculation, but no, none of it was justified. The man was not larger than life, but simply life-sized in the most ordinary sense of the word. In spite of all that had been said and written about Milken, pull back the curtain and there was no Wizard of Oz pulling levers, but an off-the-peg ordinary cookie-cutter guy on the phone. He was as if in the eye of the hurricane, and from where he stood all was still and perfectly ordinary. Instead, it was the storm that raged about him, with all its histrionic prosecutors and reports, that was so compelling.

So this book was written without the co-operation of Milken. But if I think that this was something of a blessing, that is not to say that Milken and his people did well to make himself inaccessible. They could not have done worse. Ken Lerer once told me a cautionary tale about a journalist friend who boasted about how he had screwed over a company in an article he had recently written. Why did he do that, Lerer was asked. 'They wouldn't give me access,' came the reply.

The access mess was a mistake they all made, not just Robinson Lake and Lerer, but also the high yield bond department, Drexel Burnham Lambert, and Paul Weiss Rifkind Wharton and Garrison (Milken's principal lawyers). And many more besides. For example, much has been made of the fact that Stewart only approached one of some 300 people who worked close to Milken, many of whom had been vocal enough in their support of Milken to write a letter on his behalf to the judge. But I wrote to almost one hundred key people. This was a complete waste of time. The few who did have the courtesy to respond—after a barrage of badgering calls—said they would only speak if Milken or Robinson Lake and Lerer told them to. None of them ever spoke to me. One person hit the nail on the head when he said that talking to the media was not a game you could win because you could not control the media. I could not but wonder by what right (other than grand delusion) did he expect the media to be something that he could control?

Virtually blocked, such access as was given to Milken was so maddeningly mediated it could only add fuel to the fire. Take, for example, the begrudging eleventh hour interview given to Connie Bruck, or the careful hand-picking of a handful of safe or friendly journalists whose credibility was thus immediately and unnecessarily undermined. In the end, the person who claims the access prize is Jesse Kornbluth, and I once asked him the secret of his success: 'It came as a result of living in the same building with Milken's press representative, Ken Lerer...and that would not have happened certainly in any other way because I'd been calling Milken, writing Milken and just generally beating on Drexel's door since 1986 and I had gotten nowhere.'

In my own experience, the endless procrastination and stalling not only tried the patience but made one wonder what, exactly, was trying to be achieved. But even if at the core of this access fiasco there lies an arrogant refusal to be judged—whether fairly or unfairly—by one's fellow man and be caught out in the naked vulnerability of the human condition, I think (as the overinvolved process of this interview illustrates) that this unnatural desire to control that which cannot be controlled, far from being the sinister and maniacal, plays much more like a comedy of errors.

But I digress. As I wrote the book I continued to make my requests to talk to Milken. Then finally, sometime after the deadline for the American edition of this book had passed, I fedexed a letter directly to Milken himself in prison. I felt that the reader deserved the opportunity to hear Milken speak for himself. In the letter I said that he also owed this to himself. How else could people see that he was, as he argued, a human being and not a symbol. If he did speak to me, I wrote that I envisaged a final chapter consisting of his thoughts and comments. Because I had come to believe that the Milken machine only moved when it was way past the eleventh hour or even when it was too late, I was strangely confident that he would agree.

A few days later, I received a call from Lorraine Spurge. In the Milken cosmos Lorraine Spurge is Milken's former syndicate manager, the character who was supposed to have received and then 'disappeared' the infamous blue ledger alleged to have detailed a veritable *Paradise Lost* of criminal activity. Judge Wood would not listen to Spurge's grand jury denials that she had never been given such a book because she felt that her salary and closeness to Milken tainted her testimony. After the collapse of Drexel she had founded her own company, Knowledge Exchange Inc., a high yield research and publishing venture that had published the large coffee table tome *Portraits of the American Dream*. It was, as she said herself, so outsized that if you had a pair of legs it could *be* the coffee table.

Spurge was one of the hundreds of people inside the high yield bond department whom I had repeatedly approached to speak to me. Typical of this set, her response had been no response whatsoever. She apologized for this explaining that my timing was bad and that they had all, she said, been traumatized by Milken's sentence. But now—on a brighter note—she and a colleague called Esther Rudin were brimming with ideas and suggestions. A last chapter that included an interview with Michael might also, they suggested, look at the recovery of the junk bond market, and evaluate Milken's recent testimony at the Rosenthal case. It could also include quotes culled from highly respected people that might give the book credibility, and they could put me in touch with a number of people who worked inside the high yield department. All I really wanted, I explained, was to give Milken the space to speak at the end of the book. They asked me to submit a list of questions, and asked to see the copy for the new chapter 'Verdict of History' and I agreed.

About a week later we met to review the questions. Spurge was a far cry from the fabled dragon lady I had been led to expect. She kept on telling me that since she had never done this sort of thing before she wasn't sure what the form was. At one point I suggested that Milken might like to make a list of things he disagreed with in the book that we could talk about. 'A list!' she exploded. 'Please, we'll be here till Christmas!' and she laughed uproariously. 'Michael has diarrhea—of the mouth!' she later joked affectionately about Milken.

Her colleague Esther, a writer, was also there suggesting rewording and reordering a number of the questions. She also gave me back the manuscript for 'The Verdict of History'. I said that was not necessary, but she said that she had made some suggestions; 'I'm a writer myself, and when I read something I can't help picking up a pen. Please don't be angry.' I wasn't angry, I was gobsmacked! Looking through her revisions I noticed that she had deleted about half the chapter entirely; she considered much of the Dershowitz episode, and particularly his stand on anti-Semitism, irrelevant because it did not reflect Mike's own concern. She also suggested that the chapter 'Never Mind the Reality' could be ditched completely and replaced by the interview with Mike. I declined to make any of these revisions.

A few days after that the first of several lengthy telephone interviews went ahead. Bringing the process full circle, I happened to be in Los Angeles for the first time since my poolside chat with Milken three years ago. Since then, of course, Los Angeles had burned, and it was extraordinary how Milken had argued then, as he would again, that if businesses and banks were not willing to invest in their own communities, and if the people living there did not feel that they had a future, then they would inevitably want to destroy the system instead of work with it.

Sparing me the costs of the collect calls, the interviews were held in the offices of Spurge's Knowledge Exchange, located in the old high yield bond department headquarters. Now that Gumps—the department store favored by Hollywood Wives—was gone as well as Drexel, the building had an empty feel. Walking through a labyrinth of corridors to find Knowledge Exchange, I passed the trading floor where it all went down; it was now just an empty room with a view of the Hollywood Hills. Turn a few more corners and one chances upon the offices of Milken's kid sister Joni, who runs, with her husband Noah, 'Mike's Math Club'. Together they took over the program, which goes around to schools teaching math in a fun way to inner city kids, after her brother went to prison. The office, which is across the hall from Knowledge Exchange, is decorated with Smurfs and a giant poster of Marvel's roster of Superheroes together with letters and cards from devoted kids.

To be sure, there is no such thing as a straightforward interview with Michael Milken and probably never will be, even when Milken emerges from his dependency on people who have his best interests at heart, be they salaried professionals or well-intentioned friends, and finally speaks for himself.

For Milken is not the kind of guy to let go and let it all hang out. Ask him a personal question about how he feels, and you'll be lucky to get more than a summary answer before he skips on to more comfortable ground, treading the path of one of his pet themes.

Rarely does Milken slip out of his positivist personal language with its key words of 'potential' and 'opportunity' to say anything even slightly negative about anyone. And if he does, he will always want to retract it. 'I've spent most of my life focusing on building. I'm looking for the best in people. Other people spend their lives looking for the worst in people and tearing down.' But above all Milken does not like to be seen as someone who talks off the top of his head. Reading back his answers he wanted to have the opportunity to rephrase some of them (and some of the questions too!). Concerned at all times with being clear and focused, he picks his words carefully, sometimes too carefully, for fear of being perceived to be negative or defensive.

In sum, then, Milken is determined to present himself as professional, positive, and, for want of a better word, presentable. This has been interpreted as showing how Milken is living in a massive state of denial. But watching the inanimate speakerphone emitting Milken's thin reedy voice as he talked away, I had to disagree. Occasionally a bemused irony twinkled in his voice, as if this overgrown Boy Scout wasn't quite sure how he had been transported either to the heights of the past or the depths of the present, but this was more wryness than denial.

Sometimes the voice, a tinny signal *de profundis*, was almost drowned out by the noises in the prison hallway where he stood. But Milken just rattled on determinedly like a frail bark keeping to its course in a storm, not allowing any distraction to interrupt his concentration. And as usual it was hard to get a word in edgeways to ask the next question. Reaching the end of one thought he would run straight on to the next without drawing breath, pausing only midway through, at which time you held your tongue waiting for the payoff. Here, then, was not a man who had lost his way, but someone who was making a monumental effort to keep on the course he had mapped out for himself years ago as a Berkeley student. The hatches may be battened down against the storm, but the man is far from shipwrecked. For Milken's control over himself and determination to remain the same person that he has always been is not denial but—given where he is today—all that he has left to cling to. And cling to it he does, with awesome resolve and fixedness of purpose.

AN INTERVIEW WITH MICHAEL MILKEN

WAS IT DIFFICULT TO ADJUST TO LIFE INSIDE?

Yes, it was a difficult adjustment for me. Being separated from my family is extremely painful. The adjustment seems to be hard for most inmates. Unfortunately, most people here don't have positive things happen to them during their stay. There are constant disappointments and rejections. And the system operates in a way that eliminates almost all freedoms and privacy—that's part of the way it works.

It's obviously a traumatic experience and one that I wouldn't wish on anyone. Just being here is an education, but that occurs relatively quickly; about three to six months I think is enough of an education, if one wants to look at it as a learning experience, as the opportunity to focus and think.

WHAT WERE YOUR FIRST DAYS IN PRISON LIKE?

My initial duties during the first six or seven months were as an orderly— a janitor; waxing the floors, washing windows, taking out the trash, weeding—that type of thing. When I used to come home from work it was always my duty to take out the trash, so that stood me well. On the other hand, I'm also much better at doing the laundry today than I was sixteen months ago.

WHAT IS YOUR DAILY ROUTINE?

I get up early in the morning between 4:00 a.m. and 5:00 a.m. depending on how restless I'm feeling. Breakfast is at 6:00 a.m. Currently, most of my days consist of my job—tutoring. So I adjust my day to the inmates' schedules. I tutor some inmates before they go to work in the morning. And some of the others like to study after 10:00 p.m. at night. So I generally don't get into bed until sometime between 11:30 p.m. and 1:30 a.m.

HOW'S THE FOOD; WHERE DO YOU EAT YOUR MEALS?

When I first came in, this camp did not have its own kitchen. Since then, one was built in the building in which I'm housed. All of the inmates eat together. The food is adequate. But it's not the food that's an issue. It's the lack of freedom.

DO YOU WATCH MUCH TV?

I get up in the morning and watch 'World News' on CNN, which gives a summary of what's happening internationally. I periodically watch other news shows, the Discovery Channel, sporting events and 'Star Trek—The New Adventure'. There are only two TVs, so most of the time the regular viewers decide what programs to watch. MTV and VH-1 are probably the most popular channels. From my current location, I'm obviously getting a different perspective of the cable industry than when I had the opportunity to finance it during my career.

WHAT ARE SOME OF YOUR OTHER ACTIVITIES?

There is no formal activity program, since this camp does not have as many facilities as some of the other federal prison camps. I try to keep fit, so I go out and walk, sometimes I run. I play basketball from time to time. And, as part of my tutoring, I play Scrabble with a number of other inmates, in order to increase their spelling and vocabulary skills. Many of them have become quite proficient in Scrabble and have reached a level where they could probably compete in outside tournaments.

Since I'm still involved in a lot of legal issues, I have visits periodically from lawyers. These visits require a lot of preparation, so I work on that, as well.

Over the past three to six months, I have spent time writing—and I hope to use part of my stay in prison to write a book or two.

HAVE YOU HAD A CHANCE TO DO ANY READING?

I try to read each day. I'm probably reading more now than I have read in a long time, except when I commuted to work four to five hours a day by bus. However, there's a strict limit on the number of books you can have at any one time. And I still have a great deal of reading to do that relates to legal matters. But I have had a chance to re-read, among others, works by Mark Twain and Ayn Rand. I've gone back and read a little more about Galileo, Edison and Einstein. I continue to read and study as much as I can about the field of education, as well as about Latin America and the Far East.

TELL ME ABOUT SOME OF THE NEW RELATIONSHIPS YOU'VE FORGED INSIDE.

I don't know if I would phrase it the way you have.... I've met a diverse group of people.

Even though I have spent a lot of time working in the inner-cities both of New York and Los Angeles, the diversity here still amazes me—there are people from all over the world and they have exposed me to a variety of cultures. There are people here originally from India, Pakistan, Afghanistan, Iran, various Pacific islands, Mexico, Peru and Korea.

Given that I'm not allowed to travel physically, I attempt to travel and learn what I can by spending time with different inmates. I talk to them about what it was like living and growing up in their native countries.

Shortly after arriving at camp, to augment my 'travels', I subscribed to *National Geographic*. Over the past sixteen months, I've grown to have a renewed appreciation for that magazine.

WHAT CAN YOU TELL ABOUT YOUR ROOMMATES?
They are all mature men in their forties. We all have young children and we miss our families.

WHAT DO THEY MAKE OF YOU?
I don't know, you would have to ask them that question.

However, I can tell you that in such a stressful environment, no one can keep up a 'false front' for very long. You get to know what people are like when you live in very close quarters. People get to know you for who and what you really are and not what someone else says about you. So whatever made-up stories were about me or who I was, they have, I think, been stripped away by my direct contact with the other inmates over an extended period of time. It's very hard to hide reality from another inmate.

WHAT IS YOUR CURRENT JOB ASSIGNMENT?
I am the camp tutor. The five major areas I'm responsible for are English, Literature, Mathematics, Social Studies and Science.

When I arrived at the facility, I submitted a request to work in the education department. While the camp did not have an education program I was given permission, in addition to my janitor's job, to begin evening sessions, which were open to all of the inmates, in mathematics. The initial sessions began with creating a general understanding for and relationship with numbers and logic. A few months ago I was given permission to begin a bookkeeping and accounting class that is held one night a week.

After about seven months, a formal education program was instituted and I was assigned the job of camp tutor. We have a program for inmates who do not have high school diplomas, and after nine months of hard work on everyone's part 90 percent of those that have taken the GED test have received their high school diplomas.

I was also allowed to start a remedial spelling and reading program, and the camp was able to get 2,000 books when the library closed at the military base in the Presidio. In order to motivate the inmates, I try to incorporate something that interests them. For example, like me, many of them watch 'Star Trek—The New Adventure', and so I try to make up various problems about things they can relate to like star and planet systems, different chemicals, and space and time travel, things like that.

And then to interest them in math and writing, every other week I prepare different stories and mathematical problems.

FOR EXAMPLE?

Since many of the inmates' job assignments involve construction, I have made up a number of puzzles and problems that they can put to practical use every day.

An example was a story I created about a young man named John who has been given an assignment by his father to build a fence around the largest area he could with twenty-seven yards of chain link material. John goes about planning to build his fence using different shapes: a square, a rectangle, a triangle, a trapezoid, a circle, or an oval. The object being to learn about the relationship between different shapes, and their perimeters and areas.

In solving the problem, you discover that the largest area that John could fence in, with a given amount of material, would be in the shape of a circle. That would be the shape that would afford the most efficient use of the material provided.

To make the story more interesting, I add in John's girlfriend Mary, who is an excellent math student, who comes over to his house to help with the project.

WHAT IS IT YOU ENJOY MOST ABOUT TEACHING?

I particularly enjoy interaction with children, especially that moment when you can just sense the light switch go on in a child who suddenly understands a concept or is able to solve a problem.

What I have enjoyed most in camp is creating educational puzzles and games, which inmates are allowed during visiting hours to play with their kids. One of the inmates whose children are not able to visit him sends one or two games and puzzles home to them every week. He has told me that this has provided a nice written dialogue between him and his children.

Another thing that has given me great pleasure is seeing the progress of a number of the inmates. I had one student who could not multiply 2×3 just a few months ago, and last night he was figuring out complicated algebra problems. Just watching him beam in front of the class and seeing the other inmates' disbelief at how much he has learned is really quite a rewarding experience for me. And a number of people who could not read now can read and write. I've actually had a chance to improve my motivating and teaching techniques in an extremely depressing environment.

AT WORK YOU USED TO HAVE TWO PHONES STRAPPED TO YOUR EAR AND HUNDREDS OF LINES AT YOUR DISPOSAL. HOW DO YOU COPE WITH THE RESTRICTIONS INSIDE?

I can assure you that separation from my family was much harder to cope with than not being able to pick up a telephone. But, right now, being incarcerated, the telephone is one of my only means of communicating with the outside world.

The use of the phone here is limited, since we all have to share a few phones, which are located in a hallway. You can talk to a person for ten or fifteen minutes if you want to—you might have to wait to get to a phone for a while. Calls are monitored by the prison and you can only make collect calls. I try to speak with my wife and children every evening. My children often go over their homework assignments with me.

BESIDES YOUR FAMILY, WHO ELSE HAVE YOU HAD A CHANCE TO SPEAK WITH SINCE YOU HAVE BEEN IN PRISON?

In the last year and a half, I've been able to speak with a number of people. I've called the children in my 'extended family' that I try to stay in touch with. These include a number of disadvantaged kids that I had worked closely with at the HELP Group in Los Angeles and the Milken Scholars from Harlem in New York. They also send cards and letters telling me about what's happening in school and sharing their ups and downs.

Others I've tried to stay in touch with are a number of teachers and educators I have had a chance to meet and work with over the years. This dialogue has been invaluable to me. Changes in our society can often be seen first in the classroom; this has always provided me with special insights for the future.

DO YOU EVER SPEAK WITH SOME OF YOUR FORMER COLLEAGUES?

Yes. I have spent time speaking with a number of people I've met over the years in the course of my career. I called Lee Iacocca some time when I saw the latest headlines saying that Chrysler was going bankrupt. I told him it was like old times! I told him that this was about the fourth time in my life that I had heard the same old story about Chrysler and since it didn't prove true before, I was sure it wouldn't prove true again. I was pleased to hear that he views this latest challenge as another opportunity for him to build a strong base for his company and to go forward and solve his problems.

HOW ARE YOU AND YOUR FAMILY COPING WITH YOUR CURRENT SEPARATION?

We're trying to cope as best we can, but it's tough. I saw my wife and children today. As always, it was painful to say goodbye. Plus, I'm not there with them on a daily basis to play the role I'd like to play. I've written out games and puzzles for my daughter and we might go over them on her next visit. But it's hard, not being there, to share the responsibilities with my wife. Judging by how the children are still doing, she continues to do a great job.

DO YOU GET TO SEE MUCH OF YOUR FAMILY?

Not as much as I used to; visiting hours have been reduced substantially about 60 percent from what they were when I first came in.

WHY?

I don't know, they didn't confer with me on that decision. We're allowed about fifteen to twenty hours per month. My family comes as often as possible. I also get to visit with about ten or so other family members and close friends, when time permits.

TELL ME ABOUT YOUR CHILDREN

I have three children, two boys and a girl. My oldest son is at college and continues to be interested in writing, languages and mathematics. He has a tremendous aptitude for different languages and the cultures they represent. In high school he studied Latin, Greek and Spanish, and in college he has chosen Japanese and Spanish as two of his majors. He loves to write, so maybe like my wife he'll be a writer. At one time he wanted to write mystery stories. I've never pushed him in any direction in terms of studies at all.

It's funny how things turn out. When I was young, my father took me on client visits. He was an accountant who took an active interest in the success of his clients' businesses. I learned a lot from those trips and I think that might have been one of the reasons that I became interested in financing small and medium-sized companies.

With my own children, while travelling to different cities, we have stopped in to visit a number of companies and people with whom I had relationships over the years. My oldest son and I spent some time in Mexico reviewing the Maquiladora program. We've also spent time studying and discussing the future dependence of our country on the peaceful development of Latin America, particularly Mexico. Through these discussions, both of us have had a chance to focus on the increasing similarities of our culture with the culture of Latin America. Like the influence of traveling with my father had on me, it's very possible that this exposure sparked an interest in him to learn more about the history, languages and cultures of these areas.

My other two children still live at home. My youngest son is very knowledgeable about computers and electronics. You know, every family needs at least one member of the family who knows how to work all the new appliances. So any time there's something you don't know how to work you go and call him over. Most people I would say forty and older don't like reading a five-page instruction book on how to use their new appliance. One of the great things about having teenagers in the home is that they're used to it, or already know how to work them. I've often thought that what was needed was a 900 number in the United States you can call up when you buy the new appliance and someone could tell you how to work it.

Everyone has their own interests. My daughter is particularly interested in music and dance and is extremely outgoing. She is a number of years younger than our two sons and has given the whole family a chance to see things through her eyes. One of my fondest memories is of a family trip to Italy a few years ago. In Venice, while we were all looking up, my daughter was seeing things closer to the ground. She was keeping track of all the different cats that were here and there in the nooks and crannies. She's probably one of the few people who could tell you about the cats of Venice.

HOW DO YOU EXPLAIN YOUR SITUATION TO YOUR CHILDREN?
We have family discussions about what's going on and we speak rather openly about these matters. We had spent some time talking about it before I made my final decision to plead. In our discussions, my wife and I tried to give examples of how the truth has been twisted by others from a historical perspective, and we compared that with my predicament.

WHAT ARE YOUR DARKEST MOMENTS?
There have been many. When you are incarcerated, problems at home seem to be greatly magnified. But for me the most distressing moments are when members of my family and friends are ill and I am not able to be there to help. This is one of my biggest fears and concerns. And now my wife faces this burden alone. Not being there for her, not being there to support my children, tears me apart. It's also quite depressing missing those moments in our lives which will not be repeated, like my oldest son's high school graduation.

DO YOU SEE LIGHT AT THE END OF THE TUNNEL?

Yes, I think so—I always see light at the end of all tunnels. But over the years, I have probably been too optimistic, and there have been many times when I thought I could see light at the end of the tunnel, only to discover that it was an on-coming train.

I have learned not to set my expectations too high, so that my disappointments can be kept to a minimum.

Someday this will be over and my family and I will be able to continue on with the rest of our lives. Unfortunately, that day still appears to be a long way off.

OVER THE YEARS MANY OTHERS HAVE SPOKEN FOR YOU—DREXEL BURNHAM LAMBERT, THE PUBLIC RELA-TIONS FIRM OF ROBINSON LAKE LERER AND MONTGOM-ERY, YOUR LAWYERS AND SUNDRY AUTHORS—DON'T YOU THINK THAT THIS PREVENTED THE PUBLIC FROM GETTING TO KNOW YOU AND UNDERSTANDING WHAT YOU WERE DOING?

I should have gone public a long time ago. I have made a lot of mistakes. One mistake was having others speak for me and allowing people who had never met or spoken to me and didn't have a clue as to what I believed in and stood for, create a false picture.

In my professional career, I did communicate openly with others, whether it was through direct personal contact, at speaking events, or at Drexel's Annual Conferences. Among other things, I tried to warn them that they must change with the times. I also tried hard to convince Drexel Burnham that they were headed down the wrong path. But I didn't really understand other people's objectives and agendas at that time. They figured they could make money rather than focus on the issues. Today, I understand things more clearly and possibly would have done things much differently. The frustration becomes enormous when you are blamed for the very things that you had spoken out so strongly against.

WHAT WERE YOUR EXPECTATIONS FROM THE PUBLIC RELATIONS FIRM ROBINSON LAKE AND LERER?

I don't know what my expectations were really. Contrary to what most people believe, I never had a 'PR strategy'. Sometimes I wish I had. But my first lawyer, Edward Bennett Williams—whom I identified with closely—had a simple philosophy: "Never speak to the media, just speak in the courtroom.' Obviously, one has to re-evaluate that strategy in the instantaneous media environment we live in today. And because there was a massive amount of media stories, you at least needed someone to take a phone call, so the attorneys hired Robinson Lake to handle these from a defencive position only. Their mandate was to 'do nothing' other than deal with the reporters and the stories that were being written. Obviously, with hindsight, that strategy was not successful.

BUT WHY WERE YOU SO MEDIA SHY? YOU SEEM SO COMFORTABLE AND CONFIDENT IN PUBLIC?

I don't believe I was 'media shy'. Anyone who could jump around and lead cheers in front of 5,000 people at age sixteen is obviously not shy. Many years later, at Drexel's annual conferences, I spoke in front of an audience of 3,000 through most of four days.

When I started my career I had every intention of maintaining a separation between my professional life and my private life. I didn't realize that I wouldn't have a choice. If I had been told there was a choice before joining the securities business—that if I wanted to become successful in this field, I would have to become a public figure— I might have picked another career for myself and probably would have become a full-time professor.

BUT EVEN AS PROFESSOR YOU WOULD HAVE BEEN BOUND TO END UP IN THE LIMELIGHT

Maybe, but as a teacher you have a different role than you do in the role I chose.

I really didn't understand how much power the media had. My wife has pointed out to me that during medieval times they used the rack for punishment and in modern times they use the press. I wasn't prepared for that.

My family and I are still surprised by all the lies and misinformation. For example you can say 'a' and the person writes 'b'. One of the things that quite surprised me is the ability of people to totally fabricate something, just totally make it up. Whatever you might call it—creative journalism, creative media—you can today, to get your point across, just re-enact something, like a person saying, 'You were there' and the story can be totally fictitious. The person wasn't there! By describing how people look, what they're wearing, the location, you can, by making it vivid, give the impression that it really happened even if it never did. And when it comes to finance, unlike other things like sports, journalists have a lot more latitude in what they can write, since most people don't have a basis to judge it by and will therefore believe the most unusual things.

One of the positives that came out of my first courtroom testimony in New York was that my oldest son got to sit in the courtroom, and observe what actually happened for himself versus how the press and others subsequently reported the same event.

Something that happened during the coverage of the trial typifies the sort of media reporting that has been going on. There were pictures on TV and in the papers that purported to be pictures of my 'wife' and my 'son(s)'—but the people shown were neither my wife nor my son(s)! I clipped one of these articles for posterity's sake, because it was symbolic of the stories about my case over that last five or six years.

Maybe if I had focused more on history, this would have been clearer to me. History is full of stories of people who have been maligned and misrepresented.

You know, it's very difficult to deal with images unless you speak out aggressively, and I think people underestimate the difficulty of speaking out. Even prominent national figures often can't get unbiased coverage and their point of view is incorrectly reported. And these people have much more freedom of speech than I. If someone as powerful and visible as a presidential candidate finds it impossible to deal with misinformation, you can only imagine how difficult it has been for someone like me who has an entire legal system bearing down on him. But you live and learn, and one thing I have observed watching the recent candidate, is that they have chosen to speak directly with the American public—on the news, talk shows and even MTV—at least this way they can be sure that the public sees and hears what they're saying and not what someone else says they're saying.

In the long run I still can communicate and in the long run there are ways to address people's misperceptions or mistaken current belief. But you can't do it in fifteen minutes and you can't do it in an hour; you might not be able to do it in a year, or five years.

WHY DIDN'T YOU TALK TO JAMES B. STEWART?

There are many reasons I chose not to speak with Mr. Stewart, some of them I mentioned earlier, particularly following my lawyer's advice. I also had a chance to read many of the articles that he wrote and it appeared to me that either he distorted the facts or he totally disregarded them, so my conclusion was that there was no reason to speak with him.

One of my lawyers did speak with Stewart regarding certain issues in his book and presented him with indisputable facts. Nevertheless, after being confronted with the truth, Stewart went ahead and regurgitated the same inaccurate stories anyway. I often wondered how a so-called respected journalist could get the facts so wrong.

So one of my lawyers contacted more than three hundred people whom Stewart wrote about, or who had communicated directly with the court. These people had first-hand knowledge and were involved in the actual transactions at Drexel. The results were shocking. Out of the three hundred or so people called, only one had ever been contacted by or spoken with Stewart. And even with that one person, Stewart wrote the exact opposite of what that person had told him.

But what topped it off was when I saw Stewart for the first time, on CNN's program 'Crossfire'. It was staggering to hear him say, in front of millions of people, that he had met and spoken with me. For a minute I thought I was in the 'Twilight Zone'—since I never met or spoke with this man in my entire life! The moderator Robert Novak confronted him with this fact. Realizing that he had been caught in a lie, Stewart suddenly backtracked and changed the subject to the reliability of his sources. If he could not honestly answer a simple question—like whether or not he ever met or spoke to me—imagine how he could have distorted an actual conversation with me?

WHAT IS YOUR ACCOUNT OF CONNIE BRUCK'S CLAIM THAT YOU TRIED TO BUY OFF HER BOOK?

Absurd. This allegation is not even worthy of being elevated to the level of a discussion.

WHAT ARE YOUR THOUGHTS ABOUT THE JUNK BOND MARKET TODAY?

The market has obviously recovered, but it's difficult for me to call the market's current performance a 'comeback'.

This has always been a sound, viable market. 1989 and 1990 were difficult years, due to many companies having the wrong capital structure and a panic-like environment created by over-zealous market critics, which resulted in unnecessary regulation. Because of this, many securities' prices were artificially depressed for a short period of time.

There were also transactions that had been put together earlier and were correct for their time but needed to be restructured when the environment changed by the late 80s and early 90s.

The high yield bond market has never been a homogeneous market, and how people have described it has been quite distorted. It has always been a multi-tiered market. The first tier has proven to be the most stable and even produced positive rates of return of 10–12 percent in 1990.

This recent period isn't much different from what had occurred during the 1969-70 period, 1974-75, and 1980-81. In all of these cases the market had a short term correction, only to come back stronger than ever. What was different, this time, was that the combination of rhetoric and regulation short-circuited the market's natural cycle.

This is almost as ridiculous as banning western movies because certain critics don't like westerns. Providing equal access to capital is what a free enterprise system or free market is all about. The American capital market has been the envy of all the world and what the Eastern Europeans and others are tying so hard to emulate. Unfortunately, some people in the country are trying hard to cut off this access to capital.

Today the majority of high yield or 'junk' issues have risen dramatically in price and now trade at a premium, or have been repurchased by the companies that issued them. So, much like similar periods of market downturns in the 70s and 80s, investors who held on to their investments because they understood corporate credit, profited when the high yield's market value increased by more than $80 billion over the last few years.

I have often used—when explaining this to my children—the analogy of a farmer who had his allocation of water suddenly and unexpectedly eliminated. Just as water is necessary to grow crops and maintain a successful farm, so is capital necessary to build and sustain a business.

In the case of the farmer, even though his farm is thriving, operating efficiently and employing many people, if someone with ulterior motives suddenly shuts off the water supply even the most successful well-managed farm will ultimately fail. And if the water was turned off for long enough the one who shut it down could say, 'See, I told you that land isn't any good for farming.'

What choice does the farmer have if he wants to survive? He must act quickly. He must cut back the number of acres he is farming, and because he has to reduce production, he must now lay off workers and cut back expansion plans. The farmer's primary focus has now shifted to one of survival.

In the end, turning off the water not only damages the farm, it also hurts the entire community, since many other companies and people are also dependent upon the success of that farm; consumers, supermarkets, truckers and so on. There is a domino effect. With workers being laid off and the community already in an economic slump, real estate values also drop.

One of the great misfortunes that occurred due to all the rhetoric is that people were convinced not to believe in themselves. The absolutely absurd things that some writers have said have done enormous harm to this country by making people think things totally the reverse of what they are. Even though they had to know that what they were saying was wrong, the vindictiveness directed against me, and this market, was evident in the article that appeared on the front page in *The Wall Street Journal* the day before my sentencing. In the story, they administered last rites and pronounced the high yield market 'dead', while at the same time totally distorting my philosophies and theories about investing.

It's extremely unfortunate that the *Journal*, the most prestigious financial paper in the world, was so wrong in its reporting, because it helped contribute to the severe cutback in access to capital for thousands of companies. By using pejorative terms such as 'junk', reporters helped to see to it that many corporations, who have supported communities and created jobs, were red-lined by financial institutions. If people understood what was being said, they would have felt differently. The real message was absurd: I don't want any of my money invested in a financial institution that would finance a company which could give me, my family or my neighbor a job. In other words, as Groucho Marx once commented, 'I wouldn't want to belong to any club that would have me as a member.'

Unfortunately, these misconceptions have penalized our entire country. Today, because of the cutoff of capital, is it any wonder that unemployment is up, job formation is down and our economy appears to be stuck in an unpromising static condition?

What is so ironic is that many of the loudest critics of high yield bond are now singing its praises and reaping its benefits. By the second half of 1992, only 1½ years since the market was pronounced 'dead', record numbers of new junk bond issues have come to market. It's not surprising that junk bonds, which were one of the best investments of the 1970s and 1980s, will likely prove to be one of the best investments of the 1990s.

WHAT'S YOUR VIEW OF THE SO-CALLED ROARING 80s?

My views of the last twenty years are quite different from what appear to be the popular perceptions. When I reflect on the 70s and what you refer to as the 'roaring 80s', I remember it being a period of job formation and a time of opportunity for new, growing and restructuring businesses. Many inroads were made by business people outside the mainstream—including many minority-owned companies—despite, not with, the assistance of the government.

Unfortunately, as the 80s were winding down, much of this progress was derailed by oppressive regulation and the resulting shortage of capital. By the time the 1990s began, we were pretty much back to square one. Today, it is even more difficult for innovative, talented individuals to finance the companies on which our future depends.

WHAT ARE YOU PLANS FOR THE FUTURE AFTER YOUR RELEASE?

First, I'm looking forward to spending some time with my family. I would also enjoy taking a long car trip with them, driving around the country, visiting and talking with people.

I plan to continue my active involvement in the field of education and I would like to complete and publish the books I have begun writing.

WHAT SPECIFICALLY DO YOU SEE YOURSELF DOING IN EDUCATION?

One of the first projects I look forward to working on is an education entertainment cable channel. I had begun working on this concept a few years ago, with a number of people from the entertainment industry, including Bob Pitman and Steve Ross, from Time-Warner. But those plans could not be fully developed and were put on hold when I began my prison sentence. What I envision is educators on cable TV teaching seven days a week twenty-four hours a day. The possibilities are endless.

Over the years I have had a chance to visit many classrooms and found individual teachers whose presentations were as exciting as some of today's most popular entertainers. Whether it was time spent in Jaime Escalante's math class at Garfield High in California or my visits to history classes in New England, each of them could have been exciting segments for a program. I remember one visit to a history class where the teacher would dress in the costume of the period he was teaching. If it was the Revolutionary War, he would dress up as George Washington, and, standing in the middle of the room, deliver a forty-minute monologue. These were as entertaining as one-man or -woman theatrical shows, only they were more educational.

TELL ME ABOUT THE BOOKS THAT YOU ARE WORKING ON

There are a couple of books I have been working on: One is about the private enterprise system and its relationship to society. This book will focus on how to build a community, how to build a country, how to build a company and what role capital plays in that building process. I want to demonstrate the importance of finance and how non-investment-grade companies created jobs in this country.

I want to draw upon my experience with individuals, including those I have met during my stay at federal prison camp. Here at the camp there are fewer than two hundred people and yet they represent about twenty different countries. This is not unlike the diversity we see in our inner-cities. I remember visiting a junior high school in LA where forty different languages were spoken, with English as a first language being fourth or fifth down the list. My experience then and now has reinforced for me the concept of America as a melting pot. Each individual has something special to contribute.

Sadly, this country continues to put too much value on its factories, its buildings and its real estate. Cuba also made this fatal mistake; they believed their country was great because of their sugarcane and their factories. But ultimately it was their people that made the difference. When a lot of the best and brightest left, they were in trouble. Our country needs to be refocused on its most valuable resource—our people. I want to write about how we can address that.

The second book will be a more personal story about my experiences over the last twenty-five years.

I want to give the reader the opportunity to feel and experience what I have, through my own eyes, and show them what happened from the point of view of someone who is not a lawyer, not a politician, and someone who is not seeking publicity or attention. Maybe this will prevent what has happened to me from happening to someone else, and help them from making the same mistakes that I have made. Everyone else has written about this subject from the outside, but writing about it from the inside might be much more useful.

What this book requires is for me to thrust myself back, and turn the clock back to the 70s and 80s and let people understand what was going on. Transactions do exist and are a matter of record, which is often the opposite of what people perceive them to be.

So that by taking people back to what was actually going on at the time and by showing them what I was thinking and doing they will see that this was, in fact, the exact opposite of what people have written.

It's much the same as if a person was focusing his camera, in order to capture the many different organizations who had set up tables exhibiting their particular points of view, at the corner of Telegraph and Bancroft at the University of California at Berkeley during the 1960s. If the camera-man zoomed in onone of the tables, and that group represented a very insignificant part of the entire student body (with maybe three students standing around while others might have had hundreds of students gathered around), the total picture would have been blown out of proportion. And that is similar to my situation. By focusing on a single transaction or event, the whole picture was distorted for the viewing public.

Now I am going to attempt to capture the true picture. I hope to show what actually occurred and document this in excruciating detail so that people will feel that they were there. In other words, I will rebuild the set.

DO YOU THINK PEOPLE WILL BE INTERESTED IN THE DETAILS OF YOUR STORY BY THE TIME IT GETS INTO PRINT?

I sure hope so. At least my mother will buy it. Timing is very important in getting a story out. History has often shown that a subject cannot be correctly or openly addressed if it runs counter the conventional wisdom of the period—even if that conventional wisdom is 100 percent wrong.

Sometimes people don't want to focus and don't want to know and are willing to reject everything that runs counter to their thoughts. There are many other times in history where public perception of certain events has been totally distorted and, given time, whether it be six months or ten years, the public has been awakened to the fact that their previous perceptions were incorrect.

For example, in Brecht's 'Galileo', as I recall, Galileo invited some scientists over to his house for dinner with the intent that afterwards they would all look in the telescope and see for themselves what he had seen—that the earth revolves around the sun. But his plan didn't work. Galileo assumed that they wanted to know the truth. They did not. So, even if they had seen that planets revolved around the sun, they would have refused to believe it. So there was no reason to look.

Similarly, in my case, the truth has not been lost, it just has not been given a chance to come out. I don't view this as a short term project and it will have to be written in a form that people will be able to read and understand. Maybe 1993 will be the right time for me to begin to tell the story and set the record straight.

HOW DOES WRITING COMPARE WITH BEING ON THE TRADING DESK?

Obviously I miss being on the trading desk, especially the interaction with others and seeing things first-hand. But writing has been therapeutic for me. It also gives me a chance to go back and review transactions and events from a historical perspective. Milton Friedman once told me, before I went into prison, 'be more introspective'. Writing and research have helped me do exactly that.

WHAT ARE YOUR THOUGHTS ABOUT THE L.A. RIOTS AND THE PROBLEMS OF THE INNER CITIES IN GENERAL?

I was able to watch a good six hours of the coverage of them, and my feeling was one of frustration and sadness. It was especially painful to me, since I've had a chance to spend a lot of time in South Central Los Angeles, no time recently, but a lot of time prior to this. A number of programs my family has been involved with are centered there, and so I have seen these problems first hand.

I think the unrest was a clear symbol of what needs to be done. One of the reasons I went to Wall Street in the first place was to try and address these problems. While many of my colleagues at Berkeley in the 60s chose to work in the community or the Peace Corps, I chose the securities business as my avenue to effect social change. Through my work I realized that capital was a crucial ingredient for creating jobs, increasing corporate productivity and enhancing global competitiveness. Therefore the greatest challenge was to help 'democratize' capital. My vision was to redirect capital and participation to all people.

When people who are becoming the majority feel disenfranchised, even though they live in a democracy, ultimately they will strike out any way they can out of frustration. We've got to make these people feel that they're part of this private enterprise system so they want to embrace it, work in it, not destroy it. And we are a long way from achieving that goal. And they cannot be made a part of it when they feel excluded.

Unfortunately, many of our major banking institutions, in the late 70s and early 80s, mistakenly perceive their lending opportunities to be in developing countries, rather than in the inner cities of our country.

So they forsook promising investment opportunities over here for illusionary opportunities in other countries. The trillion dollars lent by Western industrialized nations to developing countries, has resulted in hundreds of billions of dollars in both opportunity costs and actual losses. That trillion could have been invested in South Central LA. The saddest commentary of all is that these loans didn't even benefit the borrowing countries of a macro basis, but really just provided liquidity for some foreign nationals to transfer their money out of their own country. Now the losses from these loans eroded the capital base of many of our largest financial institutions, thus severely reducing the money available for our own communities, including Los Angeles.

For years, as a leader of the Western world, we've been focused on threats from abroad. But today the biggest challenges are in our own backyard. There are a lot of lessons we can learn from looking at what happened in the Soviet Union. In the end, the upheaval in that country was generated from within. I felt the minutes they gave more freedom to Eastern European countries—the satellites—that was the end of the world as they knew it. They'd never be able to reverse the process, once that process had begun.

What occurred in Los Angeles had been brewing for some time. The civil unrest rang a loud alarm that we have severely neglected the people in our urban areas. The message is clear: Our private enterprise system cannot survive without a strong society. On the other hand, it is the private sector's primary responsibility to make sure that people really have a stake in their own communities.

HOW WOULD YOU REBUILD L.A.?

There are no easy answers or 'quick' fixes. We didn't get into this situation overnight, so it will take time to rebuild.

Some of the first steps I would take would be to go to the universities and enlist the help of both professors and students. I would also try to tap into another major resource—seasoned business people, who are still in the prime of life, whom I refer to as 'the salt and pepper generation'. They have a lot of experience as well as expertise in running and managing companies, and could work as partners in inner-city ventures. We seem to have ignored this valuable group of our population. I would also go to the companies and individuals who have a vested interest, particularly those in tourism and those who own real estate in our inner-cities.

One example might be working with Disney, Universal or Time-Warner; transferring their silk screening of T-shirts from other parts of the world to South Central LA. Since each company could probably sell millions of T-shirts a year, a manufacturing operation could be set up in the inner-city, which could operate efficiently while employing and training people who live there. There's probably many more ideas like this one.

Once we've identified jobs, we have to make sure that we have a work force that is prepared to fill them. If not, the jobs will go to people who live outside of the community. Therefore it's also critical that we train the people who live in the community so that they can fill the jobs that become available.

Obviously, education has to come first. And this must begin with a realization that educators are some of the most important people in our communities. About ten years ago, my family's foundation began a program that recognizes and rewards educators. We felt it was important that people within their community acknowledge the fact that educators are critical to our country's survival. Not enough is being done for our teachers.

My vision of a town or a city is really one that is thriving because the people who live there are afforded job opportunities and they are qualified to fill them.

Providing capital to entrepreneurs in the inner cities is also important. From my own experience in establishing mentor and outreach programs in West Philadelphia at the University of Pennsylvania I have learnt that there were very few self-employed people in the surrounding urban areas, and that their businesses were quite small. Anytime that their business was poised to grow, they couldn't get the capital they needed. So they would end up selling their business or closing it down and going to work for someone else. I think one of the things you would try to do there would be to make sure people could maintain their ownership or control of their own business as they grew; give them the feeling that they could open up more stores rather than sell it to someone else and become one store of a division, one in chain.

This would also help their young people, who need more business role models and contact with members of the community who can provide them with work experience. Obviously if a family member—a cousin, uncle, aunt—has an ownership stake in a business, they're much more likely to get a summer or part-time job. This will help bring the concept of 'The American Dream' back into our inner-cities.

THERE ARE MANY PEOPLE TODAY WHO ACCUSE YOU OF
BEING IN A STATE OF DENIAL AND BLAMING EVERYONE
ELSE FOR YOUR SITUATION. WHAT DO YOU SAY ABOUT
THAT?

First they accused me of not speaking out. Now that I am speaking, the
same people are saying 'I'm in a state of denial' or 'I'm blaming others'. I
can only assume that's because I'm not saying what they want to hear. I
frankly think it would have been tough for those who used this technique
of totally twisting the meaning of the silence imposed on me by my
counsel to reverse themselves once I was able to speak for myself.
Ultimately, the public will have to make up its own mind. Since they have
never heard my side of the story, they hardly have a basis for choosing.
This sort of reversal has already happened with the press coverage of the
junk bond market. About a year ago the press began to write positive
stories, even though they had previously written off the market as a house
of cards. I hope that in time, as the truth emerges, they will start to report
it where I am concerned, as well.

BIBLIOGRAPHY

BOOKS

Ailes, Roger (with Jon Krausher), *You Are the Message*, New York: Doubleday, 1988.

Bianco, Anthony, *Rainmaker: the Saga of Jeff Beck, Wall Street's Mad Dog*, New York: Random House, 1991.

Bruck, Connie, *The Predator's Ball*, New York: The American Lawyer/Simon and Schuster, 1988.

Burrough, Bryan, and John Helyar, *Barbarians at the Gate*, New York: Harper, 1990.

Chernow, Ron, *The House of Morgan*, London: Simon and Schuster, 1990.

Dershowitz, Alan M. *Chutzpah*, Boston: Little, Brown, 1991.

Dershowitz, Alan M., *Reversal of Fortune*, New York: Random House, 1986.

Dershowitz, Alan M. *Taking Liberties*, Chicago: Contemporary Books, 1988.

Dunne, Dominick, *People Like Us*, New York: Crown, 1988.

Ehrlich, Judith Ramsey (and Barry J. Rehfeld), *The New Crowd*, New York: Little Brown and Company, 1989.

Fairchild, John, *Chic Savages*, New York: Simon and Schuster, 1989.

Frantz, Douglas, *Levine & Co.*, New York: Henry Holt and Company, 1987.

Gilder, George, *Life After Television*, Knoxville: Whittle Direct Books, 1990.

Grant, R.W., *Tom Smith and His Incredible Bread Machine*, Manhattan Beach: Quandary House, 1964.

Hofstadter, Richard, *The Paranoid Style of American Politics*, Chicago: University of Chicago Press, 1965.

Johnston, Moira, *Takeover*, New York: Bantam Press, 1987.

Lapham, Lewis H., *Money and Class in America*, New York: Ballantine Books, 1988.

Lewis, Michael, *Liar's Poker*, London: W.W. Norton, 1989.

Mills, Nicolaus (editor), *Culture in an Age of Money*, New York: Ivan R. Dee, 1990.

Smith, Adam, *The Roaring Eighties*, New York: Summit Books, 1988.

Smith, Roy C., *The Money Wars*, New York: Truman Talley Books, Dutton, 1990.

Stein, Benjamin, *Hollywood Days, Hollywood Nights: Diary of a Mad Screenwriter*, New York: Bantam, 1988.

Stewart, James B. *The Prosecutors*, New York: Simon and Schuster, 1987.

Stewart, James B. *Den of Thieves*, New York: Simon and Schuster, 1991.

Stone, Dan G., *April Fools*, New York: Donald I. Fine Inc, 1991.

Thomas, Michael M., *Hanover Place*, New York: Warner Books, 1990.

Toffler, Alvin, *Future Shock*, New York: Bantam, 1990.

Vise, David A. (and Steve Coll). *Eagle on the Street*, New York: Charles Scribner's Sons, 1991.

Winans, R. Foster, *Trading Secrets*, New York: St Martin's Press, 1986.

Yago, Glenn, *Junk Bonds*, Oxford: Oxford University Press, 1991.

NEWSPAPERS, MAGAZINES AND OTHER SOURCES

Abromowitz, Rachel, 'Why Won't the Caged Bird Sing?', *Manhattan Inc.*, June 1989.

Adler, Stephen J., 'Working Girl', *Wall Street Journal*, 24 March 1989.

Anon, 'From Milken to the Mafia, a Talk with Rudy Giuliani', *Barrons*, 26 November 1989.

Armstrong, Michael (with William Aronwald, Donald Cohn, Robert Kushner, Arthur Liman, Richard Uviller), 'Giuliani's Record as US Attorney', reprinted in *Amsterdam News*, 11 November 1989.

Berman, Phyllis (with Katherine Wesiman), 'Be Wise, Equitize', *Forbes*, 27 November 1989.

Baumgold, Julie, 'Dancing on the Lip of the Volcano: Christian Lacroix's Crash Chic', *New York* magazine, 30 November 1987.

Bianco, Anthony, 'Mad Dog', *New York* magazine, 11 March 1991.

Brenner, Marie, 'The Man Who Fell to Earth', *Vanity Fair*, August 1989.

Brenner, Marie, 'Insider Raiding', *Vanity Fair*, May 1990.

Brill, Steven, 'When the Government Goes Judge Shopping', *The American Lawyer*, November 1988.

Brown, Tina, 'Gayfryd Tales Over', *Vanity Fair*.

Budd, John F., 'Omissions Hurt CEO Ethics Rating', *Vital Speeches of the Day*, March 1989.

Bruck, Connie, 'The Old Boy and the New Boy', *New Yorker*, 8 May 1989.

Bruck, Connie, 'Billion Dollar Mind', *New Yorker*, 7 August 1989.

Burrough, Bryan, 'Just Call Me Mike: Drexel's Mr Milken Works on His Image', *Wall Street Journal*, 12 October 1988.

Burrough, Bryan, 'Self-Made Man: Top Deal Maker leaves a Trail of Deception in Wall Street Rise', *Wall Street Journal*, 22 January 1990.

Byron, Christopher, 'Sweatshirt Justice', *New York* magazine, 2 October 1989.

Byron, Christopher, 'Judgment Day', *New York* magazine, 24 September 1990.

Byron, Christopher, 'The Phantom of Wall Street', *New York* magazine, 4 December 1989.

Byron, Christopher, 'Drexel's Fall', *New York* magazine, 19 March 1990.

Coffee Jr., John C., 'Freeman's Plea Confuses Civil, Criminal Law', *Manhattan Lawyer*, 2 October 1989.

Cohen, Laurie P., 'Drexel's New Television Ads Tug at the Heart but Fudge the Facts', *Wall Street Journal*.

Cohen, Laurie P., 'The Final Days. Drexel Itself Made Firm's Sudden Demise All But Inevitable', *Wall Street Journal*, 26 February 1990.

Collins, Nancy, 'Gotcha! Cross-examining Crime-buster Giuliani', *New York* magazine, 25 May 1987.

Conant, Jennet, 'The Trials of Arthur Liman', *Vanity Fair,* June 1991.

Conant, Jennet, 'Billionaire Bashing', *Newsweek*, 30 May 1988.

Crovitz, L. Gordon, 'How the Rico Monster Mauled Wall Street', *Notre Dame Law Review*, volume 65, issue 5, 1990.

Crovitz, L. Gordon, 'RICO's Broken Commandments', *Wall Street Journal*, 26 January 1989.

Crovitz, L. Gordon, 'Mother of Mercy, Will Drexel Be the End of RICO?', *Wall Street Journal*, 21 February 1990.

Crovitz, L. Gordon, 'Milken and His Enemies', *National Review*, 1 October 1990.

Crovitz, L. Gordon, 'RICO and the Man', *Reason*, March 1990.

Dannen, Fredric, 'Arthur Liman for the Defence', *Institutional Investor*, December 1989.

Dershowitz, Alan M., 'An Open Letter', *New York Times*, 17 October 1991.

Dobrzynski, Judith H., 'After Drexel', *Business Week*, 26 February 1990.

Domenici, Pete V., 'Fools and their Takeover Bonds', *Wall Street Journal*, 14 May 1985.

Drexel Burnham Lambert, 'Financing America's Future', 1988.

Drexel Burnham Lambert, 'America's Working Capital', 1988.

Drexel Burnham Lambert, '1988 Annual High Yield Report', 1988.

Drexel Burnham Lambert, '1989 Annual High Yield Report', 1989.

Drexel Burnham Lambert, 'Building America's Industries', 1988.

Drexel Burnham Lambert, 'Building America', September 1988.

Eichenwald, Kurt, 'Wages Even Wall Street Can't Stomach', *New York Times*, 3 April 1989.

Elias, Christopher, 'Milken', *Insight* 12 June 1989.

Epstein, Edward Jay, 'Capital Punishment', *Manhattan Inc.*, February 1989.

Epstein, Edward Jay, 'How Mike Milken Made a Billion Dollars and Changed the Face of American Capitalism', *Manhattan Inc.*, September 1987.

Epstein, Edward Jay, 'The Junk Bond King's Next Move', *Los Angeles Times*, 30 August 1987.

Epstein, Edward Jay, 'The New Greed Baiting', *Manhattan Inc.*, 30 August 1988.

Faludy, Susan C., 'The Reckoning: Safeway LBO Yields Vast Profits but

Exacts a Heavy Human Toll', *Wall Street Journal*, 16 May 1990.

Forstmann, Theodore, J. 'Corporate Finance, Leveraged to the Hilt', 25 October 1988.

Friend, Tad, 'Michael Milken Free At Last!', *Esquire*, May 1991.

Fromson, Brett Duval, 'The Last Days of Drexel Burnham', *Fortune*, 12 May 1990.

Fromson, Brett Duval, 'Did Drexel Get What It Deserved?', *Fortune*, 12 March 1990.

Galen, Michael, 'Got Big Deals, Big Problems, Big Bucks? Get Arthur Liman', *Business Week*, 15 May 1989.

Gotschall, Mary G, 'The Machine Behind Michael Milken', *Regardie* magazine, January 1991.

Greenwald, John, 'A Game of Greed', *Time*, 5 December 1988.

Grose, Thomas, K. 'Offending the Rich and Famous, *TJFR*, November 1991.

Hammer, Joshua, 'Triumphant Ted', *Playboy*, December 1989.

Hertzberg, Daniel, 'Fast Growing Drexel Irritates Many Rivals with its Tough Tactics', *Wall Street Journal*, 13 June 1986.

Hosenball, Mark, 'Money-Made Mike', *Playboy*, December 1989.

Hoyt, Michael. 'Judgment Call', *Columbia Journalism Review*. January 1992.

Icahn, Carl C, 'The Case For Takeovers', *New York Sunday Times*, 29 January 1989.

Joseph, Fred, 'I Woke Up With My Stomach Churning', *Fortune*, 3 July 1989.

Kann, Peter R. 'Letter From The Publisher', *Wall Street Journal*, 9 January 1992.

Kasindorf, Jeanie. 'The Chutzpah Defense', *New York* Magazine, 11 November 1991.

Kessler, Glenn. 'An Intimate Account of the Inside Traders', *New York Newsday*, 15 October 1991.

Klein, Edward, 'Here's To You Mrs Robinson', *Vanity Fair*, May 1990.

Kornbluth, Jesse, 'Profile: the Unknown Milken', *The Trentonian*, October 1988.

Kornbluth, Jesse, 'Law Of The Jungle', *Observer* magazine, 1990.

Kornbluth, Jesse, 'The Working Rich: The Real Slaves of New York', *New York* magazine, 24 November 1988.

Lambert, Hope, 'Saul Steps Out', *Manhattan Inc.*, October 1985.

Lambert, Hope, 'The Private Life of Henry K', *Manhattan Inc.*, December 1988.

Larsen, Jonathan Z., 'The Avenger', *Manhattan Inc.*, February 1985.

Laws, Margaret, 'The Insider Story', *National Review*, 28 May 1990.

Levine, Dennis B., 'The Inside Story of an Inside Trader', *Fortune* 21 May 1990.

Lewis, Michael, 'Pointing a Finger at Wall Street', *Manhattan Inc*, 1989.

Linowes, David F., 'Is the Merger Mania Good For the Nation?', *Vital Speeches of the Day*, February 1987.

Lipman, Joanne, 'Power Broker: PR's Linda Robinson Emerges at Forefront of Image Building Art', *Wall Street Journal*, 5 December 1988.

Mannes, Henry G. (and Larry E. Ribstein), 'The Man Who Invented Junk Bonds', *National Review*, 25 November 1988.

Mercer, Robert, E., 'Terrorists in Three Piece Suits', Speech for Miami Business Forum, 3 March 1987.

McMenamin, Michael, 'Witchunt', *Reason*, October 1988.

Michaels, James W. (and Phyllis Berman) 'My Story – Michael Milken', *Forbes*, 16 March 1992.

Michaelis, David, 'The Nutcracker Suit', *Manhattan Inc.*, December 1984.

Milken Family Foundations, 'Report of Activities', 1988.

Milken Family Foundations, 'Bulletin', Fall 1990.

Milken Family Foundations, 'Bulletin', Winter 1990.

Milken, Michael, Speech to Institutional Investor Luncheon, New York, October 1988.

Milken, Michael, Speech at the Financial World's CEO of the Decade Dinner at the Waldorf Astoria, New York, 16 March 1989.

Milken, Michael (with James E. Walter), 'Managing The Corporate Financial Structure', *Wharton*, 1978.

Milken, Michael, Turnaround Management Conference Speech', 25 September 1989.

Milken, Michael, Speech to the 4th Annual Conference on Investing and Trading High Yield Debt, New York, 14 September 1989.

Nocera, Joseph, 'The Decade that Got Out of Hand' Best of Business Quarterly, Fall, 1989.

O'Sullivan, John, 'Round Up the Usual Brokers', *National Review*, 10 November 1989.

Paltrow, Scott, J., 'The New Milken', *Los Angeles Times*, 15 October 1989.

Picker, Ida, 'Picking Up the Pieces At Drexel', *Institutional Investor*, May 1989.

Proxmire, William, 'Hostile Corporate Takeovers and Raids', *Vital Speeches of the Day*, March 1985.

Queenan, Joe., 'G. Robert Blakey versus Michael Milken', *Forbes*, 1 May 1989.

Reich, Robert B., 'Leveraged Buyouts, America Pays the Price', *New York Sunday Times*, 29 January 1989.

Richman, Louis S., 'Who Is Nick Brady?', *Fortune*, 22 May 1989.

Ricks, Thomas, E., 'SEC's Failed Probes of Milken in Past Show Difficulty of Its Mission', *Wall Street Journal*, 25 January 1989.

Riley, John, 'Pro-Milken Propoganda', *New York Newsday*, 15 May 1989.

Riley, John, 'Milken: Once on Cloud, Now Under It', *New York Newsday*, 26 January 1989.

Rohatyn, Felix, 'Junk Bonds and Other Securities Swill', *Wall Street Journal* 23 April 1985.

Rosenbaum, Ron, 'The Great Gatsby of Wall Street', *Manhattan Inc.*, August 1986.

Rosenbaum, Ron, 'Meet Felix and Liz Rohatyn: Society Dissidents', *Manhattan Inc.*, April 1986.

Rudolph, Barbar, 'A Heap of Woe For the Junkman', *Time*, 5 December 1988.

Satre, Philip G., 'The Future of Gambling: You Can Bet On It', *Vital Speeches of the Day*, November 1989.

Sheehan, Jack, E., 'Michael Milken, Wall Street Wizard', *Las Vegas Sun*, March 1989.

Sheehy, Gail, 'Heaven's Hit Man', *Vanity Fair*, August 1987.

Sheinbaum, Stanley (with Nathan Gardels and Richard Rothstein), 'History is Bunk, the Future is Junk', *New Perspectives Quarterly*, Fall 1989.

Sloan, Allan, 'A Chat With Michael Milken', *Forbes*, 13 July 1987.

Stein, Benjamin, 'For My Money T Boone Pickens Is No Hero', *New York Newsday*, 12 April 1985.

Stein, Benjamin, 'Commencing Now Your Best Investment Is You', *New York Newsday*, 12 June 1988.

Stein, Benjamin, 'Betrayer of Capitalism', *Barrons*, 3 April 1989.

Stein, Benjamin, 'The New Organized Crime', *New York Times*, 2 January 1990.

Stein, Benjamin, 'The Biggest Scam Ever?', *Barrons*, 19 February 1990.

Stein, Benjamin, 'Memo to Judge Wood', *Barrons*, 24 September 1990.

Stein, Benjamin, 'A New Low? The RJR LBO', *Barrons*, 14 November 1988.

Stewart, James B. (with Danile Hertzberg), 'The Wall Street Career of Martin Siegel Was a Dream Gone Wrong', *Wall Street Journal*, 17 February 1989.

Stevenson, Richard W. (with Kurt Eichenwald), 'With Settlement By Drexel, Financier Now Stands Alone', *New York Times*, 25 December 1988.

Stewart, James B. 'Scenes From a Scandal', *Wall Street Journal*, 2 October 1991.

Swartz, Steve, 'Why Mike Milken Stands To Qualify For Guinness Book of Records', *Wall Street Journal*, 31 March 1989.

Taylor, John, 'Hard To Be Rich: The Rise and Wobble of the Gutfreunds', *New York* magazine, 11 January 1988.

Thomas, Michael M. 'On The Street Where They Looted', *New York Times Book Review*, 13 October 1991.

Vise, David A., 'Michael Milken: A Dream-Maker's "Nightmare"', *Washington Post*, 20 November 1988.

Wanniski, Jude. 'Insider Reporting', *National Review*, 2 December 1991.

Williams, Monci Jo., 'What's Legal – and What's Not', *Fortune*, 22 December 1986.

Williams, Monci Jo., 'Can Fred Joseph Save Drexel?' *Fortune*, 8 May 1989.

Welles, Chris, 'Just How Damning Is the Case Against Drexel Burnham?', *Business Week*, 28 November 1988.

INDEX